Computer Contracts

Computers...

Richard Morgan

Graham Herbert

Computer Contracts

Fifth Edition

Richard Morgan MA, FBCS, FIInfSc

Graham Stedman LL B

Solicitor

LAW & TAX

© Pearson Professional Limited 1995

Richard Morgan and Graham Stedman have asserted their right under the Copyright, Designs and Patents Act 1988 to be identified as the authors of this work.

ISBN 0752 001612

Published by
FT Law & Tax
21–27 Lamb's Conduit Street
London WC1N 3NJ

A Division of Pearson Professional Limited

Associated offices
Australia, Belgium, Canada, Hong Kong, India, Japan, Luxembourg, Singapore, USA

First published 1979
Reprinted 1994
Fifth edition 1995

Printed in Great Britain by
Mackays of Chatham

Contents

Part V: Sources of advice

Preface

This is not a book on the law of contract as such. For that, the reader must be referred to the standard legal texts. Our purpose is twofold: to illuminate the computer content of agreements and to provide usable precedents. In writing this book, we have kept before us the picture of a company secretary or legal adviser with little experience of computers who is suddenly asked to look over 'the computer contract' and comment on it. His problem in understanding the contract (let alone looking for pitfalls) arises chiefly from the computer aspects. This book may help him to understand the main types of computer contract and the provisions he may expect to find in them. We are also concerned with the lawyer or other person involved in drafting a contract and to that end have devised a set of precedents, one of the features of this book.

One new chapter has been included in this edition—Chapter 12 on public sector contracts. We have also added two new precedents—F on multiple copy software licence agreements (sometimes called site licences) and R on network service level agreements. We have taken the opportunity completely to rewrite Precedent E—shrink-wrap licence. We have also expanded the last chapter to take account of public sector sources of advice. The appendices consisting of various codes of conduct or practice have now been omitted. We felt it was dangerous to include this material in case it should change and readers would be better advised to apply directly to the relevant bodies (whose full addresses are included) for the latest version as well as any guidance on its use.

In addition the whole text has been thoroughly revised, particularly taking into account a number of recent cases, most of them unfortunately unreported, and also the Council Directive of 14 May 1991 on the legal protection of computer programs (91/250/EEC), the Council Directive 86/653/EEC on Self-Employed Commercial Agents and their respective UK implementing regulations.

A word of explanation is required as to the examples of clauses which we have used in Chapters 1–11. We have been concerned to reflect the reality of computer contracts, warts and all. We have therefore consistently kept real contracts before us, and it seemed sensible to use some of these by way of illustration of the kind of thing to expect. They are to be distinguished from the precedents at the end of the book, and originate from a number of companies in the industry, though most clauses have been substantially rewritten to achieve some measure of uniformity. In one or two cases we have telescoped clauses from more than one source, or even devised our own. The originators of these clauses are in no way responsible for their clauses as they appear in this book, though we must take this opportunity of acknowledging help and co-operation from all sectors of the computer industry in contributing material.

The last chapter is primarily concerned with what to do when things go wrong. As this is not a book on the law of contract, we have avoided all discussion of legal remedies and instead described a number of organisations to which the aggrieved party might turn. Needless to say that party must still consider his purely legal remedies as well.

The precedents are designed to give a standard form for practitioners to use in the majority of cases. Naturally there can be no attempt to cover every conceivable circumstance. In many instances, readers may have to use more than one precedent to satisfy all their needs. In particular, hardware contracts, unless they are for add-on equipment, almost invariably contain some software elements. Precedents are always potentially dangerous if followed slavishly and readers are reminded of the need to consider the circumstances of a transaction carefully before using any of the precedents in this book.

Clauses in precedents have a reference in square brackets to the point in the text at which such a clause is discussed. The reader should use this cross-reference to satisfy himself that the clause is fully relevant to his requirements and we would recommend the user to read Chapters 1–12 before using any of the precedents. In Chapters 1–11 there are also cross-references by which the reader can identify the precedent clauses which we suggest deal with the matter in the text.

Thanks are due to many colleagues in the House of Commons Library and the Vote Office for unfailing helpfulness, to Mrs Anna Kerridge and to Miss Marion Bigley.

RSM
GS

May 1995

Table of Cases

Table of Statutes

Table of Statutory Instruments

Table of European Legislation

Directives

Council Directive

Chapter 1

Introduction: the importance of contracts and the structure of the industry

1.0 Introduction

1.1 The importance of contracts
Non-disclosure agreements

1.2 Hardware

1.3 Software

1.4 PCs and word processors
1.4.1 Unsolicited disclosures

1.5 Distribution

1.6 Test agreements

1.7 Leases

1.8 Hardware maintenance

1.9 Software maintenance

1.10 Bureau services
Bureaux
Data preparation

1.11 Consultancy

1.12 Combined contracts
Turnkey agreements
Facilities management
Disaster recovery

1.13 Public sector contracts

Chapter 1

Introduction: the importance of contracts and the structure of the industry

1.0 Introduction

Computer people against Luddites is a hackneyed antithesis. Within the computer industry there are other less obvious antitheses: between the machinery and its programs; between buying a computer and buying the services of a computer; and between first time purchase and subsequent maintenance.

First some definitions: the machinery of a computer is loosely designated *hardware*. This applies to mainframe computers and PCs (personal computers) equally. The programs which run on this computer are equally generally called *software*. This is a fundamental distinction which must be grasped at the outset. No less important must be the realisation that both hardware and software are vital to the successful processing of any work on a computer.

1.1 The importance of contracts

Before considering the types of contract it is necessary to stress the importance of a written contract. The reasons for this will become obvious from further reading of this book, but it is worth mentioning at this point two cases where the supplier may be reluctant to provide detailed contracts. One is the field of PCs and word processors (dealt with in more detail below [1.4] and in Chapter 4), and the other is where the supplier gets from the customer a letter of intent which then proves to have contractual force.

Any purchase of computer or computer-related goods or services should be preceded by negotiations. Eventually there may be an exchange of letters (letters of intent) in which the customer will say that he is prepared to buy (rent or lease), subject to a formal contract being signed. The absence of the last phrase may well turn the letter of intent into a binding contract. Readers unfamiliar with computer contracts should read through the relevant sections of this book *before* signing any letter of intent, however contractually guarded.

Before ever reaching this stage a prospective purchaser will need to have thought not only about the contractual obligations he will be taking on, but also about those which he will want his supplier to undertake. In general it is highly desirable to see any supplier's standard contract early and to negotiate on its terms as part of the general negotiations, rather than to seek to change its terms after the main bargaining is complete, prices finalised, and the goods and services defined.

Particular areas which a customer should look to are:

(1) Confidentiality and the need for a non-disclosure agreement [U];
(2) Acceptance criteria [2.3.6, 3.3].
(3) Disclaimers of responsibility and their enforceability under English law [2.3.5, 3.3.1].
(4) Title and intellectual property rights [2.8, 3.8].

Non-disclosure agreements [U]

These are useful when details (particularly about software packages) are being sent to a prospective purchaser. The intention is to prevent the prospective purchaser (as far as possible) from cribbing your ideas. Such contracts usually consist of an agreement to be signed by the user not to disclose the contents of documentation sent to him, to rivals or to any other third party; to limit data to authorised members of staff; and not to copy ideas. The examples in 10.6.3 cover these points. Another type of non-disclosure agreement, whereby a software house and its staff undertake to safeguard a client's secrets, is discussed in Chapter 3 [3.7.2]. Non-disclosure is also particularly relevant to beta test agreements (see Chapter 6).

1.2 Hardware

Hardware is relatively straightforward. The companies which are generally thought of as 'computer companies'—IBM, ICL, Digital Equipment (DEC), Compaq, Dell, Amstrad, and so on—are all manufacturers and sellers of hardware. So too are a host of smaller companies which manufacture equipment to add to others' hardware. For example, in the field of visual display terminals (television-type screens with typewriter-type keyboards, attached to computers), there are large numbers of specialist manufacturers who must be thought of as hardware suppliers.

Hardware can be bought, rented or leased, the last sometimes being from specialised leasing companies rather than from the manufacturer (see Chapter 7).

Hardware can also be bought from companies who do very little manufacturing, but whose primary purpose is to assemble equipment manufactured by others. In its extreme form this assembling of pre-manufactured parts is sometimes called 'badge engineering'. In these cases a purchaser will buy from a distributor.

1.3   Software

Software is programs; and programs are the instructions to the computer. Programs may be divided into two main categories: applications programs and systems software.

Applications programs are simply the programs to do the particular job required—payroll, order entry, stock control, etc. But the computer also requires an additional set of programs for more esoteric functions: operating systems, compilers, utility programs, etc. It may be useful to summarise these briefly. An *operating system* is a program present in the computer at all times which schedules the work being done, provides a log, allocates space and peripheral equipment, and so on. Windows, DOS, OS/2, Unix and Pick are all examples. *Compilers* are programs which convert instructions written by programmers into the machine code which alone can be read and used by the computer. *Utilities* are general programs to provide useful facilities which can be incorporated into applications programs (such as the ability to sort data into ascending or descending order), or which can be used as a general assistance to the computer department (for example, a program to detect computer viruses).

After this very brief discussion of what software is, an equally cursory glance at how software is produced may not be inappropriate. Software differs from hardware in its intangibility, in the near impossibility of defining precisely what is required. Although the user may have one computer, whether it is large or small, there is no limit to the potential number of programs it may require.

The analogy with books may be pursued. At first sight the vital feature of a book is its subject matter—what does it do? The same may be said of a program—what is the application? What function does it perform? But this is only the start. There are good books and bad books on the same topics, and there are good programs and bad programs to perform the same function. Programs may be crudely bad in the

5

sense that they do not really fulfil the function at all. Here a package program (a program already written and available off-the-shelf to all comers) is like a book: if it doesn't do what you want, you shouldn't buy it. But many programs are written expressly for one particular user: if that program does not fulfil its function, where does the fault lie? It may of course be the programmer's fault—he didn't read his instructions, he doesn't understand the computer or its operating system or compiler, or simply he cannot write programs. In fact, the layman may be amazed to know that the actual *writing* of the program is in some ways the simplest part of the whole operation. What is more usually at fault is the specification of the client's requirements.

This may be made clear if the stages in program production are considered.

First, there must be a perceived need by the client for the software, and this need must be unambiguously expressed. A document embodying this is usually called a *functional specification* and it may also include performance criteria [3.3.2].

Second, this functional specification must be translated into terms of the particular hardware and software which is going to do the job; this is sometimes called the *systems specification.*

Third, the systems specification must be reduced to a detailed analysis of each software component or program, called a *program specification.*

Fourth, the programs must be written.

Fifth, they must be adequately tested. This is typically a two-stage operation: first each individual part of the program is tested alone (*program testing*); then the suite of the associated programs is tested as a whole (*systems testing*).

Sixth, each of these stages must be adequately documented both so that any residual 'bugs' can easily be identified, and also to allow for future extensions and improvements—functions covered by the general term 'software maintenance'.

The terminology to describe these stages may vary slightly from one software house to another, and the distinction between the first three is slightly arbitrary and may be blurred. But—whatever names are used and whatever the number of stages—the elements of all six stages should be present if a piece of software is to be of any value. It follows that the neglect of any of these stages can bring disaster. The functional specification, for example, often becomes a contractual document incorporated by reference, and it is essential for a client to study it rigorously to ensure that it accurately and completely embodies all his requirements. The case of *MacKenzie Patten & Co v British Olivetti Limited* (unreported, decided 11 January 1984 (QBD)) in particular arose, at least in part, from the absence of a clear specification of what was required, with both sides apparently relying on nothing better than memory to help them decide what the purchaser had or had not asked the supplier to produce. Those who wish to study this cautionary tale should read Graham Stedman: 'The MacKenzie Patten decision: Both sides of the coin' in *Computer Law & Practice* January/February 1985, pp 92–4 and GM Smith and DW Robinson: 'MacKenzie Patten: the defence view. Caveat vendor? Traps for honest salesman' Ib pp 95–6. A corrective may be supplied by *Richards Longstaff & Partners Limited v Lombard North Central plc and Welsh Business Systems Limited* (reported in *Computers and Law* 47 (March 1986) p 19). Alterations at the functional specification stage are relatively easy to deal with: later on they may prove impossible [3.5].

Too many inexperienced purchasers of software look only as far as stage four, and ignore the possibility of testing and documentation. They do so at their peril, for—as the section on software acceptance [3.3] shows—the whole question of whether or not the program can be said to be complete, and therefore acceptable, can really be decided only by testing. Of course, a client should do his own testing, but a software house willing to carry out tests on his behalf, and show him the results of those tests (lists of each condition tested for and its result), is taking its job more seriously and is likely to inspire greater confidence.

All these things have to be paid for, and as a rough rule it may be said that a cut-price software job is likely to economise on testing first and documentation second. This means that any comparison of software quotations purely on price is apt to be misleading. A potential purchaser of software should check that all these stages are adequately covered. Similarly, where a software house has been held to a fixed-price quotation, if it is in any danger of exceeding its quotation it will be sorely tempted to economise on stages five and six. For the client, a contract on which his software house is losing money is a difficult situation for he will have to make vigorous attempts to keep the work produced by all six stages up to the standard he requires.

1.4 PCs and word processors

PCs (or micros) and word processors and the associated software are best considered separately from other computers. Definitions of a PC are extremely difficult, but they certainly include all home computers, personal computers (hence PC) and word processors with only one screen—or indeed no screen at all (stand-alone word processors). Written contracts in some cases are very brief, or even non-existent, and there was at one time a general assumption that the purchaser of a PC or its software was an enthusiast rather than a business man. This has now changed, but the low cost of the goods and services associated with PCs means that suppliers and customers alike prefer a simplified contractual relationship.

1.4.1 Unsolicited disclosures

A particular problem which arises from the low cost of PC software is that of unsolicited disclosure to a company by a programmer.

In the field of computing as in any other type of technical or scientific development, the role of the amateur or freelance inventor is relevant. Stories in the press of teenage entrepreneurs who have made a fortune from a program or hardware development encourage amateurs to write in to computer companies or software houses with bright ideas.

Such unsolicited disclosures may pose grave problems if they relate to areas where the company receiving the disclosures is already at work, since there is a danger that the disclosure by the inventor may prompt the suggestion that the company has stolen his idea. Inventors should be discouraged from giving away too much about their inventions or software too readily, and equally companies receiving such disclosures must protect themselves as far as possible, and to this end we suggest a letter for such companies [V].

1.5 Distribution

We spoke above [1.2] about the arrangement whereby a manufacturer gets another company to sell his equipment to the customer. In fact many suppliers buy in part or all of their equipment from others. There is therefore a need for distribution agreements between the original manufacturer and his distributor.

This arrangement is frequently known as an OEM (original equipment manufacturer) agreement and is extremely common. From the term 'OEM agreement', the retailing supplier (distributor) is often—with a total lack of logic—called 'the OEM'. He is not actually the original equipment *manufacturer* at all.

Much the same arrangement is made for software, with the specialist software houses and even individuals producing software, though in this case it may be sub-licensed to the customer by the distributor under licence from the originator.

1.6 Test agreements

Suppliers both of hardware and of software are acutely aware that the equipment or software they wish to market must stand up to robust treatment by customers. The laboratory testing which the supplier provides, while essential, is no substitute for testing 'in the field'. The laboratory testing is usually referred to as *alpha testing*. Any test in the field is referred to as *beta testing*.

A supplier may therefore seek to release a version of his hardware or software early to a customer in return for information from the customer as to how the new product performs. In these circumstances, the customer is aware that he is taking something which is less than perfect and that he has obligations to provide additional information to the supplier. The pricing structure will reflect this.

1.7 Leases

In this kind of agreement, the supplier sells the equipment outright to a third party leasing company, which in turn hires it to the customer who intends to use it.

Although in many respects leases replicate rental agreements (Chapter 2) they do present a number of difficulties peculiar to themselves and it therefore seems best to treat those aspects of leases separately from other hardware and software contracts.

1.8 Hardware maintenance

That the machinery you buy will need to be maintained in good working order will come as no surprise. The point to emphasise here is that you should be certain you know how it is to be maintained, and what level of service to expect, before you enter into any purchase agreement.

1.9 Software maintenance

Software also requires maintenance in the sense that even the best designed and tested programs are liable to 'cough' at totally unexpected data. There is a well-known fable in the industry about an American payroll package which worked well for years until two employees with identical names (it might have been Esmé Brown) decided to marry each other—a contingency which the system designer (not unreasonably) had not envisaged. It may be said that there is no such thing as an absolutely perfect program, any more than there is a perfectly healthy man. Having said this, it is obvious that there are adequately healthy men and obviously sick men, and there are eminently usable programs and appallingly unusable ones.

But for software maintenance, the correction of errors or bugs ought not to be a major anxiety unless the original program was very cursorily tested. The more important aspect is the ability to improve, enhance or extend a program to take account of second (and better) thoughts which are bound to occur to those who use the programs regularly. It is no severe criticism of a program that it could be improved in a number of respects.

Granted that development and enhancement of programs are so important, anyone purchasing, or acquiring a licence to use, software should satisfy himself that what he is acquiring can be improved as and when he requires it. He should therefore satisfy himself as to the standard of documentation and the facilities for software maintenance. This is a particularly acute problem for the small user who has no possibility of employing programmers full-time himself (still less providing them with a lifetime's career in his organisation), but who is having programs written specially to his requirements.

The above paragraphs are appropriate for bespoke softwre—ie software written to order. For standard software supplied with the machine, the important thing is to have support from the supplier or writer—usually in the form of telephone advice—and access to the new versions of the software as and when they are made available. It is generally the case that the supplier will wish to limit the number of versions he has to support so that when a new version becomes available it means that an older one is likely to be withdrawn in the not too distant future.

1.10   Bureau services

Bureaux

A totally different approach to the market for computer services lies in the provision of bureau services. You buy time on someone else's computer. Possibly you also buy the use of his programs, or of his data preparation staff.

For those who think better in analogies, the computer industry may be likened to transport: the vehicles are the hardware and their drivers the software directing the hardware. Outright purchase of a lorry is possible, or hire purchase (hardware purchase). Drivers may be employed (software purchase). Both require some means of maintenance which in the case of drivers (software) often means extending or enhancing skills rather than correcting faults. But in contrast to this method of acquiring transport, there is the van rental business: a vehicle may be hired from its owner solely for the particular journey you want to do (bureau service). You may in some circumstances provide your own driver (software), or you may also hire the driver. These are like services of a general nature, but there are also hire services which are highly specialised (eg furniture removals), and specialised services, in particular, tend to hire both van (hardware) and driver (software).

Like any analogy this one should not be pushed too far, but it may help to differentiate between bureau services and computer systems which are in-house.

Networks whereby a number of otherwise independent computers—usually PCs—are linked together to provide the transmission of data and services between them give rise to a specialised type of bureau and a contract usually called a network service level agreement. With the emphasis on cost centre accounting and quality control in modern management the organisation providing the network services may well be in the same commercial group as the organisation using those services, but an arm's-length relationship beween them ensures that both sides understand what each can expect from the other.

Data preparation

One specialised bureau service is data preparation. For the purposes of this book *data* means the variable information given to a computer program to enable it to function. For example, in a sales ledger program the data might be the invoice information. Data traditionally has been fed into the computer in machine-readable form, in which case it will need to be prepared in advance of the running of the computer program to which it relates. This is what is normally meant by *data preparation*. When a computer is first installed in an organisation which previously has not had one, data preparation can be considerable.

For on-line services [10.1.2] the data may be input directly by the user through a terminal at the time when the program is running. The more usual term here is *data entry*. This again may be a bureau service.

An alternative to data preparation or data entry is the conversion of data from the form suitable for running on one machine to a form suitable for another. This is called *data transfer* or *data conversion*.

All the processes can be provided as a service and that service has the characteristics of other bureau service contracts. All the features relating to data [10.3] will be present though most other characteristics of bureau contracts will be attenuated or non-existent.

1.11   Consultancy

Consultancy is required most usually in one or other of two cases: feasibility and procurement studies, or remedial work for a system which is unsatisfactory. Computer consultancy contracts are constituted on the same lines as many other special consultancy agreements. As soon as consultancy is concerned with the analysis of systems, the client is embarking on the first phase of software production and, as we make clear in Chapter 11, much of Chapter 3 becomes relevant—see especially [3.0.3]. The user must define his end product—usually a report—in the same way as he defines a program. He must also satisfy himself as to the impartiality of the consultant. Many 'consultants' are also in the business of selling hardware, so it will not be surprising if they recommend that hardware. There is nothing immoral about this, provided the client is aware of it. But if he wants independent advice, he must insist on employing a consultant whose income is derived solely from consultancy.

1.12 Combined contracts

Turnkey agreements

Some users know little enough about computers and are happy to leave procurement of everything to someone else—hardware, software, data preparation/transfer, maintenance. The idea is that, at the end of the time specified in the agreement, the contractor (manufacturer or software house) offers the user the key to a sparkling new computer room and says 'It's all installed; it all works; it's all yours'—hence the name 'turnkey'. The expression is said to originate from the building and furnishing industries. The main advantage of the turnkey contract is that the customer deals with only one supplier. Thus in the event of non-performance he does not have to decide whether the failure is one of hardware or of software. He simply turns to his supplier for a remedy. This contrasts with the situation where a customer has two contracts, one for hardware and one for software, and each supplier may be tempted to blame the other. These contracts, though important, do not merit a separate chapter since they are simply combinations of Chapters 2, 3, 8 and 9—or they should be. Before entering into a turnkey agreement, the user should satisfy himself that these aspects will all be carried out.

Facilities management

This is a complex idea to grasp initially. User A buys a computer system from supplier B. B then enters into a management contract to run the system on A's behalf. The idea is that a company can own its own system without relying on a bureau and at the same time leave the running and technical headaches to professionals. Such agreements are still not that common (except between companies in the same group where one company within the group handles all the management of the computers for the group as a whole, in the same way that property management is often handled in a specialised fashion for a diverse group) and will contain hardware (Chapter 2) and bureau (Chapter 10) elements.

Disaster recovery

It sometimes happens that two organisations (or two parts of the same organisation) have similar hardware and sufficient spare capacity to enable them to enter into a mutual agreement for disaster recovery. Thus if a fire puts Company A's computer out of action the work can be processed on Company B's machine. Similarly if Company B suffers a disaster, Company A's resources can provide at least a minimum of support to Company B. It will be seen that where such an arrangement is possible, the two contracts will largely be mirror-images of each other and must cover such things as the use of the computer, the hours of its availability, the storage and loading of software and data, access by personnel, etc.

1.13   Public sector contracts

Since our accession to the European Union, a steady stream of directives has been issued which define the rules for public sector procurements and hence have contractual implications. At the same time there are other aspects of public sector contracts which set them apart from all other contracts, mostly dictated by the greater need for accountability in public sector contracts.

These various requirements may affect all aspects of computer contracts and readers who have to deal with such contracts should study the relevant chapters about their *type* of contract first (hardware, software, maintenance, bureaux, consultancy, etc) and then read the chapter on public sector contracts afterwards and modify their clauses and procedures accordingly.

PART I   HARDWARE AND SOFTWARE ACQUISITION

Chapter 2

Hardware

2.1 Equipment to be supplied
2.1.1 Equipment
2.1.2 Location

2.2 Payment
2.2.1 Outright purchase
2.2.2 Rental
2.2.3 Rental with option to purchase
2.2.4 Prices
    Currency rates
    Price adjustments on long deliveries
2.2.5 Discounts

2.3 Delivery and acceptance
2.3.1 Delivery
2.3.2 Pre-delivery tests
2.3.3 Packing and carriage
2.3.4 Post-delivery tests
2.3.5 Performance
2.3.6 Acceptance
2.3.7 Liability for delay
    Supplier's delay in delivery
    Customer's delay
2.3.8 Defects

2.4 Termination
2.4.1 Sale
2.4.2 Rental

2.5 Alterations

2.6 Customer's duties
2.6.1 Providing information
2.6.2 Confidentiality
2.6.3 Site preparation
2.6.4 Care
2.6.5 Miscellaneous
2.6.6 Supplier's remedies

2.7 Supplier's duties
2.7.1 Confidentiality
2.7.2 VDUs and health
2.7.3 Electromagnetic compatibility
2.7.4 Telecommunications approval

2.8 Title and intellectual property rights
2.8.1 Title to the hardware
2.8.2 Patent and other intellectual property rights
2.8.3 Integral software

2.9 Miscellaneous
2.9.1 Export control

Chapter 2

Hardware

A book dealing with computer contracts must inevitably begin with contracts for the acquisition of the computer itself. The common industry term to cover all equipment is 'hardware' and this term will be used in future in this book since it covers not only a complete computer but also ancillary or peripheral equipment associated with the computer's performance.

Many contracts dealing with hardware will also cover programs (software), maintenance and other topics which are covered by separate chapters in this book. Anybody purchasing a computer would be advised to examine the other chapters and see whether they are not equally as appropriate as this chapter.

Hardware contracts may involve:

(1) complete computer systems;
(2) parts of, or additions to, computer systems.

The form of payment in such contracts may be:

(1) outright purchase;
(2) rental;
(3) rental with the option to purchase;
(4) lease.

The relation between the supplier and his customer may be:

(1) supplier to end user;
(2) contractor to a customer who will himself be a potential supplier to other end users (distributor). Distribution agreements are dealt with in more detail in Chapter 5;
(3) supplier to leasing company which will lease the equipment to the end user — see Chapter 7.
(4) supplier to the supplier of test facilities — see Chapter 6 and Precedent J

It should be pointed out that most suppliers use more or less standard contract forms, and the prospective customer should not expect that they will necessarily be enthusiastic about re-writing their contract. It is therefore essential that he understand the nature of the contract he is being asked to sign, so that negotiation can focus on the areas where he has a good case. The standard form may be a contract explicitly or may be in the form of a proposal, quotation or tender which becomes a contract on acceptance and signing by the customer. The reader is advised not to accept a proposal and then hope to iron out the contractual difficulties later when all bargaining power has been eroded. The pages that follow should be taken as a guide to the implications of a contract rather than as an opportunity to question every clause in a standard form.

2.1 Equipment to be supplied

2.1.1 Equipment [A1, A2; B1, B25; O2]

A computer hardware contract is an agreement for the delivery of goods. Hardware suppliers have a certain amount of flexibility in defining the goods to be supplied and, except for the very smallest and simplest equipment, there is no such thing as a standard model of a particular machine. The exact description of the goods is therefore most usually set out in a schedule which is incorporated as follows:

> The Supplier agrees to sell and the Customer agrees to purchase the equipment listed in Schedule *A* hereof at the prices stated therein and upon the following terms and conditions.

In the schedule will usually be a list of pieces of equipment, giving for each:

(1) the quantity of such items;
(2) the manufacturer's description—usually in the form of a number and narrative such as DEP 117X Disk Drive;
(3) the price.

The customer must satisfy himself first that the hardware is sufficient for his needs. By that we do not simply mean that the equipment must be capable of handling his volumes of data, but more fundamentally that the disk drive in the above example may be attached to a disk drive controller which must appear implicitly or explicitly in the list; and provision must also be made for the disk packs too. A cynical colleague of mine once likened a contract with this kind of deficiency to purchasing a car only to find out the wheels were extra! The customer must therefore check any such list extremely carefully with any orders or correspondence to ensure that it is complete.

The equipment list does not usually include operating supplies or disposables (eg disk packs, toner cartridges, etc). One supplier explicitly excludes them:

> Operating supplies such as disk packs stationery printing cartridges and similar accessories are not supplied as part of the Equipment.

Even if no such clause appears, the customer should assume that he will have to order these separately, and he should seek his supplier's advice on the type, quality and quantity of such accessories as well as their price.

The list may well have some software (programs) added at the end. The most likely candidate is the operating system—the program described above [1.3] and supplied usually by the manufacturer and intended to schedule work on the computer and ensure the smooth and efficient utilisation of the peripheral devices such as disk drives, printers, and so forth. If this item is absent, the customer should ensure that it will be provided at some stage—perhaps in a second, related agreement for software. If it is present, the customer should be aware that he is purchasing a software package, and that the relevant provisions for a software contract should apply to that item at least (see Chapter 3) though the price is 'bundled'. The provision of hardware with embedded or integral software is discussed further in 2.8.3 below.

It should also be observed that the supplier sometimes reserves to himself the right to substitute other equipment:

> The Supplier reserves the right to make substitutions and modifications in the Specifications of the Equipment designed by him provided that such substitutions or modifications will not materially affect the performance of such equipment in the intended application.

If this clause merely means that the supplier is constantly improving his equipment and wishes to incorporate such improvements, it cannot be objected to. But it is worth pointing out that performance [2.3.5] is not guaranteed in most contracts anyway. A cautious customer might ask for a list of such modifications and substitutions on delivery, but he should be warned that it will probably be both lengthy and technical. In practice, the customer can do little about this clause, and should not be too anxious, though the better he defines the performance level required in the application, the more secure his position will be.

In rental agreements there may be a limitation on the use of the hardware, since the supplier may be concerned to preserve some resale value in the equipment or possibly also to limit his maintenance obligation, in which case a clause such as the following, though unusual, may occur:

> Payment by the Customer to the Supplier of the monthly charge as set out in Clause X hereof shall entitle the Customer to use of the Equipment for up to any 180 hours in each calendar month and to the benefit of maintenance in accordance with Clause Y hereof. Use beyond that limit shall be subject to an additional charge at the rate defined in Schedule A hereof.
>
> The Customer shall report to the Supplier at the end of each calendar month the total time of use of the Equipment during that month. Use of any part of the Equipment shall be deemed to be use of the Equipment. Any hours unused below 180 hours in any calendar month cannot be carried over into any subsequent month.

A word about second-hand equipment. Any proposing purchaser of second-hand equipment will not expect to find any manufacturer's warranties. There may also be difficulties about export control even though the vendor is in the same country as the purchaser. If software (eg an operating system) is included there could also be serious problems which are dealt with in 3.0.2 and 7.4.2 below.

2.1.2   Location [A1; B1]

A hardware contract should specify precisely where the goods are to be installed, since this can affect delivery [2.3.1] and transport costs [2.3.3], and is also relevant to the customer's duty to prepare the site [2.6.3]. This is usually covered either by including an identification of the installation site in a schedule and referring to:

> . . . at the installation site described in the *Third* Schedule hereto

or else quite simply by saying in an ordinary clause:

> The installation site is. . .

Sometimes—for instance for an OEM agreement on a cumulative discount basis [2.2.5; Chapter 5]—it is not possible to define the installation site(s) in advance, in which case a clause such as this is suitable:

> Delivery of each piece of Equipment shall be made to any address within the United Kingdom designated by the Customer in writing to the Supplier at least one week before the estimated date of delivery.

In a rental agreement it is usual to stipulate that the hirer cannot alter the equipment or move it to another location during the continuance of the agreement:

> No movement or alteration to the Equipment shall be made except with the Supplier's written consent which may be revoked if the performance or maintenance of the Equipment is thereby impaired. In the event of such revocation the Customer shall at his own expense relocate and reinstate the Equipment in its original position and to its original condition and standard of performance.

In practice, movement of equipment after installation (whether in a sale or rental agreement) is usually prohibited or limited in this way by a maintenance agreement (see Chapter 8). Any customer wishing to obtain equipment to move frequently (eg for demonstration purposes) should notify the supplier and maintenance contractor before signing any contracts. Different considerations of course apply to PCs and portables (see 8.1.1).

2.2   Payment

2.2.1   Outright purchase [A3]

Sometimes goods can be supplied 'off the shelf' ('ex-works' may be the preferred term), in which case it is anticipated that delivery will follow shortly on the signing of the contract:

> The Supplier shall issue an invoice for the Equipment upon its shipment. Payment of such invoice shall be made in full within ten days of the issue of a certificate of test for the Equipment.

But see Post-delivery tests [2.3.4], since this example fails to deal with acceptance.

Occasionally the hardware is a special piece of equipment, designed to the user's particular requirements and so will not be built until after the signing of the contract. In that case it is usual to make payment in two or more stages, the first being on signing the contract and the last usually on delivery and acceptance. For example:

> Invoices for payment of the Contract Price will be presented as follows:
> (i) 30 per cent on signature of this Agreement;
> (ii) 40 per cent on issue of a certificate by the Supplier that the manufacture of major items is complete;
> (iii) 30 per cent on delivery and acceptance in accordance with Clause 6 hereof.

It will be observed that the supplier has complete control over stage (ii) (by which time he has secured 70 per cent of the price), and that 'major items' are not defined.

Where the purchase price is payable by instalments the parties should be careful to clarify whether any instalment is to be made by way of a part payment or a deposit. If an instalment is made by way of a deposit then it will not be recoverable by the customer if, in breach of contract, he does not perform his side of the bargain, even though the actual loss suffered by the supplier as a result of such breach is less than the amount of the deposit.

Chapter 6 on test agreements gives other examples of contracts for experimental or development work.

2.2.2   Rental [B1, B2, B13, B14, B15]

The earliest computer contracts were almost all for a rental from the manufacturer, and for some people this is still the preferred method. It gives some protection against obsolescence and if an internal capital budget is exhausted equipment can be rented against a revenue budget. It may be particularly useful also where the project is of a research or experimental nature with the possibility of its being either abandoned or changed significantly on completion. However, some suppliers—particularly of peripheral equipment or of small systems—decline to consider rental agreements, so a customer should not assume this option is open to him. In the case of a rental, payment is usually monthly in advance.

Rental usually commences on the date of delivery, which is often not identified in the agreement. The usual procedure is for the supplier to hand over a delivery note and the first invoice on delivery, and then date them:

> The charges for the Equipment shall commence on the day following the day of issue by the Supplier of a certificate that the Equipment is or but for the Hirer's non-compliance with his obligations under this Agreement would have been installed and ready for use.

Rental is typically for an initial period of 2 years with a proviso that it will be continued thereafter, terminable on 3 months' written notice:

> The period of rental under this Agreement shall continue for an initial period of two years from the date of commencement specified in Clause *X* above and will remain in force thereafter until terminated by at least three months' written notice given by either party to the other.

Alternatively the agreement may be terminated at the end of the initial period or at any time thereafter:

> The period of rental under this Agreement shall continue for an initial period of 2 years from the date of commencement specified in Clause *X* above and will remain in force thereafter unless or until terminated by at least 3 months' written notice given by either party to the other expiring at the end of the said initial period or at any time thereafter.

Agreements for one year are uncommon, and for less than one year almost unknown. For a longer rental period (3 years or more), it is probably more advantageous to both sides to consider an outright purchase or leasing agreement (see Chapter 7), since the rental price may well amount to the equivalent of purchase over 3 or 4 years.

In the case of a rental, where title to the equipment remains with the supplier, it is usual for the supplier to stipulate that the hirer must have the equipment maintained only by the supplier or supplier's nominee. Most rental agreements include the maintenance clauses in the same document and specify monthly payments of both rental and maintenance charges, but some have a separate but related maintenance agreement. For convenience, all maintenance clauses are dealt with in Chapter 8.

2.2.3   Rental with option to purchase [B34]

An agreement of this type may be particularly useful if the customer is not quite sure whether the equipment will be able to perform the particular functions he has in mind, and wishes to prove the equipment for a period. It will have all the clauses of an ordinary rental agreement and will in addition contain a clause such as:

> At any time after the expiry of one year from the date of commencement hereof the Hirer may upon giving 3 months' written notice purchase the Equipment at the price described in the *Second* Schedule hereto.

Then follow clauses appropriate to a purchase agreement, or alternatively:

> The Equipment shall be purchased by the Hirer on the Supplier's standard terms and conditions of sale for the time being in force.

In the case of such an agreement, the purchase price usually reflects some (but not all) of the payments made under the rental agreement. An alternative way of having a similar agreement is by terminating the rental and having a new rental-to-purchase agreement. Such an agreement defines the date of the rental-to-purchase conversion, and then might proceed:

> The Supplier shall raise an invoice for the Equipment on the Rental-to-Purchase conversion date. Payment of such invoice shall be made in full by the Customer within 10 days of the date of the invoice.

2.2.4   Prices

These are often based on a published price list (almost invariably quoted exclusive of Value Added Tax), and will be taken from a proposal or quotation. As such, they are not likely to change except in the cases mentioned below.

Currency rates [A3(2)]

Large numbers of manufacturers are based abroad, and the wildly fluctuating exchange rates for foreign currencies have had a damaging effect on the UK suppliers of goods manufactured abroad. This has prompted one supplier to add, in the days when the pound was falling against the dollar, the clause:

> In the event that the prevailing exchange rate between the United States dollar and the English pound sterling has fluctuated in excess of two per cent from the time the quotation is tendered to the time payment is received the Supplier reserves the right in its sole discretion to adjust any prices or authorised quotations or published price lists and to apply such adjusted prices or quotations or price lists to all customers of the same class and the Customer agrees promptly to remit the amount of any such adjustment.

The basic intention is understandable, but we have to admit the drafting of this example is particularly poor. Two per cent of what?—is this two cents in the dollar? Then, too, 'fluctuate' could mean an increase of 1 per cent followed by a decrease of 2 per cent, bringing the exchange back to 1 per cent below the starting price. The business of applying adjustments to other customers of the same class (and what is a class?) is of no interest in this agreement. Also, the adjustment is not geared to the changeability. And what if the rate goes up? Can we perhaps try:

> The prices in this Agreement are based on an exchange rate between the United States dollar and the English pound sterling of $1.60 to £1. If from the date hereof to the date the last payment is received the pound shall fall 2¢ US or more below that rate the Supplier

reserves the right to increase any prices for equipment still unpaid to take account of the new exchange rates.

It is perfectly reasonable to quote an actual exchange rate in the agreement since presumably the original English price lists have been based on such a rate.

Price adjustments on long deliveries [A3(3)]

Apart from quotation of exchange rates, the right to adjust a price is likely to figure in any contract for specially commissioned hardware which is not ex-works. This may reflect some uncertainty on the part of the supplier as to how exactly he is to construct the equipment, but more usually it is simply to protect him from the effects of inflation on his own suppliers:

> At any time before the three months immediately preceding the Estimated Delivery Date the Supplier shall be entitled to vary this Agreement to accord with any changes in the Supplier's price list current from time to time and to give notice of such variation to the Purchaser. This Agreement shall be deemed to be varied accordingly by such notice of variation unless the Purchaser shall within 14 days of receipt of such notice terminate this Agreement by giving notice to the Supplier.

This clause does not permit the supplier to increase his price beyond the date specified even though the actual delivery may be late, and it links any such increase to published price lists. As such it is quite a fair clause, though the option to terminate is not very realistic since the purchaser's preparations for receiving the equipment [2.6.3] will probably be so far advanced as to be irreversible.

2.2.5 Discounts

In a book of this sort it would be inappropriate to deal in detail with the different discount agreements. In general terms a discount of, say, 10 per cent is not unusual where the customer is buying (or enhancing) more than one machine; and sometimes much larger discounts are available when a customer is purchasing several machines either for himself or for customers of any computer-based service he provides. Some contracts have a complicated sliding scale based on the number of machines ordered within a particular year, and a provision for unearned discount (ie discount which has been allowed in expectation of a sales target for the year which has not been achieved) to be billed back to the customer. The benefit of such an agreement to the supplier is not simply that he enjoys greater turnover but also that, on the basis of such agreements, he can more accurately schedule the demand for and manufacture of his equipment. There are some manufacturers virtually all of whose output is available only under discount on OEM agreements, so that they have no interest in a purchaser of a single system. This is particularly true of the PC market.

2.3   Delivery and acceptance

2.3.1   Delivery

Most contracts expect payment on delivery of the equipment, although a customer will naturally not wish to make any payment until acceptance. In fact, 'delivery' proves on examination to be a succession of different episodes each of which is necessary to establish the efficient functioning of the equipment in its new environment. The customer's obligation to prepare the site is dealt with below [2.6.3] and will not affect the delivery itself unless he has failed to complete his preparations. The supplier, on the other hand, is required to assemble all the equipment, test it before it leaves the factory, arrange and effect transport and delivery to the customer's premises, assemble it there and do any further testing. Any software delivery [3.3] takes place after this. The hardware stages deserve examination in detail.

2.3.2   Pre-delivery tests [A7]

Once the supplier has assembled the equipment he will test it before delivery. Most manufacturers are happy to tell the customer precisely what these tests consist of, and may allow him or his representative to be present:

(*a*)   The Supplier shall submit the Equipment to his Standard Works Test ('the Test') before despatch to the Customer. The Supplier shall supply to the Customer on request copies of the Test Specification and certification that the Equipment has passed the Test.

(*b*)   If the Test is held in the presence of the Customer or his representatives the Customer will be charged therefor. In the event of any delay by the Customer or his representatives in attending the Test after 7 days' notice the Supplier reserves the right to proceed with the Test and the Test will be deemed to have been conducted in the presence of the Customer and the results thereof shall be deemed to have been accepted by the Customer.

Such tests are often called 'diagnostic tests'. Their purpose is to test the circuitry and all mechanical aspects of the equipment. For example, a test on a matrix printer will test the printing of each character in every print position so that if there is a defect either in the type itself or the print mechanism this can be identified. Engineers use the same or similar tests when checking equipment for maintenance. The customer is of course at liberty to ignore these tests (and save himself the cost of them), but by so doing he may possibly prejudice his ability at some future time to suggest that the equipment was in any way defective.

2.3.3 Packing and carriage [A8, A9; B5, B6]

Some suppliers themselves bear the costs of transportation, but some of the larger manufacturers will charge the customer:

> All costs of transportation within the United Kingdom and the Republic of Ireland and all delivery charges (including but not limited to heavy gang, handling and hoisting charges) and insurance costs until acceptance will be paid by the Customer.

The restriction of this clause to the UK and Ireland is not intended to benefit an export customer; rather it is because the supplier is American and is not charging separately for delivery from his factory to the UK but only from the airport to the customer's site.

Some manufacturers reserve the right to select the carrier, and at the same time exclude any liability for delay or loss by the carrier during delivery:

> (*a*) The Supplier shall select the Carrier but by so doing shall not thereby assume any liability in connection with shipment nor shall the Carrier in any way be construed as an agent of the Supplier.
>
> (*b*) The Supplier shall not be liable for any damage for delay in delivery or failure to deliver when such delay is due to delays in transportation or any other cause beyond the Supplier's control.

If the supplier does not charge for delivery he will in fairness have the right to choose the carrier:

> The Contract Price includes the cost of all delivery charges to the Installation Site by any method of transport selected by the Supplier.

But even here 'delivery' usually means only delivery to the door of the purchaser and not the actual putting of the equipment on to the site. The reason for this is simply that the cost of doing this will vary enormously depending on the position of the site and whether hoists and other plant are necessary:

> The Supplier shall not be responsible for offloading the Equipment and moving it to the Installation Site.

The packing materials, including polystyrene boxes and padded cases (called 'muffs' in the trade), are often expensive since they will have been specifically built to the supplier's requirements. Some suppliers therefore ask for their return:

> All packing cases, skids, drums and other packing materials used for delivery of the Equipment to the Customer must be returned by the Customer to the Supplier's works in good condition and at the Customer's expense. The Supplier reserves the right to charge for any such packing cases and materials not so returned.

Because the equipment ceases to be under the supplier's physical control after delivery it is usual for risk, and hence the obligation to insure, to pass to the customer even though he has not yet accepted the equipment.

2.3.4   Post-delivery tests [A1, A11; B1; O11, O14]

The pre-delivery tests are not necessarily available to the customer and their purpose is primarily for the supplier. However, the prudent customer will seek to check that the equipment does indeed do what it is supposed to do, and is not defective or damaged. It is, in theory, open to the customer to devise any tests he thinks appropriate, and some customers will be capable of designing their own tests. If they do, they would be well advised to agree them with their supplier in advance, so that both sides can be clear that the tests are fair. But, for most commercial customers without specialist engineering and programming skills, it is simpler to use the existing diagnostic test packages which the supplier has himself used before delivery. As the test is often the process which determines acceptance—and hence payment—it is in the supplier's interest that such tests should be commenced promptly:

> (a) Standard Tests on Installation ('the Tests') shall be performed by the Supplier in accordance with the Supplier's Standard Test Specifications within 7 days of the Supplier having given written notice of completion of installation of the Equipment. If the Tests have not been performed completely within that 7-day period by reason of any action or omission of the Customer then the Tests will be deemed to have been performed correctly and the Customer to have accepted the Equipment.

(*b*) If any portion of the Equipment fails to pass the Tests on Installation the Tests on the said portion of the Equipment shall if required by the Customer be repeated within a reasonable time and upon the same terms and conditions.

This last clause is bound up with the question of defects [see 2.3.8], but it is included here to point out that, before an installation can be considered complete and the equipment commissioned, each part of it must have passed (or be deemed to have passed) the acceptance tests.

It is important for the customer to ensure that the tests are carried out to his satisfaction. If he fails to carry the tests out at all, he may well be deemed to have accepted the equipment, either when he starts to use it or very soon afterwards. Failure to notify the supplier of defects may be deemed acceptance:

'Commissioning Date' is the date on which the Supplier's standard tests on the Equipment have been satisfactorily completed at the Customer's premises or one month after operational use of the Equipment by the Customer begins, whichever is the sooner.

Unless accepted earlier, the Equipment is deemed accepted by the Customer on the Commissioning Date.

In one example, the supplier, in stressing the importance of prompt payment, may not explicitly within the contract draw the customer's attention to his need to test the equipment. The relevant clauses say:

The Supplier will upon delivery and installation of the Equipment issue the Customer with a Commissioning Certificate certifying the date that the Equipment or any part thereof is ready for use.

The Supplier shall issue an invoice for the Equipment upon its shipment, payment of such invoice to be made in full within 14 days of the date of the Commissioning Certificate. Interest on overdue amounts will become payable at a rate of 3 per cent per month or pro rata for parts of a month on invoices not fully paid.

The customer faced with such a clause should vigorously defend his right to have the equipment tested in his presence.

2.3.5   Performance

Questions of performance—how many transactions the storage devices can hold, how quickly they can be processed, how many terminals can be handled, and what response time can be expected in a single transaction—all depend on the interaction of hardware and software. It is unlikely that there will have been any exactly analogous situation with which a proposed system can be compared. Any relatively small change in either hardware or software is liable completely to upset previous calculations. This matter is dealt with again under software [3.3.2], but it is worth repeating here that no respectable manufacturer is likely to allow performance to be a criterion of acceptance unless the opportunity is given (and paid for) to have very extensive performance tests on both hardware and software before delivery. A clause such as the following is sometimes used:

> The Supplier accepts no liability for failure to achieve any performance figures he or his servants may have given to the Customer unless:
> (a) the Supplier has specifically guaranteed them subject to specified tolerances in an agreed sum as liquidated damages and
> (b) the environmental conditions specified in the Supplier's quotation are maintained.
> The payment by the Supplier of the said liquidated damages shall be in full satisfaction of any such liability for failure by the Supplier to attain such performance figures.

In practice performance figures are very rarely admitted as a part of the requirement for a commercial system. The contract from which this example has been adapted might more readily be used in a non-commercial environment.

With interactive or on-line systems where system response time [3.3.2] is important, it is of course incumbent on the customer to use telecommunications equipment at the right speed:

> Where any data transmission speeds are given by the Supplier in relation to the Equipment, such speeds are at all times subject to conditions attached by the relevant telecommunications authority to the use of the relevant modem[1] or other telecommunications equipment at the speeds indicated and to the capability of such modem or other telecommunications equipment to achieve such speeds.

2.3.6   Acceptance [A12; O14]

If we recapitulate the procedures for delivery so far, we see that a likely sequence of events might be:

---

[1]Modem: communications equipment designed to connect terminals and computers to telecommunications lines.

(1) notice from supplier that the equipment is ready and invitation to customer to witness standard hardware tests at the supplier's premises;

(2) running of standard hardware tests at supplier's premises with or without the presence of the customer or his representative;

(3) delivery of equipment from a UK site to the customer's premises (using a carrier approved by the supplier)—sometimes involving an additional charge for delivery to the customer;

(4) offloading of equipment from the carrier's vehicles to the actual installation site on the customer's premises—usually at the customer's additional cost. Risk passes and the customer must insure;

(5) on-site running of standard hardware tests by the supplier's staff on the delivered equipment in the presence of the customer or his representative, following which the hardware is said to be commissioned.

It should be noted that:

(*a*) it is not always possible to examine both tests. In the case of equipment imported from abroad, the first one will usually be invisible to both the customer and the supplier's UK representative;

(*b*) the pre-delivery test may even be left to the supplier. This is particularly the case where a small peripheral device (as opposed to a whole computer) is involved;

(*c*) performance figures are unlikely to be accepted by the supplier as having any overriding relevance.

Acceptance by the customer of the equipment usually follows the successful completion of the last phase of this sequence: on-job running of the standard hardware tests; and, following such acceptance, the purchase price (or first rental payment) immediately becomes due. In the absence of any more specific directions in a contract (and it is amazing how vague some contracts are in these matters), it is reasonable to assume that the above procedure is what is involved.

At the end of stage (3) above (delivery to the customer's site), the carrier is likely to produce a delivery note to be signed when the equipment is handed over by him. The customer should satisfy himself that this delivery note is not, in fact, an acceptance form from the supplier.

Ignoring for the moment this unpleasant possibility, we may give as an example a payment clause implying acceptance:

> Payment for the Equipment shall be made by the Customer on acceptance of the Equipment by the Customer after completion of Tests in accordance with Clause *X* hereof.

Where part only of the Equipment has been tested delivered and accepted as aforesaid the sums required to be paid under this Clause shall be the relevant percentage of the part of the Contract Price which represents the price of the part of the Equipment which has been so tested delivered and accepted.

A more formal but basically similar approach is provided by a large manufacturer:

After transporting the Equipment into position at the Installation Site the Customer will provide access to and the Supplier will undertake the installation and commissioning of the Equipment and will carry out the current Standard Hardware Test Programs details of which will have been given to the Customer prior to the start of such tests. This work will be done during normal working hours and will be at the Supplier's expense. When the Equipment or any item thereof is commissioned and the Standard Hardware Test Programs have been successfully completed the Supplier will issue a certificate to the effect as set out in Schedule *C* hereto (hereinafter referred to as the Commissioning Certificate).
. . .The Supplier shall issue an invoice for the Equipment on the day the Equipment is shipped from the Supplier's factory. Payment of such invoice by the Customer shall be made in full within 10 days after the date of the Commissioning Certificate.

2.3.7   Liability for delay [A1; B1; O15]

Having considered what ought to happen, we must now examine the possible delays and hindrances which may occur in this process, and how the contracting parties may envisage meeting them.

Supplier's delay in delivery [A10]

The first delay may arise if the supplier has failed to assemble part or all of the equipment ready for delivery, or if—having assembled it—he finds it cannot pass his own standard hardware tests. When some or all of the hardware is imported, the chances of delay here can be considerable and, without accusing foreign manufacturers of negligence or any malfeasance, it is easy to see the opportunities for damage in shipment, hold-up in customs, and so on. Most manufacturers exclude liability for delay. One of the simplest and fairest such clauses is of a manufacturer who, after giving an estimated date of delivery, adds:

> The Supplier shall not be liable for any delay or for the consequences of any delay in performing any of its obligations under this Agreement if such delay is due to any industrial dispute or any cause whatsoever beyond its reasonable control and shall be entitled to a reasonable extension of the time for performing such obligation.

A customer should naturally look for a clear implementation schedule from the supplier for the performance of the contract. If delays are caused by an event outside the control of the supplier then the position is usually covered by a clause such as the example set out above—called a *force majeure* clause. This is not unreasonable, of course, but what happens if the delay is due to the default of the supplier? The customer's remedy will depend on whether the time for performance was 'of the essence' of the contract. If so, he will be entitled to cancel the contract, and recover damages. If not, his remedy will be confined to damages.

Time will be of the essence if there is an express provision to that effect in the contract. The same result may also be achieved in commercial contracts by simply specifying a date for performance, as it is generally accepted that, without any express stipulation to the contrary, time will be of the essence in a commercial contract. Even if time is not initially made of the essence, this does not mean that the customer has to wait forever for performance. If the supplier fails to complete by the agreed date, the customer may make time of the essence by serving notice on the supplier, requiring him to complete within a reasonable time. If the supplier fails to meet that deadline, the customer may treat the contract as discharged and recover damages.

Some contracts do not mention a date for completion of the contract at all. Although this is unsatisfactory, it does not mean that the supplier may perform when he chooses. The law will imply an obligation on the part of the supplier to complete within a reasonable time.

It is rare for a supplier to allow time to be of the essence in a contract, either by agreeing to an express provision or committing himself to a particular completion date. However, suppliers are sometimes prepared to give a firm date for completion if the customer agrees to confine his remedy to liquidated (ie estimated) damages in the event of a delay. Such an arrangement entails the parties' making a genuine pre-estimate of the loss likely to be suffered by the customer in the event of the supplier's delay. Such an estimate may in some cases be provided by costing a bureau service which the customer would need to use to tide him over the delay. The contract will then provide for the contract price to be reduced by a stated amount (reflecting the estimated damage) each week, or other period during which the delay continues, up to a stated maximum. The advantage to the supplier is that his overall liability is limited to the stated maximum. The customer may also benefit, because it will be possible to obtain a reduction in the price without resorting to litigation. An example is as follows:

(1) The Supplier shall complete this Agreement on or before 31 December 1995 ('the Completion Date')

(2) For the purposes of this Clause 'complete this Agreement' means to deliver and install the System and to complete successfully the Supplier's standard tests in accordance with Clauses X and Y hereof

(3) If the Supplier fails to complete this Agreement by the Completion Date then the Supplier shall pay to the Customer as and by way of liquidated damages for any loss or damage sustained by the Customer resulting from delay during the period from the Completion Date to the date on which the Supplier completes this Agreement the aggregate sum of 1 per cent of the total Contract Price for each week of such delay and pro rata for parts of a week up to a total maximum of 15 per cent of the total Contract Price. The payment of such sum shall be in full satisfaction of the Supplier's liability for delay in completing this Agreement. The payment of liquidated damages shall not relieve the Supplier from the obligation to deliver the Equipment or from any other liability or obligation under this Agreement.

A word of warning, however, about such clauses. The pre-estimate of damage must not be penal, for otherwise the clause will be unenforceable. The customer should, therefore, resist any temptation to agree to an arbitrary figure, but instead be prepared to show that the pre-estimate was reached on a justifiable basis.

Customer's delay [A16]

It is of course possible for the customer to cause delay by failing to prepare his installation site. That obligation is dealt with below [2.6.3], but it is worth pointing out that any such delay will have serious consequences for the supplier since it will mean that he cannot proceed to commissioning, acceptance and payment; and also that he has to store and insure the equipment until it can be delivered. The same problem may also arise if the customer has failed to prepare test data in time [3.3.1; 10.3]. Accordingly the clause on delay is often expressed in mutual terms:

Neither the Supplier nor the Customer shall be liable for delay in performance or failure to perform their obligations if such delay or failure is caused by circumstances beyond the reasonable control of the party so delaying or failing.

The question of storage of equipment which cannot be delivered through the customer's fault is covered by:

If by the Delivery Date the Supplier has not received from the Customer instructions sufficient to enable the Supplier to deliver the Equipment the Supplier shall be entitled to arrange storage of the Equipment on the Customer's behalf. All such storage charges insurance and other associated costs which may be incurred by the Supplier shall be discharged or repaid by the Customer and the risk of deterioration and damage to the Equipment so stored shall lie with the Customer.

The contract may also go on to provide for the compensation of the supplier generally:

If the Supplier is unable to complete this Agreement by the Completion Date due to the neglect or default of the Customer then:

(*a*) the Customer shall pay to the Supplier all reasonable costs, charges and losses of the Supplier attributable to such delay; and

(*b*) notwithstanding the Supplier's inability to complete on the Completion Date the remaining balance of the Contract Price shall fall due to be paid on the Completion Date.

If payment is due on completion the supplier would obviously be prejudiced if he could not complete due to the customer's default; hence the reason for the specific provision dealing with accelerated payment.

2.3.8 Defects [A19; O24]

Neither side would usually pretend that the on-site testing will discover every possible defect in the hardware. Many defects will become apparent only after extensive use. The usual procedure in the industry is for the supplier to guarantee the hardware for a limited period of either 6 or 12 months against faulty design, workmanship or materials, but to exclude all other conditions that may be implied in the customer's favour by law:

The Supplier will repair or at his option replace all defective parts which under proper use care and maintenance appear in the Equipment within 12 calendar months after the issue of the

Commissioning Certificate and arise solely from faulty design materials or workmanship.

Except as expressly provided in this Agreement, no warranty, condition, undertaking or term, express or implied, statutory or otherwise, as to condition, satisfactory quality, performance, durability or fitness for purpose of the Equipment is given or assumed by the Supplier and all such warranties, conditions, undertakings and terms are hereby excluded.

The warranty offered under clauses like this is often 'off-site'—ie the customer must at his own expense return the faulty piece of equipment to the maintenance contractor or supplier. Full maintenance contracts usually provide for 'on-site' maintenance—ie the maintenance contractor comes to the customer's premises when equipment needs maintenance. So a warranty of this sort is rarely directly comparable to a full maintenance service.

Most contracts emphasise the proper use, care and maintenance aspects, and the customer who does not have a maintenance agreement (see Chapter 8) with the supplier is obviously in a weaker position. It is also common for the contract to exclude from the warranty any equipment which has been modified by the customer:

This warranty is contingent upon proper use of the Equipment in the application for which the Equipment is intended and does not cover Equipment which has been modified without the Supplier's written approval or which has been subjected to unusual physical or electrical stress or on which the original identification marks have been removed or altered. Nor will this warranty apply if adjustment repair or parts replacement is required because of accident hazard misuse failure of electric power air conditioning humidity control transportation or causes other than ordinary use.

The inclusion of transportation in this list is significant and not unusual. If insurance during transportation is the supplier's responsibility, the customer should satisfy himself that it covers defects caused by transportation but not apparent till later.

Electrical stress is a reminder of the damage power surges can cause and customers in any doubt about this should either endeavour to obtain a 'clean' power supply and/or be prepared to fit a constant voltage transformer, 'smoother' or uninterruptable power supply (UPS). These matters should be discussed in advance with the supplier.

The removal or defacement of identifications is primarily directed at OEM customers who purchase the equipment in order to sell it as a mixed configuration with their own or someone else's equipment. The practice of an OEM supplier affixing his own badge or identification to all the equipment he supplies is quite common; in its simplest form, where an OEM supplier does nothing but package disparate pieces of equipment under his own label, this practice is derogatively called 'badge engineering'. But it is natural that the supplier should want his own labels to be intact. Any customer purchasing a mixed configuration from an OEM should be on the watch for traces of defaced or removed labels, and should question his OEM as to his authority to do so—particularly if his maintenance is performed by somebody other than the OEM.

The customer may, of course, attempt to rely on his statutory rights and here the Unfair Contract Terms Act 1977 provides protection against unreasonable warranty exclusion or limitation clauses. This was demonstrated in the recent case in the High Court of *St Albans City and District Council v International Computers Ltd, Computers and Law* NS 5, No 5 (December 1994/January 1995) 14–16, (1994) *The Times*, 11 November, where it was held that a contractual limitation of £100,000 was unreasonable in the context of losses flowing from a defective computer system of £1,300,000. Suppliers will now have to reassess their contracts in this area, and cannot assume that the same considerations will apply at all times and to every customer. Much may turn on the relative strength and resources of the parties, the contract value, the insurance cover available to each party, the options available to the customer to seek a similar system elsewhere, any inducements offered to the customer to accept the limitations and public policy considerations. There has in the past been some doubt as to whether the Act would apply to software in every case but the courts have construed the relevant exemption in the Act in a fairly restrictive way such that customers for software should in most cases be able to rely on the Act's protection—see 3.3.3.

2.4   Termination

2.4.1   Sale [A17, A18]

Many hardware contracts are curiously reticent about the possibility of termination. From the supplier's point of view, this is probably deliberate policy since he is concerned primarily in off-loading his equipment and claiming payments. Any attempt to fail to perform a contractual duty can be interpreted as a delay caused by the customer [2.3.7] rather than an attempt to terminate, and may even add to the cost [2.5]. To the extent that suppliers are very unwilling to vary their contracts, a customer should ensure that there is no possibility of his changing his mind before purchasing. If he is in any doubt he should seek a rental agreement which foresees an end to the agreement. Otherwise the price adjustment clause [2.2.4] provides an opportunity to terminate; or, of course, total failure of consideration may do so.

Nevertheless, a supplier with a full order book and long delays in delivery may find it worthwhile to include a termination clause which will enable him, if the customer wishes to cancel the order, to realise some money immediately from the customer and, by passing the equipment to another customer, bring forward the payment on that order also.

> If the Customer wishes to terminate this Agreement in whole or in part at any time before the Delivery Date (other than for any breach by the Supplier which would entitle the Customer to terminate) then the Supplier shall agree to the termination of this Agreement in respect of the equipment cancelled upon the Customer paying to the Supplier as agreed and liquidated damages:
> (a) a sum equal to 6 per cent of the contract price of the equipment cancelled; and
> (b) a sum equal to 12 per cent of the said contract price reduced by 1 per cent in respect of each complete calendar month unexpired between the date of termination and the Delivery Date.

As mentioned above [2.3.7], a contractual provision of this nature will be enforceable only if it represents a genuine pre-estimate of the loss likely to be suffered by the supplier. An alternative would be to provide for the payment of a deposit by the customer which would not then be returnable in the event of a cancellation by the customer [2.2.1].

2.4.2   Rental [B31]

Here termination is usually visualised either as a result of the customer's breach of an obligation (most usually to pay rent) or if his company commences to be wound up, and so on:

> Without prejudice to any other remedy which may be available to the Supplier under this Agreement, the Supplier may by written notice to the Hirer forthwith determine this Agreement:
> (a) if the Hirer commits any breach of this Agreement which is not remedied within 30 days after the Supplier has given written notice thereof to the Hirer; or
> (b) if the Hirer, being an incorporated company, shall have a receiver, administrative receiver or liquidator appointed or shall pass a resolution for winding-up or a court shall make an order to that effect or being a partnership shall be dissolved or being an individual shall commit any act of bankruptcy or shall die

or the Hirer (whether an incorporated company or not) shall enter into any voluntary arrangement with the Hirer's creditors.

A clause which deals with termination of rental begins with the same preamble as the example quoted above [2.4.1], and itemises the damages as given in that clause where the termination is before delivery. Where the termination is after delivery (by which time the equipment will no longer be new and thus cannot be delivered as new to another customer), the following is appropriate:

Where the Customer wishes to terminate this Agreement at any time after delivery of the Equipment, there shall become payable by the Customer to the Supplier 75 per cent of the hire charges due for the balance of the minimum hire period, subject to a minimum payment equal to the full hire charges for a period of six months.

Again, such a clause may be unenforceable if it is considered to be penal.

2.5   Alterations [B17, B26]

In the case of most standard hardware contracts the question of alterations should not arise except in so far as the supplier may himself improve, substitute or modify his own equipment [2.1.1]. However, sometimes the customer changes his mind about the equipment he requires, either because his own perception of his computing requirements has changed or because the supplier has offered an alternative new system. If the change is substantial it is probably best to tear up the old contract and start again with new estimated delivery dates and time scales; but if the alterations are small the old contract may stand with appropriate modifications.

However, the customer should be aware of the likely effect of his change of plan. Each item of equipment requires a different length of time to prepare for despatch, and a change of plan is likely to affect delivery periods. If the new equipment does not affect the viability of the previous configuration (eg a contract for two more terminals), the late delivery of these items causes very little problem. But if the equipment is fundamental (a larger or faster disk drive and controller to replace an older model), the entire delivery period and all that follows on that will have to be replanned. This might be interpreted as a customer's delay [2.3.7] and the customer should clarify this point when he orders the new equipment. A clause visualising such a change runs:

Should the Supplier incur extra cost owing to variation or suspension of the work by the Customer's instructions or lack of instructions or to interruptions delays overtime unusual hours mistakes or work for which the Supplier is not responsible all such extra cost shall be paid by the Customer.

If in a rental agreement, new equipment is required which does not involve a complete replacement of existing equipment, but is simply in addition, the period of rental for the new equipment will probably be made to coincide with the unexpired portion of the existing rental agreement.

The Customer may hire equipment (subject to the availability of such equipment) from the Supplier in addition to that listed in Schedule *A* hereof by written order to the Supplier referring to this Agreement, and by receipt of written acceptance of such order by the Supplier. The rental period for such additional equipment shall continue until the expiry of the rental period defined in Clause *X* hereof, unless the parties otherwise agree in writing. Monthly rentals initially payable for such additional equipment shall be those in effect when such additional equipment is delivered and accepted.

2.6 Customer's duties

The customer's duties, apart from the duty to pay the contract price or rental, include:

(1) providing information;
(2) keeping confidentiality;
(3) preparing the site;
(4) care and maintenance;
(5) miscellaneous and general provisions.

2.6.1 Providing information [A6]

This requirement is chiefly relevant where some feature is required in the system peculiar to the contract. In most commercial applications such features are provided by software [3.6] and to this extent a clause to this effect is not usually included in a hardware contract. Where it is relevant the clause might read:

The Customer undertakes promptly to provide to the Supplier all necessary information that the Supplier may reasonably from time to time require to permit him to proceed uninterruptedly with the performance of this Agreement. In the event that the Customer

42

fails or delays in providing such information so that the work is delayed or increased thereby the Supplier reserves the right to increase the Contract Price to cover the cost of such delay or increase.

2.6.2   Confidentiality [A21]

This also is included in contracts which include some novel or unusual hardware feature which the supplier wishes to keep from his competitors. In the case of American companies, the early announcement of an enhancement or a new piece of equipment may even be interpreted as an unfair act under anti-trust laws, and it is therefore essential to the supplier that confidentiality shall be preserved until he is ready to make a public announcement. Sometimes also the customer may, wittingly or unwittingly, learn something of the supplier's other customers. In a tender, also, the unsuccessful tenderers do not want their ideas to be plagiarised by others. Such a clause as the following is therefore appropriate:

> The Customer undertakes that he and his staff will keep confidential and not disclose to any third party without the Supplier's prior consent in writing any drawings design or information (whether of a commercial or technical nature) acquired from the Supplier in connection with the work the subject of this Agreement.

2.6.3   Site preparation [A5]

Computers can be large pieces of equipment and some require special environments both for technical reasons (free of dust, with controlled temperature or humidity, and so on) and because of the sensitivity of the information they handle (requiring security checks, smart cards, and so forth). This can imply either a totally new building or a considerable refitting of an existing building. It is the customer's duty to ensure that such an environment is ready before the equipment is to be delivered, and he cannot expect the supplier to bear the cost of any storage and/or insurance caused by delay due to his failure to have his computer room ready on time [2.3.7]. Accordingly it is reasonable for a supplier to stipulate that:

> The Customer shall at his own expense prepare and provide all proper accommodation and facilities including proper environmental conditions for the Equipment and its maintenance in accordance with the Supplier's specification 30 days before the Estimated Delivery Date. For this purpose the Supplier will make available to the Customer free of charge the advice of a site engineer.

This last point is a good one, for it means that the customer should get adequate on the spot advice from the supplier. The customer can hardly be blamed for failing to prepare the site if the supplier has not advised him of what to do, nor checked that he has done it.

Another example of the same requirement, but also bringing in the question of supplier access, is comprised in:

> To enable the Supplier expeditiously and properly to fulfil his obligations under this Agreement the Customer shall provide the Supplier and his staff or agents with suitable access to and uninterrupted use of the site to prepare foundations and satisfactory environmental conditions for the Equipment and shall provide any electrical power lighting and hoisting necessary and all other necessary facilities.

2.6.4 Care [A24; O20]

In a rental agreement the hirer undertakes to maintain the equipment [2.2.2], usually using the supplier or his approved maintenance contractor for the purpose:

> The Customer hereby undertakes to enter into a Maintenance Agreement with the Supplier in the Supplier's standard form current at the date of this Agreement in respect of the Equipment.

2.6.5 Miscellaneous

These points, which need not be given in detail, include:

(1) undertakings not to assign or mortgage [A30];
(2) undertakings not to deface or remove badges or labels [2.3.8; A23; B27];
(3) undertakings to insure [B18]; and
(4) undertakings not to jeopardise the insurance of the equipment.

2.6.6 Supplier's remedies

A customer who defaults on payment or fails to assume his other obligations may well not terminate the agreement but simply render himself liable to surrender the equipment to the supplier while still fully liable for the contract price:

> If after the date of this Agreement the Customer shall fail to perform any of his obligations under Clause *X* hereof the full amount of the Contract Price remaining to be paid by the Customer under this Agreement shall immediately and without notice become due

and payable and the Supplier shall have the right to repossess the Equipment without notice on demand and without any let or hindrance on the part of the Customer.

2.7   Supplier's duties

2.7.1   Confidentiality [A21]

This clause is common to both hardware and software agreements, but, since it is usually more relevant to software, it is dealt with in Chapter 3 [3.7.2].

2.7.2   VDUs and health [A19(2)]

An obligation on a customer owed to his own staff should be supported by a duty on the supplier. Under EC Council Directive 90/270/EEC employers have to comply with certain standards for staff who use display screens. Under art 3 employers are obliged to analyse the workstations from a health and safety point of view and remedy the risks found. For all new workstations they should obtain low radiation screens (these are now available) and each customer should ensure that his screens comply with this. A warranty from the supplier that the equipment complies would be an appropriate clause in a hardware contract. It should be noted that old equipment already installed before the directive came into force (31 December 1992) must be replaced not later than 31 December 1996.

For completeness we mention the customer's remaining obligations to his staff, though they do not need any change to the contract between the supplier and the customer. Article 6 requires the customer to provide information and training to his staff. Article 7 requires that there must be breaks or changes in activity. Article 8 requires workers' consultation and participation. Article 9 provides for eye tests.

These various requirements embody no more than good practice already put into operation in most responsible companies, but it should be noted that they are now backed by law.

2.7.3   Electromagnetic compatibility [A13]

The Electromagnetic Compatibility Regulations 1992 (SI 1992 No 2372), implementing EU Directives 89/336/EEC, 91/263/EEC and 91/31/EEC, apply to nearly all electrical or electronic apparatus sold in EU states on or after 28 October 1992. Manufacturers and distributors are obliged to ensure their equipment meets certain standards of compatibility and this usually requires certification of compliance by the manufacturer or supplier. The legislation applies to assemblers (ie OEMs—see 1.5) as well as manufacturers and applies when the apparatus is first put on sale as well as when it is first used and continues to be applicable thereafter. Exemptions are few—simple components such as integrated circuits, second-hand equipment and equipment which is or will be covered by other directives dealing with electromagnetic compatibility. The obligation continues even after installation. Apparatus which is suspected not to be compliant and whose sale is prohibited or suspended cannot be provided by a supplier and failure to observe this is an offence. There is no Crown immunity in the legislation.

There are four years of transitional arrangements which will expire on 1 January 1996. From that date full compliance will be required but until then contractors can choose between compliance with the directive or compliance with such earlier legislation as may have existed in the member state before the directive. In the UK this means the Wireless Telegraphy Act 1949, s 10. It would seem easiest and most sensible to comply fully with the directive now.

It should be noted that there is a second 1992 statutory instrument on this topic (the Electromagnetic Compatibility (Wireless Telegraphy Apparatus) Certification and Test Fees Regulations 1992 (SI 1992 No 2373)). As its name suggests, it is confined to wireless telegraphy apparatus and in particular to such apparatus as is not covered in SI 1992 No 2372 by defence, civil aviation or ordinary telecommunications through the BABT [2.7.4]. We doubt whether it can therefore apply to IT telecommunications apparatus and have therefore ignored it.

2.7.4 Telecommunications approval [A1, A14; B1]

No equipment can be connected to a telecommunications system which is, or is to be, connected to a public system in the UK unless it is approved by the Secretary of State for Trade and Industry (Telecommunications Act 1984, s 22) on advice from the British Approvals Board for Telecommunications (BABT). The BABT is, in practice, responsible for inspecting and testing equipment which is proposed to be connected to a public telecommunication system and for recommending acceptance or rejection to the Secretary of State. Readers are no doubt familiar by now with the 'BABT Approved' and 'red triangle' stickers which are placed on telecommunications equipment pursuant to the Telecommunication Apparatus (Marketing and Labelling) Order 1985 (SI 1985 No 717) indicating either that they are or that they are not approved.

Despite the existence of such stickers there can be no harm in asking the supplier to warrant that his equipment is approved. The wording of such a warranty is likely to follow the wording on the sticker:

The Supplier warrants that at the date hereof the equipment is approved for use with the telecommunication system run by [British Telecommunications plc] in accordance with the conditions in the instructions for use.

'Equipment' would include instruments, modems and other communications devices.

There may also be a clause restricting the customer from modifying any approved equipment:

The Customer undertakes that he will make no modification to any part of the Equipment connected to any public telecommunication system without the prior written consent of the Supplier.

The supplier may also envisage the possibility that the Secretary of State may at some later stage alter the requirements, in which case he may be obliged to change his own equipment:

If at any time the Secretary of State pursuant to the provisions of the Telecommunications Act 1984 requires the Supplier to modify or alter the Equipment or any part thereof as a condition of the Secretary of State's continued approval of the Equipment or part thereof then the Customer shall allow the Supplier from time to time to do so at the Customer's expense.

In practice it is not likely to be a very onerous clause, since the possibility of it ever being invoked is remote.

Additionally, the supplier might protect himself from inadvertently seeming to usurp the Secretary of State's authority:

The Supplier does not warrant the continuation of the consent of the Secretary of State pursuant to the provisions of the Telecommunications Act 1984 to the connection of the Equipment to any public telecommunications system.

2.8 Title and intellectual property rights [A4, A26; P16]

2.8.1 Title to the hardware

It is usual in a sale agreement for title to the hardware to pass to the customer after the final payment, but the insurable risk usually passes on delivery:

Title to each item of the Equipment shall remain with the Supplier until the total Price for the item has been received by the Supplier. Risk shall pass to the Customer on delivery of the Equipment at the Installation Site.

This may also be followed by a warranty as to title:

> The Supplier warrants that upon the payment of the full Contract Price and any other charges payable under this Agreement the Customer shall acquire good clear title to the Equipment free from all liens or encumbrances.

Title remains with the supplier in a rental agreement.

2.8.2   Patent and other intellectual property rights

A separate clause as to patents giving the customer an indemnity against any possible infringement of patents is also usual:

> The Supplier will indemnify the Customer against any claim for alleged infringement of any Letters Patent by the normal use or possession of the Equipment or any part thereof provided that the Supplier is given immediate and complete control of any such claim.

Often the clause seeks to cover all intellectual property rights together:

> . . . Letters Patent registered designs design rights trade marks or copyright

and this is particularly likely when the clause seeks to cover software rights as well as hardware rights.

It should be noted that indemnities of this nature are usually limited to the liabilities incurred by the customer to the third party and do not extend to compensating the customer for loss of use of the equipment. It is fairly common for the supplier to reserve the right to replace the infringing equipment with non-infringing equipment or, where this cannot be done, to buy back the infringing equipment at the original price paid by the customer less depreciation.

2.8.3   Integral software [A4(3–5)]

It is becoming increasingly common for computer equipment to be supplied to the customer with embedded or integral software or with software already loaded on to the hard disk. Typically, this would include operating systems and possibly applications software as well. Where the equipment is special equipment designed for a particular task, its functions may be controlled by a piece of specially formulated software which, because it is not likely to be changed, is embedded in the equipment in a board or in the form of a chip. The customer may be unaware that he is using such software or 'firmware' and may not care as long as the machine performs the task he desires. In other cases, the supply of accompanying software will be a marketing feature and it is now commonplace for retailers of PCs and PC software [4] to advertise 'bundled' offers of a PC and a range of third party applications software for sale.

The contractual approach to integral or embedded software varies enormously. To take an everyday example, the 'computer' contained in the modern motor vehicle is very unlikely to be accompanied by a licence agreement authorising the user to use it in a defined manner. It is embedded in the vehicle and commercial expediency dictates that a licensing agreement is impractical. The owner of the intellectual property rights in the firmware merely relies on his rights at law which, in that example, are probably perfectly adequate in relation to what is a relatively low value item. The law will imply a right in favour of the purchaser or user to use the embedded software for the purpose for which it is intended and nothing further is required. This is equally true of sophisticated computer equipment containing integral software of high value but in that case the owner of the rights may be anxious at least to assert such rights by an acknowledgment from the customer that they exist and are protected and to go even further by incorporating express licence terms in any sale agreement. This may be the case particularly where the software owner is concerned that the embedded software may be extracted and used for a purpose other than the one which he intends. The right to terminate any licence will give the owner added protection in that event. Where licence terms are incorporated the points raised in 3.8.1 will be relevant.

In theory when the owner of a car with embedded firmware comes to sell the car, the question of how the software licence can be passed on to the new owner arises. This is treated in more detail in 7.4 where the problem is particularly acute. In the present instance, the owner of the intellectual property rights is likely to be the same as the manufacturer of the hardware and therefore there is an implied right for any subsequent purchaser of his car to use the software on the same terms as the original purchaser.

The ownership of the intellectual property rights in the integral software will help to determine the nature of the contractual documentation. Package software belonging to third parties which is supplied with hardware will often be accompanied with its own shrink-wrap licence agreement [5.3.6.4]. It may be a term of any related distribution agreement that the distributor must take steps to draw to the customer's attention that he is required to abide by the terms of such licence agreement. Where the integral software is of high value, the owner (if not also the supplier of the software) may insist that the hardware supplier must require the customer to sign an express licence agreement before the software can be supplied as part of the equipment. In such a case, the sale agreement may include a term that the customer must execute the licence agreement before the equipment (including the integral software) will be delivered. If the software owner and the hardware supplier are one and the same, then the terms of any express licence may be incorporated in the sale agreement. In either case the licence agreement may include a term requiring the purchaser to ensure that any subsequent purchaser agrees to abide by the terms of the licence.

2.9   Miscellaneous

2.9.1   Export control [A25]

Mainframes and mini-computers are generally supplied for use in one particular location. If the equipment is subsequently to be installed at a different location it is as well to advise the supplier, if only because otherwise maintenance agreements may be invalidated [8.5.1]. If the customer wishes to re-export the equipment, he will have not only to cover maintenance, but also to obtain the necessary export licence. So far as the regulations are concerned, this is covered by the Export of Goods (Control) Order 1994, SI 1994 No 1191, as amended by SI 1994 Nos 1632, 2518 and 2711. Computers and software fall under Part III Group 3 (Industrial Goods) especially Sections 3 (Electronics), 4 (Computers) and 5 (Telecommunications and Information Security) and their re-export can be prohibited to certain countries.

But the export or re-export of computers was not always simply a UK matter. UK representatives met colleagues from other governments in a Co-ordinating Committee called CoCom. The governments in question comprised all the NATO states except Iceland but included Japan and Australia. The purpose of CoCom was to co-ordinate exports so as to prevent certain proscribed countries from obtaining technology which might have had a defence application. Each government agreed to give effect to the export bans through national legislation. As a result of the reforms in Eastern Europe considerable relaxations in the rules were implemented, particularly in relation to the export restrictions on computers. CoCom itself was finally disbanded by common consent of its members on 31 March 1994 because the strategic threat from the Eastern bloc had disappeared but all CoCom members agreed to maintain national export controls based on CoCom lists of goods and technologies. SI 1994 No 1191 and its amendments specify the present licensing controls.

Countries in the current list include states locked in civil war (Angola, Rwanda, Somalia, Sudan); countries involved in local wars (Armenia and Azerbaijan); 'those territories recognised by Her Majesty's

Government in the United Kingdom as having been comprised within the Socialist Federal Republic of Yugoslavia on 25 September 1991 which are not specified in Article 3B1.(i)'; and oppressive regimes such as Myanmar (formerly Burma). Intending exporters must apply to the Department of Trade and Industry for up-to-date information.

Further complications arise in equipment of American origin, or equipment which contains US components or know-how. In the first edition of this book an example of such clauses was included from a contract with a US manufacturer:

> The Customer agrees that he will not resell, ship or otherwise dispose of the Equipment to the People's Republic of China, North Korea, Cuba, Uganda, Rhodesia or the USSR or any of the Soviet Bloc countries (as defined in the prevailing United States Export Regulations) without the prior written consent of the Supplier.

In the intervening years since that edition, the situation has become more complicated. The US Government at the time of writing is very unlikely to grant any export orders to a number of countries including several Communist and Middle Eastern states, but now seeks to prohibit re-export of US equipment to *any* country without a valid order from the Bureau of Export Administration in the US Department of Commerce. Accordingly, such clauses as the following may be found in contracts for US manufactured goods:

> The Equipment is subject to Export Controls defined by the Department of Commerce in the USA and is restricted to sale in the UK.

Needless to say, this policy is arousing violent protest.

Despite this there is now a requirement from some US companies to non-US OEMs that the US manufacturer be allowed to audit the OEM's books to ensure that US Department of Commerce regulations are being complied with. It has even been alleged that US companies use such a clause to acquire full knowledge of the business of their foreign OEM and thus be in a good position to curb the OEM or take other commercial action against them.

Chapter 3

Software

3.0 Introduction
 3.0.1 Importance of software
 3.0.2 Packages
 3.0.3 Commissioned software
   Time and materials contracts
   Fixed price contract
   Estimated maximum price contract

3.1 Service to be performed

3.2 Payment
 3.2.1 Milestones
 3.2.2 Logic bombs for non-payment

3.3 Delivery and acceptance
 3.3.1 Acceptance tests
 3.3.2 Performance
 3.3.3 Error correction

3.4 Termination
 3.4.1 Termination by performance
 3.4.2 Termination or breach by the client
   Voluntary termination
   Infringement of title
   Failure to pay
   Client's incapacity
 3.4.3 Termination by the software house

3.5 Alterations
 3.5.1 Packages
 3.5.2 Commissioned software

3.6 Client's duties
3.6.1 Co-operation on systems design
Liaison and nominees
Information
Office facilities
Computer facilities
Expenses
3.6.2 Poaching staff

3.7 Software house's duties
3.7.1 Staff
Nomination
Dress and conformity
3.7.2 Confidentiality
3.7.3 Staff training

3.8 Title
3.8.1 Licences
Back up copies
Decompilation
Analysing the ideas underlying software
Copying and adapting software and correcting errors
Severability
Ownership of rights
3.8.2 Bespoke software

Chapter 3

Software

3.0 Introduction

3.0.1 Importance of software

When a computer is bought, the purchaser usually goes to a great deal of care in examining the contract for the machinery (hardware) itself, but may be tempted to examine the contract for programs (software) less critically. Yet software contracts are at least as important as hardware contracts because:

(1) the software may be tailor-made to your requirements and, if so, will involve estimates of future capabilities and hence uncertainty;

(2) the cost of hardware is falling, but the cost of software (whose production must necessarily be labour-intensive) is rising so that, on some small computer systems, the software cost will actually outstrip the hardware cost;

(3) bad hardware will sometimes retain some capital value and hence re-sale value, but bad software is unsaleable: conversely, good software may prove to be a very valuable asset;

(4) good software can get something useful out of poor or obsolescent hardware, whereas bad software can do nothing with even the finest hardware.

A further important aspect of software is that it may not be eligible for capital allowances. This point applies equally to contracts of purchase as to leases, but because of the other special aspects of leases it is dealt with in 7.4.1.

In speaking of tailor-made software, we are dealing with programs written at the user's request, and not dealing with 'packages'—the unlovely term used to describe off-the-peg programs where the user purchases merely a non-exclusive licence to use someone else's program. The first thing to establish, when purchasing software, is whether you are treating for a licence, or whether you are embarked on a piece of software written exclusively to your own requirements. A third possibility also exists—a package with a few modifications specifically asked for. In that case, the user has to consider the contract both in its package aspect and in its tailor-made context.

The distinction between packages and bespoke (or partially bespoke) software is an increasingly important one. Package software is becoming simply a commodity and as such marketed like hardware. This is particularly true of PC software [Chapter 4]. Bespoke software, however, is a service and so more akin to consultancy. Public sector rules seem to be tending towards treating package software as procurable under a supplies contract whereas bespoke software is more likely to come under a service contract—see 12.1.

3.0.2   Packages [C2; O2]

Package contracts are usually fairly straightforward. The user should have had an opportunity to see and even test the package in advance of procuring it. Typically, package contracts will stress that the user is acquiring only a licence—which may be revoked, is non-exclusive, and cannot be passed to a third party without the package owner's agreement or, alternatively, subject to the condition that the transferor must deliver the package and its documentation to the transferee on terms that the transferee agrees to abide by the package owner's licence. Often the package may not even be used on any other computer than the one specified, even though the user may own more than one machine. Packages are usually priced to provide a licence for use on an individual machine ('machine licence'). This maximises the licensor's fees but more importantly warns the customer that he cannot simply copy the package to another machine. When the customer has several appropriate machines, there may be economies of scale in seeking a 'site licence' for all suitable machines to use copies of the package at a single site. The package owner (licensor) reserves all title to the software and to its documentation (not only program lists, but also operating instructions, user manuals, etc, all of which are copyright material). There is often an installation charge and the amount of advice and instruction the user can expect from the package owner is defined, together with undertakings as to future maintenance of the package.

Sometimes the user receives the full source listing of programs, which theoretically might enable him to alter or amend it himself. Some contracts expressly forbid him to do this, or allow him to do so only with the consent of the package owner. Whether or not he is allowed to do this, it is likely to have a serious effect on any maintenance contract for the software, which usually stipulates that the user cannot alter the package in any way. Sometimes the user is not given the listing of the program at all, but only the program in a form ready to load and run—known as the object code; in this condition it is, for all practical purposes, impossible for all but the most expert user to amend (or even understand) the internal workings of the program.

Sometimes the package may itself contain software written by a third party. Such software may be a file handler within a general system, for example. The user should satisfy himself that any package he buys is *entirely* the property of the purported owner and, if other software is involved, should enquire into the nature of the licence, any additional fee he may have to pay to the licensor of the original package, and the availability of instructions and maintenance (as required) for the package. He is justified in asking for an indemnity against any future copyright infringement claim in respect of the package (or part of it) from a third party [C12].

Some suppliers have different categories of software with different levels of support. The variations in support might cover such topics as:

(1) A guaranteed minimum time for which the package will be maintained (this might be Category I).
(2) A guarantee that the software will be compatible with any future releases of other software from the supplier, eg operating systems (this might be Categories I and II).
(3) A particular level of maintenance—or lack of it (Category III might have no maintenance).

> Any package supplied in Category III to the Customer is to be taken and accepted by the Customer on an 'as is' basis and the Supplier does not thereby undertake any obligations in respect of its support, except in respect of error or malfunction in a package formerly in Categories I or II, where notice of such error or malfunction was given by the Customer to the Supplier before it was reclassified as Category III.
>
> The Supplier shall give to the Customer not less than 60 days' notice of any reclassification of the Package. The Customer shall then have the right to terminate this Agreement on one month's notice.

When software is being purchased along with second-hand equipment, there may be particular difficulties. Has the vendor the right to pass on his software licence to the purchaser? This problem arises acutely in the case of leases where a lessor attempts to resell the equipment and the arguments rehearsed in the chapter on leasing [7.4.2] appear equally to apply to any other second-hand purchase involving software.

For a case in point, readers are referred to *Intergraph Corporation v Solid Systems Cad Services Ltd* [1993] FSR 617.

3.0.3 Commissioned software [D2, D5]

By this term is meant programs written expressly for a particular user. Such software is also referred to as 'tailor-made' or 'bespoke'; it is the opposite of the 'package'.

It is the nature of contracts for commissioned software that the user is buying something which does not yet exist (in contrast to packages which can be tested before purchase) and this is likely to increase the cost, time scale and risk. Most users will therefore prefer packaged software whenever possible.

Such software may be purchased under any of three main types of contract:

(1) time and materials (including contract programming);
(2) fixed price;
(3) estimated maximum price.

Such contracts are usually between a user (called a client) and a programming company (software house) or a manufacturer.

Time and materials contracts

These are the simplest type of contracts, whereby the client promises to pay the software house for all time spent and expenses incurred. From the software house's point of view, providing they have adequately costed their staff's time, and kept accurate time and expense records, they run no risk of being out of pocket on the job. They will usually bill the client on a monthly basis. Two types of time and materials contracts should be distinguished.

Contract programming (or 'bodyshopping' as it is more usually and vulgarly known) is a primitive form of time and materials contract whereby the client hires the programmer from the software house on a *per diem* basis. In this case, no actual program is specified, nor even mentioned: the sole requirement is that the programmer will be available to program at premises specified by the client on particular dates. Weekly rates for an experienced but not very senior programmer might be from £2,000 to £4,000, plus expenses. Staff with deeper or more esoteric experience and skills will naturally command higher rates. If contract programming is offered at rates substantially below these figures, then either a very small software house (whose overheads, and probably skills and profits, will be meagre) will be involved; or it may even be a case of 'moonlighting'—a term of art which covers the case of a programmer working for company A and selling his skills to company B in his spare time (or even in A's time). This will almost certainly be in breach of his contract of employment with A, and will involve severe risks for B. Whatever the status of the individual concerned, he should always be put under contract [11.2; T].

A time and materials contract (as opposed to contract programming) involves the software house in the responsibility of delivering a finished program. Materials in this context may include computer time, storage charges (for programs and test data on the computer)—unless, of course, the client can himself provide these. Although the cost is charged on the basis of time and materials, this should not preclude the software house from giving as realistic an estimate as it can of the time and cost.

Such an estimate may also include 'milestones'—particular stages in the work to be reached by particular dates [3.2.1]; and these, while primarily serving as a trigger for payment, give both parties a chance to monitor progress, and to review or even halt the proceedings if the original estimates seem to be too far astray. The client should also expect regular progress meetings to monitor development—at least once a month.

Although such a contract seems a little vague, it is probably the commonest type of commissioned software contract in the computer industry. It depends on complete confidence between client and software house, but then no software contract is worth making without such confidence.

Fixed price contract

A fixed price contract states that the software house will write a program to perform certain functions at a particular price. The existence of such a contract (other than for packages) presupposes that a realistic price for the work can be estimated in advance, but, in practice, this is possible only after the software house has done a good deal of investigative work. It is therefore common for a software house to charge for such investigative work on a time and materials basis, and then set off all, or part, of the cost of this work against the fixed price for the programming. For example, C may ask S to write a program, and insist that it be on a fixed price basis; S will say that the price can be fixed only after an investigation, and suggest an estimate of £3,000 for the investigation. At the end of it, he may say that the program could be written for £19,500, but allow the £3,000 already spent against this. Thus, if C accepts that estimate, he pays £3,000 now and a further £16,500 later; if C rejects the estimate, he simply pays £3,000 now and the work goes no further. It may sometimes be worth entering into more than one such agreement with shortlisted suppliers and rejecting all but one estimate at the end.

It is worth pointing out that many software houses, including the most reputable, refuse to handle fixed price contracts at all unless the value of the work is trivial. The client who insists on such a contract is usually a first-time user, who doesn't trust the boffins; such caution is understandable, particularly as in the early days of computing many time and materials contracts went completely out of control, and involved their hapless clients in hideous expenditure. Fortunately, the number and scale of such catastrophes have decreased. But the client will find that a fixed price contract may give him peace of mind and budgetary certainty, but it will not give him the best deal. Because the contract price cannot be varied in the light of work done, the software house must add on a substantial contingency budget, which they expect never to have to use. This sounds harsh, perhaps, but it must be realised that a fixed price contract implies a lack of confidence between client and software house. (How do solicitors react when asked for a fixed price for a court action?) Furthermore, the definitions of milestones [3.2.1] and acceptance of the programs need to be stricter. If a client prematurely terminates a fixed price contract and allows the software house to do any further work, he could find that he is faced with a time and materials contract in any case.

In an extreme case, the software house may have failed to add on sufficient contingency. In this event, the software house is obviously in dire trouble, but so too is the client. For the software house, the most probable recourse will be to skimp the quality. The most likely areas to do this will be in the testing and documentation, with the result that the client will be asked to take delivery of software which still contains serious bugs and has insufficient documentation to enable the bugs to be traced. Possible deficiencies of this sort illustrate clearly the dangers of comparing two software quotations, unless it is absolutely certain that the testing and documentation are to similar standards.

Estimated maximum price contract

This contract is an attempt to avoid the rigidity of the fixed price contract and the fluidity of the time and materials contract. The basis for the work is time and materials, *but* the software house quotes a maximum for their costs (though not always for their expenses), and agrees to warn the client as the costs approach the maximum and not to exceed it without the client's express authority. If the software house does not reach the maximum the client pays only for the work performed. A contract for an investigation is often of this type.

Like the fixed price contract, the estimated maximum price contract will usually have a substantial contingency budget. Such a contingency could well be 25–50 per cent above any estimate, since it must take into account the worst possible combination of circumstances.

As with the time and materials contract, the software house will submit records of time taken and disbursements and will expect to attend regular progress meetings.

3.1 Service to be performed [D2, D4]

The software house is presumably either writing a program or supplying a completed program. The wording to cover this is often terse, uncouth and even misleading. We have seen companies promising to '*program a program*' and even '*do a program*'! The more usual term is, of course, to '*write a program*'. The simplest way of defining the purpose for which the program is written is by reference to an existing document which lists all functions in detail: '*. . . to write a program to perform all the functions more particularly described in the document entitled "Bloggs Ltd . . . Stock Control-Functional Specification" and dated 25 November 1995 . . .*'. In this way the specification becomes a part of the contract.

3.2 Payment [C3; D5]

Time and materials contracts, and estimated maximum price contracts, depend on the software house keeping accurate and complete records, and the client should satisfy himself on the adequacy of those records. He should also satisfy himself as to the records of expenses. The best opportunity to do this lies in regular progress meetings.

Under time and materials, and estimated maximum price contracts, accounts are usually rendered monthly. The alternative, which is the norm in the case of fixed price contracts, is for payment to be either once, on delivery—as also in a licence for an existing software package—or by instalments on reaching milestones.

3.2.1 Milestones [D5(1)]

A milestone is a defined stage in reaching the objective of a complete program. The first milestone is usually on signing the contract; the last is usually the client's acceptance of the software. Between those stages the definitions of what the milestones are, and how both sides will know when they are reached, are up to the two parties. A milestone could be the completion of part of the design phase—eg delivery of a system specification; or a successful demonstration of a particular part of the work. The problems of definition are analogous to the problem of defining acceptance [3.3.1].

On achieving a milestone, it is usual for a proportion of the total cost to fall due. It is thus essential for the client to satisfy himself as to the reasonableness and value of any milestones, and as to the ease (or otherwise) of saying whether or not they have been achieved. It may also be possible in certain circumstances for the client to have an option to terminate at a milestone. Any timetable for development should allow the client sufficient time for examination and review at each milestone.

Unless the contract states otherwise, money paid on achieving a milestone will not be recoverable from the software house if a later (or final) milestone is not achieved.

3.2.2   Logic bombs for non-payment

Sometimes a supplier of software has included within it a 'logic bomb' whereby after a period of time the software will become inoperable. The purpose of this is that if the customer fails to pay the supplier, the bomb can come into effect. If, however, payment is effected satisfactorily, the supplier can disable the bomb and allow the software to continue functioning. Apparently at least one such case has been considered under the Computer Misuse Act 1990. Section 3 of the Act provides for an offence of unauthorised modification of computer material and is usually thought of as designed to deal with viruses. In a case heard by the Scunthorpe magistrates' court in 1993, the supplier of the software was convicted in that his software modified the contents of the computer on which it was running. It should be noted that the software supplied was apparently actually modified by the supplier at the time of installation and further that title to the software remained with the supplier until such time as the customer had paid for it. This case was unfortunately never appealed despite much expectation at the time that it would be (the Computer Law and Security Report [1994] p 39; PLC December 1993 and reported in *IT Law Today* vol 1, issue 8, September and *Computer Weekly* on 19 August 1993). The magistrate held that had the supplier informed the customer contractually of the existence of the logic bomb, he might have been cleared. No case has yet come before the courts to test this assertion, but it would seem prudent for the supplier to include such a clause in the contract if he intends to use a logic bomb [D5(3)].

3.3   Delivery and acceptance [C4; D9; O12]

3.3.1   Acceptance tests [C6; D10; O14]

When the work is completed, the client may expect:

(1) delivery of the program in a usable form ready to load onto his computer—eg by disk or tape—or indeed actually loaded by the supplier;
(2) evidence of adequate tests performed on the programs (though for a software package this may well have been done before the signing of the agreement);
(3) manuals necessary to use the software;
(4) commencement of training (see below, Staff training [3.7.3]—the schedule of training should already have been completed);

and in the case of bespoke software:

(5) the programs ready to load, whether in source code or object code form. This will usually consist of:

   (*a*) the source code. This is the actual programs as written and before compilation [1.3];
   (*b*) flow charts and diagrams;
   (*c*) other documentation, possibly to an agreed standard; and possibly also
   (*d*) the object code—ie the programs after compilation [1.3].

   Items (*a*) and/or (*d*) will probably be in the form of a tape or disk, and there will also be a printout.

This will be essential if anyone is to maintain the program in the future (see Chapter 9) and its safeguarding will protect the client from piracy of his software [3.8]. Alternatively, where the title to the software is to remain with the software house, the source code may be deposited with a third party from where the client can retrieve it in the event of the software house going into liquidation, or failing to maintain in cases where (as is usual) maintenance is carried out by the original supplier. [N]

As with milestones, so *a fortiori* on completion of the program it is essential that there should be an agreed basis for deciding whether or not the programs are complete and perform their functions adequately. For example, one contract reads:

Acceptance by Licensee
The Licensee's acceptance of delivery of the Software shall be conclusive evidence that the Licensee has examined the Software and found it to be complete in accordance with the description

> in the Specification in good order and condition fit for any purpose
> for which it may be required and in every way satisfactory.

An adumbration of an unachievable Utopia, the cynic may say, but it emphasises the point that after acceptance of the software it is difficult for the client/licensee to make complaints about the software's performance which he could have investigated before acceptance.

In the case of software packages, the prospective user can, of course, devise such tests of the packages as he thinks necessary before signing any contract. But where bespoke programs are concerned, the nature and extent of the tests can be, and should be, defined in advance of the completion of the software. On the one hand, the tests must be agreed by both sides to be fair and reasonable: if they are not, then it would seem that the software house has written a program other than the one the client required—perhaps the design specification was at fault? On the other hand, if the software house knows the full nature and content of the tests before the programming is far advanced, the program may be designed too specifically for the expected data, failing to cope with the unexpected. In fact, this last problem is of a theoretical rather than practical nature, since the programming is defined by the specification, prepared in advance, rather than by the test data. Nevertheless, it follows that in many contracts three separate batches of test data are envisaged: test or control data delivered at an early stage by the client to the software house and used to test the individual programs or parts of programs (program testing); further data to test the linkage of the various different programs which constitute the whole contract (systems testing or link testing); and acceptance test data prepared by the client and not shown to the software house or made available until after the completion of the programs. If this test data is at all large—and it should be if it is to test the capacity of the system—it may well need to be prepared by someone other than the client, and the data preparation contract in 10.3 may be relevant.

The running of this acceptance test data through the programs must ideally be performed jointly by both client and software house, since any error or unexpected result must be resolved by both sides; both must agree that the test is fair, that the condition the test reveals is an error, and that it is one which it is the software house's duty to rectify. It will be observed that each of these terms is open to discussion, but, in practice, both sides will have an interest in completing acceptance tests successfully—the software house so as to be able to invoice a satisfied customer and release staff for other assignments, and the representative of the client since the choice of software house (and often many other aspects of the system) has been his own personal responsibility and he is usually anxious to demonstrate within his own organisation that he can obtain a satisfactory result in the notoriously hazardous business of software contracts.

The test data itself will also have to include some description of the results to be expected, if the tests are to be at all meaningful. The preparation of test data and expected results is an exceedingly laborious and unenjoyable task.

This discussion of acceptance tests is by way of background to their relatively brief appearance in contracts, for it is most unusual to include a detailed description of the test data, even in a schedule. Instead, there is merely a brief acknowledgement of the existence of test data, usually included by the supplier as a way of defining acceptance. For example, in a licence agreement:

> The Licensee shall supply to the Software House test data suitable to test all aspects of the Software, and the Software House shall process such data on the Licensee's computer by way of acceptance testing. Immediately after correct processing of such test data as aforesaid the Licensee will be deemed to have accepted the Software.

Here the software house's desire to fend off awkward questions from the licensee is a little too apparent. Who decides whether (or not) data is suitable? But then this clause is for a package, where the licensee has presumably already had a chance of examining the software before any question of contract is raised.

Another clause from a licence states:

> Where the specifications do not include agreement with control information supplied by the Licensee or where the Licensee has failed to provide such control information all results shall be accepted by the Licensee as full and satisfactory performance by the Software House without being so agreed.

'Control information' here is presumably the expected results from test data. This clause puts the onus of providing test data and results on the licensee (as is reasonable), but does not preclude a diligent licensee from devising exceptionally rigorous tests if he so wishes. In practical terms, a licensee or client should devise test data and expected results as soon as his requirements are sufficiently defined to allow this, and should seek from the supplier full facilities for trying them out.

Finally it should be pointed out that acceptance tests usually depend on the completion of training and if this is delayed or neglected [3.7], the whole timetable for acceptance may be endangered.

3.3.2 Performance

So far we have considered only the question of data input and expected results output. But there is a second, and more controversial, aspect to program testing: for, in addition to checking design logic, error checking, file maintenance, report generation, and so on, the licensee/client may be concerned with the throughput performance. In an operating system or other 'pure' software, this may involve rigorous timing of the throughput (length of time taken to compile a program of x statements, length of time taken to link-edit y subroutines, etc) or timing of performance (the execution time of a compiled program, etc), or perhaps measurement of the program size after compilation.

Tests such as these are usually more appropriate to a software package which is to be compared against similar rival packages from other organisations, or even a simultaneous comparison of hardware and software of rival systems. For example, manufacturers A and B each claim to be able to supply a computer with a sort program and a compiler. The prospective customer devises a program with a sort phase. Program, sort phase and data for the program are all typical of the work the prospective customer hopes to use the computer for and the volumes of data are also realistic. Both manufacturers are given the program and are required to demonstrate the compilation. Following this, both manufacturers are given the data and required to demonstrate the execution of the program and the sort. All demonstrations must be performed in the customer's presence, and information is logged about timings, program size, disk area needed for the sort, and so on. The customer then compares the results and uses them to help him to decide between rival suppliers. Such 'benchmark' tests are not usually mentioned in software contracts, but rather tend to be performed before the contractual stage is reached since they are usually concerned with existing software packages.

For bespoke applications software, a client *may* also seek such guarantees of performance to a particular standard. It is fair to add that there is no area of computer performance so difficult to estimate as throughput (timing, program size, etc), and few software houses would dare to give any guarantees in this area.

Performance may be included in the functional specification and in this way incorporated by reference in the contract. For the client able to look for such guarantees, the way ahead is extremely thorny. Performance criteria may include:

(1) Volume capacity in terms of

(*a*) storage of data in terms of its rate of entry and the length of time it is stored;

(*b*) throughput—ie speed of processing records;

(*c*) storage and parallel processing of particular programs;

(*d*) number of terminals and other active peripherals which can be linked to the system without degrading response time;

(*e*) speed of individual components—eg telecommunications lines or printers.

(2) Response time—that is to say in an interactive system the elapsed time between the depression of a message key and the appearance of a meaningful message on the screen, other than a wait message. This time will depend on the full interaction of hardware, software and telecommunications equipment and on the volumes of data and numbers of other simultaneous users.

(3) Maintenance and back-up cover (see Chapters 8 and 9).

3.3.3 Error correction [C8; D11; O23]

Software contracts are often reticent about the subject of error correction after acceptance, and for that reason the topic must be considered here, rather than as a software house's duty [3.7]. If immediately upon acceptance of the software, the client enters into a software maintenance agreement with the original supplier, the absence of any mention of error correction in the software contract does not matter, since any errors in the program which have not been discovered by acceptance tests can be put right under the maintenance contract. Chapter 9 discusses such contracts and indeed the whole question of error correction and enhancement of software. It is suggested in that chapter, and repeated here, that anyone contemplating purchasing software should ensure that he knows how it will be maintained and by whom.

However, if there is no maintenance contract, the client can only fall back on the various statutory provisions loosely included in the term 'consumer law', while being aware that his own acceptance tests (or lack of them) may be likely to be interpreted as affirmation of the contract. In practice, a reputable software house may remedy small bugs which come to light quickly. These cannot consist of any major rewriting of the software, since the client should surely have discovered the need for this before acceptance, or indeed before acceptance of the functional specification. Certainly, the correction cannot extend to anything which involves a change to the functional specification. A practical difficulty which tends to delay the rectification of bugs is that the software house will have redeployed the staff who wrote the original program and have no one available to do the work without a considerable effort in studying the workings of the program first. In the absence of any maintenance agreement (and the client would do well to ask himself why there is no maintenance agreement) the client should look for some such clause as:

> Up to 6 months from the date of acceptance by the Client of the Software the Software House undertakes to rectify free of charge all faults and defects in the Software of which the Client has notified them in writing provided both that such correction will not depart from the Functional Specification of the Software and also that such faults or defects were not and could not reasonably have been discovered by the Client before acceptance of the Software.

The time scale can of course vary from 6 months, but a software house is unlikely to wish to enter into an open-ended contract which could suddenly be re-activated years later when the original programmers have long since left, and all knowledge of the application or machine is dim, and it is not unreasonable to expect the client to find all serious bugs as soon as possible after acceptance.

In some cases a distinction may be made between significant and non-significant bugs:

> For the purposes of this Agreement, failure to conform to a specification, and error or malfunction of the Package shall mean only significant deviations from the specification for the current release of the Package.

It is not unreasonable for the supplier to protect himself from some perfectly frivolous fault, and it is certainly reasonable to confine rectifications to the current release, but whether this clause in its failure to define 'significant' helps at all must be open to question.

As mentioned above [2.3.8], the Unfair Contract Terms Act 1977 might be thought to be of use here to limit the effectiveness of contract terms which purport to exclude or limit liability for defects. However, the Unfair Contract Terms Act 1977, Sched 1, para 1 provides for a number of exemptions from the provisions of ss 2–4 of the Act, including:

> (c) Any contract so far as it relates to the creation or transfer of a right or interest in any patent, trade mark, copyright, registered design, technical or commercial information or other intellectual property, or relates to the termination of any such right or interest.

Software is now copyright [3.8]. But Schedule 1, para 1(c) has given rise to difficulties of interpretation. Does it mean that exclusion clauses in software contracts (or even contracts with software elements) will never be affected by the Act or does it only affect provisions which themselves create, transfer or terminate intellectual property rights or interests thereby leaving the other clauses in the contract unaffected? Judicial guidance on this issue was received from Judge Thayne Forbes in *The Salvage Association v CAP Financial Services Limited* [1992] *Computers and Law* NS 4.4 (October/November 1993) 15–17. In his view, the nugatory effect of para 1(*c*) only concerned those clauses in an agreement that dealt with the creation or transfer of a right or interest in an intellectual property right. It did not touch or concern terms which related to other matters such as the quality of the software, the competence and performance of the supplier's employees or liability for breaches of the agreement or in negligence which are still subject to the controls of ss 2—4 of the Act. In the context of software, this would seem to confine the operation of para 1(*c*) to the clause granting the right to use the software or assigning the copyright in the software to the customer, such that if there is some defect in the supplier's copyright ownership, the supplier could exclude his liability for such eventuality without being subject to the controls of ss 2—4. Whether this line of judicial thinking will be maintained remains to be seen but it is to be welcomed that the court has thus far adopted the narrower interpretation, for otherwise the provisions of the Act would easily be evaded by providing in a contract for the creation, transfer or termination of a relatively minor intellectual property right or interest. In any event, it is always safer for customers to treat exclusion clauses in software contracts (including also hardware [2.3.8] and turnkey [1.12] contracts with software elements) with care and to endeavour to negotiate appropriate relaxations if they are thought to be onerous.

3.4 Termination [C21; D26, D27]

An effect of the termination of a package program licence will probably be the delivery to the licensor or the destruction by the licensee of all copies of the software and its documentation [3.8.1]. In the case of bespoke software, the client will require copies of the software or specifications to date and in particular any source code to date [3.3.1].

3.4.1 Termination by performance

Satisfactory discharge of a software contract will usually be by the delivery of the programs by the software house, and acceptance and payment by the client. However, the contract will inevitably have to visualise less happy eventualities.

3.4.2 Termination or breach by the client

Voluntary termination

Like any other agreement, a software contract may provide for termination at the wish of either party. Logically (if not lawfully), such a contract can also be frustrated by the client—at least, in the earlier stages—since the software house tends to be largely dependent on the client for information about his system, test data and often, of course, machine time and other facilities, though the clauses with regard to acceptance tests [3.3.1] mean that the client must take positive steps to reject any program the software house produces. If a client wishes to terminate early, the damage he can do to the software house goes beyond mere monetary loss, since the software house will have scheduled its future work on the basis of the staff for a particular project being gainfully occupied (and hence not available for other work) right up to the end of the project; it may not be able to find sufficient work at short notice if numbers of experienced staff are suddenly back on its hands. It is therefore not uncommon to specify a period of notice the length of which will probably take into account the number and experience of the staff working on the job—eg, for a time and materials contract:

> The Client shall give to the Software House not less than 4 weeks' written notice of any cancellation and any such cancellation shall be without prejudice to the Software House's rights arising from antecedent breach by the Client and to recover costs incurred or committed prior to the date of such cancellation's taking effect or at the election of the Software House to recover the full contract price less any stage payments already paid. Any such cancellation shall be without prejudice to the Software House's remaining and continuing rights under this Agreement in relation to confidence and title to the Software.

The provisions relating to the payment of the full contract price are particularly usual in a fixed-price contract.

Infringement of title

If the software house reserves title to the software, either explicitly or implicitly, any act or attempted act calculated to interfere with or jeopardise that right is, in some contracts, deemed to be a condition justifying the software house in terminating the contract, while still allowing it to pursue any other remedies that may be appropriate. This is especially likely to be the case in a licence for an existing piece of software:

If the Licensee shall do or allow to be done any act or thing which in the opinion of the Software House may jeopardise the Software House's rights in the Software or any part thereof and in particular but without prejudice to the generality of the foregoing if the Licensee shall make or allow to be made unauthorised copies of the Software or if the Licensee imparts or divulges the contents of the Software without the prior written consent of the Software House, then in each and every such case the Software House may by notice in writing sent to the Licensee at the Licensee's registered office forthwith or at any time thereafter and for all purposes terminate the rights granted to the Licensee under this Agreement and the licence thereby constituted, such termination to be without prejudice to the rights of the parties arising out of antecedent breaches and without prejudice to the Licensee's remaining and continuing obligations under this Agreement in relation to confidence and the Software House's property in the Software.

A clause that relies purely on the software house's opinion seems gratuitously vague, and it is not easy to define 'contents of Software'. But the general intention is clear enough.

Failure to pay

Similarly, failure to pay is likely to result in termination:

If the Licensee shall fail to pay any sum payable under this Agreement within 7 days of written demand made on or after the due date the Software House may terminate this Agreement.

Client's incapacity

Clauses about death, bankruptcy, winding-up, etc, in software contracts do not differ from similar clauses in other contracts which permit termination.

3.4.3   Termination by the software house

In the absence of fault on the part of the customer, clauses in this category are rare since termination by the software house before completion of the contract leaves the customer in an unsatisfactory position. In a very long and complicated development such a clause may be appropriate, provided it is firmly linked to milestones [3.2.1] which give the customer some return on progress to date.

3.5 Alterations

3.5.1 Packages [C16]

For some standard software there will be a total ban on the customer modifying the package, although, as mentioned in [3.8.1], this may be ineffective to prevent the customer lawfully making modifications for the purpose of error correction. A ban is, however, likely to be the case if the customer also has a maintenance agreement with the supplier [9.6.1].

Nevertheless, the supplier may allow modification in some cases and provided the customer can maintain the package himself:

(1) The Licensee may modify the Package (other than . . .) and may merge the Package or parts thereof with other data and/or programs. This Licence applies to all parts of the result which are or were the Package or part or parts thereof;

(2) The Licensee will notify the Licensor of all such modifications or mergers and without charge to the Licensor supply all necessary documentation of such changes including specifications and source code. This material will be used by the Licensor for the purpose of sub-clause (3) only;

(3) If the Package or any part or parts thereof so modified or merged by the Licensee are used on the Equipment and adversely affect it, then the Licensor will not be responsible for any resulting loss and may make an extra charge to the Licensee for any assistance the Licensor may provide at the request of the Licensee to investigate the Package so modified or its results.

Some agreements provide for ownership of the modifications to vest in the licensor and for copies to be provided to the licensor on expiry of the licence, or else for the copies to be destroyed and a certificate of such destruction to be given to the licensor. The agreement may well provide that the licensee include on all copies (including modifications) of the licensed software the licensor's copyright notice.

3.5.2 Commissioned software [D7]

An astonishingly large number of software contracts fail to cover the possibility of the client's wishing to modify his requirements after the software house has already started on its task. In practice, this is an extremely common occurrence the effect of which on the work to date can range from trivial to catastrophic. The reason for its frequency is that, as the date of delivery approaches, the client thinks more and more deeply about the nature of what he has ordered, and how he has got to use it; as a result he has second, and better, thoughts about exactly what he wants. A competent software house will endeavour to provide additional unused fields in record formats to cope with this, but even so relations are easily soured by the absence of any express provision to cover this—and, worst of all, the absence of any realisation or understanding by the client of quite how disruptive any change of mind may be. A clause such as the following can save a lot of trouble:

> Any request by the Client for alteration to the Software shall be examined by the Software House who reserve the right to terminate this Contract or amend it in any way they think necessary to give effect to the said alteration. Price modification of the Specification and delivery of any such alteration shall be agreed in writing between the Software House and the Client before the Software House commences work on the alteration.

Many contracts refuse to consider any alterations unless they have been submitted in writing by the client.

Whatever the contract may or may not say, it is very much in the client's interest that:

(1) All such alterations are clearly specified.
(2) Any such specifications have been notified to, and agreed with, the software house at the earliest opportunity.
(3) Any resultant variations in price, timescale, performance, etc, are fully discussed and agreed.

Because of the frequency of clients requiring changes (modest or otherwise) after a system has been specified and agreed, less competent software houses have sometimes agreed orally to changes, failed to discuss the implications of the change for the fulfilment of the contract, and then used the change as a 'let-out' when they have been unable to deliver the software on time. It is nearly impossible for a client to gauge the truth of an assertion such as: 'We could easily have finished the work by 1 June, as originally agreed, but you asked us to implement changes and this upset our time schedules.' Correct documentation of both change and its effect on the contract is essential for both sides. An effective clause in the contract on the lines of that given above protects the client from the expensive and unsatisfactory results of an oral request by his staff ('. . . just put this in, will you?'). Junior staff working for the client may easily be tempted to do this, and imagine they are furthering the client's interest, unaware that they may be doubling cost, timescale and complexity of the software, and even, in extreme cases, rendering it impossible to implement. An explicit requirement for requests for changes to be in writing is very valuable, such as:

The Software House shall not accept or implement any changes to the Software requested by the Client or his servants unless requests for such changes are made in writing and submitted in the manner prescribed in Clause *X* hereof.

Having said all this, it is not open to a contracting party unilaterally to alter an agreement and, in the absence of an agreed change control procedure embodied in the contract, a customer cannot compel the supplier to implement alterations.

3.6 Client's duties

For an existing package the main client's duties relate to alterations [3.5.1] or title [3.8.1]; but for bespoke software it is essential that the client appreciates the extent of his duties.

3.6.1 Co-operation on systems design

Software houses are dependent on the goodwill of their clients if they are to produce successful systems to fit their clients' requirements. A lawyer whose client withholds co-operation and confidence is at best at a grave disadvantage, and the analogy with software holds good.

Liaison and nominees [D17]

The first requirement is for the client to nominate a member of his staff to supply information to the software house. The original negotiations between the two sides will probably have included the client's directors or partners, or at least very senior management concerned with policy and contractual matters rather than detailed implementation. System design requires the participation of the data processing staff, and a nominee should be as closely as possible concerned with the day-to-day working of the system. For instance:

The Client shall within one week of the date hereof nominate in writing to the Software House the representative who will supply any information which may be needed by the Software House to fulfil the provisions hereof. The Software House cannot be held responsible for any delay caused by non-availability of such nominated representative.

The client's advantage from this will be that his nominee can control the progress of the project. Alterations to the system [3.5.2] make a nominee particularly important.

Information [D19]

If the software house is to perform any useful function, it needs a good deal of information about the client. Very often successful systems design depends not just on accurate knowledge of the particular application (eg stock control) performed in the client's business, but of the whole background of the client's work. Withholding of information can, therefore, seriously impair the software house's effectiveness and disrupt schedules. Hence:

> The Client shall provide all information and documentation requested by the Software House in order to allow the Software House to design and write the Software. Such information and documentation shall be subject to the provisions of confidentiality contained in Clause X hereof. In the event that work is delayed or the extent of the work increased by delay or failure in providing such information or documentation the Software House reserves the right to amend the price and timescale of this Agreement to take account of any increased cost or timescale of the delivery of the Software caused by such delay or failure.

Office facilities [D23]

The nature of systems analysis and design usually requires that the software house's staff will have to work on the client's premises. At least a desk per person is required, and many contracts cover provision of stationery and facilities like photocopying or even typing. It is customary for these to be provided free of charge:

> Typing facilities equivalent to the services of one full-time copy typist shall be made available to the Software House's team at the Client's premises in Northtown . . .

Or, more succinctly:

> The Client undertakes to provide to the staff of the Software House such desks and office facilities as may be necessary to enable the Software House to fulfil their obligations under this Agreement.

Computer facilities [D22]

With regard to machine time, if the client already has a suitable computer installed, the contract will usually require him to make it available for program development. This is usually free of charge:

The Client undertakes to provide the Software House with all computer time necessary to write install and test the Software during normal working hours or at such other time or times as may be agreed free of charge.

Sometimes the machine time may be more precisely defined (. . . *not less than* n *hours a day including* x *hours in prime shift* . . .) and there may also be a minimum configuration defined:

Throughout this contract the Client shall provide at Northtown the machine time itemised below on an ICBM of the following specification:
8M bytes of memory
printer
etc . . .

However, such detail is not usually necessary unless the work has an experimental (or at least unusual) character.

If a software house is under particular pressure to complete a job quickly, it may seek to do so by increasing the number of staff on a project. It must be admitted that such a manoeuvre rarely has a beneficial effect unless introduced at a very early stage in the project; nevertheless, the client should be prepared to find that the use of his machine during the project will fluctuate wildly.

He should also be aware that failure to provide machine time, even though it is not his fault, may seriously increase costs and timescale.

If a client does not provide machine time this is usually either because he has not (yet) installed a suitable computer, or else because the computer is already too heavily used during ordinary daily operating, the time required for programming not being necessarily commensurate with the time required to run the completed program.

Occasionally computer time is required on a different machine because the client's computer is too far from the software house's staff, and a remote terminal is for some reason not feasible. In this situation, either the client can buy machine time elsewhere or, more usually, he deputes the software house to do this for him, in which case the charges to be levied by the owner of the computer must be defined and agreed in advance, and both sides should visualise the situation when the third party's computer is not available—through machine failure or some other reason. One would normally expect the client to bear the cost of any delay caused by the failure of the third party's computer, just as he would for failure of his own computer, but it is essential that this situation be considered at contract stage:

FT Law & Tax
FREEPOST
21-27 Lamb's Conduit Street
London
WC1N 3BR

Computer Contracts on Disk

 New

By Richard Morgan & Graham Stedman

Computer Contracts on Disk is the perfect companion to *Computer Contracts* (5th edition), and a unique time saving tool. In ready-to-use WP format, the disk contains all 22 precedents (comprisive 360 pages) printed in the book, covering everything from a beta test agreement and software licences, to a network service level agreement and bureau service agreements. It is the disk that allows you to:

- produce computer contracts quickly and efficiently, saving time in drafting, keying, checking and amending documents.

- have a full selection of expertly drafted precedents instantly available in your everyday practice.

The disk conveniently allows you to have the entire text of the precedents ready to hand on a computer, and because they correspond with the precedents and the commentary in the book, you can cross refer between the two.

Each precedent is fully set out on the disk, with all clauses which in the book are abridged or merely refer to other precedents, provided in complete form on the disk. You will find the amount of compilation and amendment to be done has been reduced to a minimum.

By using this disk, you can ensure that whatever document you need is ready at your fingertips, so an even more efficient and effective service can be offered.

Place your order today for this unique time-saving tool!

○ **Yes!** Please send me _____ copy/ies of **Computer Contracts on Disk** (**Word 2** or above) by Richard Morgan & Graham Stedman.
  December 1995 • 075200 2791 • £50.00 (including p+p) + VAT

○ **Yes!** Please send me _____ copy/ies of **Computer Contracts on Disk** (**WordPerfect 5.1** or above) by Richard Morgan & Graham Stedman.
  December 1995 • 075200 2805 • £50.00 (including p+p) + VAT

○ Please send me further details about **Computer Contracts on Disk.**

Please note: the disk is not available on approval

(Prices and dates are subject to change without prior notice.)

NAME

POSITION

FIRM

ADDRESS

TEL

FAX

Return to:
FT Law & Tax
FREEPOST
21-27 Lamb's Conduit Street
London
WC1N 3BR

For more urgent orders call:
FREEPHONE 0800 289 618
OR
FAX: 0171 831 8119
Please quote reference
DD/0006

No stamp needed if posted in the UK.

FT LAW & TAX

DD/0006

The Software House shall not be held responsible for any delay
or increase in costs caused by any failure in securing machine time
for writing, installing and testing the Software.

Apart from machine time, the software house will also, in theory,
require storage space for tapes, etc, and consumables (stationery, floppy
disks, and so on). This is often assumed as part of Office Facilities.
Similarly, data preparation facilities may be required:

During the subsistence of this Contract the Client will provide free
of charge all such data preparation facilities as may be necessary
for the staff of the Software House to design write install and
test the Software.

As with other clauses, there may be a rider spelling out the ghastly
effects of delay or failure on the overall cost and timescale. With the
growth of interactive or on-line systems, accessible directly through a
keyboard, such facilities are becoming of less importance.

Expenses

If the software house's staff are working away from home, the client
is usually expected to bear the cost of their expenses (travel,
accommodation, etc). The definition of expenses varies and is often
surprisingly vague. If in doubt, the client should negotiate with the software house maximum figures or, if this is possible, himself provide
accommodation. Many software houses have a maximum scale which
their staff must adhere to, and will be happy to make this available
to the client. In the light of this, a clause like:

Invoices for expenses properly incurred by the Software House
in fulfilment of this Agreement will be submitted to the Client
monthly in arrears.

can be perfectly effective.

3.6.2   Poaching staff [D25]

At the end of a successfully completed project, a client may find that
his confidence in the individual members of the software house's staff
has grown to the point where he would wish to employ them full-time.
They probably know both his programs and his business rather better
than any of his own staff and as full-time employees they would cost
the client far less than the fees the client is paying to the software house,
since those fees contain the software house's overheads and profits. From
the software house's point of view, such a loss of staff can be serious,

since staff expertise is their sole asset. It is therefore quite common for a software house to include a clause such as:

> The Client accepts that the Software House will suffer loss if a member of the Software House's staff employed on work on the Client's behalf accepts an offer of permanent employment with the Client within 6 months of the termination of the work which is the subject of this Agreement. If such a member of the Software House's staff accepts such offer of employment in such circumstances the Client agrees to pay to the Software House the equivalent of 3 months' employment at the highest rate for that member of staff.

Software houses do not necessarily charge any one member of staff out at a standard rate to all clients. Like many other professionals, they have to take into account factors other than the time expended and the salary of the individual concerned—in particular they will consider the degree to which highly specialist knowledge is a requisite for the task. This explains the reference to 'at the highest rate' above.

In one instance we have found the prohibition against poaching staff expressed in terms mutual to the parties:

> It is agreed that neither of the parties hereto shall approach employees of the other with offers of employment for the duration of this Agreement and for 6 months thereafter.

This is a little disingenuous, since the likelihood of the software house's wishing to employ the client's staff is usually minimal.

Clauses which purport to prevent poaching of staff are *prima facie* void and unenforceable as being in unreasonable restraint of trade (*Kores Manufacturing Co Ltd v Kolok Manufacturing Co Ltd* [1957] 3 All ER 158 and *Hanover Insurance Brokers Ltd v Shapiro* [1994] IRLR 82; (1993) *The Times*, 17 November). However, they may be valid if two conditions are fulfilled. First, the restraint must be reasonable in extent and afford no more than adequate protection to the person seeking to rely on it. Second, it must not be against the public interest. A restraint of this nature will be against the public interest if it restricts an employee's freedom of choice of employment without constituting a fetter which the employer reasonably requires for his protection. The onus is on the person seeking to rely on the restriction to show that it is reasonable.

Such a restraint will stand more chance of being held valid if it is limited in duration and applies only to those staff which the software house reasonably needs to protect against poaching. It would be unnecessary, for example, to apply such a restriction to unskilled manual workers. The restriction could be limited, say, to persons working on the project and either earning in excess of a stated salary level or above a certain seniority, or even to named individuals.

A software house would be well advised to consider two restrictions, one prohibiting the client from soliciting his employees and one prohibiting their employment by the client. If the two restrictions are made severable then, in the event of one being found to be invalid, the courts will be able to apply what has become known as the 'blue pencil' test and sever the offending restriction but enforce the other. The courts may be more sympathetic to a non-solicitation clause which prevents an employee from being head-hunted than to a non-employment covenant which could prevent an employee taking up employment as a result of a voluntary response to an advertisement.

In short, the software house should only seek to impose restrictions which are necessary to protect it. The temptation to impose wider restraints should be resisted: the validity of the clause will be put at risk as a result. A suitable clause might be in the form of that contained in D25.

Restraint clauses like these, though common, are by no means universal.

There is a further point that to a large software house hoping for repeat orders from a corporate client, the loss of a single member of staff in return for the placing of a member of staff trained in their methods in the enemy's camp could be highly advantageous, since he will tend to think in terms of the skills and personalities of his old firm when new software is required.

3.7 Software house's duties

In bespoke programming, many of the software house's duties will correspond in essence or in form, [3.6] above, with the client's duties.

3.7.1 Staff

Nomination [D17, D20]

It is usual to allow the client to know who the individuals are who will be working for him. A good software house is proud of its staff and anxious to show the client how relevant the individual members of staff's experience is to the work they will be doing for the client. It is also essential that the staff are personally acceptable to the client, since the success of the project depends on the client's confidence in those who are working for him. The client should therefore satisfy himself on this point and should expect to meet at least the more senior staff assigned to his project before starting the work. If the staff fail to inspire confidence, the client is quite at liberty to reject them. At the same time, he should realise that a software house's staff are not numerically inexhaustible and, like a counsel objecting to jurors, he should limit his fastidiousness—unless, of course, he loses confidence in the software house as a whole, in which case he should at once seek another. This element of confidence cannot be overstressed. In certain cases, the client may be justified in insisting that only a named individual should be considered competent to do the job; this can particularly happen with software evaluation and consultancy (rather than programming), where the named individual has specialist knowledge.

We have been unable to find examples in formal contracts of a named individual being insisted on as the only competent person to do the work, but the client should feel at liberty to insist on such a clause if he believes it necessary. Some such wording as this might be suitable:

> The Software House agrees that the work more particularly described in Clause X hereof shall be performed by Mr Fred Nurk or such other person as may be approved by the Client in writing.

Dress and conformity [D24]

Some computer personnel have acquired a reputation for unconventionality in dress and appearance. It is possible that this is derived largely from visits to computer installations where the operators have been much in evidence. The antisocial hours many operators are obliged to work naturally require an individual who eschews the 9-to-5 image in dress as well as hours. Programmers are sometimes as unconventional, and the inspirational type (writing his programs, like Coleridge composing *Kubla Khan*, in some drug-induced trance in the early hours of the morning) is not quite extinct, though most software houses will avoid him like the plague. The majority of programmers from reputable software houses are smartly or unimaginatively conventional in their dress. Nevertheless, fears still persist of computer staff showing large quantities of hair where skin should be, and large quantities of skin where clothing should be, and some clients require reassurance. It is, therefore, by no means unusual to find clauses like this:

> Whilst the Software House's personnel are attending the Client's premises such personnel will conform to the Client's normal codes of staff practice.

It will be observed that such clauses also include implicitly time-keeping and less easily definable norms of behaviour on the client's premises, as well as dress and appearance. There is an implied duty on the client to advise the software house of what those norms are.

There is, however, a more technical aspect of conformity. Many computer installations have rigid standards of procedure and documentation within their programming departments, designed to produce a uniformity of approach and design for all their software and hence a corresponding ease in updating and maintaining it. The documentation system referred to in 3.3.1 is relevant here. The introduction of contract programmers who do not know these standards and yet are experienced staff working on their own can give rise to problems. In extreme cases, some installations where there have been unpleasant experiences of this refuse to use contract programmers to supplement their own staff, and instead insist that each programming job must be done either entirely by in-house staff or entirely by an outside software house. Without going to this rigid position, it can be said that it is perfectly possible for a client to use a clause of this nature and notify the software house well in advance:

(1) That he has such standards.
(2) That he will specify them to the contract programmers.
(3) That he will interpret this clause as requiring their conformity with his standards.

3.7.2   Confidentiality [C20; P15; U]

The duty of the client to furnish information about his business [3.6.1] must imply a like duty on the part of the software house to respect the confidentiality of such information. However, it is usual to include some statement of this duty explicitly in the contract:

> The Software House undertakes not to divulge or communicate to any person firm or company any confidential information however acquired which refers to the Client without first obtaining the written consent of the Client.
>
> The Software House shall ensure that all its employees and sub-contractors are bound by the provisions of this clause.

In practice this may best be done by requiring all the software house's relevant individual staff to sign a non-disclosure agreement [U]. Or, a little less generously:

All information or data passed by the Client to the Software House shall be treated as confidential by the Software House and not knowingly divulged to any third party without the Client's prior consent.

To be fair, the second is primarily intended for a bureau service rather than a software house as such, but it is noticeably less strict (*a*) in limiting the confidentiality to information expressly *passed*, (*b*) in excepting unknowing breach of confidence, and (*c*) in not stipulating that any consent to a waiver of this clause should be in writing.

Since the coming into force of the Data Protection Act 1984, the parties will also need to consider the extent to which the software house will require real data about real human beings. Some programs, of course, will not need the names of living identifiable individuals as data, and in such cases the Act is not applicable. But in most cases, human beings will be identifiable—personal customers, employees, members of some association, and so forth. In these cases, the software house may be acting as a bureau [10.3.3] and the clauses normally appropriate to a bureau and its customer may have to apply to the software house and its client [P15].

Sometimes the work of the software house may entail access not only to the client's confidential information but also to that of the client's own clients. A clause which recognises this can be helpful:

The Software House recognises that in the course of carrying out the Contract Works it will have access to confidential information belonging to third parties including clients of the Client and that the Client is under a professional obligation of confidence towards its clients and in respect of some other third parties. The Software House undertakes to the Client that it will treat all such information including for emphasis only and not by way of limitation, the names and addresses of the clients of the Client, as confidential and secret and will not use or divulge any such information. It further undertakes to draw the attention of all its officers, employees and agents involved in carrying out the Contract Works to the provisions of this clause and to ensure that each of them is also bound by it.

3.7.3 Staff training [C18, C19; D12, D13; O22, O23]

This area is often surprisingly neglected. Yet for a client whose staff are (as is often the case) new to the job and technically unsophisticated, adequate information on how to work the system is essential, and—even for a client who already possesses experienced computer staff—the exact workings of the new system (whatever it may be) must be learned in detail. We believe it to be one of the hallmarks of a good software house that they pay special attention to the way that a particular client's staff will use the system, and bear in mind the staff's level of experience and the other pressures that work may put on them.

In practice, instruction is usually provided in two separate but related ways: (*a*) supply of operating manuals; and (*b*) staff instruction. Often operating manuals may be explicitly promised by the software house:

> On acceptance of the Software, the Software House undertakes to provide the Client with two copies of the Manual and Operating Instructions relating to the Software.

This allows the software house to charge for additional copies should they be required. The client must ask himself how many copies of the manual he is likely to need.

Staff instruction varies. Some offer complicated arrangements allowing the client *x* course credits each worth one day's instruction for up to *y* members of staff. This may be difficult for the client to understand, and insufficiently sensitive to the fact that different systems (and different clients) require varying amounts of instruction. There are also more vague clauses like:

> The Software House undertakes to instruct the Client's employees and provide such technical advice as may be necessary in the use of the Software.

In practice, once the software is complete the client has an interest in using it to its full potential, just as the software house has an interest in satisfying his client and being paid. The best course is undoubtedly to draw up a detailed list of all staff likely to need any form of training and familiarisation, and incorporate a full training programme in a schedule. Where possible a training course should train at the same time all staff performing similar functions. In practice this is limited, first by the fact that usually the client cannot spare all staff performing similar functions simultaneously, and secondly by the fact that any training involving a terminal cannot really be made available to more than two staff per terminal at any one time if they are to have adequate opportunity for hands-on experience.

It is desirable (a) that all staff be trained before the system is delivered, and (b) that use of their training be as soon after their training is completed as possible—ie all training should be immediately before the software is delivered. If the drawing up of a full training schedule is neglected or delayed, it may be that there is no way of completing all the training without changing the date of delivery.

3.8 Title [C9, C11; P16]

This section touches on a crucial point all too often given limited treatment in software contracts. Who owns the software? What is the nature of the right to use it which appears to be conferred? The vexed question of whether software is copyright, patentable, or simply nothing more than a trade secret was solved so far as the UK was concerned by the Copyright (Computer Software) Amendment Act 1985. That Act, which came into force on the 1 September 1986, declared that the owners of software are in the same position as regards copying as are the owners of literary works. The position has been reinforced by the Copyright, Designs and Patents Act 1988 and now, throughout the European Union, by the Council Directive of 14 May 1991 on the legal protection of computer programs (91/250/EEC) ('the Software Directive'). UK law to a large extent already complied with the Software Directive but its provisions were implemented in the UK by the Copyright (Computer Programs) Regulations 1992 (SI 1992 No 3233) ('the UK Regulations').

However, as the law has provided better protection, suppliers have found the problems of enforcing the law are considerable. The association of suppliers called FAST (Federation Against Software Theft) provides advice on this. The problem is particularly acute with PC software so we deal with it in that chapter [4.3]. FAST's address is to be found at 13.2.2.

In the case of a licence for an existing package, the licensor has potentially the most to lose by neglecting to protect his rights, for his customer may wittingly or unwittingly connive at proliferating the package (or the use of it) to other potential customers. In the case of bespoke software, the situation may be reversed, for the client is paying full price for new software which he hopes will give him a commercial edge over his competitors, and any attempt to make his package available to them at a reduced price (since it has once been paid for) will harm him doubly. However, if the software is not of a kind to give him any commercial edge over his rivals, there may be benefit in allowing the software house to keep title since they may then increase the number of users of the package and thereby increase the viability of maintenance and software support facilities to be provided by the software house [3.8.2].

3.8.1 Licences [C9, C11, C12, C13, C14, C21; L7; R12]

The unsatisfactory nature of legal protection as regards software before the passing of the Copyright (Computer Software) Amendment Act 1985 led many suppliers to include a general clause such as:

Patent copyright and other industrial property rights in the Package and its programs and any associated documentation shall be vested in the Licensor who reserves the right to give licences to use the Package to any other party or parties.

This would at the least have provided copyright in the manuals and so forth and it may still be appropriate for international contracts in dealing with countries which do not have adequate protection. The same contract continues:

The Licensee hereby agrees:

(1) that the Package is the sole property of the Licensor and that the Licensee will take all reasonable precautions to maintain the confidentiality of the Package its programs and documentation;

(2) that it will not assign transfer mortgage charge pledge or sublet any of its rights or obligations under this Agreement;

(3) to make no copies of or duplicate the Package or any part or parts thereof by any means or for any purpose whatever (except as may be necessary for normal security storage) without the prior consent in writing of the Licensor;

(4) that it will not modify, adapt, translate or decompile the Package or any part or parts thereof or attempt to analyse the Package in order to understand the ideas underlying any part or parts thereof;

(5) to use the Package solely at the installation described in the Schedule hereto;

(6) to instruct all its staff from time to time having access to the Package not to copy or duplicate the Package or any part or parts thereof or to make any disclosure relating thereto to any third party;

(7) to effect and maintain adequate security measures to safeguard the Package from theft or access by any person other than employees of the Licensee in the normal course of their employment;

(8) in the event that any of the programs comprising the Package or any part or parts of the associated documentation should come into the hands of a third party through the Licensee or any employee or former employee of the Licensee, the Licensee shall forthwith pay to the Licensor the price for the entire Package ruling for the time being as would be charged such third party for a Licence to use the Package.

This is about as complete as human ingenuity can make it. Notice that the mention of 'former employee' in clause (8) stops up a loophole which is not otherwise dealt with, and effectively lays upon the licensee the duty to add a clause as to the security of this package to his contracts of employment with his employees. Yet it appears that the licensor is fully justified in this stricture, for cases have been known where a disreputable rival service bureau has recruited staff from a licensee expressly to learn about a licensor's package.

Sometimes the licensor is happy for the licensee to pass the package to third parties, provided he does so as the licensor's agent:

> The Licensee may act as agent for the Licensor in the grant of other Licences for the Package:
>
> (1) The Licensee shall have no power express or implied to bind the Licensor in any way whatever;
> (2) If such licence to a third party is granted through the efforts of the Licensee the Licensor shall be entitled to the full price for the time being of the Package from such third party and in the event of any default in such payment the Licensee hereby agrees to indemnify the Licensor for the full price for the time being of the Package;
> (3) If such other licence is granted to a third party for a fee wholly through the efforts of the Licensee then upon the Licensor receiving the full price for the time being of the Package (whether from the third party or from the Licensee) the Licensee shall be paid by the Licensor a commission of x per cent of the price for the time being of the Package;
> (4) The Package shall be supplied only by the Licensor and upon the terms and conditions contained herein and the Licensee has no authority express or implied to vary add alter or amend such terms and conditions in any way whatsoever.

In the case of standard software—not least software being supplied by the equipment supplier—it is usual for the licence to apply to only one machine. Yet if that machine is unusable, the customer will probably seek a back-up machine [8.1.2], so although the customer is usually prohibited from running the software on any but the designated machine, the restriction may be relaxed:

> If the Package cannot be used with the Equipment because the Equipment is not yet commissioned or because of any equipment failure as defined in Clause X hereof, this Licence will be deemed to be temporarily extended without additional charge to use with

any other suitable equipment until installation of the Equipment or remedying of the failure.

Suppliers should be careful about insisting that the use of their software should be tied to the use of their own proprietary equipment; such provisions could well offend relevant competition law.

The prohibition against copying has been a common one and in practice is not very realistic in its extreme forms, for it is a sound operational practice to keep spare copies of all important programs in case of damage to the original copies, since the magnetic media on which copies are kept are highly vulnerable to dust, temperature change and other ills, and the equipment on which they are run, especially disk drives, can by malfunction damage the media. A more reasonable clause is:

> The Licensee may make only as many copies of the Package or parts thereof as are reasonably necessary for operational security and use. The Licensee will ensure that printouts and documentation of all such copies acknowledge the Licensor's copyright. This Licence applies to all such copies as it does to the Package delivered. No copies of the documentation of the Package may be made without the written consent of the Licensor. The Licensee must reproduce and include the copyright notice on all such copies.

It follows also on termination that all such copies must be accounted for, either by surrender to the licensor or by destruction:

> Upon the termination of this Agreement the Licensee will return to the Licensor all such software and documentation including that modified by the Licensee and all copies thereof in whole or in part or, if requested by the Licensor, the Licensee will destroy all such software, documentation and copies and certify in writing that they have been destroyed.

Back up copies

The right for a licensee to make a back up copy has now been given legal force by the Software Directive. In implementing the requirements of the directive, reg 8 of the Copyright (Computer Programs) Regulations 1992 (SI 1992 No 3233) inserts a new s 50A(1) in the Copyright, Designs and Patents Act 1988 ('the CDPA'):

> 50A(1) It is not an infringement of copyright for a lawful user of a copy of a computer program to make any back up copy of it which is necessary for him to have for the purposes of his lawful use.

This right is absolute. It may not be excluded by contract and any term which purports to do so is void. The language of the provision is somewhat curious, though. As mentioned above, it may be 'desirable' or 'sensible' to take a back up copy but can it always be said to be strictly 'necessary' for the purposes of the lawful use of software? In many cases, quite possibly not. Quite how far this advances the rights of licensees remains unclear. One supplier who obviously cannot be bothered with such legal niceties simply gives his licensees the right:

> Either (a) to make one copy of the Software solely for back up or archival purposes or (b) to transfer the Software to a single hard disk of a personal computer provided the Licensee keeps the original solely for back up or archival purposes.

It is becoming increasingly common for software owners expressly to permit licensees to make back up copies and this trend is likely to continue.

Decompilation

The restriction on decompilation is more problematic. Generally speaking, the decompilation of software from its object code form to a higher level language such as COBOL or BASIC is a restricted act for copyright purposes and may not be carried out by a licensee without the software owner's permission. Nor is the decompilation of a program 'fair dealing' for the purposes of the CDPA (see s 29(4) CDPA as introduced by reg 7 of the UK regulations). However, the European Commission thought that a right to decompile for the limited purpose of achieving interoperability with other programs was something which a lawful user of software ought to be able to undertake.

This decompilation right was conferred by the Software Directive and is enshrined in UK law by s 50B of the CDPA (as introduced by reg 8 of the UK Regulations). Section 50B provides that it is not an infringement of copyright for a lawful user of a copy of a computer program expressed in a low level language to convert it into a version expressed in a higher level language or, incidentally in the course of so converting the program, to copy it (ie to decompile it), provided two conditions are met. These conditions are first that it is necessary to decompile the program to obtain the information necessary to create an independent program which can be operated with the program decompiled or with another program (this is described as 'the permitted objective'), and secondly that the information so obtained is not used for any purpose other than the permitted objective. However, these two necessary conditions are expressed *not* to be met in four situations:

(1) Where the lawful user has readily available to him the information necessary to achieve the permitted objective;

(2) Where he does not confine the decompiling to such acts as are necessary to achieve the permitted objective;

(3) Where he supplies the information obtained by the decompiling to any person to whom it is not necessary to supply it in order to achieve the permitted objective;

(4) Where he uses the information to create a program which is substantially similar in its expression to the program decompiled or to do any act restricted by copyright.

Again, this limited decompilation right is absolute. It may not be excluded by contract and any term purporting to do so is void.

The response from software owners has been varied. One, in its standard licence, simply refers to the statutory provision:

> Save to the extent and in the circumstances permitted by Section 50B of the Copyright, Designs and Patents Act 1988, the Customer must not decompile the Software (nor permit any third party to do so).

Another, who obviously has found customers for his software in other countries of the European Union, stipulates that:

> You may not alter, merge, modify or adapt the Software in any way including disassembling or decompiling. This does not affect your rights under any legislation implementing the EC Council Directive on the Legal Protection of Computer Programs. If you seek interface information within the meaning of Article 6.1(b) of that Directive you should initially approach [*Supplier's contact and address*].

To make available the necessary interface information might be one means of preventing licensees from decompiling programs. The argument will run that because a licensee has readily available to him the information necessary to achieve the permitted objective, the legislation does not permit him to decompile the software.

With this aim in mind one supplier provides:

> To the extent that local law grants you the right to decompile the Software in order to obtain information necessary to render the Software interoperable with other software, the Supplier hereby undertakes to make that information readily available to you. The Supplier has the right to impose reasonable conditions such as a reasonable fee for doing so. In order to ensure that you receive the appropriate information, you must first give the Supplier sufficient details of your objectives and the other software

concerned. Requests for the appropriate information should be directed to [*name and address*].

There seems to be no reason why this approach should not work; it is after all expressly envisaged by the legislation that the decompilation right should not apply where the licensee has the necessary interface information and, since the software owner is likely to be the only fruitful source of such information, an offer by the software owner to make it available seems to meet the desired objectives of the legislation. However, the information should be 'readily' available and not subject to burdensome conditions. Whether the software owner is entitled to charge for the information is a moot point. A licensee may argue that it is not readily available if it is unreasonably expensive. If that argument is correct then the decompilation right will continue.

A question of timing also arises. A restrictive view of the legislation might be that information is not readily available unless it is available to the licensee at the same time as the program is supplied or, at least, at the same time as the licensee wishes to decompile the program for the permitted objective. A licensee who has to make a request to the software owner, provide information and then wait for a response may not be said to have the information readily available to him. In this context, a curious difference in wording appears between the language of the Software Directive and that of the UK Regulations. Article 6.1(b) stipulates that one of the conditions which must be met in order for the decompilation right to apply is 'the information necessary to achieve interoperability has not *previously* been readily available to [the licensee]'. The word 'previously' was not imported into s 50B of the CDPA. Whether this means that the legislation will be construed restrictively as mentioned above remains unclear. It is to be hoped that common sense will prevail. By no means every licensee will wish to decompile the software licensed to it to achieve interoperability with other software. The mass circulation of interface information with software would seem an unwarranted expense. A genuine offer by a software owner to make interface information available in response to a licensee's request should, it is submitted, be sufficient to be construed as making that information 'readily available' provided it is not subject to burdensome conditions. Certainly, no reasonable licensee ought to complain at such treatment. Whether this view will be adopted by the courts remains to be seen.

Analysing the ideas underlying software

The prohibition on the licensee's analysing the package in order to understand the ideas underlying the program also causes a problem. Generally speaking, copyright law protects the expression of an idea and not the idea itself and it should not therefore be offensive for a licensee to discover the ideas underlying the working of the program in his possession. As a consequence of the adoption of the Software Directive, new s 269A was inserted in the CDPA by reg 11 of the UK Regulations, which provides that any term or condition in an agreement shall be void in so far as it purports to prohibit or restrict the use of any device or means to observe, study or test the functioning of a program in order to understand the ideas and principles which underlie any element of that program. A term of a contract, such as the example given above, which attempts to prevent a licensee's analysing software to discover its underlying ideas will consequently now be void and unenforceable. Licensees should be cautious, however, as this does not mean that the expression of those underlying ideas can be copied. This is recognised by the Software Directive and the UK Regulations, and new s 3(1)(c) of the CDPA (as inserted by reg 3 of the UK Regulations) makes it clear that the 'preparatory design material for a computer program' is itself protected by copyright as a literary work.

Copying and adapting software and correcting errors

Much debate has arisen as to whether the lawful user of a computer program has a legal right without the permission of the copyright owner to copy or adapt it in order to run the program, or in order to correct errors in it. Certainly, he now has the right to copy for back up purposes if that is necessary for his lawful use, as mentioned above. Certain copying of a program is necessary if it is to be used in the manner intended and this is usually expressly permitted by a software licence. The position at law is governed by new s 50C of the CDPA (as inserted by reg 8 of the UK Regulations). This provides that it is not an infringement of copyright for a lawful user of a copy of a computer program to copy or adapt it, provided that the copying or adapting is necessary for his lawful use and is not prohibited under any terms of an agreement regulating the circumstances in which his use is lawful. The section goes on to say that it may, in particular, be necessary for the lawful use of a computer program to copy it or adapt it for the purpose of correcting errors in it.

The lawful user of a computer program who is not bound by an agreement governing its use, but instead is regulated only by copyright law, will consequently have the right to copy and adapt it where this is necessary for his lawful use, including for the purpose of correcting errors in it. This would certainly apply to the lawful acquirer of mass-produced software where no separate agreement governing its use is applicable. Given the uncertainty surrounding the enforceability of shrink-wrap licences [5.3.6.4], this position may also pertain even though the software owner purports to impose such a licence. Moreover, a 'licence' may not always be an 'agreement'.

The opportunity for a software owner to restrict copying and adaptation in this fashion appears only to arise where there is a licence agreement between the owner and the licensee. It may at first sight seem perverse that a licensee with an agreement should have fewer rights, but presumably the law takes the view that it is open to a licensee with an agreement to negotiate the terms of that agreement as he sees fit and that if he wishes to accept restrictions that it is up to him. A licensee should nevertheless ensure that he is granted sufficient rights to permit him to use the software for its intended purpose and that the issue of future error correction, whether by a separate maintenance agreement or otherwise, is adequately addressed.

Unfortunately, the debate does not end there. There is an argument that the UK Regulations do not correctly implement the intention of the Software Directive and that the UK courts might need to have regard to the purpose of the directive in determining the rights of licensees. The source of the problem lies in art 5(1) of the directive which reads:

> In the absence of specific contractual provisions, the acts referred to in Article 4(*a*) and (*b*) shall not require authorisation by the right holder where they are necessary for the use of the computer program by the lawful acquirer in accordance with its intended purpose, including for error correction.

One interpretation of the phrase 'in the absence of specific contractual provisions' is 'in the absence of specific contractual prohibitions to the contrary' such that if an agreement specifically prohibits the licensee from copying or adapting the software that will be effective to exclude such rights. This seems to be the interpretation adopted by the draftsman of the UK Regulations. The other interpretation which could be put on the phrase is 'in the absence of specific contractual provisions granting the necessary rights' such that, to the extent that a licence agreement does not expressly grant the necessary rights to copy and adapt for the use of the computer program by the lawful acquirer in accordance with its intended purpose including for error correction, then the directive fills in and grants such rights to the user. If the latter interpretation is correct, the question then arises as to whether a contractual provision which nevertheless prohibits copying or adaptation is effective. Regrettably, the directive is none too clear on the issue. Article 9(1) renders void any contractual provision which attempts to exclude the rights conferred by the directive to make back up copies, to observe the underlying ideas of a program and to decompile for interoperability purposes but is silent about art 5(1), perhaps suggesting that a contractual prohibition would be valid. However, Recital 18 to the directive presents another view:

> Whereas this means that the acts of loading and running necessary for the use of a copy of a program which has been lawfully acquired, and the act of correction of its errors may not be prohibited by contract.

Confused? So are we. It seems a pity that this apparent inconsistency has been allowed to arise and, if Recital 18 reflects the intention of the directive, that the language of that recital was not expressly imported into the main body of the directive.

One software owner who obviously suffers from a headache over the whole thing, and wishes to save time and money on updating his licence terms in response to developing judicial interpretation, opts for simplicity:

> Except as expressly permitted by this Agreement and save to the extent and in the circumstances expressly required to be permitted by law, the Licensee shall not rent, lease, sub-license, loan, copy, modify, adapt, merge, translate, reverse engineer, decompile, disassemble or create derivative works based on the whole or any part of the Software or use, reproduce or deal in the Software or any part thereof in any way.

Severability

Software owners concerned that some of their contractual terms could possibly be held to be void will not wish the illegality of one provision to infect the remainder of the contract:

> Notwithstanding that the whole or any part of any provision of this Agreement may prove to be illegal or unenforceable the other provisions of this Agreement and the remainder of the provision in question shall remain in full force and effect.

Ownership of rights

Finally, the licensee should satisfy himself that the licensor is, in fact, the originator and owner of all parts of the package being sold, and it is not unreasonable for him to demand an indemnity in case of any future dispute:

> The Licensor shall indemnify the Licensee against all claims demands costs charges and expenses arising from or incurred by any infringement of copyright patent or other title in respect of the Package or any part thereof provided that such infringement is not caused or contributed to by any act or acts of the Licensee

other than the use of the Package in accordance with the provisions of this Agreement.

3.8.2 Bespoke software [D14; M9]

From the software house's point of view, the chief aspect of title is the anxiety that in parting with all rights in the software the software house may limit its ability to profit from the programming skills (as opposed to the applications knowledge) which the software house's staff may have acquired during the course of the work. One solution is simply to have no clause on title at all—in which case the software house will retain the title, giving the client only a licence. This is not necessarily a bad option for the client. He may indeed wish the software house to retain title so as to encourage the software house to keep the software maintained. In particular, there may be merit in the idea of the software house selling the software to other users (provided they are not direct competitors of the client). In this way, the software will acquire a larger number of users, which, at the very least should ensure that its bugs are more readily found. There may even be a user group and certainly maintenance spread over several users should work out cheaper for each particular user. The original user may even expect a rebate on the price he paid whenever the software house effects another sale.

However, if the client insists on a clause formally passing title to him, the following example—allowing the software house to retain and use the skills it has incidentally acquired, while passing title in the software to the client—seems appropriate:

(1) Software is defined as programs written directly for the Client by the Software House under this Agreement. Title to such Software passes to the Client immediately after acceptance.

(2) Any programming tools and skills used by the Software House for the development of such Software remain the sole property of the Software House and are not available for use by any other person other than employees for the time being of the Software House.

Points remain to be defined in this example: 'acceptance' must be defined [3.3.1]; 'programming tools' are different from 'skills'. The former include actual coding—a sequence of instructions for handling a particular type of file, which has become standard within that software house for work on that machine and in that language, for example. It is this sort of thing which may be relevant when considering 'conformity', [3.7.1] above. 'Skills' seem to be much wider and embrace not so much solutions to particular programming or design problems, as the approach to programming and design. 'Software development' presumably means 'work undertaken under the provisions of this Agreement', since it must include analysis and design, as well as programming.

To return to programming tools: we have here a problem if, as we believe, they include actual coding, since (2) implicitly contradicts (1) without that contradiction being resolved. We suggest that if (1) is left unchanged, we may rewrite (2) as follows:

> (2) Notwithstanding anything contained in section (1) of this clause, the Software House hereby reserves to itself the right to use in any way it thinks fit any programming tools skills knowledge and techniques acquired or used by the Software House in performing its duties under this Agreement.

It may be objected that by rewriting the clause this way, we have merely granted the software house a licence to use, as programming tools, some of the software, the title to which they have passed to the client, which is all right, so long as the software house does not actually try to re-use those tools for another client, since they cannot then give him full title to the software. This may be covered by amending (1) to read, in place of 'Title to such Software', 'Title to such Software insofar as it is the property of the Software House'. The reader will by now realise that we are in a somewhat rarified air, so far as software contracts are concerned. There is still no entirely satisfactory clause which covers this point. Fortunately, it does not appear ever to have become an issue between the parties, and if both sides are fully awake to the points being dealt with at this stage, interest will remain academic.

Chapter 4

PCs and word processors

4.1 Introduction

4.2 Hardware

4.3 Software

Chapter 4

PCs and word processors

4.1 Introduction

Personal computers (PCs) are small computers for individuals to have on their desks. In this book we consider portables as PCs and also all the personal computers which do not run the operating systems/graphical interfaces (eg DOS or Windows)—ie contractually Apple computers, for example, are not greatly different from other PCs.

Many of the first micros (predecessors of the PCs) were word processors, ie systems designed for only one application. Such systems still exist, though increasingly word processing is sold simply as a software licence, the software to run on an existing PC which may or may not be used for other purposes.

In theory there is no compelling reason why contracts for PCs or word processors should differ from any other hardware and software contracts. In individual cases some of the provisions of contracts for larger machines may be irrelevant: environmental conditions are less onerous, and heavy lifting tackle and hoists may not be needed. But in general the contracts in Chapters 2 and 3 are perfectly applicable. Some suppliers recognise this by using the same contracts for both large machines and small and to that extent it is a question whether the subject merits separate treatment in a chapter of its own. Originally it was because there were other companies whose contracts were inadequate or slip-shod—even non-existent—that this chapter was needed. There then came into being a mass market of home computer enthusiasts. They were not primarily business users and they tended to purchase their equipment and software from High Street retailers rather than business equipment suppliers. They were not likely to let corporate lawyers loose on the fine print of contracts but instead trust to ordinary consumer protection law for redress in case of any contractual difficulty.

Suppliers responded to this new market and a great deal of hardware and software—particularly software—changed hands in a comparatively casual way in this market, and such methods have spilled over into business applications. This is especially the case with small software items designed for a mass market where the cost is low and not worth the scrutiny which lawyers and company secretaries and computer managers must give to mainframe installations costing hundreds of thousands of pounds.

The first and most important question is therefore as to whether there is a written contract at all. The intending purchaser of a word processing system is seeking to buy hardware (Chapter 2), software (Chapter 3) and maintenance (Chapters 8 and 9) and must satisfy himself that all these aspects are covered. The purchaser of a PC may be buying his software separately, though the chances are that there is some software with his hardware so that he too is buying a turnkey system [1.12]. He may also buy additional software alone and will need to consider Chapter 3. There is every reason to use the relevant chapters as a guide to the purchase of these smaller systems. However it has to be recognised that for purchases of single machines—especially from High Street retailers—lengthy negotiations are not appropriate. Orders for multiple machines, especially linked in networks, will give the parties much more reason and opportunity to examine contractual terms in the way set out in Chapters 2 and 3. Readers should bear these points in mind when using this chapter.

4.2   Hardware

Detailed examination of PC and word processor hardware contractual conditions has not uncovered any major surprises. Because of the low cost of the equipment the margin for rental or leasing agreements is very small and such agreements are much less usual than with larger machines. One clause puts the onus on the customer to make his own leasing arrangements since the supplier cannot help.

> The Customer may enter into a leasing agreement with a third party acceptable to the Supplier provided that:
>
> (*a*) the terms of such agreement do not adversely affect the obligation of the Customer owed to the Supplier hereunder;
>
> (*b*) the Customer has notified the Supplier in advance of such intention; and
>
> (*c*) the Supplier has notified the Customer in writing of the acceptability of the third party, such acceptance not to be unreasonably refused.

The hardware clauses in PC and word processor contracts tend to be vague about the customer's right to refuse to accept equipment which is not satisfactory. The last example given in the section on post-delivery tests [2.3.4] is typical, although it is not in fact taken from a PC or word processing contract. The customer should of course point out to the supplier that he will accept the equipment only when he is satisfied.

4.3 Software

Software on word processors and PCs usually means package software [3.0.2] for which the customer is granted a licence.

The most common deficiency in these contracts is a clear definition of what the software is supposed to do. Again this is a frequent fault in package software contracts generally and the remedy often involves incorporation of another document by reference '. . . more particularly defined in document entitled *Scrabble 200 Word Processor User's Manual Version 3.7*, 14 March 1995'. In this way there should be no doubt as to whether or not the software includes a particular feature that the customer has asked for.

Software sold for personal computers in the rapidly increasing number of computer shops is usually sold under licence terms directly with the software owner in the form of a 'shrink-wrap' licence [5.3.6.4; E]. In these circumstances, the customer's only recourse must be exhaustive testing of the software in the shop before he purchases the programs. If this makes purchasing software at some shops seem an unsatisfactory business venture, the reader can draw his own conclusions.

Another aspect of this unsatisfactory type of sale is reservation of title and protection of that title [3.8.1]. Software sold on floppy disks is held on a cheap electronic medium and can easily be copied, thereby infringing copyright [3.8]. People confidently assert that a piece of PC software is 'in the public domain' and there is therefore no question of indemnity against infringement of title or payment of a licence fee. Public domain is appropriate to copyright material where fifty years have elapsed from the author's death. Although programs are now copyright, the newness of the computer business means that 70 years cannot yet have elapsed from the death of the author. There is therefore at present no such thing as 'software in the public domain' and rights, though dormant, unenforced and even untraceable, still exist. However, increasingly copyright owners make their software available with a statement that it is 'in the public domain' whereby they expressly waive any right to enforce their copyright. The user has no opportunity of knowing whether the person who makes the statement is indeed the copyright owner of all the software and of course there is no contract between the user and the person making the statement so there is no indemnity, actual or implied, to protect the user against any claim by a third party for copyright infringement.

It is also by no means clear whether the copyright owner having made such a statement of waiver is entitled to revoke it again at some future date and if so what would constitute notice to the user.

Such 'public domain' software or 'freeware' is discussed further below.

An ordinary software licence for PCs allows the user to load the system on to his PC and use it there. In practice, he may well write it to the hard disk and leave it resident on the PC more or less permanently. He still has the original floppy disk from which he loaded it available to use as a back up.

In the case of software designed for virus protection, practice may vary as to how the software is to be used. For a company, it may well make sense to dedicate a single PC as a 'quarantine' machine on to which all new software will be loaded and a virus protection program or series of programs run to check it, before the software is re-loaded on to its destination machine. The problems of 'shrink-wrap licences' are discussed further at 5.3.6.4. In theory such agreements assume that the software will only ever be loaded and used on one machine. The use of a 'quarantine' machine means that in fact the software will be loaded first on to the 'quarantine' machine and then on to its destination machine. Usually there is no specific wording in the 'shrink-wrap licence' which prevents this and it follows, if that is the case, that the user can in fact move the software from one machine to another, provided it is available on no more than one machine at any time.

Where virus-protection software is sold to a company or individual with more than one machine but not able to dedicate a single machine as a 'quarantine' machine, the user cannot, of course, simply copy the same software onto all his machines if he has licence only for a single machine. The simplest method of working will be for him to load the anti-virus software on to a machine immediately before other new software to be tested by it is loaded. Following the completion of the anti-virus test, he may well wish to eliminate the anti-virus software from his machine so as not to take up valuable memory. One software supplier who has fully grasped this has interesting wording to alert the user to his obligations as a licensee and at the same time recognises realistically how the software will actually be used. Consider the following:

Licence

You have not become the owner of this software—you have purchased the right to use the software. You may make one copy of this software and you should keep that copy in a safe place; use the original write-protected disk as a working disk. You must not copy this manual. You must treat this software just like a book. You can use it in more than one place, but only at one place at a time. You may lend it to someone else, but if you do, you cannot use it at the same time, just like a book cannot be read by two people at different places at the same time. If you choose to install the programs on a hard disk, they may not be used on any other machine.

We regard this as both realistic and helpful. However, it has to be said that the enforcement of terms like this can only be left to the honesty and good sense of the licensee.

However, the flood of amateur producers of software—a sort of New Grub Street of schoolboys, hackers and home computer enthusiasts generally—means that copyright in software is frequently infringed and the culprit can rarely be traced. It is also true that a substantial number of the amateurs are not particularly interested in the money. Such people may wish to waive their copyright or at least dilute it by claiming that their software is 'freeware' (ie copyright waived) or 'honorware' or 'shareware' (or some similar term) with a polite invitation to anyone into whose hands the software falls to experiment with the software free of charge, but if the user intends to keep the software on his system, he should send a fee to the originator of the software. In some cases he will then be eligible for copies of future upgrades of the software. It may be suspected that not everyone is entirely scrupulous about honouring such an arrangement.

It must be admitted that 'freeware' or 'shareware', while drawing the user's attention to the existence of copyright in software, probably weakens the overall enforceability of software protection under the Copyright, Designs and Patents Act 1988. The Federation Against Software Theft (FAST—see 13.2.2), an association of companies concerned about this, offers excellent practical advice to companies wishing to safeguard their software, including the clear incorporation of copyright notices, the placing of a 'fingerprint' (ie some hidden notice or word readily identifiable by the owner but unlikely to have got there other than by the deliberate act of the copyright owner). The 'fingerprint' may be either physically put onto the disk or other medium in some ineradicable form, or encoded, or both, the recording of serial numbers issued to authorised licensees (again put on the disk or other medium). This helps trace the source of any unauthorised copies, and the retention of manuals and documentation. Further details on these and other techniques may be obtained from FAST [13.2.2].

Amateur software writers are not all as casual about software rights and there are some well-publicised stories of some who have made substantial sums from their ideas. To do this they will usually have to interest one of the larger software distributors, and this means hawking the idea round suitable companies to get the necessary backing for commercial exploitation of the idea. It is therefore not uncommon for software houses to receive unsolicited disclosures of allegedly new ideas from individual programmers.

Such disclosures can cause problems for the company receiving them. In the first place they must satisfy themselves that the programmer really does have full right to dispose of the idea. If it has been developed in his employer's time, or on his employer's equipment, then *prima facie* the rights in the software will belong to the employer and not the programmer [11.0.2]. The disclosure may also consist of ideas either already known to the company or readily discoverable by the company through its own efforts. If the company subsequently uses the ideas (even though both its knowledge of the ideas and its decision to use them are earlier in date than the disclosure by the programmer), the programmer will inevitably cry 'Foul!' when he sees 'his' ideas being exploited.

From the programmer's point of view, he must establish that the disclosure was for the sole purpose of enabling the company to assess the feasibility of entering into an arrangement with the programmer for the exploitation of his ideas. The courts, once they are satisfied that the programmer treated the information as confidential, will restrain the company's use of the material (the leading case is *Johnson v Heat and Air Systems Ltd* [1941] 58 RPC 229). The company's defence can only be if it can *demonstrate* that it already had possession of the information.

Faced with a letter offering unsolicited disclosures, a company should be extremely cautious about how it acts. At the risk of seeming bureaucratic, the safest course for both sides is an agreement, in the form of an exchange of letters, setting out the rights and obligations of both sides. In particular it should state that the company will treat the information as confidential only insofar as it is not already known to the company or is not independently developed by any of the company's employees who have not had access to the programmer's ideas. A sample of such a letter to a programmer is provided as Precedent V.

Chapter 5

Distribution and marketing

Chapter 5

Distribution and marketing

5.0 Introduction

5.0.1 The need for distribution and marketing

So far in this book we have dealt almost entirely with contracts between the supplier of a product or service and the end-user. Behind that simple arrangement there may be many more complex ones which have led up to the supplier being in a position to supply the end-user. Distribution and marketing arrangements are often of little concern to the end-user. He will acquire his product from one party and will be blissfully unaware of the agreements underlying the relationship between his supplier and the owner or manufacturer of the product. Occasionally, however, the end-user does become aware of a wider relationship. One example which springs to mind in relation to computer software is the end-user licence. Here, the end-user acquires his computer system from his supplier under a contract in the normal way but is also asked to enter into a licence agreement with the owner of the software whereby he undertakes directly with the owner to use the software in accordance with the licence terms. Of course, the end-user immediately becomes aware that the software is not owned by his supplier and this may lead him to question whether the supplier is in a position to provide appropriate software maintenance services or to arrange for a deposit of source code. This is particularly so in the case of leasing contracts.

While distribution and marketing arrangements can complicate matters contractually, they are in widespread use and reflect a growing need for manufacturers of products to appoint intermediaries to help them penetrate consumer markets. Not every business has the resources both to manufacture the product and to market it effectively to the end-user. At one extreme, one might find an individual inventor who has no resources to manufacture or market his product but who, in return for a royalty, agrees that this should be dealt with by a commercial organisation with the appropriate resources. At the other extreme a multinational company having almost limitless marketing resources may nevertheless find itself in a position where it has to appoint a distributor or agent in a particular territory in order to overcome local political or legal difficulties. Between these extremes there is scope for many different kinds of relationship but each reflects the need for one party to acquire the marketing skills of another.

5.0.2   Distributor or agent? [G2, G14; H2; I2]

One of the first questions which will need to be answered is whether it is desired to appoint a distributor or an agent. In the former case, the relationship between the manufacturer and the distributor will be that of buyer and seller. The distributor buys from the manufacturer and sells on at a margin to his customers. There is no direct contract of sale between the manufacturer and the end-user. The distributorship agreement will include terms governing the sale of the products between the manufacturer and the distributor, but with the distributor being largely free to contract with his own customers as he sees fit:

> Sales of the Products to the Distributor shall be governed by the Company's standard conditions of sale in force from time to time

Clearly, such a clause gives the seller of the products an opportunity to revise its standard conditions to the disadvantage of the distributor and will usually be resisted by the distributor for that reason. Being an independent contractor, the distributor assumes a greater degree of risk than an agent, particularly in respect of bad debts, carrying stock and liability to customers.

An agent, on the other hand, is in a very different position. He acts as the intermediary between his principal and the customer in return for a commission, and it is these latter two who are the contracting parties. The agent will not normally incur any personal responsibility under the contract and can expect to be indemnified by his principal for any loss which may arise which is not due to his neglect or default. Some agents merely procure orders for the products and then leave the principal to enter into a contract with the customer. Others are given authority to negotiate and enter into contracts on the principal's behalf. An essential part of an agency agreement is a clear statement of the authority (if any) given to the agent to contract on the principal's behalf.

> Except as expressly provided in this Agreement the Agent has no authority to commit the Company to any obligation and shall indemnify the Company against any loss or damage which the Company may sustain or incur as a result of any unauthorised act of the Agent

An agent who exceeds his authority will be liable to his principal for any loss suffered. Precedents G and H illustrate some of the differences between an agent and a distributor, and the reader is referred to these for examples of the types of obligations which commonly arise [G14; H2].

In the European Union, special legislation affords protection to commercial agents. This is dealt with in 5.9 below.

5.1   Responsibilities of the parties [G7, G8; H7, H8; I9, I10]

A distributorship or agency agreement usually does two main things. First, it establishes the contractual relationship of the parties, so that in the case of a distributorship agreement it would stipulate that the relationship is that of buyer and seller, and the agreement will incorporate terms similar to those found in any contract of sale (eg retention of title, passing of risk, provisions for late payment etc). Secondly, it stipulates the responsibilities of the parties regarding the products themselves and their marketing to the end-user.

Commonly, the agreement will need to stipulate who will be responsible for:

(1) *Manufacturing and packing the products.* If this is to be done by the distributor, the agreement becomes more complicated, as the distributor will need to have in his possession all the necessary technical information to enable him to manufacture. The owner will be concerned to ensure that he has sufficient control over the distributor's activities to ensure compliance with specifications and quality control and to protect his intellectual property rights.

(2) *Licensing.* If the product is software which is to be licensed to the end-user, the owner will need to decide whether to license the end-user direct [H] or grant the distributor rights to sub-license the end-user [I]. In the former case, the distributor will undertake to procure the end-user to enter into a standard form end-user licence with the software owner.

(3) *Maintenance and support of the products.* If this is to be undertaken by the distributor he will need to be provided with all the necessary information and spare parts to enable him to perform his obligations properly. Software maintenance can cause problems, and this is discussed in 5.3.6.6.

(4) *Compliance with local laws and regulations* [G7 (22, 23)]. Clearly, it is important that the products should comply with the laws and regulations of the territory in which they are to be sold.

109

Commonly, the responsibility for this is divided. The distributor advises the manufacturer of the local requirements and the manufacturer undertakes to manufacture them in accordance with those requirements.

(5) *Advertising*. It is obviously in both parties' interests to maximise sales in the territory in question, and advertising will be a key feature. The parties may agree elaborate provisions for determining who will be responsible for the costs of advertising or alternatively say nothing, leaving commercial pressures to play their part. As a general rule, an exclusive distributor is more likely to be asked to commit resources to advertising, whereas a non-exclusive distributor, who is one of many in the territory, is more likely to look for a national strategy from the manufacturer.

Example:

The parties shall cooperate in regard to the promotion and marketing of the Products. The Company undertakes to spend such reasonable sums on advertising and marketing activities as may be necessary sufficiently to promote the Products in the Territory.

5.2   Price and payment [G1, G4, G16; H9; I11]

Price and payment terms are a key aspect of any long-term purchasing arrangement and distribution agreements are no exception. Unlike a one-off sale, there must be a mechanism for establishing the price for each consignment of the products ordered. Commonly, the basic price is determined by reference to the seller's published prices from time to time less an agreed discount whereby the distributor makes his margin. A distributor looking for price protection might be inclined to seek controls limiting price increases to demonstrated increases in costs of manufacture. However, prices can go down as well as up and sometimes it is as well to leave the seller to determine his prices freely; after all, it is not in the seller's interests to set prices which unduly restrict sales. The distributor is more likely to be concerned that he is being treated fairly in comparison with other distributors, particularly in his own market. If another distributor is being treated more favourably, then this immediately undermines the distributor's position. He may therefore seek a 'most favoured customer clause' whereby the seller undertakes that the prices charged to the distributor will be no more than those charged to the seller's other distributors purchasing similar volumes.

The Company warrants and undertakes to the Distributor that the prices to be charged for the Products will be no greater that the lowest prices charged to the Company's other distributors in the Territory purchasing the Products in similar volumes

Volume discounts are a common feature of distribution arrangements. In addition to the basic discount on published prices, the distributor is given the opportunity to obtain additional discounts by achieving predetermined sales targets. Such provisions require careful thought, however, and the seller should remember that in his effort to earn additional discounts the distributor may be inclined to spend fewer resources on such matters as after-sales support.

Pre-payment or prompt payment discounts also appear quite regularly in distributorship agreements. The seller offers an agreed discount for payment on order or within a short period after order, failing which the distributor has to pay the higher price. Cynics might argue that the seller merely adds on the amount of the discount to his 'real' prices to ensure early payment and that late payment is really a bonus for the seller who receives something he did not otherwise expect to have!

The seller will invariably reserve the right to increase or reduce prices, usually by giving the distributor an agreed period of notice. The price is then expressed to be that prevailing at the time of delivery of the products to the distributor. This could work unfairly against the distributor if the seller deliberately withholds deliveries until a price increase becomes effective. This situation can be guarded against by a provision that if the distributor orders products with a requested delivery date prior to the effective date of the price increase, then the lower price will be charged notwithstanding that the products are actually delivered after the effective date. Similarly, price decrease protection can be given to the distributor by providing that if a delivery is made during the notice period of the price decrease the distributor will nevertheless be charged the lower price.

Unlike distributors, agents usually earn their living by charging a commission, often expressed as a percentage of the net sales price of the product. In these cases, the agent is perhaps more concerned in maintaining the price of the products lest his commission be reduced, although increasing volumes of sales will also increase his income. It will be important to establish exactly what the agent will apply his percentage to. Clearly, it will be in the seller's interests to express the agent's commission as a percentage of the net amount payable to the seller, and any definition of 'net sales price' will normally exclude such items as VAT, customs duties and transport and insurance charges.

> For the purpose of this Clause 'Net Sales Price' means the price invoiced to the Company's customers excluding import duties and other levies, transport and insurance charges and Value Added Tax or other applicable sales tax.

Adjustments are sometimes made so that the agent is not entitled to his commission until payment is actually received by the seller or for the agent's commission to be paid in the same instalments as the purchase price is payable, but see also 5.9.

Where prices are expressed in currency other than that in which the distributor sells the product, the currency rate considerations of 2.2.4 [A3(2)] may be relevant.

5.3   Types of distribution system

5.3.1   Territory or market sector [G13; H12, H13; I14, I15]

A distributor is normally employed for his marketing expertise either in a particular geographical territory or a particular market sector. The appointment will usually reflect that fact and will be limited to the area where the seller thinks that the distributor will have an impact. If the distributor has been over-optimistic in his ability to market the product, he may well find that the seller subsequently wishes to reduce the distributor's area of operations or terminate the contract.

5.3.2   Exclusive distribution [G2]

The most valuable agreement from a distributor's point of view is one which gives him the exclusive right to distribute the products in a particular area. This advantage may be cut down by the seller's insistence on being able to sell direct to certain customers in the distributor's market or by a short notice period for terminating the agreement.

> Notwithstanding the Distributor's exclusive appointment the Company reserves the right to sell the Products direct to end-user customers situated in the Territory.

Exclusive arrangements are inherently anti-competitive [5.10], but this does not mean that they are necessarily against the public interest. A distributor with exclusive rights may be inclined to put much greater resources into training, maintenance and after-sales support than one whose profit margins are continuously under attack from competitors dealing in the same products.

5.3.3   Non-exclusive distribution [H2; I2]

From the seller's point of view, the grant of non-exclusive rights to a number of distributors in a particular market has two advantages. First, the seller is not reliant on one distributor who may perform badly. Second, the existence of competition between distributors should ensure maximum sales effort. Excessive competition in a market can be counter-productive though and may lead to the emergence of the 'box-pusher' distributor who provides little service or support and could not care whether the end-user uses the computer as a computer or a door stop!

5.3.4 Selective distribution

In an effort to encourage competition yet keep out the discount stores a number of manufacturers have put in place selective distribution systems. These systems work by requiring retailers who wish to become dealers to meet certain pre-determined qualitative criteria relating to such matters as the technical qualifications of their staff and the suitability of their premises and training and after-sales support. Once appointed, these qualified retailers are then permitted to purchase the products from one or more national distributors appointed by the manufacturer. Conversely, the distributors are only allowed to sell to those retailers who meet the qualitative criteria and who have been appointed as qualified dealers. In this way the manufacturer can ensure that certain minimum standards of training and support are maintained. Attempts to restrict competition by quantitative criteria (ie by merely restricting the numbers of resellers of the product) are highly likely to offend relevant competition law [5.10] and even qualitative criteria must be applied fairly and uniformly so as not to exclude a dealer who can demonstrate that he meets them. This does not mean however that the manufacturer has to sell to anyone who meets the criteria; generally speaking a manufacturer who is not in a dominant position in the market can sell to whom he chooses. What he cannot do is prevent his distributor from selling on to a retail dealer who meets the criteria.

5.3.5 Hardware distribution [G7]

In some respects hardware distribution hardly merits a separate mention as it is not that different from the distribution of any other product. If anything its distinguishing feature is the complexity of the product. In comparison with the domestic kettle, computers are difficult to use, and to many the term 'user friendly' has yet to become a reality. An efficient distributor will be able to provide expert advice to his customers, helping them to make the appropriate choice and then ensuring that they receive effective after-sales support. It will be in the interests of the seller to ensure this happens by providing training courses for the distributor's personnel, spares for maintenance services and by monitoring the standard of service he provides.

5.3.6 Software distribution [G10; H4; I4]

The distribution of computer software presents a number of difficulties to the owner and it is important that these are considered before embarking on a distribution strategy.

5.3.6.1 Types of software

The practicalities of distributing software in a particular way often depend on the nature of the software to be distributed. Broadly speaking, one can identify three categories:

(1) Specialist bespoke programs [3.0.3]
(2) General commercial software [3.0.2]
(3) Mass marketed software [4.3].

It is fair to say that the first category of programs is unlikely to be relevant to distribution arrangements. They are usually developed for a particular customer and may not have a general application. The cost of producing them is therefore borne entirely by that customer.

On the other hand, commercial programs with a general application are more ideally suited for distribution. The cost of development is, in effect, spread across a number of customers and once a user base is established the producer can afford to spend additional resources on developing and enhancing the software. While the software may be used by a number of customers it may still be valuable enough to be worth protecting from general disclosure by the use of confidentiality undertakings and in these circumstances will be subject to a licence agreement governing its disclosure and use.

Mass marketed software presents the greatest number of difficulties, some of which have been mentioned in 4.3—see also Chapter 9. It is widely available and is probably not, for this reason, protected by the law of confidence. It has been subject to the same problem of unauthorised copying as has afflicted the music industry and the problem is likely to persist, particularly as it is almost impossible to keep track of every copy which is sold. Asking the purchaser of a £50 piece of software to sign a licence agreement governing its use is about as feasible as asking the purchaser of a compact disc to do the same.

5.3.6.2 Copyright protection [3.8; H10; I12]

Section 3(1) of the Copyright, Designs and Patents Act 1988 confirms that computer programs are treated as 'literary works' for the purposes of copyright law. Any copying of a program is therefore an infringing act unless the act is licensed by the copyright owner or it is specifically authorised by the Act. For instance, s 50A gives a lawful user of a program the right to make a back up copy which it is necessary for him to have for the purposes of his lawful use. Furthermore, s 50C stipulates that is is not an infringement of copyright for a lawful user of a program to copy or adapt it, provided that the copying or adapting is necessary for his lawful use (which may include copying or adapting for the purpose of error correction) and is not prohibited under any term or condition of an agreement regulating the circumstances in which his use is lawful, although the possibility of the latter contractual opt-out may not be a correct implementation of the Software Directive [3.8.1]. Having said this, most programs are accompanied by an express licence permitting storage of the programs on a designated computer and also the taking of copies for security and back up purposes.

Given the existence of copyright protection, why do software owners still require end-users to enter into licence agreements? The answer to this is as follows:

(1) To impose an obligation of confidence on the user. However, as mentioned above, this is probably not applicable to software which is widely available to the public.

(2) To impose limitations and exclusions on the liability of the software owner for the program. A defective package costing £100 could result in consequential losses to the end-user considerably greater than the price of the program.

(3) To restrict the way in which the end-user may use the programs (eg to use the software on a designated computer and to use it for the end-user's internal purposes only and not for the purpose of operating a bureau service). Clearly, this is only necessary if the particular use is not restricted by copyright law.

(4) To permit acts which might otherwise be an infringement of copyright (eg to take a back up copy whether this is necessary for the purposes of lawful use or not).

(5) Specifically to draw to the attention of the end-user the restrictions imposed by copyright law.

(6) Where the extent of any implied licence to use is uncertain.

(7) In the event of a breach of the licence, the copyright owner may terminate the licence in accordance with its terms and enforce the remedies conferred by the licence agreement. This is in addition to the copyright owner's remedies of damages and injunctive relief for breach of copyright.

5.3.6.3 *Licensing* [H4; I4]

The software owner who wishes to distribute his software through intermediaries and at the same time impose licence terms on the end-user has to face up to the problem that unless special arrangements are put in place there will be no direct contractual nexus between the software owner and the end-user. Direct covenants from the end-user will ensure that the owner can enforce the licence terms himself rather than rely on an intermediary to do so.

One method of achieving this is to appoint the intermediary as the agent of the software owner, authorised to enter into a standard form licence agreement with the end-user on the owner's behalf [I]. Alternatively, the agent can procure end-users to enter into a licence agreement which only comes into effect once it is submitted to and accepted by the owner [H]. The latter method gives the owner more control over who the software is licensed to while at the same time permitting more flexible negotiations between the owner and the end-user over the terms of the licence agreement.

Problems arise, however, where it is not feasible to secure a written contract with the end-user. This is particularly so in relation to mass marketed software where customers are used to going into a retail shop and buying software off the shelf with the minimum of formality. It would be administratively burdensome and, indeed, impractical to ask each individual customer to sign a licence agreement before purchasing the software.

5.3.6.4 *'Shrink-wrap' licences* [E; G10]

In an attempt to impose licence terms on the end-users of mass marketed software without the need for a written agreement, software owners have employed a device which has become known as the 'shrink-wrap' licence. This is a short licence agreement which is contained within the packaging for the software. It may actually be printed on the packaging or alternatively be a loose form secured between the packaging and the film. A variant is the 'tear-off' licence which is printed on a sealed cardboard packet containing the diskette on which the software is recorded and is expressed to be accepted by the user by his tearing open the packet. A copy of the licence agreement often appears in the user manual. It is expressed to be made between the software owner and the end-user.

Legal commentators have identified two main difficulties with shrink-wrap licences under English law:

(1) *The doctrine of privity of contract.* This provides that no one except a party to a contract can acquire rights under it and no one except a party can be subject to liabilities under it. Where the end-user purchases a package from a distributor the contract of sale is clearly between the distributor and the end-user (we say 'sale' because the end-user will own the physical article, namely the media on which the program is recorded and may use it as he wishes short of infringing copyright). The shrink-wrap licence is, however, expressed to be made between the software owner and the end-user. Every contract has to be supported by consideration, and it is difficult to see sometimes what benefit flows to the end-user from the software owner under most shrink-wrap licences which merely impose additional restrictions or limitations on liability.

(2) *Incorporation of terms.* Many shrink-wrap licences contain a condition to the effect that they are deemed to be accepted by the customer if he opens the package and breaks the wrapping. The difficulty that has been identified with this procedure is that in many cases the contract of sale will have been made before the act of acceptance has taken place. It is a clearly established principle of English law that all the terms of the contract have to be brought to the parties' attention before the contract is made otherwise those terms which are not will not be validly incorporated into the contract. Where the end-user purchases the package in a retail shop the contract is usually made at the till when the cashier accepts the customer's money, and there can be no guarantee that he will have read the licence terms prior to that time. Proving that he did is equally difficult.

In the case of a mail order transaction the contract is probably made over the telephone (in the case of credit card transactions) or when the distributor commits some act of acceptance (eg cashing the customer's cheque or posting the goods to him) in response to the customer's written order. Mail order sales would appear to present particular difficulties in ensuring that the customer is aware of the licence terms before the contract is made.

How then does one circumvent these problems? The honest answer is probably with some difficulty. Software owners have sought to find the solution in copyright law rather than contract law, attempting to create a collateral copyright licence agreement between the software owner and the end-user which arises independently of the contract of sale and where it does not matter that the terms of that agreement are not communicated before the contract of sale is made.

117

The argument has been run in the past that copying a computer program by storing it in any medium by electronic means (eg by loading it into the hard disk of a computer) is a restricted act for copyright purposes and may not be performed without the copyright owner's permission (see the Copyright, Designs and Patents Act 1988, s 17(2)). So too, it was argued, was making a back up copy although, as mentioned above, a statutory right to make a back up copy is now conferred by s 50A of the Act. The software owner then sought to impose his licence terms on the end-user by pointing out these restrictions and granting him a licence permitting the requisite use subject to the other terms and conditions of the licence. The end-user was deemed to accept the terms by some act of acceptance, whether it be tearing off the wrapping or loading the program onto the hard disk of a computer.

The hapless consumer who purchases his package software in a retail shop may complain with some indignation that, having paid his money and purchased his copy of the program from a reputable retailer who is presumably authorised to sell it, he should be entitled to use it for the purpose for which it is intended without any further restriction or limitation. The law, it seems, might agree with him in two ways.

The first is the argument that at common law, and without notice to the contrary, such a purchaser has an implied licence to use and copy the software for the purpose for which it is intended. Such an implied licence probably exists and it would therefore be necessary to bring to the purchaser's attention specifically the fact that the copyright owner does not intend such a licence to be granted but instead an express licence on the terms offered.

The second argument is even more problematic. As mentioned in 5.3.6.2, new s 50C of the Copyright, Designs and Patents Act 1988, provided by the Copyright (Computer Programs) Regulations 1992 (SI 1992 No 3233) now provides that it is not an infringement of copyright for a lawful user of a program to copy or adapt it, provided that the copying or adapting is necessary for his lawful use and is not prohibited under any term or condition of an agreement regulating the circumstances in which his use is lawful. Rather unhelpfully, s 50A(2) defines a 'lawful user' of a computer program as someone who has (whether under a licence to do any acts restricted by the copyright in the program or otherwise) a right to use the program. It is at least arguable that a person who buys a copy of a computer program legitimately is a lawful user particularly if it can be said that an implied licence arises in his favour at the time of purchase. Moreover, art 5(1) of the Software Directive (91/250/EEC) which the regulations implement in fact refers to the lawful *acquirer* not user which is an altogether different concept. A person who purchases a copy of a program lawfully could be described as a lawful acquirer without having any licence, express or implied, to use the program. The UK courts may be compelled to interpret the expression 'lawful user' in the light of the intention of the directive as synonymous with 'lawful acquirer'. In fact, the draftsman of the UK legislation may have had the implied licence at common law in mind when using the expression lawful user and perhaps did not intend to deviate from the objective of the directive. If, in fact, lawful acquirer and lawful user are synonymous for these purposes this means that a person who purchases a copy of a program lawfully (and does not sign or accept an agreement regulating his use beforehand or contemporaneously which prohibits copying or adapting) becomes entitled to copy and adapt it for his lawful use as a result of s 50C.

If either of these arguments is valid, it means that a person who purchases a copy of a computer program lawfully will already have the right to use it in accordance with its intended purpose. The offer of a licence from the software owner is therefore unnecessary and this casts doubt on whether an offer of a licence in return for restrictions and limitations in favour of the software owner is the basis for a valid agreement. Consideration must flow both ways, but if the purchaser already has the rights which the software owner is purporting to confer it is difficult to see what consideration flows in favour of the purchaser. In order to fall within s 50C, the instrument prohibiting the copying or adapting must be an 'agreement' and not a mere 'licence'. Moreover, the agreement must be one 'regulating the circumstances in which his use is lawful'. If the purchaser already has the right to use the program lawfully it is perhaps difficult to argue that a subsequent agreement itself regulates his lawful use. One possible solution might be for the software owner to offer the user some additional benefit not conferred on him by law (perhaps an absolute right to make a back up copy or the offer of help-line support) but there seems little compulsion on a user to accept this if it means agreeing to burdensome restrictions or limitations. Some software owners make the provision of help-line support conditional on the user signing and returning a registration card which includes a confirmation that the user agrees to be bound by the terms of the licence agreement. One further obstacle to the enforceability of the shrink-wrap licence is the argument, mentioned in 3.8.1, that s 50C is an incorrect implementation of the Software Directive in permitting the right to copy or adapt a computer program in order to use it for its intended purpose to be prohibited by a contract to the contrary at all.

One can see that the enforceability of the shrink-wrap licence does remain in some doubt, which will continue until there is judicial guidance on the issue. The trend appears to be in favour of the tear-off licence, with a physical act of acceptance (namely, the tearing open of the packet containing the diskette) accompanied by an offer to refund the purchase price if the user does not accept the licence terms. It is a clearly established contractual principal that the terms of an offer can be accepted by a prescribed form of conduct provided the offeree is aware of the terms and he does the act with the intention of accepting the offer. Whether a lawful user of a program opens the packet containing the diskette solely in order to use the program for its intended purpose or with the intention of also accepting the licence conditions will, we are sure, be a point which will be argued in any case attempting to establish the enforceability of such agreements.

The position is improved for the software owner where he is granting a site licence or multiple copy licence [5.3.6.5] and where there is some real additional benefit flowing from the software owner to the user. Such licences are often the subject of formal written agreements which avoid the need to rely on the device of the shrink-wrap agreement or, alternatively, confirm the user's agreement to be bound by the terms of the shrink-wrap agreement [F].

A form of shrink-wrap licence agreement is offered in Precedent E. However, it must be regarded as being accompanied by a strong health warning as to its likely enforceability.

Where software is distributed, it should be made clear in the contract between the software owner and the distributor that it is the responsibility of the distributor to ensure that each copy of the package is sold with the accompanying shrink-wrap licence. It is common to find distributors who, when demonstrating software to a potential customer, open up the package and throw away the shrink-wrap licence. This practice may be reduced by providing the distributor with a sufficient number of demonstration versions of the package [G5].

Shrink-wrap licences commonly permit the original licensee to sell the diskette and transfer the licence to another user provided the user accepts the terms of the licence and the original licensee ceases to use the software. This is consistent with the exhaustion of distribution right contained in s 18(3) of the Copyright, Designs and Patents Act 1988 and such express transfer provisions will replace those implied by s 56(2) of the Act.

While a shrink-wrap licence *may* help the software owner to limit or exclude his liability to end-users it does little for the distributor who is not a party to it. The distributor would have to have his own contract with the end-user. However, the likelihood of an end-user signing a written agreement with a retailer for package software is remote.

5.3.6.5 *Networks and site licences* [F; I Sched 1]

Site licences have been introduced by the industry in response to two problems. First, the reluctance of multiple users of a program to pay the full price for each copy of the program they use. Second, the use of network systems where several processors are linked together and where the software can be resident at any time in any one of those processors.

The demand for multiple copies of a program can be met by bulk discounting. The more copies the customer purchases the less he pays for each individual copy. This requirement can quite easily be fulfilled by the distributor, who prices accordingly. However, it does not answer all the problems as it still means that the customer is required to purchase a series of single user licences. What may be preferred is a licence which enables the user to copy the program for use on all his computers without signing a separate licence for each copy [F]. A wider definition of 'use' would be required and a change in pricing structure. Site licences need not be ruinous to the software owner and, indeed, may tempt business users with only one valid copy of a program to seek legitimacy by applying for a site licence.

A single user licence which permits use of the program on one processor only is clearly not appropriate for a network system. Again, the definition of 'use' will need to be redrafted in a wider fashion while at the same time introducing an appropriate pricing structure.

Site licensing can be viewed as a specialist form of distribution. Because it entails redrafting the single user licence it is not something which the distributor can usually handle alone, unless the software owner has agreed upon a standard form of site licence (but even that may not cope with every situation). We are beginning to see larger corporate customers going direct to the software owner to negotiate special arrangements for site licences. Their purchasing power may be such that the software owner cannot ignore them. In these circumstances distributors are likely to be left to service the smaller users unless they can negotiate exclusive distribution rights with the software owner, but even then the owner might reserve the right to supply end-user customers direct. The future is uncertain, but we doubt whether distributors are always going to view the introduction of the site licence with enthusiasm.

5.3.6.6 *Support* [G6, G8; H6, H8; I6, I7]

For a full discussion of maintenance readers are referred to Chapters 8 and 9. Maintenance of hardware by a distributor does not cause any particular difficulties. The distributor has to be trained, of course, but he can quite easily be supplied with a stock of spare parts, and this does not give him much more information than he could obtain by dismantling the machine.

Software maintenance is a different matter. If the distributor is to provide effective maintenance he will need access to the source code of the software and will need to employ skilled programmers to carry out the work. For this reason, one often finds that responsibility for software maintenance is retained by the software owner so that the distributor's duties are confined to supplying and installing the software. In this way the software owner protects his software by not revealing the source code.

It is only in cases where there is a great deal of commercial trust between the parties that the software owner will release his source code. This may arise, for example, where the software owner and distributor are parent and subsidiary or members of a joint venture.

5.4   Termination [G3; G15; G16; H15; I17]

Like most term contracts, provisions will be incorporated giving one party the right to terminate in the event of the default or insolvency of the other. Additionally one might find a right given to the seller to terminate if the distributor or agent fails to meet any agreed minimum sales targets.

The appointment of a distributor or agent is often considered as a personal relationship such that the distributor cannot assign or delegate his rights and obligations.

> The Distributor shall not be entitled to assign, sub-contract or delegate any of its rights or obligations under this Agreement.

A change in control of a corporate distributor might similarly be regarded as unacceptable by the seller (particularly if the new owner of the distributor is a competitor of the seller), and accordingly the contract might provide the seller with a right to terminate in that event.

Special obligations can arise on the termination of the appointment of a commercial agent. These are considered in 5.9.

5.5   Alterations [G8; H8; I7]

Alterations can occur in both the specification of the products and the range of products offered by the seller.

It is clearly in the seller's interests to ensure that the distributor is kept fully informed of all enhancements and changes to the products so that he can properly market and support them. To this end the seller may offer the distributor's personnel a free training programme in respect of any major enhanced product.

It will be important to establish exactly what products will be sold by the seller to the distributor. The seller may not want to sell his entire product range through the distributor, as the latter may not have the necessary expertise to demonstrate and support the whole range. On the other hand, the distributor's position could be seriously affected if the seller is given the absolute right to discontinue selling products to the distributor. A compromise which is often agreed is that the seller will initially offer the distributor an agreed range of products which is identified in a schedule to the agreement. If the seller discontinues selling any of the products to the distributor then he must discontinue selling them altogether in the distributor's territory. If a new product is introduced which can reasonably be regarded as a successor to any existing product, then the distributor will be offered that successor product in lieu of the old one. (It will usually be in the seller's interest to discontinue sales of the obsolescent product as swiftly as possible.) Entirely new products are then left to be offered by the seller at his discretion.

Most sellers will wish to reserve the right to discontinue selling a product, not least to ensure that they can minimise the risk associated with product liability.

5.6 Distributor's duties [G7; H7; I9]

The distributor will usually undertake to:

(1) Use his best endeavours to maximise sales in his territory.
(2) Achieve minimum sales volumes.
(3) Employ trained staff to demonstrate and support the products.
(4) Keep the seller advised of matters material to the exploitation of the products in the territory.
(5) Install and maintain the products.
(6) Provide training to end-users.

As regards (1) and (2), the distributor will be cautious about agreeing to these if the seller reserves the right to refuse to accept the distributor's orders. Clearly, the distributor will not wish to be put in a position where he is deemed to be in breach of the agreement merely because his orders are not fulfilled by the seller.

5.7 Seller's duties [G8; H8; I10]

The seller's obligations will normally include:

(1) Fulfilling the distributor's orders as soon as practicable.
(2) Training the distributor's personnel.
(3) Providing technical and commercial assistance.
(4) Keeping the distributor advised of technical changes to the products.
(5) Advising the distributor of any proposal to discontinue products or introduce new ones.

One of the main risks of dealing in high technology products is obsolescence. Entire ranges can dramatically decrease in value on the announcement of a successor product and a distributor can be faced with selling off large quantities of stock at a loss. It is vitally important, therefore, to the distributor that the seller agrees to keep the distributor informed of any proposed new products, thus allowing an orderly running-off of stocks.

5.8 Liability [G18; I22]

Sellers will invariably seek the same type of limitations on liability as one would expect to see in any contract of sale. In particular, one often sees a limited one or two-year warranty for defective products being offered in lieu of the statutory implied terms. The distributor should remember that he will be expected to extend similar warranties to his own customers and may find himself squeezed in the middle if the products have to be held in stock for a lengthy period of time. Some companies require their distributors to pass on the benefit of warranties:

> The Distributor shall offer to its customers a warranty in respect of the Products no less favourable then the warranty given to the Distributor by the Company under Clause X.

More and more manufacturers are now offering 'guarantees' direct to the end-user which tend in practice to absolve the intermediary from responsibility. Whilst these are not guarantees in the strict legal sense of the word, they are probably enforceable by the customer as collateral agreements where it can be shown that the customer was induced into the contract with the distributor because of the guarantee. If the manufacturer is also the copyright owner and the end-user has acquired a licence direct from him rather than from the distributor this may possibly further strengthen the enforceability of the guarantee. Some contracts actively encourage distributors to arrange for defective products to be sent back to the manufacturer:

> The Distributor shall not attempt to repair any defective Products returned to it by its customers but instead shall assist them in completing the appropriate guarantee claim form and returning such products direct to the Company.

Other areas of liability that can arise are infringement of intellectual property rights and failure of the products to comply with local laws and regulations. Appropriate indemnities are usually taken.

An agent can usually expect a blanket indemnity from his principal, because the contract is not made with the agent but between the principal and the customer and is entirely transparent so far as the agent is concerned. However, where the agent has undertaken to the principal to perform certain of the principal's obligations under the contract, the agent may incur some liability to the principal against which he should not expect to be indemnified.

5.9   Legal protection for commercial agents

Special legal protection is afforded in Great Britain to commercial agents (as distinct from distributors) by the Commercial Agents (Council Directive) Regulations 1993 (SI 1993 No 3053). These were implemented pursuant to the European Council Directive 86/653/EEC on Self-Employed Commercial Agents and came into force in Great Britain on 1 January 1994. Separate regulations cover Northern Ireland.

Prior to the regulations coming into effect, English law adopted a largely *laissez faire* attitude towards the principal–agent relationship. The parties were mainly left to devise their own contractual relationship, subject to competition law, and very few terms were implied by law into an agency contract. This was in marked contrast to some other countries of the European Union where commercial agents were treated as more akin to employees with rights to compensation on termination (as under unfair dismissal and redundancy). The purpose of the directive was to harmonise the laws of the EU countries in this area.

The regulations give commercial agents important rights which cannot be excluded by contract. Chief among these are the right to a minimum period of termination notice, a right to commission on transactions concluded after the termination of the agency agreement where the transactions are mainly attributable to the efforts of the agent and a right to indemnification or compensation for any loss suffered as a consequence of the termination of the agency agreement by the principal. The regulations govern the relations between commercial agents and their principals in relation to the activities of commercial agents in Great Britain, but do not apply where the parties have agreed that the agency contract is to be governed by the law of another member state. It should be remembered, however, that there is similar implementing legislation in the other member states.

Readers should be aware of the following:

(1) The regulations only apply to commercial agents. A commercial agent is defined as a self-employed intermediary who has continuing authority to negotiate the sale or purchase of *goods* on behalf of another person ('the principal') or to negotiate and conclude the sale or purchase of *goods* on behalf of and in the name of the principal.

(2) It is generally believed that the regulations extend to agents which are corporations or partnerships as well as individuals.

(3) Contracts for the supply of *services* are not governed by the regulations. However, some of the other EU countries have extended their national legislation to cover supplies of services and consequently the local position should always be checked.

(4) Genuine distribution agreements where the distributor buys and sells goods on his own behalf are not affected by the regulations.

(5) Commercial agents do not include officers authorised to commit companies or associations, partners authorised to commit partnerships, insolvency practitioners acting as such, unpaid agents, commercial agents operating on commodity exchanges or markets, Crown agents for overseas governments or persons whose activities as commercial agents are secondary to some other primary purpose. Mail order catalogue agents for consumer goods and consumer credit agents are presumed, unless the contrary is established, not to be commercial agents for these purposes.

(6) A commercial agent and his principal are deemed to owe certain duties to each other which cannot be excluded by contract. A commercial agent must look after the interests of his principal, act dutifully and in good faith, make proper efforts to negotiate and, where appropriate, conclude the transactions he is instructed to take care of, communicate to his principal all the necessary information available to him and comply with reasonable instructions given by his principal.

(7) A principal must also act dutifully and in good faith, must provide his commercial agent with the necessary documentation relating to the goods, obtain for him the information necessary for the performance of the agency contract, notify him within a reasonable period once the principal anticipates that the volume of commercial transactions will be significantly lower than that which the agent

could normally have expected and must inform him within a reasonable period of his acceptance or refusal of, and of any non-execution by him, of a commercial transaction which the agent has procured.

(8) Where the level of remuneration has not been agreed between the principal and agent (which is likely to be rare), the commercial agent is entitled to that customarily paid or, in the absence of a customary practice, reasonable remuneration.

(9) Where a commercial agent is remunerated, wholly or in part, by *commission*:

(a) he is entitled to commission on commercial transactions concluded during the period covered by the agency agreement both where the transaction is concluded as a result of his action and where the transaction is concluded with a third party whom he has previously acquired as a customer for transactions of the same kind (ie repeat orders, even where the agent was not instrumental in obtaining them);

(b) he is also entitled to commission on transactions concluded during his agency where he has an *exclusive* right to a specific geographical area or to a specific group of customers and where the transaction has been entered into with a customer belonging to that area or group (even where the customer was not procured by the agent). The directive, in fact, gave member states the other option of giving a commercial agent this right where he is 'entrusted with a specific geographical area or group of customers', that is on a non-exclusive basis, and implementing legislation in other member states may cater for this possibility;

(c) he is entitled to commission even after his agency contract has terminated in respect of a transaction concluded within a reasonable period following such termination if that transaction is mainly attributable to his efforts during his agency or where the order reaches the principal or the agent before the termination of the agency contract;

(d) commission payable to him as mentioned in (c) above will not be shared with a successor agent unless it is equitable that this should be done;

(e) he is entitled to his commission when one of the following events occurs, namely (i) the principal executes the transaction (presumably when he delivers the goods), (ii) the principal should, according to his agreement with the third party, have executed the transaction or, at the latest, when (iii) the third party executes the transaction (presumably when he pays for the goods) or should have done so if the principal had executed his part of the transaction as he should have. The commission must be paid by the last day of the month following the quarter in which it became due. These rights cannot be taken away by contract;

(f) his right to commission can only be extinguished if it is established that the contract will not be executed and the principal is not to blame (eg the third party defaults or becomes insolvent or the contract is frustrated), in which case the commission must be returned. Again, the agent's rights cannot be diminished by contract;

(g) he is given rights to be supplied with statements of the commission due to him and extracts from the principal's books in order to check the commission due to him. These rights may not be excluded by contract.

(10) The commercial agent and the principal may demand from each other a written document setting out the terms of the agency contract, including terms subsequently agreed. This right may not be excluded. The directive entitled member states to provide that an agency contract shall not be valid unless evidenced in writing. Great Britain did not adopt this option.

(11) Where the agency agreement is concluded for an *indefinite* period, either party may terminate it by giving certain minimum notice. This is one month for the first year of the contract, two months for the second year commenced and three months for the third year commenced and for the subsequent years. The parties may not agree on shorter periods of notice. Member states were given the option of fixing the notice period at four months for the fourth year, five months for the fifth year and six months for the sixth and subsequent years and to decide that the parties could not agree on shorter notice, but Great Britain did not take up that option. If the parties voluntarily agree to a longer period of notice, the period of notice to be observed by the principal must not be shorter than that to be observed by the commercial agent. Unless otherwise agreed, the end of the notice period must coincide with the end of a calendar month.

(12) An agency contract for a *fixed* period which continues to be performed by both parties after that period has expired is deemed to be converted into an agency contract for an *indefinite* period, with the consequence that the minimum periods of notice referred to above must be given (the earlier fixed period being taken into account in calculating the period of notice). A party to an agency contract should therefore be careful not to perform it following the expiry of a fixed term if it is not intended to confer the entitlement to further notice.

(13) The regulations do not affect any statute or law which allows the immediate termination of an agency contract because of the default of one party or where exceptional circumstances arise.

(14) The directive stipulated that on the termination of an agency contract, member states were required to ensure that the commercial agent be entitled to *either* (i) an indemnity or (ii) compensation in prescribed circumstances. The following points should be noted:

(a) the agent is entitled to an *indemnity* if and to the extent that he has brought to the principal new customers or has significantly increased the volume of business with existing customers and the principal continues to derive substantial benefits from the business with such customers and the payment of the indemnity is equitable having regard to all the circumstances and, in particular, the commission lost by the agent on the business transacted with such customers. The amount of the indemnity may not exceed a figure equivalent to an indemnity for one year calculated from the commercial agent's average annual remuneration over the preceding five years and if the contract goes back less than five years the indemnity is calculated on the average for the period in question. The grant of an indemnity does not prevent the agent from seeking damages;

(b) the agent is entitled to *compensation* for the damage he suffers as a result of the termination of his relations with the principal. Such damage is deemed to occur particularly when the termination takes place in circumstances depriving the commercial agent of the commission which proper performance of the agency contract would have procured him while providing the principal with substantial benefits linked to the commercial agent's activities and/or which have not enabled the commercial agent to amortise the costs and expenses that he had incurred for the performance of the agency contract on the principal's advice;

(c) most member states have chosen to give commercial agents an indemnity. For Great Britain, however, the regulations stipulate that the indemnity will only be payable where the agency contract provides and that consequently commercial agents will be entitled to compensation unless the parties have opted for the indemnity in the contract;

(d) while there is a maximum limit on the calculation of the indemnity, neither the directive nor the regulations stipulate how any compensation will be calculated and this is left to the national courts to assess;

(e) the agent must notify the principal of his claim for compensation or, as the case may be, indemnity within a year of the termination of the agency contract, otherwise the entitlement will be lost. This leaves the onus on the agent. If the claim, once notified, is not met the agent will have to pursue his entitlement in the national courts;

(f) there is no need to make any reference to compensation in the agency contract but if the parties wish to opt for the indemnity this must be provided for expressly;

(g) the parties may not derogate from the right to compensation or, as the case may be, indemnity before the agency contract expires. Any attempt to limit or exclude the amount of compensation or indemnity in the contract will therefore be ineffective. However, once the contract has expired there seems nothing to prevent the parties from reaching a binding settlement or, indeed, waiving the entitlement altogether;

(h) the entitlement to compensation or indemnity arises not only when the contract is expressly terminated but also where it terminates as a consequence of the death of the commercial agent;

(i) the entitlement to compensation or indemnity is lost if the principal terminates the contract because of the agent's default justifying immediate termination at law, if the agent himself terminates the contract (other than a justified termination as a consequence of circumstances attributable to the principal or other than on grounds of the age, infirmity or illness of the agent in consequence of which he cannot reasonably be required to continue his activities) or if the agent, by agreement with the principal, assigns his rights and duties under the contract to another person;

(j) it seems that the entitlement to compensation or indemnity may depend on who terminates the contract. For instance, the principal may terminate the contract for a breach which has arisen as a consequence of the incapacity of the agent. In such circumstances, no compensation or indemnity would seem payable. But if the agent terminates on grounds of infirmity or illness the entitlement will survive;

(k) although the right to compensation or indemnity cannot be excluded by contract, there seems to be no reason why the principal could not insist that the agent take out at the agent's cost life assurance and/or health insurance and assign the benefit of the policy to the principal to protect the principal against compensation or indemnity claims in the event of the death or illness of the agent.

(15) Finally, the regulations provide that a restraint of trade clause (that is, an agreement restricting the business activities of a commercial agent following termination of the agency contract) shall not be valid unless it is concluded in writing, relates to the geographical area or the group of customers and the geographical area entrusted to the commercial agent and to the kind of goods covered by his agency under the contract and does not exceed two years' duration. This is without prejudice to any statute or law which otherwise restricts the enforceability of such clauses.

The extent to which the regulations and the directive affect computer contracts depends on the products concerned and the nature of the relationship between the parties. There seems little doubt that hardware will be 'goods' within the meaning of the regulations and that the regulations will apply to commercial agency agreements relating to such products. On the other hand, a genuine distributorship arrangement where the distributor buys and sells computer products on his own account, such as that envisaged by Precedent G, will not be caught by the regulations. Marketing of software by agents is more problematic. It raises the old argument, largely unresolved, as to whether software is 'goods' for these or, indeed, other purposes. The authors' personal view is that it will be hard to deny that mass-produced package software which consumers are used to purchasing in retail outlets should be regarded as goods for these purposes. However, software which is furnished under a written copyright licence agreement, particularly where property in even the media on which the software is recorded is reserved to the copyright owner, should, it is submitted, not be regarded as a sale of goods for the purposes of the regulations and consequently outside the scope of the regulations which only apply to agency contracts relating to the sale or purchase of goods. Precedents H and I are examples of agreements to which the regulations may be said not to apply. Software owners should be cautious, however, when dealing with commercial agents in other countries of the European Union where local law is to govern the contract. The local legislation should be checked to see whether the protection afforded to commercial agents extends beyond the sale and purchase of goods to services or other supplies, in which case even the marketing of copyright licences may be caught. Even English law may not be entirely clear cut in this area. For instance, in *St Albans City and District Council v International Computers Ltd* [1994] *Computers and Law* NS 5.5 (December 1994/January 1995) 14–16 the judge remarked *obiter* that software could be regarded as goods for the purposes of the Sale of Goods Act 1979. It remains to be seen whether the courts draw a distinction between software media sold as goods and the provision of copyright licences where not even title in the media passes to the customer.

5.10 Competition law

As illustrated by 5.3.4, distribution arrangements can give rise to anti-competitive practices by the parties and for this reason such arrangements have for a long time been subject to competition law designed to prevent such practices. Some systems of law are highly developed in this field (particularly in the US and EU) and anyone who is considering entering into a distributorship agreement is strongly recommended to seek professional advice. It is not within the scope of this book to deal with competition law in the UK or elsewhere; for that the reader is referred to the standard legal texts dealing with the subject.

Chapter 6

Test agreements

Chapter 6

Test agreements

6.1 Types of test agreements [J]

As explained in 1.6 above, it is customary for both hardware and software to undergo two separate tests: the alpha tests at the manufacturer's or software house's premises; and field tests or beta tests which allow the product/software to undergo testing by a real customer in circumstances as realistic as possible. The purpose of the testing is of course to provide the manufacturer or software house with information about how the hardware or software performs, any bugs encountered, and how robust it is. In return the company providing the beta tests may have the advantage of obtaining earlier than usual a new and possibly more advanced product. They may also expect some financial inducement such as a discount or even free use of the hardware or software for a period.

On many occasions the arrangements are informal, and may even be in the form of an exchange of letters, rather than a more formal contract. However, there are sufficient differences from ordinary purchase contracts (eg, the date at which insurable risk passes) and issues of confidentiality which make a formal agreement desirable.

Quite a different form of test agreement may arise where an intending purchaser is to test out some software before deciding whether to buy. For many software packages a test version is available which either has some of the features atrophied or non-existent, or may even have a self-destruct module to prevent the user from making use of it too long [J6(4)] (for such 'logic bombs' see 3.2.2). For this kind of agreement it is usual for no money to change hands and for there to be a strict time limit during which the intending purchaser has to complete his evaluation.

6.2 Payment [J1, J3]

Beta test agreements differ from evaluation tests in that the test is for the benefit of the manufacturer, rather than the end-user. This means that the end-user will pay a reduced fee or even none at all for the privilege of testing out the hardware or software. It also means that the manufacturer will wish to learn as soon as possible of any defects or problems with the equipment or software and will therefore expect to provide a very high level of maintenance and support. It is usual for this maintenance or support to be provided at no further cost to the user.

So far as evaluation versions of software packages are concerned, the benefit is entirely for the end-user and although they are usually provided free, the supplier will ensure that if this free test is abused he will automatically receive a full licence fee.

6.3 Delivery and acceptance [J2, J4, J9]

It is the nature of the beta test product or service that it almost certainly contains undetected errors or faults. The customer is well aware of this and takes the equipment 'as is' and is in no way able to rely on its performance, robustness or anything else though he should have taken reasonable steps to inform himself of its general condition beforehand. Full acceptance procedures are inappropriate here, particularly as the user is not taking full title to the equipment or software but merely a limited licence. It is therefore reasonable for the agreement to begin from the date of delivery and to have no separate acceptance. Another way of looking at it is to describe the evaluation itself as an extended acceptance procedure.

In some agreements—particularly those which tend more towards the software evaluation type—the user is required at the end of the test period either to return the hardware or software being tested or to place an order, and failure to do either is deemed to mean that he is willing to place an order. Consider the following:

> The Customer is expected within 7 days of the expiry of the Test period either to return the Product to the Company or to place an order for its procurement. If the Customer fails to do this after a further 14 days' written notice from the Company to the Customer requiring it so to do the Customer shall be deemed to have agreed to purchase the Product. The terms and conditions applicable to the procurement of the Product, howsoever invoked, shall be those that apply to the supply by the Company of their existing hardware

as applicable or those of the Company's then current commercial 'Hardware Agreement' whichever is the later.

A particular point to notice is that in the case of hardware the insurable risk remains with the manufacturer since title does not pass to the customer and indeed the customer is performing a favour for the manufacturer in testing the equipment at all. There remains, nevertheless, an obligation on the customer to take all reasonable steps to ensure that the equipment is safeguarded against obvious hazards.

6.4   Termination [J6]

Almost all agreements of this type have a definite termination period that could of course be extended if the parties agree. In the preceding section we have already considered the possibility that on termination the product tested must be either returned or purchased. As the period is very short premature termination is not usually a problem and need not be considered here.

When a product is ready to launch on the market it is unlikely that the supplier will wish to leave any beta test versions in the hands of third parties. Accordingly a right is often reserved to recall test versions when the final product launch is imminent. Alternatively, a logic bomb [6.1 and 3.2.2] may be used to destroy the software.

6.5   Alterations [J7]

Again the short period of the trial means that changes are not very likely. Sometimes the agreement may be for a range of products to be tested either in succession or simultaneously but this does not usually constitute a change to the arrangement once it has been signed. In a longer-term arrangement the parties may anticipate an improved beta test version becoming available and the supplier may reserve the right to substitute this for an existing version to get the full benefit of the customer's evaluation.

6.6   Customer's duties [J5]

The first duty will of course be to test the equipment or software. It is important from the manufacturer's point of view that this test begin as soon as possible and to this extent the test partakes somewhat of the character of an acceptance test following delivery. Failure by the customer to make proper use of the hardware or software would be of no use to either side.

A related requirement is for the customer to report as rapidly as possible to the manufacturer any defects or problems which he may encounter with the product. As he can anticipate a high level of response from the manufacturer this should operate in the interests of both sides.

It is the nature of beta tests that they relate to new products or software and confidentiality will therefore be very important. The supplier will wish to keep secret from its competitors not only the functions and capabilities of the new product but also its very existence. The premature announcement of a new product can have a dramatic impact on sales of existing products and may significantly reduce the value of stocks held by the supplier and its distributors. There may therefore be far stricter and higher levels of confidentiality exacted from the customer than would normally be the case.

Some agreements seek to limit the use of the hardware or software to evaluation purposes only. This is not entirely sensible since it is the nature of the tests that it should be as realistic as possible and the only way to do this is with real data. It is therefore reasonable for the customer to wish to process genuine workloads and have the benefit of such processing.

Where dealing with an evaluation version of a software package, it will be particularly important for the customer to ensure that it does not fall into other hands and if he allows it so to do, he may find himself deemed to have acted as an agent for the original supplying company and obliged to provide them with an appropriate fee.

6.7 Supplier's duties [J2, J8]

These include delivery of the product, its insurance while still on the customer's premises, and the provision of a high level of support and maintenance.

There will not be any liability on the supplier for the experimental hardware or software in terms of its performance, capacity, or even fitness for purpose.

The supplier will of course retain all title to the product right to the end of the test period and after, unless the customer purchases. The supplier will therefore require the customer to deliver up the product, destroy copies (if for software), or purchase it outright, as appropriate or he will use the logic bomb to destroy it.

Intellectual property rights will be relevant in a testing context and the customer should insist on the usual indemnity against claims by third parties of infringement of their intellectual property rights.

138

Chapter 7

Leases

Chapter 7

Leases

7.1 Types of lease

Under a third-party lease, the equipment is purchased from the supplier by a third party leasing company (lessor), which then hires it to the customer who intends to use it (lessee). Usually, it will differ from a rental agreement principally in that the lessor will be a separate entity from the supplier of the equipment.

The problems with leases involve an understanding of hardware and software contracts (Chapters 2 and 3). The present chapter presupposes knowledge of those chapters and assumes that the kinds of clauses described in those chapters are, where relevant, incorporated. As leases give rise to different types of problems, the structure of this chapter necessarily differs from that of the previous chapters in order to focus on those differences.

Broadly, leasing agreements can be classified into two types. One is simply an arrangement enabling the lessee to enjoy the use of the equipment (operating lease) whilst the other is primarily a source of finance (finance lease).

7.1.1 Operating lease

This type of lease either runs for a short fixed period or is subject to termination by the lessee on short notice at any time (or after a stated initial period). The lessor will charge a rent fixed by market rates and will expect to re-lease the equipment to other customers before the end of its useful life. Operating leases are popular where there is a buoyant second-hand market for the equipment or where it is subject to rapid changes in technology; the customer may, in these circumstances, not want it for the whole of its useful life.

The lessor will normally purchase the equipment before being approached by the lessee and will usually be experienced in its technology. He will also bear the burdens and risks of ownership and will usually

141

maintain and insure the equipment. The risk of obsolescence of the equipment will clearly be reflected in the lease rentals but where the lessor is associated with the manufacturer he may be better informed than the user about anticipated obsolescence and will be able to price accordingly.

Operating leases are similar in many respects to rental agreements [2.2.2], and are therefore not dealt with separately further in this chapter though the problem of software licence transfer [7.4.2] applies equally to them.

7.1.2 Finance lease

Under Standard Statement of Accounting Practice 21 a finance lease is defined as 'a lease that transfers substantially all the risks and rewards of ownership of an asset to the lessee'. This is deemed to occur where the minimum lease payments amount to substantially all of the value of the leased equipment.

Under SSAP 21, a finance lease is required to be shown in the balance sheet as an asset with the obligation to pay future lease payments being shown as a liability. Operating lease rentals, on the other hand, are charged to the profit and loss account over the term of the lease on a straight line basis.

The finance lease, as its name suggests, is essentially a source of medium to long-term finance and provides the customer with an alternative to borrowing on an outright purchase. It runs for a minimum fixed period which reflects the estimated useful life of the equipment so that there will be only one lessee. In contrast to the operating lease, the rentals are calculated on the basis of the cost to the lessor of purchasing the equipment plus his desired return on capital, after taking account of such variables as the lessor's entitlement to capital allowances and grants (and the delay between incurring the expenditure on the equipment and receiving the benefit of such allowances and grants) and rental cash flow.

The lessor will purchase, own and eventually sell the equipment. In practice, however, it is the lessee who accepts the burdens and risks of ownership (such as obsolescence, defects and loss). The lessee usually initiates the transaction by choosing the equipment and the supplier, and by arranging for the lessor to buy the equipment and then lease it to him. The lessee will normally also be responsible for negotiating the sale contract with the supplier.

The popularity of finance leasing diminished as a result of the abolition of first year capital allowances with effect from 31 March 1986 and the reduction in the rate of corporation tax over recent years. Until the abolition of first year allowances, the finance lease compared favourably with alternative forms of finance. The lessor was in effect able to give away a large percentage of the tax saved as a result of the first year allowance by passing this on to the lessee in the form of reduced rentals. Expenditure on plant and machinery now qualifies for an annual writing down allowance of only 25 per cent on a reducing balance basis. This has resulted in an increase in the effective rate of interest payable under leasing agreements. This notional interest rate is greater for short-term leases where the writing down allowances do not absorb the full purchase price of the equipment.

Finance leases are not dead and one still finds lessors willing to give away at least some of their writing down allowances to lessees in order to offer reduced rental payments. Because of the reducing nature of writing down allowances, it is unlikely that lessors will enter into leases for more than 5 years, as by that time 76 per cent has been written down and it is unlikely to be cost-effective to continue thereafter.

If the equipment is likely to be scrapped or sold for nominal value within 5 years of first use then it may be advantageous to the lessor to elect for the equipment to be treated as a 'short life asset' (Capital Allowances Act 1990, s 37). The residue of expenditure not written down at sale or scrapping can be deducted as a balancing allowance as opposed to remaining in the 'pool' of expenditure being written down at 25 per cent per annum. However, the penalty is that every piece of equipment must form a separate calculation in the capital allowance computation and increased administration costs will be incurred.

7.2 Advantages of leasing

In view of the reduced advantages of the finance lease the user of equipment will now need to consider carefully whether he should lease or buy his equipment. Operating lease rentals will usually be a fully deductible expense for tax purposes for the year in which they are payable. On the other hand, finance lease rentals will be a tax deductible expense as they are charged to the accounts in accordance with the normal principles of commercial accountancy under SSAP 21 (*Gallagher v Jones, Threlfall v Jones* [1993] STC 537). Capital allowances arising on a purchase will not be of immediate benefit where the lessee is currently carrying on business at a loss and it may be advantageous to permit a lessor to claim these while at the same time passing some of the benefit on to the lessee in the shape of reduced rentals. If a company does wish to purchase but at the same time ease its cash flow hire purchase may be the answer. The hirer is entitled to writing down allowances on the full cost of the equipment. If a company does purchase its equipment outright any interest paid on borrowings will be tax deductible.

Generally speaking, where the lease term equates with the useful life of the equipment it is more advantageous to lease than it is to borrow. Rental payments are lower because the lessor has the residual value of the equipment and can also afford to give away some of his writing down allowances. However, the lessee should remember that when he commits to a leasing agreement the 'notional interest rate' is fixed, whereas by borrowing (especially where he foresees a fall in interest rates) the lessee may be able to take advantage of loan finance at variable interest rates.

Unlike hire purchase or bank borrowings, leasing companies can sometimes offer more flexible payment terms. In addition, lessors are less inclined to seek guarantees or other security for their contracts.

When acquiring computer equipment obsolescence can be a key factor in determining whether the user opts to buy or lease, or indeed whether to take a finance or an operating lease. If a significant change in technology does take place the lessee who holds his equipment under an operating lease can quickly change his old computer for a new one at a marginally increased rental. This may override all other considerations.

It should not be forgotten that the finance lease is essentially not a short-term arrangement. There will be few opportunities to terminate before the contractual term and even then the lessor will usually look to be compensated for the rentals he has forgone. Rental increases are also a possibility. Because the lessor's return can be affected by such matters as changes in the law relating to capital allowances, leases often provide for a variation in rentals to compensate for any loss caused to the lessor in such circumstances.

7.3 Lessee's enforcement of warranties

In circumstances where the lessor is not involved in the selection of the equipment or the supplier and relies on the lessee to use his own skill and judgment, the lessor will not usually give the lessee any warranties in relation to the equipment and will attempt to exclude any implied in the lessee's favour by law. The effectiveness of such an exclusion will be subject to the Unfair Contract Terms Act 1977. It might be thought that because the lessor has little responsibility for or control over defects in the equipment the courts will regard such exclusions as reasonable. However, this appears not to be the case for in *Lease Management Services Limited v Purnell* [1994] 13 TrL 337 the court held that an exclusion clause is not rendered reasonable because it is imposed by a finance company rather than the original equipment supplier. The lessee cannot take advantage of any warranties given by the supplier to the lessor in the sale contract as he is not a party to it. In an attempt to overcome this problem lessors often assign their rights to such warranties to the lessee or agree to enforce them for the lessee's benefit. Unfortunately, in most cases this is little more than useless because the lessor cannot recover more than *his* own damage (the actual loss suffered by the lessee is irrelevant). If, as is usual, the lease provides that the lessor is entitled to his rentals come what may, his loss will be negligible. The answer in practice is for the lessee (if he is able to do so) to procure direct warranties from the supplier.

The lessor usually acquires title to the equipment in one of three ways:

(1) By himself entering into a contract with the supplier.
(2) By appointing the lessee as his agent to contract with the supplier.
(3) By taking over the contract already entered into by the lessee with the supplier by means of a contract called a novation agreement between the supplier, the lessor and the lessee.

In its simplest form the novation agreement provides for the supplier and the lessee to be released from their respective obligations and for the lessor to purchase the equipment from the supplier in the lessee's place. Such an arrangement does not, however, address the problems connected with the lessee's enforcement of warranties.

An alternative is for the three parties to enter into a hybrid of the novation agreement. Such an agreement provides for the lessor to take over the lessee's obligation to pay for the equipment (and consequently for the lessor to acquire title) in return for the lessee agreeing to lease the equipment from the lessor. In other respects the sale agreement remains intact. The lessee is entitled to the benefits of the sale agreement (including warranties and delivery and installation obligations) subject to his complying with its burdens. Apart from enabling the lessee to procure direct warranties, this type of agreement has the important practical advantage of resulting in relatively little disturbance of standard documentation. All the obligations to be performed will be the same as in any ordinary sale agreement and will be performed by the same parties (namely the supplier and the lessee). The lessor's involvement is minimal—he simply has to pay the price and take title in accordance with the terms of the sale agreement once the equipment has been accepted. The lease will also be simplified because all the lessor need do is to impose an obligation on the lessee to comply with the terms of the modified sale agreement, rather than set out the lessee's obligations (as to preparation of installation site, taking of delivery, acceptance testing, etc) in detail.

In entering into a novation agreement the parties should ensure that title to the equipment has not already passed to the lessee (this is unlikely as most contracts provide for title to pass only on payment of the purchase price in full) and that the contract is wholly unperformed. Failure to do this may have adverse tax consequences. Needless to say, the lessee must ensure, prior to his signing the contract of sale, that the supplier and the lessor will enter into the novation agreement.

7.4 Software

Finally, two points in relation to software are worthy of special note.

7.4.1 Capital allowances

Regular payments akin to a rental are allowable revenue expenditure, the timing of deductions being governed by normal accountancy practice.

A lump sum payment is capital if the licence is of a sufficiently enduring nature to be considered a capital asset in the context of the lessor's trade. Equally the benefit may be transitory (and the expenditure revenue) even though the licence is for an indefinite period. Inspectors of Taxes will in any event accept that expenditure is on revenue account where the software has a useful economic life of less than two years, timing of the deduction again depending on normal accountancy practice.

Expenditure on a package containing both hardware and a licence to use software must be apportioned before these principles are applied.

Capital expenditure incurred on the acquisition of computer software for the purposes of the lessor's trade, if it would not otherwise be expenditure on machinery or plant (eg where the software is acquired by electronic means), is treated as such for capital allowance purposes. Similarly, capital expenditure incurred in acquiring for the purposes of the lessor's trade a right to use or otherwise deal with computer software, is similarly treated as expenditure on machinery or plant and (so long as entitlement to the right continues) as belonging to the lessor (see Capital Allowances Act 1990, s 67A).

The term 'computer software' is not defined by the Capital Allowances Act 1990. It is understood that the Inland Revenue considers that the term includes both programs and data. Expenditure qualifying for capital allowances by virtue of the Capital Allowances Act 1990, s 67A may also qualify for the special treatment for expenditure on 'short life assets', as described in 7.1.2 above.

7.4.2 Software licensing

Special arrangements will have to be made regarding the licensing of software in a leasing transaction.

The lessee will, of course, require a right to use the software during the continuance of the lease but the lessor will also wish to acquire rights. The lessor's need is not so much a right to use the software as a need to protect his investment. If the lessee defaults on rental payments the lessor will usually hope to recover his investment by proceeding against the lessee for the rental payments due in respect of the remainder of the lease (suitably discounted) or, if there is one, by claiming under a third party guarantee. If, however, the lessee is insolvent or there is no guarantee, then, in order to recover as much of his investment as possible, the lessor has one of three options:

(a) sell the equipment back to the supplier; or
(b) sell the equipment to a third party; or
(c) re-lease the equipment to a third party.

The first option does not cause a problem but the effectiveness of the other two may depend on the lessor being able to license the purchaser or subsequent lessee to use the software, as the equipment may be virtually useless without the software. If the lessor cannot grant such a licence then the purchaser or subsequent lessee will have to acquire a licence direct from the supplier at a fee. This would mean that the lessor would be unable to recover his investment on software, which could be serious if software represents a significant part of the value of the system.

The lessor will therefore need to negotiate an appropriate arrangement with the supplier to protect himself. One means of achieving this would be for the supplier to grant to the lessor a licence to use the software, together with rights (a) to grant sub-licences to lessees; and (b) to assign the benefit of his licence to a purchaser (but so that the licence in the hands of the purchaser will not be assignable) during a period equal to the minimum period of the first lease. In this way the lessor can recover his investment in full.

A supplier may argue that a purchaser or subsequent lessee should pay an additional licence fee. However, the lessor can point out with some justification that if the supplier sold the equipment direct to the customer he would not reasonably expect to obtain more than one licence fee during the useful working life of the equipment.

A lessee will also be concerned to see that a purchaser can be licensed to use the software, so that on a voluntary termination of the lease by the lessee prior to the expiry of the minimum period, the resale value of the equipment will be as high as possible, thus ensuring the maximum set-off against the termination payment due under the lease. However, in these circumstances the supplier may argue more forcibly that an additional licence fee should be paid.

PART II   MAINTENANCE

Chapter 8

Hardware maintenance

8.1 Services to be performed
8.1.1 Equipment and location
8.1.2 Service
Preventive maintenance
Corrective maintenance

8.2 Payment

8.3 Limitations and exceptions
8.3.1 Frivolous calls
8.3.2 Out-of-hours maintenance
8.3.3 Amount of usage
8.3.4 Delays

8.4 Termination
8.4.1 Term
8.4.2 Termination by notice
8.4.3 Other terminations

8.5 Variation
8.5.1 Variation of equipment
8.5.2 Variation of charges

8.6 Customer's duties
8.6.1 Use and care of the equipment
8.6.2 Access
8.6.3 Notification
8.6.4 Spares
8.6.5 Miscellaneous

Chapter 8

Hardware maintenance

In Chapter 2 on hardware we have seen that it is usual in a rental agreement for the supplier to require the customer to maintain the equipment in good order [2.6.4]. In the case of a lease, the supplier or third party leasing company usually specifies who shall perform this maintenance. Generally it is the supplier himself. In this chapter we consider such a hardware maintenance agreement; in the next we examine the more nebulous concept of software maintenance.

For convenience, we refer to the company performing the maintenance as 'the supplier' since in many cases the supplier is the sole maintainer. The alternative where this is not so (the 'mixed shop') is discussed below [8.5.1].

For PCs the most important question is whether maintenance is provided at all. Contracts for PCs when they exist are much like contracts for other hardware maintenance, the most significant difference being that the low capital cost of the equipment usually means that 10 per cent per annum of capital cost [8.2] produces too high a figure for what is a mass market—6–7 per cent is more usual.

The possession of large numbers of PCs in a company means that the company can now seek across-the-board contracts for maintenance of several machines from a single contractor at competitive rates.

8.1 Services to be performed

8.1.1 Equipment and location [K1]

These are usually defined in exactly the same way as in a hardware contract [2.1.1 and 2.1.2].

For PCs and portables, the concept of a location is slightly difficult. It is the nature of a portable that it is moved around. This may also be true of some PCs. This inherently exposes the portable to additional risks, and the best that can be arranged here is either that portables (which are basically fairly reliable machines) are supported only on a call-out basis—that is to say the user pays separately each time he requires an engineer to attend—or at best the equipment is only maintained at a single location, which means that the user must bring his portable back to base (ie the location identified in the contract) before the maintenance contractor can deal with it.

8.1.2 Service

Maintenance is usually concerned with two separate types of engineer service:

(*a*) preventive maintenance; and
(*b*) corrective maintenance.

Preventive maintenance [K2(1)]

Preventive maintenance is concerned with the regular testing and treating of the equipment. This includes the running of the diagnostic programs (which will probably be the same as those used for pre- and post-delivery tests [2.3.2], [2.3.4]), the adjusting of those features which may through use have got out of tune (for example, on an impact printer the tension of the paper is critical: if it is too taut the type will pierce it; if it is too slack the impression will be unclear or smudged and the paper may not feed properly), the oiling of those few mechanical parts which need oiling, and generally advising the customer of the condition of the equipment, including the likelihood of his requiring replacements. On this basis, the installation site will be visited regularly (say every six months) by a suitable engineer. For example:

> The Supplier shall make visits for the periodic servicing of the Equipment to test the functions thereof and make any adjustments the Supplier deems necessary to keep it in good working order. Such visits shall be on Mondays to Fridays (public holidays excluded) between the hours of 9am and 5pm.

Notice first that the definition of 'servicing' means that the customer's ideas of how the equipment should work are irrelevant unless shared by the supplier. The customer should agree in advance criteria to define working. Second, the supplier stipulates that the maintenance shall be during ordinary working hours. For a machine which will be worked round the clock, this may present problems, and any scheduling should take account of engineers' visits. In practice, this is unlikely to be too serious a problem, since it will often be possible to run the engineer's diagnostic test programs at the same time as other programs—providing either that they use different peripheral devices or that slightly slower running of the customer's application programs is possible. In practice, a supplier will, as far as possible, fit in with a customer's schedules.

Corrective maintenance [K2(2)]

Corrective maintenance means the remedying of defects or mechanical faults which arise. Visits for this kind of maintenance are usually in response to a service call from the customer to say that some particular piece of equipment does not work:

> The Supplier shall make emergency service available on request on Mondays to Fridays (public holidays excepted) each week throughout the year between the hours of 9am and 5pm to rectify a breakdown or malfunction of the Equipment and on receipt of such a request from the Customer shall send an engineer to the Installation Site as soon as reasonably practicable at the said times to test adjust or repair the Equipment as may seem to him appropriate.

Notice again the emphasis on ordinary working hours. If the customer is likely to be performing time-critical work outside ordinary working hours, he should take this up with his supplier. If it is merely a question of running the payroll program on Thursday nights, the supplier will probably point out that, even if the agreement allowed the customer to telephone for an engineer at 2am, there would inevitably be a delay of some hours before the engineer arrived, and more time would elapse before the problem was cured; in other words, the customer would do better to replan his schedules to envisage the possibility of interruption or delay. The most likely candidates for truly time-critical programs are real-time applications—for instance, a traffic flow system controlling the use of traffic lights in a large city. In this case, the stand-by facilities are likely to be very much more copious than in ordinary commercial processing, and might include a duplication of part or all of the system. It is worth pointing out that failure is most likely in devices which have numerous moving parts—like printers—and printers are not usually devices running in real time. The time taken by a supplier from receipt of the customer's request for corrective maintenance to having an engineer on the customer's premises is called 'response time'—a term to be distinguished from systems response time defined above [3.3.2].

Should a customer have an application like the traffic flow system and have taken the supplier's advice about duplicating part or all of his system in the interests of stand-by facilities, he must then seek to negotiate with the supplier for a special maintenance agreement. He may also seek a back-up agreement with the owner of another installation similar to his own and geographically near it. It is usual for two users of similar configurations of equipment to enter into mutual back-up agreements, whereby in certain circumstances each undertakes to provide spare capacity on his machine to the other. Such agreements are in effect bureau agreements (see Chapter 10) and must:

(1) define the circumstances;
(2) define the configuration and capacity available;
(3) define any timescale or other limitations on the use of the service;
(4) specify personnel and define access to the premises;
(5) specify price (if any—in mutual agreements there may be no price).

Both sides should try the arrangements out rather than await the disaster which will make them necessary. Compatibility of the two systems is essential. In practice such agreements are difficult to set up, unless the alternative machine is very lightly used and can easily accommodate the new load as well as its existing load. As to how to find an appropriate installation, see below on User Groups [13.6].

In other cases the agreement is often more specific about the speed with which an engineer will arrive at the installation. This will in fact depend on the distance the installation site is from the supplier's nearest service area, but a typical example might be:

> In this Agreement 'working hours' means the time between 9am and 5pm on all Mondays to Fridays except public holidays . . .
>
> The Supplier shall make emergency service available to the Customer who requests such service within Working Hours and on receipt of such request will despatch an engineer to assist at the Installation Site within the next eight Working Hours after such request was received . . .

In other words, if a customer telephones for an engineer at 3pm on a Tuesday afternoon, the engineer may turn up at any time between 3pm and 5pm on Tuesday, or 9am and 2 pm on Wednesday. This kind of agreement is extremely common, and is what is usually meant by an 'eight-hour maintenance agreement' ('four-hour' maintenance agreements are also common). It does *not* mean that the engineer will arrive within eight elapsed hours after the call is put in if any of those hours are outside working hours. Still less does it mean that the fault will be *rectified* in eight hours—or, indeed, in any particular number of hours.

The supplier will need to schedule his maintenance services by priority (four-hour response before eight-hour, for example). This means that customers with no formal agreement who simply pay on a call-out basis often receive a poor response time.

In many instances on-line diagnostics are now being used, whereby the customer's machine can be linked by telecommunications to diagnostic programs and equipment on the supplier's premises. In this way the fault can often be pinpointed by telephone and it may even be possible to cure the fault by telephone in some instances. Sometimes the supplier is prepared to provide the modem free of charge to facilitate this. Nevertheless, the clauses described above guaranteeing response time should still appear in the contract, as a safeguard.

The question of what spare parts may reasonably be kept, and who will keep them, must be considered. Sometimes the supplier will look after this:

> The Supplier will keep a stock of spare parts at his Service Centre nearest to the Installation Site.

Sometimes the supplier will require the customer to keep spares. A clause to this effect is described below [8.6.4]. There we notice that the purpose of the clause is probably to reduce the service charge to the customer; it may also reflect the distance of the customer from the nearest service centre.

A word about the location of suppliers' service areas: when negotiating with his supplier, the customer should always enquire where the nearest service area is. In practice, the supplier may offer to open a new service area (ie take on a new engineer) specially for one particular customer, if the customer's business is big enough. At any rate, if the service area seems uncommonly distant, this will be a good reason for the customer to query the credibility of the maintenance service being offered.

8.2 Payment [B15; K3]

Payment for both preventive and corrective maintenance is usually by a single annual charge spread over monthly or quarterly payments in advance. The annual charge varies, but may typically be at or near 10 per cent of the purchase price of main frames and minicomputers. (A rate of 6–7 per cent is more usual for PCs). However, such a figure cannot necessarily be maintained in the future (see Variation of charges [8.5.2]) since inflation and fluctuating exchange rates may increase the list price and make the original proportionate maintenance seem unrealistic. It is also true that obsolescence and technological advance may reduce the list price of the equipment, but the effect of this will probably be to increase the maintenance cost since spares will probably be produced in smaller quantities and it will be less worthwhile for the supplier to train and maintain engineers who can repair equipment at only one or two installations.

A typical payment clause reads:

> The Customer will pay to the Supplier monthly in advance the sum of £x charge for the Service the first such payment falling due promptly on the commencement of this Agreement.

8.3   Limitations and exceptions [K5]

The maintenance service provided by the supplier is subject to numerous limitations and exceptions. Many of these are breaches of the customer's duties which are more particularly described below [8.6]—eg failure to use and care for the equipment properly. Others (like *force majeure*) are common to all agreements. But some may be considered here.

8.3.1   Frivolous calls [K7]

Most agreements have a clause preventing the customer from summoning an engineer on a frivolous pretext:

> If the Customer requests the Supplier's service without good reason the Customer will be liable to pay to the Supplier in accordance with the Supplier's then subsisting scale of charges for such calls such charges being in addition to any other moneys due under this or any other agreement from the Customer to the Supplier.

Most examples of such clauses all omit to define 'good reason' or say in whose judgment a reason may be good. In practice, it is doubtful whether this clause gives rise to any such difficulty between supplier and customer: it is there to protect the supplier against extreme cases.

8.3.2   Out-of-hours maintenance [K4, K7]

Despite what has been said relating to service [8.1.2], a customer may have an ordinary '4-hour maintenance' agreement and still wish on a particular occasion to have a service call out of hours. Many agreements cover this by adding a clause to the effect that:

> If the Customer requires to make a Service Request out of Working Hours he shall become liable to pay to the Supplier such charge as may be in force for the time being for such service calls in addition to any other charges due under this Agreement.

8.3.3 Amount of usage

The contract is for a particular period, but it may be that the user wishes to use the equipment so heavily that signs of wear will show early. (Purchasers of cars will recognise that mileage, as well as age, is relevant to the car's reliability.)

> Maintenance under this Agreement does not cover any reconditioning required after a period equal or equivalent to 5 years' single shift usage.

With increasing hardware reliability, the less reliable elements of a system become more conspicuous and it is reasonable to assume that such elements will become still less dependable with age. Accordingly, some agreements stipulate that equipment over a particular age which contains moving or mechanical parts will not be maintained under the same agreement as that for the rest of the system, but will either attract a higher premium, or be maintained only on a 'call-out' basis—that is to say the supplier charges separately for each call, rather than on a fixed price basis monthly, quarterly or even annually in advance.

The cost of maintenance to the supplier has been worked out on the basis of the mean time between failures (MTBF to engineers—or, as a slightly mealy-mouthed alternative, mean time between systems incidents (MTBSI))—for each separate piece of equipment. After a long period the MTBF could be alarmingly short: the supplier is therefore protecting himself. But notice that this limitation may sometimes be based on single-shift working—that is, working in ordinary office hours (or the equivalent). Some machines are worked on a double or even treble shift system and in those cases the agreement would for all practical purposes expire after 2 years and 6 months or 1 year 8 months. If you expect to use your equipment as heavily as this, and your manufacturer includes a clause of this nature, you should seek clarification from him. If you think the above clause is hard, consider this variant:

> When in the Supplier's opinion reconditioning of any part of the Equipment is considered necessary the Supplier will submit to the Customer a cost estimate for such reconditioning such costs being in addition to any charges within this Agreement. If the Customer declines to accept this cost estimate then the Supplier reserves the right to cancel this Agreement forthwith so far as it relates to that piece of Equipment or to terminate this Agreement forthwith if in the Supplier's opinion failure to recondition that piece of Equipment impairs the satisfactory operation of the whole of the Equipment.

The MTBF tells you the number of times, on average, that a piece of equipment is out of action, but not for how long it is out of action. This is dealt with by another set of initials—MTTR or mean time to repair.

8.3.4 Delays [K18]

Most suppliers will do their best to keep to the timescales within which they expect to be able to respond to a call for emergency maintenance for a customer. Nevertheless a supplier is likely to seek to exclude at least some of the responsibility for his failure to do so:

> The Supplier shall not be liable for any delay or the consequences thereof in performing any of his duties under this Agreement if such delay is due to any industrial dispute or any cause whatsoever beyond his reasonable control.

In this particular case the exclusion is not unreasonable.

8.4 Termination [K14]

8.4.1 Term

Normally a maintenance agreement will be for a particular period; three years is common, though other periods often occur—66 months occurs in one clause. We have already seen [8.3.3] that the equipment is likely to need more maintenance as it gets older, so this is one reason for a time limitation. But many agreements visualise the supplier increasing the charges [8.5] and therefore that is not necessarily the whole story. The truth is that where the company effecting the maintenance is the manufacturer or supplier, they will not wish to have to commit engineers to the task of maintaining obsolete equipment for perhaps a handful of customers—particularly as the supplier hopes by then to have a newer (and more easily maintained) machine available.

Some agreements are not for a fixed term but for a minimum term with the agreement continuing from month to month or year to year thereafter until determined by one or other party [8.4.2].

In the case of linked rental and maintenance agreements, maintenance will terminate at the same time as the rental.

8.4.2 Termination by notice

This may be after a minimum term, in the form:

Subsequent to the Minimum Period either party shall be entitled to terminate this Agreement by giving to the other not less than 3 months' written notice to expire on the last day of a calendar month.

Three months' notice is easily the commonest notice period. For example, a supplier will sooner or later wish to terminate when the equipment is completely obsolete. The last provision in the example (for termination at the end of a full month) is to avoid apportionment of the charge for part months, but this is not so common. If an annual charge is paid the customer might expect reimbursement of part if the contract terminates otherwise than on the anniversary, but many contracts are silent on the point.

8.4.3   Other terminations

An agreement can also be determined by breach of the customer's duties [8.6], or in some cases by failure of the customer to allow the supplier to recondition equipment (see the second example in 8.3.3), or to increase charges [8.5.2].

8.5   Variation

8.5.1   Variation of equipment [K1, K6]

The standard arrangement is that the agreement excludes any change in the equipment as defined (usually in the schedule). In practice, however, provided the equipment comes from the original supplier and maintenance charges have been negotiated in advance, it is generally possible to vary the charges and the list of the equipment. The dangerous situation from the point of view of the customer arises when new equipment is to be added which comes from a different supplier. An innocent-looking clause, eg:

> The Customer shall not make any movement of or alteration addition or attachment to the Equipment except with the Supplier's written consent

is designed to cover a complex situation. Obviously,

(*a*)   it is very much easier and more efficient for a supplier to maintain equipment which is well-known to his staff; but

(*b*)   it is in the supplier's interest to lock the customer into an agreement whereby the customer can buy his equipment only from the supplier.

Nevertheless, a flourishing market has grown up of suppliers whose equipment is fully compatible with, and designed to look like, that of major suppliers. Such equipment is often marketed by companies whose level of support and profit margins are lower than those of the main manufacturers, with the result that they can be offered at prices which are much lower than those of the manufacturers they are imitating. The big manufacturer's maintenance agreement with his customers is his most powerful weapon in keeping out the 'plug-compatible' equipment. Any customer who wishes to take advantage of plug-compatible low prices must first decide how he is to cope with maintenance in an installation which becomes, in the jargon expression, a 'mixed shop'. The solution is basically either to do all maintenance himself—and for some large customers it is practical for them to have their own engineers and maintenance staff; or to give the work to a third party maintenance company who may be the supplier of the plug-compatible equipment or who may be a separate maintenance company. No customer should consider the possibility of a mixed shop unless he can deal with the question of maintenance.

Another aspect of variation is the way in which many maintenance suppliers 'swap out' equipment. The principle works like this: a customer contacts the supplier to ask for an engineer to call. The engineer does so, and either diagnoses a major fault or is unable with certainty to diagnose the precise fault at all. He exchanges the equipment for another one more or less identical while he takes the faulty one away for more detailed examination. The advantage of swapping out is that the customer has the fault cured very quickly while the supplier's engineer, instead of working under pressure, has all the time in the world to examine and correct the fault, and he can also more readily compare this fault with other faults in similar pieces of equipment which he is dealing with. However, the contractual aspect of this can be fairly serious and deserves careful thought.

In the first place if the equipment list identifies each particular item of equipment by serial number, the supplier may actually be in breach in swapping out.

Second, at the very least the supplier may be exchanging a new piece of equipment for an old one and in some cases exchanging equipment for something which is not quite the same—eg an earlier model of the same piece of equipment or one whose performance is in some way more limited.

Third, it may prove very difficult to decide at any one time who owns what. In an extreme case where a receiver is called in for a supplier's business, the receiver could require the customer to surrender part or all of his equipment to him.

Enough has been said to show that swapping out, whether of whole pieces of equipment or of their components, may have practical advantages, but is something of a contractual minefield, and while it is reasonable for the supplier to require (as in the sample clause above) that the customer should not alter his equipment, it seems no less reasonable that the customer should have the same safeguard against the supplier altering his equipment for the worse. The problem of ownership can be fairly readily dealt with by an appropriate clause [K6], but even with this safeguard the customer may still wish to think before agreeing to swap out.

Where the agreement is to maintain a number of PCs it is probably the case that the owner of the machines is constantly adding to their number, replacing older machines by more modern ones or increasing machines' memory or other features. There is thus not a fixed list of the equipment to be incorporated into a schedule. Clearly the parties must as far as possible be agreed as to how many machines there are and of what type, but inevitably sooner or later a new machine will have been acquired which is not on the list and requires urgent maintenance attention.

The most helpful way for this to be dealt with is for the maintenance contractor to treat it as a valid machine to be maintained and sort the details out later. The customer is thus expected to advise the contractor after the maintenance has been effected when he acquired the machine so that the relevant maintenance charge for that machine can be backdated [K3(3).]

8.5.2   Variation of charges [K3(4)]

Many agreements visualise the possibility of varying charges. As the equipment becomes older and obsolescent, the number of staff the supplier will wish to use for its maintenance is likely to drop, and consequently the cost will rise. Inflation will also ensure that what was (say) 8.5 per cent of the list price last year may not be so high a percentage at next year's prices for the same equipment. Some such clause as this may appear:

> The maintenance charges specified in the *x*th Schedule hereto are based on the Supplier's Scale of Charges in force at the date hereof. After the initial period of this Agreement all maintenance charges may be adjusted on one month's written notice by the Supplier to the Customer to correspond to the Supplier's Scale of Charges then in force.

To prevent the supplier from simply forcing the customer to terminate by quoting excessive new maintenance rates, in some long-term maintenance contracts the parties agree that the maintenance charges shall be increased by reference to the Retail Prices Index. The following is an example:

> After the initial period of this Agreement has expired the Supplier shall be entitled to increase the maintenance charges at any time and from time to time by giving to the Customer not less than one month's notice in writing but any such increase shall not exceed a percentage equal to the percentage increase in the Retail Prices Index for the relevant period plus 3 per cent.

It should be noted that no definition of the 'relevant period' is given and that there is no limit on the number of times that the Supplier may increase the charges.

Such clauses are of course appropriate in any contracts involving regular payments, but are particularly suitable in hardware maintenance agreements where the lifetime of the contract may be many years. It may also happen that the customer is dilatory in purchasing (and paying for the maintenance of) the original equipment. A manufacturer may therefore state:

> At any time before the x months immediately preceding the date of commencement of the term of this Agreement the Supplier reserves the right to vary the charges to correspond to the Supplier's Scale of Charges then in force by written notice to the Customer. If the Customer does not accept these charges he may treat the Agreement as discharged by giving to the Supplier one month's notice in writing within 2 weeks of receiving the notice of variation of the charges.

This clause is usually of little effect unless there is an unusually long lead time.

8.6 Customer's duties

Many of these—such as the duty to pay [8.2] and not to attach other equipment [8.5.1]—have already been dealt with. However, there remain others which, while related to the last, are best considered here.

8.6.1   Use and care of the equipment [K9(1)–(8)]

In addition to promising not to add to the equipment, the customer is also likely to be required to maintain the electricity supply and/or any environment, and to use the equipment properly. The first of these may be phrased negatively:

> Such repair or replacement shall be free of additional charge to the Customer unless caused by fluctuation in the electricity supply.

Power surges can be extremely damaging. Lifts which involve intermittent heavy use of electricity are the principal culprits, and customers would be well advised to obtain a power supply separate from that used by the rest of the building.

In general a customer is likely to be required to undertake:

> . . . to maintain in good order the accommodation of the Equipment the cables and fittings associated therewith and the electrical supply thereto

and he must also expect to be required:

> . . . to keep and operate the Equipment in a prudent and proper manner in accordance with the Operator's Manual issued by the Supplier with the Equipment;

and:

> . . . to use for the operation and servicing of the Equipment only those materials and supplies approved by the Supplier and listed in the Operator's Manual.

This is primarily concerned with printer ribbons, stationery and so on. It follows also that he will:

> . . . not allow the Equipment to be repaired serviced or otherwise attended to except by the Supplier's staff or by the Customer's own staff working according to the Supplier's Operator's Manual.

Finally, the customer may not move his computer [8.5.1].

8.6.2   Access [K9(9)–(12)]

The next group of clauses refer to facilities to be provided by the customer to the supplier's staff. The first is obviously access and accommodation usually described as 'full and fit' but the agreement may more specifically ask for:

. . . adequate working space around the Equipment for use of the Supplier's staff and adequate facilities for storage and safekeeping of test equipment and spares.

If the customer has had his site inspected by the supplier before delivery [2.6.3] and the supplier is, as is usually the case, the maintenance contractor, this should present no difficulty.

The agreement may also specify:

. . . a suitable vehicle parking facility which is free of any legal restrictions and immediately close to the Installation;

or:

. . . handling or lifting tackle scaffolding together with any labour required to move plant and equipment.

A further sensible precaution might be the following:

In the interests of health and safety the Customer shall ensure that the Supplier's personnel whilst on the Customer's premises for the purposes of this Agreement are accompanied at all times by a member of the Customer's staff familiar with the Customer's premises and safety procedures.

This places the onus on the customer to ensure that the supplier's maintenance engineers are properly supervised and do not inadvertently cause damage by being ignorant of safety procedures. If damage does arise as a result of an engineer not being properly supervised then the blame will attach to the customer not the supplier.

8.6.3   Notification [K9(13)–(17)]

An important requirement is usually that the customer will:

. . . promptly notify the Supplier if the Equipment needs maintenance or is not working correctly.
   Failure by the Customer to notify the Supplier within 6 months of becoming aware of any such need for maintenance or any such failure to work correctly shall free the Supplier from all liability to investigate such need for maintenance or correct such fault.

This is designed to prevent the customer relying on some such vague complaint as that the equipment 'has never worked'.
   A further aspect of notification is that the supplier will reasonably wish to know how the equipment has been used. As it is usual to keep a log of all usage the customer may find this embodied as an obligation

on him. This is particularly likely where the equipment does not belong to the customer—eg in rental and leasing agreements [2.1.1].

> The Customer will at all times keep a record of the use of the Equipment in a form to be approved by the Supplier and at the Supplier's request provide the Supplier with copies of the entries and allow the Supplier to inspect such record at all reasonable times.

This is in any event a sound precaution and will enable the customer to check on the speed with which the supplier deals with matters. It is usual for the supplier's engineer to leave a copy of a form for each visit which records the date and time of notification of the fault, of the engineer's arrival, the type of fault, its cure and any action taken by the engineer, and the time of the engineer's departure. It is in the customer's interest to reconcile this with his own log and notify the supplier of discrepancies, if possible before the engineer has left.

For third-party maintenance of PCs the contractor will require the customer to advise him as soon as possible of the date of acquisition or at least installation at the customer's premises of new machines [K9(17)].

8.6.4   Spares [K10]

Some agreements require the customer to keep spares; this is usually feasible only on sites which are either very large or very distant from the supplier's depot—or both:

(a) The Customer shall purchase from the Supplier and hold available to the Supplier such spare parts as the Supplier shall recommend such spare parts to be supplied at the Supplier's List Prices then in force.

(b) The Supplier may draw on this stock of spare parts for maintenance and repair of the Equipment. The Supplier shall not be liable for any delay in performing maintenance or repairs under this Agreement if any such spare parts as are recommended to be held are not available and shall be entitled to charge the Customer for all additional expenses and costs incurred by the Supplier as a result of such delay.

(c) Any spare parts which are not in the recommended list shall be supplied by the Supplier at the then current List Price.

A maintenance agreement like this is not particularly common. The advantage to the customer lies partly in his maintenance being quicker and more reliable, and partly in the lower charges.

An alternative system allows for the supplier to hold all spares, but:

. . . the Customer will if so required by the Supplier provide storage space at the Installation Site for a reasonable stock of spare parts.

8.6.5   Miscellaneous [B23; K6, K9(18)]

If the customer holds spares, then it may well be that:

Any parts removed from the Equipment by the Supplier in pursuance of maintenance or repair shall be the property of the Customer.

Otherwise, more usually:

When replacement parts are fitted the parts removed shall become the Supplier's property.

This of course refers to the practice of 'swapping out' [8.5.1].

With systems involving telecommunications apparatus supplied by British Telecom or some other telecommunications supplier it may not be possible to test the computer supplier's equipment without also using some telecommunications apparatus. We therefore find a clause like the following:

The Customer will at his own expense provide such telecommunications facilities as are reasonably required by the Supplier for testing and diagnostic purposes and will bear the charge for the use of such facilities by the Supplier for such purpose.

Chapter 9

Software maintenance

9.1 Services to be performed
9.1.1 Standard packages from the manufacturer
9.1.2 Other suppliers' standard packages
New releases
Legal requirements
9.1.3 Other software—bespoke systems
Error detection and correction
Advice and information
Enhancements
9.1.4 Response time

9.2 Payment

9.3 Limitations and exceptions
9.3.1 Scope of maintenance
9.3.2 Performance
9.3.3 Loss and consequential loss

9.4 Termination

9.5 Variation

9.6 User's duties
9.6.1 Not to alter
9.6.2 Use current release
9.6.3 Notification
9.6.4 Information and services

9.7 Supplier's duties

Chapter 9

Software maintenance

Any computer program which is being used regularly will inevitably put its user in mind of ways in which it can be improved and enhanced. A program which is never expanded in this way is a fossil. Software maintenance is therefore to be directed to the business of improvements and enhancements. It may be for an off-the-peg package, in which case the series of improved versions will usually be known as 'Releases' and numbered sequentially; alternatively the software being maintained may be a tailor-made system which the user is unwilling or unable to maintain himself: a small company with a few programs to maintain, and few opportunities for promotion or for working on interesting new projects, will experience the utmost difficulty in recruiting or retaining good programming staff, since maintenance has acquired a reputation of being the saltmine of the software industry and programmers can, and do, change employers to avoid what is seen to be dreary work. In these circumstances a company will probably turn to the software house who designed the program and ask them to provide maintenance.

Whether or not the maintenance of bespoke software is performed by the software house which wrote it, in any case the *source code* (ie the form in which the program is written) is essential to effect maintenance. As mentioned in 3.3.1, the client may well wish to ensure that in any failure by the software maintenance contractor (whether a failure of capacity—eg liquidation—or a failure to fulfil the terms of the contract), the current version of the source code can be recovered. For standard software one method is to have each version of the source code deposited with a third party who then is placed under an obligation to deliver it to the customer if any disaster overtakes the maintenance contractor. For his part, the client will probably be required to agree not to attempt to resell the source code or make it available to anyone else or otherwise exploit it, but simply to use it on his system [N].

For software available through a distributor, there are particular difficulties in leaving the maintenance aspects to the distributor [G6, G8; H6, H8]. If the distributor is to provide effective maintenance he will need access to the source code of the software and will need to employ skilled programmers to carry out the work. For this reason, one often finds that responsibility for software maintenance is retained by the software owner so that the distributor's duties are confined to supplying and installing the software. In this way the software owner protects his software by not revealing the source code.

For PCs, software maintenance contracts *per se* are rare. The customer who buys his software over the counter of a home computer shop is likely to have no software maintenance at all. It is tacitly assumed that those who use such shops can probably write or rewrite their own software and will not need such a thing as software maintenance. Again, the low initial cost of the product must inevitably mean that maintenance is relatively expensive. However, new releases or upgrades are becoming more usual—and not now solely for word processing software—and suppliers can use this as a further weapon in their fight against 'piracy' (copyright infringement). The user into whose hands the software comes can obtain information about maintenance and new upgrades by completion of a simple form and sending a licence fee. It will be noted that this is applicable to 'shareware' [4.3] and software generally which changes hands by methods other than ordinary purchase from an authorised dealer. It is also, of course, a chance for the user to regularise his position on copyright infringement. However, much of the software is American and the opportunity to obtain maintenance information by a transatlantic telephone call will not always be appropriate.

In general, when offered a new version of software, the customer must satisfy himself that manuals will be provided where relevant, and either that the new release requires no new training or that it will be provided, free or at a reasonable price by the supplier (unless the user thinks he is capable of training himself).

For the question of levels of support in different software categories from the same supplier and for possible changes in the levels of support see above [3.0.2].

Increasingly for PC software although there is no formal maintenance contract as such suppliers will provide helpdesk facilities, answering queries about the use of the software. This is not really maintenance since the majority of the enquiries will not be reporting a bug, but simply asking for help in the use of the software. In theory, the enquiries could have been dealt with by the user's finding the relevant place in the manual or invoking the on-line (often supposedly 'context-sensitive') help facilities, but in fact both manuals and on-line help facilities are notoriously unhelpful. Initially some software houses provided this service free but increasingly now (with the use of PCs in companies rather than purely by the home market) this is a charged service.

Contractually it may or may not be greatly different from traditional software maintenance services and may still contain 'bug-fixing' provisions, but the main service will be the manning of a helpdesk between particular hours and the provision of information over the phone. For this aspect of the work the precedent for a network service level agreement [R] may be appropriate.

9.1 Services to be performed [C17; D16; L5]

The service will be limited to one or more particular pieces of software (usually defined in a schedule) and also for non-PC software to one or more particular installations. In part this last feature is dictated by the fact that the maintainer of a software package is usually the licensor and he is anxious to prevent the user from making use of the system on more than one machine without taking out a second licence. But it is also dictated by the physical distance between supplier and user, and the desire to be certain about any minor variant versions which may be in use, since each additional site may have differences of configuration which require different versions

9.1.1 Standard packages from the manufacturer

For off-the-peg manufacturers' software packages, maintenance—like the licence itself—is often bound up in the hardware contract:

> The Supplier's Maintenance Service for Software includes the installation of the Software and subsequent Software Releases in accordance with the Supplier's usual procedures.

This may be the first and last mention of software maintenance in the entire contract, as opposed to any other clauses referring to the licence. The supplier is not committed either to producing new versions or to supplying them to the customer; on the other hand, the correction of faults and bugs should be covered elsewhere in the contract (see Chapter 3).

The release of new versions is important because the supplier of the software will wish to keep as much uniformity as possible in the versions in use. This will mean that he is not maintaining too many different versions, and that the effect of any changes can be gauged on all versions now out. He will therefore put pressure on all customers to use the new releases as soon as they are available, and customers may be told that, after a certain time, the old version(s) will no longer be maintained. Sometimes a new release is found to be so defective that a customer declines to change to it from an older release; in these circumstances he would be well advised to contact all other users (perhaps through a user group, [13.6]) so as to present a united front to the supplier.

Where a manufacturer's standard package is to be maintained by someone other than the manufacturer the customer will need to satisfy himself that the maintenance contractor can get hold of the new versions of the software as soon as they are available and learn enough about them to be able to provide a credible service.

9.1.2   Other suppliers' standard packages

It will be anticipated that a software support contract from a software house which has no interest in the hardware will be both a more complex and more comprehensive agreement. The usual services offered cover:

(*a*) release of new versions, and
(*b*) legal changes;

as well as services more appropriate to a tailor-made package.

New releases [L5(2)]

A more detailed clause to cover the provision of new releases is:

> The Supplier shall make available to the Customer such improvements and modifications to the standard version of the Software as the Supplier shall make and release from time to time and which are compatible with the version installed for the Customer.

This clause visualises the possibility that the customer may already have a version which is not in every respect standard, and therefore a new release may be inappropriate. The standard version will usually be described in a schedule.

Legal requirements [L5(4); M6; Q13]

Some software packages reflect legal requirements and could be affected by statutory changes. Alterations of the standard rate of VAT to 18.5 per cent might be required, for instance. An intelligently designed program will be able to cope with this, but it is possible to imagine more far-reaching changes which might involve software modification. This is especially true of payroll programs, and it is therefore usual to include in any agreement for the maintenance of such programs a clause such as:

The Supplier will modify the Software so that it conforms to any change of legislation or new legal requirements.

This clause places no time limit on the speed with which such a modification would be required, and the speed with which such changes can be published and made effective by a Chancellor makes it impossible for any maintainer to wish to give any undertaking in this respect. It is to be hoped that by now all governments are aware of the time that must be taken to design, produce and test software in order to implement changes.

9.1.3   Other software—bespoke systems [M2]

The clauses considered in this section will also be found in an agreement for standard package software, and provide for error detection and correction; provision of advice and information; and facilities for the customer to have enhancements and improvements introduced.

Error detection and correction [L5(1); M5]

The supplier will need to investigate and correct errors, and this is usually covered by some such clause as:

The Supplier shall correct any faults in the Software in so far as they are due to faulty workmanship on the part of the Supplier.

This is of course much the same as the clause on error correction in a software contract [3.3.3], but extends the period of free correction for the duration of the maintenance contract.

The supplier may also reserve to himself the incorporation of enhancements at his own discretion; this could be necessary because the package incorporated some obsolescent facility or is written in a version of the computer language which is no longer implemented in that form:

The Supplier may at his own discretion introduce into the Software such minor amendments as he shall from time to time consider necessary.

The only anxiety from the user's point of view should be that he is informed of such changes, and that his documentation is brought fully up to date. Documentation may be covered by:

The Supplier shall supply to the Customer such documentation as may be necessary to reflect all changes to the Software.

A clause of this nature is essential if the user is to be able to keep track of all changes to the system—whether introduced by the supplier or the user.

Advice and information [L5(3); M7]

The writing of software involves a good deal of consultancy and giving of advice by the software house to the client, and this is reflected in such clauses in software contracts as seen in 3.6.1. Where the software has been accepted, this giving of advice is often liable to continue. As stated at the outset of our discussion of software maintenance, a regular user of a software package will inevitably think up ways of improving the package and, when he has done so, he will need technical advice to see whether his ideas are technically and commercially feasible: can this improvement be done at all? Will it fit within the confines of the existing software? How will it affect that software and the rest of the client's work? How much will it cost, and how long will it take? How valuable are the expected benefits? The client faced with these questions will inevitably turn to the supplier/manufacturer. The satisfying of these questions is likely to take a good deal of time for it may require a lot of investigation to determine the precise effect of a proposed change. This is particularly so if a proposed change is liable (as they frequently are) to change the client's clerical or other non-computer procedures, since this will involve visiting the client's own premises and interviewing relevant staff. For this reason a software maintenance contract will often provide only for giving advice by telephone—or at least not attending the client in person. If a client insists on an investigation which involves anything more than this, then this would be considered by the software house as a proposal for a new study contract.

   Such advice is also usually limited in scope to elucidating the use or worth of the existing package:

> The Supplier will provide the User with such technical advice by telephone, fax or mail as is necessary to resolve the User's difficulties and queries in using the Software.

Anything beyond this is usually limited to a few days per annum:

> The Supplier will provide technical assistance to the User at the Installation Site for a maximum of 5 man-days per annum during the continuance of this Agreement.

If the user does not take all his days' worth of what is in effect pre-paid consultancy in any one year, there is no facility for crediting this for any succeeding year. Conversely, if he uses more time, he will find himself paying for it, over and above the maintenance charges, at the supplier's standard rates.

Enhancements [M7]

The boundary between advice, whether on site or not, and proposals for enhancements is a narrow one, and the clauses in the last section might equally as appropriately have been considered under the present head. However, a clause like the following may also be included:

> The Supplier will undertake at the Supplier's sole discretion the study and/or implementation of enhancements to the Software for the User.

'Sole discretion' is a phrase to raise the hackles and blood pressure, but it is difficult to devise a valid alternative. The supplier could limit his involvement to a particular number of days, or to a particular cost value of work, but as the assessing of the number of days or the cost value of doing some work for the user must perforce be entirely under the supplier's control, the milder form of words does not correspond to any reality more favourable to the user.

9.1.4 Response time

Response time—the speed with which a manufacturer starts to rectify an error of which he has been notified—was discussed above [8.1.2].

Surprisingly, the concept is less common in software maintenance contracts which are often silent on the rapidity with which the work or correction/enhancement will begin. The user will infer—correctly, no doubt—that the maintenance function does not have particular staff associated with it, but is done by any dogsbody who happens to be around and can spare the time to bone up on the user's software. A clause which takes this point seriously and implies that staff are permanently assigned to the maintenance function is therefore very refreshing:

> Upon receipt of the User's request for support or rectification of a defect the Supplier shall (subject to its then current commitments) normally begin work on such support or defect not later than the first working day thereafter and shall diligently continue the work during normal working hours or at such other times as may be mutually agreed until the work is accepted by the User as completed satisfactorily. If the User requests support in an emergency the Supplier shall use all reasonable efforts to fulfil the request as quickly as possible.

Acceptance has been dealt with [3.3], and need not be recapitulated here. Indeed, it is not normally recapitulated in any software maintenance contract, though it is obviously relevant. Ideally such contracts should cover it.

9.2   Payment [L3]

Payment for software maintenance can be extremely simple in the case of a manufacturer's standard package, and rather more complicated for bespoke software.

To deal with the manufacturer's package first, the usual arrangement is for the original licence charge to include such software maintenance as is provided [3.2], though there may be a charge for the installation and the magnetic media on which new releases are sent to the customer.

For bespoke software the payment will usually be monthly or quarterly, and will often represent an annual percentage of the original software cost (say 10 per cent):

> The Supplier shall charge and the User shall pay the Standard Maintenance Charge due monthly in advance.

So far, so good. But when it comes to work beyond the standard maintenance period of x days, some contracts will also specify the rates for work over and above the standard maintenance charge. Where this is so, the software house may further distinguish between ordinary office hours and overtime:

> The Supplier shall charge and the User shall pay fees at the standard or overtime rates specified in the Schedule hereto in respect of all time spent by the Supplier's Staff in initial familiarisation work and in other work required by the User under this Agreement over and above 5 man-days' consultancy per annum.

For maintenance provided by the software house who wrote the original system, the familiarisation period should be negligible. For the other work, the software house is in effect providing a contract which differs from ordinary software contracts in that it does not give an overall estimate of the cost of the work. A maintenance contract of this sort is then a hybrid between a pure maintenance contract and software contract, and Chapter 3 should be consulted for many of the terms and conditions which it will contain—including expenses, the ability to vary the charges, and so on.

9.3 Limitations and exceptions

9.3.1 Scope of maintenance [L5(1); M5(5)]

As with hardware maintenance contracts, the supplier often specifies what is not covered by the service. This will include breaches of the user's duties, eg:

> The Supplier's Maintenance Service for Software excludes service in respect of:
>
> (*a*) failure caused by equipment or software not supplied by the Supplier;
>
> (*b*) failures resulting from the Customer's modifications of the Software;
>
> (*c*) mis-use of the Software or operator error;
>
> (*d*) software releases earlier than the Supplier's then current release;
>
> (*e*) tests and checks requested and specified by the Customer which are outside the Supplier's normal test specifications and procedures.

9.3.2 Performance

Whether the software maintainer has or has not written the program to be maintained, the question of the performance of that program (even after amendments made under the maintenance agreement) is liable to be excluded:

> The Supplier disclaims all liability for the performance of the Software the usefulness of the results produced or its possible effect on the User's business.

'Performance' is probably wider than in 2.3.5 and 3.3.2, and means simply the system's working without any guarantees as to its achieving any particular measurable standard

9.3.3 Loss and consequential loss [L14; M16]

It is usual for contracts of this type to limit (so far as the law will allow) loss and consequential loss. These clauses are usually very general and do not differ in form or enforceability from such clauses in other contracts for services.

9.4 Termination [L10]

Many software maintenance contracts remain in force until revoked, a situation which would become embarrassing to a supplier who has no adequate clause to increase his charges [9.5] since he would then be under the necessity of revoking it himself simply to increase his fees when a combination of inflation and obsolescence of the hardware made a price rise inevitable.

Most contracts provide for termination on notice by either party. The minimum notice period is likely to be at least a month.

Apart from this, most contracts allow termination for the user's non-payment or incapacity. Again, these clauses are not any different from similar clauses in other contracts for services.

However, as with hardware where new equipment is available which replaces obsolete equipment [8.4.3], so also with software packages from a supplier, the supplier may reserve the right to terminate in order to encourage the customer to use new software. This should of course be distinguished from the case where the supplier is encouraging the customer to use a latest version of an existing package—see 9.1.2 New releases.

9.5 Variation [L3(3)]

None of the contracts we have examined visualises the possibility of any change in the identity of the software. This is hardly surprising, though the fact that they also fail to envisage any change in the location of the computer on which the software is to run is perhaps more unexpected. In practice, of course, this will usually be covered in the software licence [3.5].

The charges are a different matter. Some clauses are virtually the same as those for hardware maintenance [8.5.2]; a more complex clause provides in effect for annual negotiation:

> Any alteration to the charges shall be subject to negotiation between the parties hereto commencing not later than x days and ending not later than y days prior to the anniversary date in each year. Failing agreement the Supplier shall specify the alteration to the User and give written notice thereof not less than 2 days prior to the anniversary date. Such alterations shall become effective for the year beginning with the anniversary date.

9.6 User's duties

9.6.1 Not to alter [L6(4)]

Obviously in this type of contract a first care must be that the program is not tampered with by anyone other than the party maintaining it. Any alteration, however trivial, will automatically invalidate the contract:

> The User will not permit anyone other than authorised representatives of the Supplier to change in any way the Software its operating instructions or manuals.

This is the standard view, though it is occasionally relaxed by the licensor to the extent of requiring authorisation for any changes.

> The User may with the Supplier's prior written consent modify the Software or its documentation at his own expense and on his own responsibility provided that the Supplier shall immediately have sole rights in any such changes and that the Supplier's copyright notices are incorporated. The User agrees that the Supplier will have the right to charge for all services resulting from the User's modification of the Software and documentation.

9.6.2 Use current release [L6(1)]

The question of releases is discussed above [9.1.1 and 9.1.2]. A manufacturer will normally impose uniformity on his customers.

> The User shall use only the current release of the Software. Without prejudice to the Supplier's other remedies the User agrees that the Supplier will have the right to charge for all services resulting from the User's failure to use the current Software release.

9.6.3 Notification

The user is usually obliged to notify any defect, cf 8.6.3:

> The User will give written notice to the Supplier of any defect in the Software within seven days of such defect becoming apparent.

9.6.4 Information and services [L6(7)]

Finally, the user is expected to provide information, office and computer facilities as for a full software contract, and pay expenses [3.6.1]:

> The User shall make available free of charge to the Supplier all information facilities and services usually required by the Supplier for the purpose of his obligations under this Agreement including but not limited to computer-runs print-outs discussion with User's staff data preparation office accommodation typing and photocopying.

This is a comprehensive list but no more than required in software contracts.

The question of information may be amplified by clauses relating to nomination of representatives exactly as in ordinary software contracts [3.6.1] and [3.7.1].

9.7 Supplier's duties [L8, L9]

These are identical in intention (if not in form) to corresponding clauses in a software contract, and will relate to liaison and nomination [3.7.1 and 9.6.4]; conformity and dress [3.7.1] and confidentiality [3.7.2] and possibly data protection [3.7.2; 10.3.3 and P15]. Confidentiality requires a further example since under a maintenance agreement the software, and therefore its documentation, are already in existence at the time the contract comes into force and belong to the user:

> The Supplier shall be entitled to retain a copy of all appropriate documentation of the Software on its premises for the duration of this Agreement. Such documentation shall be held in confidence and only for the purposes of this Agreement and returned to the User at the expiry of this Agreement.

Staff poaching [3.6.2] is less likely in a maintenance situation and is not often included.

Staff training [3.7.3] is not relevant unless the modifications are very substantial, in which case the modifications will probably be part of a new software contract (as opposed to a software maintenance contract).

PART III COMPUTER SERVICES

Chapter 10

Bureau services

10.1 Nature of the service
10.1.1 Batch bureaux
10.1.2 Time-sharing bureaux
Terminals
10.1.3 Network service level agreements
10.1.4 Volumes

10.2 Payment
10.2.1 General bureaux: batch
10.2.2 General bureaux: time-sharing
Data stored and other peripheral usage
Time
10.2.3 Specialised bureaux

10.3 Data
10.3.1 Batch systems
Delivery
Safe-keeping
Return of data
Retention of data
10.3.2 Data transfer
10.3.3 Data protection

10.4 Termination

10.5 Variation
10.5.1 Variation of charges
10.5.2 Variation of service

10.6 Customer's duties
10.6.1 Batch services: data
Provision of data
Quality of data

Chapter 10

Bureau services

Some years ago a company selling computer bureau services ran an advertisement with the slogan: 'You don't need to buy a cow if all you want is a pint of milk'. This is the essence of the bureau business: that a company with computer resources makes them available to others in return for payment. Within this broad concept a number of distinctions is possible of which two main types seem to us interesting from a contractual point of view. The first type of distinction is between a generalised bureau which is not particularly interested in what is done on its equipment, the customer simply providing his own programs and data, and a specialised bureau providing a specific service, where the fact that a computer is used may well not be the most important aspect. The second distinction is between a batch bureau and an on-line one [10.1.2]. The first of these distinctions affects the application: the second is technical and thus these two types of distinction may interact with each other producing batch general services, on-line general services (usually loosely called 'time-sharing bureaux'), batch specialised services and on-line specialised services. Networks are the latest form of bureau service and a network service level agreement is really only an on-line bureau service of a particular kind. The reader of this chapter will need to be clear which of these types of service he is considering.

10.1 Nature of the service

10.1.1 Batch bureaux [Q2, Q8]

Batch bureau agreements are in sharp decline but not yet finally extinct, and are therefore included in this book for completeness. At the risk of slight boredom, the reader may find it easier to consider batch bureau contracts first where the physical separation of the bureau and customer makes the issues clear, before examining on-line and network agreements.

Most agreements have proved amazingly vague as to exactly what is being provided:

> The Bureau shall perform such services for the Customer as are expressly agreed between the Bureau and the Customer.

—agreed when? In what form? Does 'expressly' mean 'in writing'? Does this clause permit the agreement to be varied in the future after it has come into force?

> The Bureau shall provide computing services in accordance with its current literature . . .

This is surely better in that it refers to an identifiable document (although again the question of variation is relevant), but then this example is from a specialised bureau whose precise service may be expected to be defined in some detail in its current literature. The simple answer to this problem must be a schedule, and in the schedule the following might be relevant, at least for a specialised service:

(*a*) commencement date of service;
(*b*) general content and form of customer's data (eg standard forms as prescribed by bureau/DAT tape containing customer's accounting information/mailing list/etc);
(*c*) processing by bureau defined either by result (to produce payslips and other payroll information for the customer) or run such programs as the customer shall deliver to the bureau, etc;
(*d*) timescales—of delivery, of processing, of re-delivery—expressed both as to days of the week or month and as to times of day.

For the casual bureau user, who does not want a regular service but simply the opportunity to run program X now and again, other considerations apply. In this case he usually knows the performance of his program well, and simply wants to read Y records or print Z pages. Provided the charging structure is based on some such criteria as this, a vaguer clause is possible:

> The Bureau shall make available to the Customer the facility of running the programs more particularly described in the Schedule hereto on the Bureau's computer upon the charges hereinafter described.

It should also be noted that the bureau may well wish to charge for time booked and not used:

> A charge of 25 per cent of the standard rate will be made for computer time booked and not used (whether because the Customer has failed to ensure that his data is delivered on time or otherwise)

unless the Customer has given to the Bureau at least 12 hours' notice of cancellation.

10.1.2 Time-sharing bureaux [Q2, Q3]

The basis of a time-sharing bureau is that the customer has access to the bureau on-line, either through a terminal specially supplied by the bureau (as is usual for most specialised services) or through any suitable terminal or PC (a common arrangement with general time-sharing bureaux). Very occasionally the customer may even take his data to the bureau's premises and there input it through the bureau's own terminal though this is not much different contractually from a batch bureau.

The generalised clause suggested in the previous section is suitable here, but the charging structure will be concerned not with physical records or pages but with the concepts of data stored, connect time, CPU time, etc—these concepts are explained below [10.2].

Terminals [P1, P6]

If the customer provides his own terminal, the bureau may well not be too concerned as to its precise nature. A clause requiring the customer to use only equipment which has been BABT approved would not be inappropriate and could follow the pattern of those in ordinary hardware contracts.

Apart from this, the bureau will be concerned only with the customers' correctly using their terminals, see 10.6.2 below.

Sometimes, however, the customer also hires a terminal from the bureau; this is usually optional in a generalised contract, but for a special contract it is very common. This is usually because a specialised service may well have a specialised terminal with functions peculiar to that application shown on the keyboard. A contract of this sort must therefore have a hardware hire component containing some of the elements of contracts in Chapter 2. In particular, it will probably allow for hire, installation, restriction on use, and return by the customer on termination. The last two of these may be dealt with under customer's duties [10.6]; the first two are considered as part of the bureau's duties [10.7.4].

It will be noticed that the bureau will usually be responsible for maintaining the terminal [10.7.4]: terminals are generally reliable devices but the on-line bureau services contract may well have elements of a hardware maintenance contract.

If it is a PC the only questions of interest will be the operating system (Windows, DOS, OS/2, etc) and its speed and capacity.

10.1.3 Network service level agreements [R]

A network service level agreement is really only a form of on-line agreement, whereby the bureau services to be provided will be those usual in networks such as electronic mail, certain retrieval services, perhaps a fax service, virus protection service, etc. The terminal is usually the user's own PC with hardware or software items added to it to enable it to gain access to the network. The user will probably be heavily dependent on the network and will therefore be looking for a high level of availability. He will also typically expect to have training provided by the network provider, as well as a helpdesk which he can contact by telephone if he has any difficulties or queries.

10.1.4 Volumes [Q15]

Remarkably, very few contracts specify any limitation on volume. Some allow a sliding scale of charges to benefit the high volume user, or at least discourage very small volumes, but few seem to envisage the predicament when the customer gives them a larger volume than they can cope with. The following clause is therefore interesting:

> All the work (provided that it does not exceed in volume the Customer's specified maximum volumes as set out in Schedule 3 hereto) shall be performed by the Bureau in accordance with Schedule 1 hereto. Any work in excess of the maximum volume or volumes set out in Schedule 3 hereto shall be performed by the Bureau as soon as is reasonably practical for the Bureau having regard to the other commitments of the Bureau.

A clause like this is obviously vital if the bureau gives any indications as to speed of processing or delivery.

10.2 Payment

Payment is usually monthly. In this section no sample clauses are given since the charging systems vary widely and are usually incorporated in a schedule.

10.2.1 General bureaux: batch [Q3]

The basis on which charges are calculated can vary a good deal. Originally, machines were available to a single user who was charged purely on time, regardless of how much of the machine or its facilities he used. With more sophisticated machines it was based on both time and peripheral usage. The operating system gave the time used by each program on a printed log and also after each printout on the line printer, and this was generally taken as evidence of the time taken. Peripheral usage was usually expressed in a measure appropriate to that peripheral (£x per 1,000 records read, £4 per page) or simply per number of characters transferred—whether to disk, tape, printer or other peripheral. Data preparation or transfer (if any) would also be charged for [10.3]. Sometimes a bureau would also charge for consumables (paper used, etc); it was of course up to the customer to provide these himself for use on the computer.

10.2.2   General bureaux: time-sharing [P4]

These bureaux customarily charge on some mix of three main bases: data stored (and sometimes other peripheral usage), connect time, and CPU time.

Data stored and other peripheral usage

This is the easiest basis for charging and should therefore be dealt with first. The customer is charged for all the data he stores on disk or tape. It is usually measured in bytes (ie characters) or words (a longer unit whose relation to bytes/characters varies from machine to machine), and is sold in units of so many 'K', 'M' or 'G'. 'K' stands for 'kilo' and means, loosely, 1,000: more precisely, 1,024 (binary 2^{10} for those who are interested). 'M' stands for 'mega' and means 1,000,000. 'G' is 'giga', ie 1,000,000,000 (American billion). It is also measured per day (or per working day). Sometimes charging may also be by other peripheral usage—usually the printer, though if the terminal has (or can have) a printer attachment this may more easily be monitored there. If the main computer's printer is used, this is essentially a batch function and some time-sharing bureaux prefer to have a separate scale of charges for batch work. These will, of course, be charged like other batch services, see 10.2.1 above.

Time

'Time' on the computer may be simply the elapsed time taken to run the program (elapsed or, for on-line systems, connect time). Or it may be the actual fraction of the elapsed time during which the computer actually executed the customer's program (CPU time). A brief explanation may clarify the last concept: a time-sharing bureau may be running programs for three customers, A, B and C, simultaneously. What is actually happening is that the Central Processing Unit is switching rapidly between A's, B's and C's programs. The time spent on each will not be exactly even, since the computer will take advantage of delays in the various peripheral devices to service other programs. It follows, therefore, that, in a single minute, the CPU may have executed A's program for 21 seconds, B's for 27 seconds and C's for 12 seconds. A charging system based on elapsed or connect time would charge all three customers for 1 minute; a charging system based on CPU time would charge A for 21 seconds, B for 27 seconds, and C for 12 seconds.

A further complication is the question of program size. Under older operating systems each user was allocated a single partition and all partitions were of the same size. This saved the bureau needing to differentiate between programs of differing size. For other bureaux whose operating systems allocate program space on a more flexible basis depending on the size of programs to be run, the scale of charges will be by CPU time for so many 'K' or 'M' words or bytes of core. It is also possible that the operating system may obligingly work out some combination of CPU time and program size to produce a new unit of x seconds per y 'K'.

10.2.3 Specialised bureaux

In specialised bureaux, it is generally easier to charge in terms of the transactions handled. A payroll service might be on the basis of the number of employees in any run (weekly or monthly) and the number of additions, changes and deletions. An accounts program might be charged per 1,000 postings.

Joining fees are also usual in this kind of service. In the case of an on-line service, the joining fee will also cover the cost of installing the terminal. There may also be a charge structure for taking on the customer's data before the system can operate. There may also be delivery charges.

Frequently there is a minimum charge. In the case of an on-line system, this minimum charge will include (but not necessarily comprise) terminal rental.

Finally the contract may specify a charge for 'dumping' the customer's file. 'Dumping' is an inelegant term of art meaning the reproduction on an appropriate peripheral of a file. This is likely to become relevant if the customer wishes to leave the service, since he will not necessarily automatically have the right to transfer his data in computer-usable form. Whether or not the bureau can withhold his data from him is discussed below, but in many cases it is perfectly legitimate for them simply to give the departing customer a printout (charged at normal printout rates) of all his data, which he must then go to the expense (and delay) of preparing afresh for a new service with another bureau. If, on the other hand, the bureau are prepared to dump his file on magnetic tape or some other computer-usable medium, the customer should expect that the charge may well be on the high side so as to discourage him from leaving the service. This is a point which a customer should consider not only when contemplating terminating the service [10.4], but also before beginning.

10.3 Data

A point to be clear about is whether data means that which goes from the customer to the bureau, that which is stored and processed by the bureau, and/or that which the bureau sends to the customer. A contract will need to differentiate.

This section must consider the data handling separately for batch programs and on-line. With a batch system the data actually leaves the customer's premises, is held by the bureau for the purpose of inputting it, and then may or may not be returned to the customer; in an on-line system no physical document leaves the customer's premises, and the contract will be concerned solely with the data in its computer-usable form [10.2.2].

Contracts purely for data preparation or data transfer (see 1.10) with no other processing element are also relevant here. The batch system described in 10.3.1 is of course far less common than it used to be, but it may arise when new hardware and/or software are being purchased and the customer wishes to get a backlog of data on the system quickly, so that he can begin acceptance testing as soon as possible after delivery.

10.3.1 Batch systems

In a batch system, the usual procedure is for the customer to deliver his data to the bureau's premises; for the bureau to input it to the computer; and then for the bureau to send the results, and sometimes also the data, back to the customer. This part of a bureau's work is virtually indistinguishable from an ordinary data preparation bureau's work, except that in the latter case the results will consist of magnetic tape or some other computer-readable medium rather than a printout.

Delivery [Q7]

Delivery is typically effected by the customer himself, by post, or by a courier service. If the customer performs the delivery himself, the contract is often silent on the question of delivery—though it is to be noticed that failure by the customer to deliver data could seriously disrupt the bureau's operation. For such a clause see 10.1.1 above, or this general clause on frustration:

> If this Contract or any part thereof shall become impossible of performance or otherwise frustrated the Bureau shall be entitled to reasonable remuneration for any work done or prepared to be done by the Bureau.

This last phrase is designed to cover, at least in part, time booked on a machine, the payment of overtime to operators and so on. The clause also covers poor quality of data—see 10.6.1. However, the customer's failure to deliver data might also be covered by the service being on a minimum charge basis. It is also to be noted that silence on this point, and an apparently tolerant attitude to this point, facilitate a bureau's exclusion of liability for any delay in processing the data—usually within a more general exclusion clause such as:

> The Bureau will not accept any responsibility for loss or damage or delay . . . etc.

Some contracts deal with delivery in the more general context of incidental expenses:

> The cost of transporting data or supplies necessary to the performance of this Contract . . . shall be borne by the Customer.

Safe-keeping

It is quite common for a bureau to exclude any responsibility for the safe-keeping of data while on their premises:

> The Bureau shall not be responsible for the loss of or damage (howsoever arising) to any documents or data supplied by the Customer while on the Bureau's premises nor for any consequential loss arising therefrom.

At first sight this seems gratuitously harsh, but it might serve to remind a customer that he will usually need to be able to check that the data he supplied is the data which was used, and in his own interests he should keep a duplicate copy of that data. Otherwise, should any dispute arise as to what data was actually run, he has no evidence on his side. The reader should bear this in mind when considering return of data (see below).

Return of data [Q8]

It is by no means usual for data to be returned to the customer. If data is to be returned, this should be expressly provided for:

> After completion of the processing all Data and documents supplied by the Customer to the Bureau shall be returned to the Customer.

In this connection the case of *Re Kingsley (decd)* (1978) 122 SJ 458 is important. It concerned a firm of solicitors using a specialised bureau for their time-recording records. They had claimed costs in respect of 815.5 hours' work but the bill was taxed (ie assessed for allowable costs) for only 777.5. After processing on the bureau's machine the original records had been destroyed. Payne J suggested that all the data (including the non-computer data such as attendances) should be kept intact until after taxation or any review of taxation. This is a case which all bureau users should study.

Retention of data [P8]

So far we have considered data only in its tangible form as human-readable or computer-readable material delivered from the customer to the bureau (and sometimes returned after use). But of course the processing usually involves the bureau storing the data in some different form such as disk on their computer. This storage has been considered in its cost aspects above [10.2.2], but there is also an ownership aspect:

> The data held by the Bureau on computer files as a result of a service provided by the Bureau to the Customer shall become the property of the Customer only upon payment of all the Bureau's invoices in full.

This clause is of course designed to prevent a customer's leaving a bureau without paying. The clause continues:

> The Bureau shall at its normal charges for the time being make all reasonable facilities available for the transfer of the data as the Customer may desire.

In other words, if a customer leaves the service (and has paid his bills), the bureau will provide print-outs, tapes or whatever of the data to facilitate its transfer elsewhere, but reserves the right to charge for it—a not unreasonable precaution; and this cost is one which any customer contemplating changing bureaux must consider, as well as the cost of re-inputting the data with the new bureau.

It will always be prudent from a customer's point of view to take and keep copies of the total data file from time to time. If there is a dispute the bureau may unreasonably withhold the master tape which would leave the customer in a very difficult position.

10.3.2 Data transfer

If a customer is moving from one type of hardware and/or software to another he may need to have his existing data transferred to the new system. To do this he will need to test that the transfer can be done successfully by sending a test sample of his existing data to his supplier or other data transfer contractor and asking him to produce data in the form for the new system which must then be run successfully on that new system. Only after a careful and accurate test of this sort should the customer negotiate a data transfer agreement.

Having satisfied himself that the transfer is feasible and that the contractor can actually perform it, the customer will need to define the service contractually. Usually the contract envisages the customer's real data leaving his premises (probably in tape or disk form), being taken to the contractor's premises, the transfer being effected, and the original data together with its new format being returned, or just possibly being kept for further processing. The types of clause described in 10.3.1 for delivery [Q7], safe-keeping, return [Q8] and retention of data [P8] are likely to be relevant here.

10.3.3 Data protection

Schedule 1, Part 1 of the Data Protection Act 1984 enshrined certain principles about the holding of personal data. These are:

Personal data held by data users

(1) The information to be contained in personal data shall be obtained, and personal data shall be processed, fairly and lawfully.

(2) Personal data shall be held only for one or more specified and lawful purposes.

(3) Personal data held for any purpose or purposes shall not be used or disclosed in any manner incompatible with that purpose or those purposes.

(4) Personal data held for any purpose or purposes shall be adequate, relevant and not excessive in relation to that purpose or those purposes.

(5) Personal data shall be accurate and, where necessary, kept up to date.

(6) Personal data held for any purpose or purposes shall not be kept for longer than is necessary for that purpose or those purposes.

(7) An individual shall be entitled:

(a) at reasonable intervals and without undue delay or expense
  (i) to be informed by any data user whether he holds personal data of which that individual is the subject; and
  (ii) to access to any such data held by a data user; and
(b) where appropriate, to have such data corrected or erased.

Personal data held by data users or in respect of which services are provided by persons carrying on computer bureaux

(8) Appropriate security measures shall be taken against unauthorised access to, or alteration, disclosure or destruction of, personal data and against accidental loss or destruction of personal data.

It will be apparent that these provisions will affect bureau contracts. If the data to be processed does not contain personal data within the meaning of the Act, the customer should say so and indemnify the bureau accordingly. If there is or could be any personal data within the meaning of the Act, each side must undertake to the other that it will comply with the provisions of the Act and that it will register appropriately, and must indemnify the other against any breach of the provisions of the Act [P15]. It seems appropriate when dealing with an Act such as this which has a code (the Principles in Schedule 1) to show the spirit as well as the letter of the law, for contracting parties to bind themselves to observe that spirit and refer to their obligations to observe the Schedule.

10.4   Termination [P19]

Termination of bureau services is usually a fairly simple matter, being triggered either by incapacity (eg receivership), effluxion of time, by notice or by breach. The first two need hardly detain us: a typical clause on notice might read:

> Either party to this Agreement may at any time after the date of commencement by giving three months' written notice to the other terminate the service period under this Agreement.

For breach:

> The Bureau shall be entitled to terminate the service period under this Agreement by notice in writing to the Customer in the event of the Customer's being in arrear for a period of 30 days after any payment to be made hereunder has become due or if the Customer shall commit or allow to be committed a breach of any of the terms of this Agreement and shall fail to remedy such breach

within 30 days of notice by the Bureau requiring such breach to be remedied or if the Customer shall become bankrupt or insolvent.

Sometimes also a contract may permit a customer to terminate if he refuses an increase in charges (for the increase itself see 10.5.1 below):

> If the Bureau shall give to the Customer notice to alter any charges in accordance with Clause *X* hereof the Customer may within the period of one month commencing on the date of such notice give to the Bureau notice in writing of the Customer's refusal to agree to such alteration and the Bureau's notice shall then be deemed to be notice to terminate this Agreement to take effect 3 months after the Bureau's notice.

Termination may also sometimes be triggered by the customer reducing his volume of work by more than a certain amount.

> Any notice given by the Customer to the Bureau under Clause *X* hereof which seeks to reduce the specified minimum volume of work by more than 30 per cent of the volumes specified in Schedule *Y* hereof shall be deemed to terminate this Agreement.

10.5 Variation

10.5.1 Variation of charges [P4(4)]

> The Bureau reserves the right to vary any of the charges due under this Agreement upon giving to the Customer not less than 3 months' notice in writing of such alteration.

This is a fairly standard clause and merits no special analysis, though it should be noted that sometimes the contract allows the customer to terminate the contract if he refuses to accept the alteration in the charges—see 10.4.

10.5.2 Variation of service

The disparate nature of the services which can be the subject of a bureau contract means that a variation of almost any clause is at least conceivable. In practice, there is often no variation clause as such, since it is simpler for one party or the other to give notice and negotiate a fresh contract. However, the following example is an interesting attempt to allow for this, while allowing the customer to terminate if the alterations are unacceptable:

Any change in any element of the services the subject of this Agreement may necessitate other changes to the Bureau's charges or otherwise whether such change of an element is made under the following clause or otherwise agreed between the parties hereto.

This clause is followed by:

The Customer may request the Bureau to vary any element in the service the subject of this Agreement by giving 3 months' notice in writing to the Bureau specifying the variation required provided that if the Bureau consider that such variation is not technically practicable or desirable or ambiguously or inadequately specified the Bureau may within 10 working days of such notice give further notice to the Customer to that effect whereupon the notice given by the Customer shall be cancelled.

This clause does not, of course, spell out the cost of implementing the alterations which is not necessarily the same as the cost of performing the alteration. In other words, the customer's request might well require a software alteration which would need specifying in writing. Finally, if the alteration reduced the volume of data below a particular point, this might be construed as termination (see 10.4).

10.6 Customer's duties

Customer's duties may be divided into three classes: batch service duties (mostly concerned with the submission of data); on-line service duties (mostly concerned with the usage and abuse of the terminal); and general duties.

10.6.1 Batch services: data

This section should be considered closely with section 10.3.

Provision of data

We have already considered [10.3.1 and 10.1.1] the effect of a customer's failing to deliver data. The point is reinforced in some contracts by imposing on the customer a direct obligation to provide data and the programs to be run if they in fact are the customer's:

The Customer shall provide the Bureau with all programs operating instructions and data necessary to enable the Bureau to perform its services under this Agreement.

Quality of data

It also follows that the programs and data must be of adequate quality. Strictly speaking, the customer's *duties* extend only to the provision of data sufficient to enable the bureau to execute its side of the bargain; in practice, this is usually expressed negatively with the bureau excluding liability for faulty or illegible or otherwise defective data:

> The Bureau does not accept responsibility for loss or damage arising from or consequential upon the Customer's act or default in relation to errors in the coding of information, illegible information or documents, faulty damaged incompatible or incorrectly encoded computer media supplied to the Bureau, the late arrival or non-arrival of data, incorrect data, data out of sequence or in the wrong form, variations in data from that originally agreed to be supplied. The Bureau reserves the right to charge for any additional work needed to be run as a result of any of the faults listed in this clause.

This is a formidable and alarming list, and one which is well worth considering in detail, if only because these considerations apply to all data preparation contracts.

Errors in the coding of information includes illegible information: data preparation costs are based on assumptions as to the number of key-strokes an hour which can be performed by an operator. This obviously depends on the physical speed and dexterity of the operator, and also on the quality of the data. The customer should insist on the bureau seeing representative samples of the data *at its worst* before the contract is signed, so that the bureau are aware of what they will be receiving. But if the data actually submitted after the contract is noticeably worse in quality (illegible, badly laid out, etc), the bureau's operator is likely to produce results which are not only unsatisfactory (in terms of characters misread and so forth) but also more expensive since the operator will have had to spend more time wondering whether the figure is a 0 or a 6. The correct analogy here is with typesetting where a printer will charge extra for the setting of 'bad copy'—a term of art which for some reason has not permeated to the computer industry.

Faulty, damaged, incompatible or incorrectly encoded computer media: whereas the previous problems were concerned with data written on sheets, these words are concerned with computer media: eg magnetic tape. The problems which can arise here are complex, technical, and often highly intractable. 'Faulty' media are the easiest to consider. A magnetic tape has on it magnetised particles arranged in a pattern. If the tape drive which produced it failed to reproduce the code correctly, it obviously cannot be read. 'Damaged' is also straightforward. 'Do not fold staple or mutilate' used to be a common litany when punch cards were used. Cards which had been folded, stapled or mutilated could not be read. 'Incompatible' is more complicated. The codes which represent each character are not always identical for each machine and nor is the density in which the codes are packed. The customer who intends to supply data in computer-usable form should satisfy himself that his data will run on the bureau's machine, and the simplest way to do this is to ask the bureau to let him have a trial run with a fair sample of the data. For *late arrival* and *non-arrival*, see 10.3.1 above. *Incorrect data*—is the stuff which is being delivered to the bureau the right data for the run of which the customer expects to receive the results? *Data out of sequence* applied chiefly to punched cards where the recurring nightmare had always been the box of cards tipped on the floor. The remaining categories (*wrong form, variations of data*) are blanket definitions to cover any other imaginable forms of defective data.

10.6.2   On-line services: terminals and modems

With on-line services where the customer has a terminal, the quality of the data does not really arise since, if the customer inputs rubbish, only he knows and only he is involved. Nor is the provision of data really relevant since charging is not usually dependent on booking computer time at a particular time [10.2.2].

Limitation of terminal use

If the customer provides his own terminal for the service, the rest of this section is irrelevant. If, however, as is common, the terminal is provided by the bureau, the bureau is in effect hiring a terminal to the customer, and many of the clauses will come straight from a hardware hiring contract covering the correct use of the terminal, duty to insure it, and so on [2.6]. However, in addition to these duties, the customer may be restricted from attempting to gain access to the system by any other terminal:

> The Customer shall not utilise or attempt to utilise any equipment other than that provided by the Bureau under the terms of this Agreement for the purpose of using the services of the Bureau.

The reason for this clause may be complex. At its crudest, the clause may do no more than reflect the profit the bureau makes on hiring terminals. But there are other more justifiable reasons: the bureau may wish all users to have a standard terminal so as to simplify maintenance and staff training among the customer's employees. These considerations apply particularly where the customer lacks deep experience of computer applications, and needs a good deal of both support and training. The design of standard operating instructions (which may be enshrined in a manual) becomes very difficult if the terminals vary. The terminal may also have special features (particular function buttons peculiar to one application) which cannot easily be simulated on any other terminal. For example, an information retrieval system might have a special button marked 'SEARCH' enabling the user to look for the terms he has already specified.

Limitation of service availability

In a similar way, most bureaux will seek to prevent their customers from using the terminal for services provided by other bureaux:

> The Customer shall use the terminal equipment solely for the purpose of the service provided by the Bureau under the terms of this Agreement.

The purpose of this clause is straightforward: no bureau providing a terminal to enable customers to use their service is likely to be enthusiastic about that terminal being used to give his customer access to a rival system, and, in practice, pretty well the only way to seek to stop it is by contract. It is also designed to prevent the customer from gaining access to the bureau's other services and data.

This problem arises because the bureau cannot actually see what is done with the terminal, or who uses it. So a bureau may also seek to use the contract to prevent the customer from using the service on behalf of someone else. This is particularly likely to be so when the charging structure has a joining fee, specialised terminal charge, or other charging basis apart from machine usage and storage charges:

> The Customer shall not use the service provided by the Bureau under the terms of this Agreement for the benefit of any person or organisation other than the Customer.

This clause is a little difficult to define without becoming too specific about the service, and perhaps the most satisfactory way to define it is in those terms. For example, a bureau providing a sales ledger service might draft the following:

> The Customer shall use the Sales Ledger service provided under the terms of this Agreement solely for his own sales ledger and shall not use it for the sales ledger of any other company organisation or body whatsoever.

Another clause designed to deal with a related problem is the following:

The Customer shall not sell lease assign transfer or otherwise make available for any purpose whether gratuitously or for a valuable consideration the system or any part thereof or any information with respect thereof to any person firm or company (other than his own employees for the sole purpose of enabling the Customer to use this service within the terms of this Agreement).

This clause deals not only with the customer effectively running the service as if he were a bureau for others, but also with the mischief which could arise where a customer revealed information about the system to someone else which enabled this third party to gain access to the system. Time-sharing systems are usually accessed by telephoning the correct number of the computer (thereby setting up the communication line) and the inputting of user name and code word to identify the particular user. It follows that an unauthorised person, obtaining these three pieces of information (telephone number, user number and code word), and already possessing a terminal or PC and modem, could get into the system. For an ordinary time-sharing system, where each user builds up his own files on the computer, this is bad enough, though at least, in theory, it is detectable when the customer whose number has been used without authorisation identifies files as not being his own. But for a retrieval system where the customer is not building up data files, the danger is even greater since it is virtually undetectable. Failure to guard against this may in some circumstances be a breach of the Data Protection Act 1984. The damage to be guarded against is twofold: unauthorised access ('hacking'); and damage to data or programs ('virus'). Both these activities are criminal offences, under ss 1 and 2, and 3 respectively of the Computer Misuse Act 1990 [R3(7)].

Incidentally, this clause provides the bureau with further protection for his software [3.8], a point which is considered below [10.6.3].

Modems and network cards [R6]

On a network a customer is likely to wish to attach a PC and the mechanism for this if the customer's machine cannot be directly cabled to the network is by modem—'modulator/demodulator'—which converts data signals to voice signals for transmission over the public switched telephone system and then converts them back to data on receipt after transmission.

Rental for a modem is possible though the cost may be merged with the general network costs. It is impossible for a bureau or network provider to know what the modem is used for and as it has no moving parts it cannot be said to be harmed by being used for other services. So restrictions on terminal use described in the preceding section are not usual with modems. However, the contract will need to ensure that on termination the modem is surrendered or that the customer pays for the modem's retention.

If the customer's PC can be directly cabled to the network (this usually arises when customer and network provider are part of the same group of companies), there will probably be a network card to be installed in the customer's PC. Again, there will probably be no separate rental for this, no restriction on its use, but procedures for its return to the network provider on termination of the contract.

10.6.3   General duties [P13; Q19]

Protection of the system

Software protection [3.8] is often relevant to bureau services since it has been known for a bureau's customer to hand over as much information as he can gather about the service program (operating manuals, forms, print-outs of runs, and so on) to a third party in order to get them to write a program for him to run on his own machine. Therefore the clauses considered in Chapter 3 [3.8] are relevant here. A variant of this to cover the situation for an accounting program may be of interest:

(*a*)   The Bureau is the sole owner of all rights in connection with the programs to provide the Services and the Customer shall not pass information about such programs or the Services to any person or body except the Customer's own staff, auditors, HM Inspector of Taxes, HM Customs & Excise and similar persons and bodies having a right duty or obligation to know the business of the Customer and then only in pursuance of such right duty or obligation.

(*b*)   The Customer shall not at any time hereafter (whether or not the Services are still being used by the Customer) pass any information about the Programs and Services their working methods structure nature or content to any computer service company software house bureau consultant or to any other person except as mentioned in (*a*) of this clause without the written permission of the Bureau and upon such terms and conditions as the Bureau may specify.

Like most such clauses it is not perhaps completely watertight. A customer with considerable ingenuity and dishonesty could probably get round these clauses, though after notice like this he would have to admit that he was warned.

In view of this situation, an indemnity clause is not inappropriate:

The Customer hereby agrees to indemnify the Bureau in respect of any breach by the Customer or any of its employees servants or agents of any terms or conditions of this Agreement resulting in any loss damage liability costs or expenses which the Bureau may suffer.

The clause itself is usual enough in all kinds of contracts for services, and in no way peculiar to computers, but—considered in conjunction with the preceding clauses—it adds up to a formidable attempt by a bureau to protect its property.

Communications software

A network provider may also supply software for the customer to run on his PC to facilitate communications. Contractually this is not much different from providing applications software for the customer to run on a bureau's equipment, except that the software once installed on the customer's PC is no longer directly under the control of the bureau. However, the licensed software continues to belong to the bureau (network provider), and so must be either surrendered or destroyed on termination of the contract.

Data protection

The obligations under the Data Protection Act 1984 are binding on both the bureau and the user and each will need to indemnify the other against failure to comply with the Act. Details have already been set out in 10.3.3 and an example of such an indemnity is at P15.

Duty to pay

This duty is virtually indistinguishable from such clauses in other contracts. It is usual to bill customers monthly in arrears for payment in thirty days.

> The Customer shall pay to the Bureau all charges due under this Agreement within 30 days of the last day of the month in which the Service was performed.

Report of defects

We shall be considering below [10.7.3] the circumstances in which the bureau may be obliged to re-run work. For this to be remotely practicable, it is essential that the customer report any defects, faults or imperfect runs as soon as possible:

> Full charges shall be payable by the Customer for time used if the Customer shall not have reported any machine errors within

2 days of the Customer's receipt of the data produced by the run in which such machine errors are alleged to have occurred.

Leaving aside for the moment the question of whether machine errors could possibly include operator errors or other malfunctionings within the control of the bureau, we see that this clause, in effect, seeks to impose on the customer a duty to check all his results within 2 days. It is therefore essential that he keeps records (duplicate entry forms?) of all data he submits, and that the service prints out an audit trail of all data it has received (whether or not it has been able to process it successfully—see 10.3).

This situation is usually covered by a very general clause excluding the bureau's liability in the event of *force majeure* (and thereby admitting it in cases of negligence and the like on the bureau's part) or even by a more explicit offer to replace or reprocess data negligently handled (see 10.7.3 below), provided it is in a reasonable time. We feel a more explicit clause is desirable to impress on the customer a duty to report errors, faults and mishandlings, with a like explicit clause requiring the bureau to reprocess in such an event. For instance:

> The Customer shall notify the Bureau within 7 days of all claims in respect of replacement or reprocessing made necessary whether as a direct result of the negligence of the Bureau their servants agents or sub-contractors in the performance of the Service or otherwise.

Do the 7 days flow from the date of occurrence of the error, or from the customer's becoming aware of it? For the bureau's clause, see 10.7.3 below.

10.7 Bureau's duties and liabilities

10.7.1 Confidentiality [P15; Q17]

Many of the bureau's duties in specialised services mirror a software house's duties [3.7], including confidentiality [3.7.2], and need not be recapitulated here.

An aspect of this confidentiality is the obligation alluded to above [10.3.1] on return of the data after processing. A further aspect is Data Protection [10.3.3].

10.7.2 Helpdesk and training

A network agreement will frequently include a helpdesk facility. The helpdesk will be manned—usually not for the full time the network is available since many networks are available 24 hours a day, 365 days a year. Instead a helpdesk may be manned during ordinary business hours. The staff on the helpdesk will provide telephone advice to the customers' users trying to gain access to the network and use its services. The staff will keep records of all reported faults and difficulties which can provide valuable analysis as to how satisfied the users are with the network.

Training is a related service. Section 3.7.3 provides information about this which is equally appropriate to network training.

10.7.3   Replacement and reprocessing [Q14, Q16]

This has already been mentioned above in discussing the customer's obligation to report errors and defects [10.6.3]. Many contracts are altogether silent about even the possibility of replacement of data which has been faultily prepared, or the reprocessing of runs lost through machine malfunction or operator error. Nevertheless, there is a well recognised custom that negligence or fault of this kind should be rectified by replacement or re-run:

> If the results produced by the Bureau for the Customer are incorrect by reason of a fault occurring in the computer or of a mistake due to negligence or inadvertence of the Bureau or their servants agents or sub-contractors then the Bureau shall reprocess the data to produce correct results without further charge to the Customer but the Bureau shall not be under any further liability to the Customer in respect of the said incorrect results or their consequences.

This is the usual form of this obligation, and it allows reprocessing for only two types of error: machine malfunction (eg a printer fault preventing the data from appearing legibly), or negligence and inadvertence (eg operator mishandling or loss or damage of the results). This clause is appropriate only where the bureau owns the program since, if they do not, the error may have been due to programming error in a piece of software supplied by the customer. It follows, of course, as has already been emphasised, that the customer must keep his data (or accurate records of it) and secure his audit trail in order to be able to prove his point. It should be noted that:

(1) Reprocessing is limited to these situations, and most bureaux exclude *force majeure.*

(2) It is up to the customer to complain promptly of any faults [10.6.3].

(3) Most contracts seek to limit the obligation to reprocessing, and decline to entertain any further claims for consequential loss.

In this last connection, it is clear that consequential loss is likely to increase rather than decrease the longer the error remains undetected, and this again reinforces the customer's interest in complaining as soon as possible. A comprehensive clause in this area runs:

(*a*) The Bureau will replace free of charge and as soon as is practicable having regard to the Bureau's other commitments any materials spoilt destroyed or lost as a direct consequence of the negligence of the Bureau its servants or agents or subcontractors in the performance of the Service.

(*b*) The Bureau will correct free of charge and as soon as is practicable having regard to the Bureau's other commitments any errors in results produced by them solely through their negligence provided that such errors are notified to the Bureau in writing by the Customer within 2 days of the Customer's receipt of such results.

(*c*) Save as expressly provided in *x*(a) and *x*(b) above the Bureau shall be under no liability whatsoever in respect of any loss damage or delay of any nature whatsoever and however caused whether direct or consequential and whether or not caused by the negligence of the Bureau its servants agents or subcontractors.

10.7.4   Maintenance [P6, P11]

Maintenance of the terminal or modem (if hire is involved, see 10.1.2) and of the software is covered in Chapters 8 and 9.

10.7.5   Performance and availability

Guarantees as to performance of a bureau system are extremely rare [3.3.2], but the checklist of points there may be equally applicable to bureau contracts. To those should be added availability—ie a measure of the times of day when the system must fulfil the minimum performance criteria.

In networks performance criteria are rather more usual. The users of the network will want a guarantee that the electronic mail messages will reach their destination in a reasonable period of time, that faxes initiated on the network will be sent at the specified time and that if there is to be any delay or a fax cannot be delivered (eg a non-existent fax number), they will be notified swiftly. Most of all they will want a guarantee that the network will be up at specified hours, which often means in practice 24 hours a day, 365 days a year, and if there has to be any downtime they are notified of it well in advance. They will also want a guarantee that the helpdesk is available within specified hours (not usually the same hours as the network—see 10.7.2).

Chapter 11

Consultancy

11.0 Introduction

11.1 Services to be performed

11.2 Payment

11.3 Completion of the consultancy

11.4 Termination

11.5 Alterations

11.6 Client's duties

11.7 Consultant's duties

Chapter 11

Consultancy

11.0 Introduction

11.0.1 The nature of consultancy

Consultancy—the calling in of expert advice on a short-term basis—can happen in almost any conceivable type of commercial or professional matter. On the one hand it can be far wider than computers, covering scientific process, marketing, personnel, asset realisation and thousands of other activities. On the other hand it can be argued that bespoke programming by a software house is itself a form of consultancy, and it is certainly a fact that much of what has been said in Chapter 3 is directly applicable to consultancy generally. The problems, therefore, of defining computer consultancy for the readers of this book are formidable.

Nevertheless, it can be argued that as a minimum it should embrace the use of consultants to assist the client or organisation in choosing a system, and this is the aspect we have concentrated on in this chapter and in precedent S.

There are numerous unkind jokes about consultants, such as the one about their being the people who are paid to borrow your watch in order to tell you what the time is. In fairness to consultants it can be suggested that if all the client employing the consultant wanted was to find out the time, the consultant's response was perfectly correct. There is a danger of assuming their omniscience.

In classical drama, the problems that arise in this world were sometimes depicted as being solved by divine intervention. Many modern managers, faced with technological perplexities, look for divine help and the modern *deus ex machina* is the consultant—an omniscient being who is above this mortal world. After his brief intervention all should come right and even if it does not the blame can safely be laid at the door of somebody else other than the manager.

(Richard Morgan and Brian Wood: *Word Processing*, 2nd edition Pitman Publishing Limited 1985.)

The authors went on to suggest that choosing a consultant must be largely on the same basis as choosing a good employee—namely by looking for the right combination of experience (relevant to your work), knowledge (of the wider and more technical aspects of your problem), skill (particularly in management) and temperament (the consultant's sensitivity to the character and ethos of your organisation).

11.0.2   Consultant or employee? [S18]

There are a number of significant legal differences between independent contractors (such as consultants and freelance programmers [T]) and employees which are worth emphasising:

(1) Generally speaking, the intellectual property rights in any work produced by the consultant will vest in the consultant unless the contract otherwise provides. In the case of an employee such rights usually vest in the employer.

(2) A duty of confidentiality on the part of the employee is implied into the employer/employee relationship. While the circumstances surrounding a consultancy may give rise to such a duty it is usual to incorporate an express provision in the contract.

(3) Unlike the employee, the consultant does not owe a duty of fidelity to the person engaging him unless the contract so stipulates. This may give rise to a number of express provisions in the consultancy contract, covering such matters as working for competitors, accounting for commissions and secret profits and publicity.

In view of these differences it is essential to establish the relationship of the parties before a contract is entered into. In many instances the position will be clear and this will be particularly so in cases where the independent contractor is other than an individual.

Companies are more likely to run into difficulties where they engage the 'regular casual' who is an individual. In these cases the distinction between an employee and an independent contractor can become blurred and legal advice should be sought as to whether the individual concerned should be regarded as one or the other. Apart from the matters referred to above, employees are entitled to certain employment rights (such as those relating to unfair dismissal and redundancy) and the employer is liable to deduct PAYE. The independent contractor, on the other hand, makes a taxable supply for VAT purposes and where he is registered for VAT he should add this to his fee.

11.0.3   Independence [S5]

The independence of the consultant will usually need to be established. Some 'consultancy' is provided by organisations which have a financial interest in the equipment they recommend.

Clauses in the contract whereby the consultant warrants his independence of suppliers and agrees not to accept commissions from them may sometimes be appropriate [S5].

11.0.4   Contract or letter?

A large number of consultancies are undertaken on the basis of an exchange of letters rather than a full-blown contract. As it is the nature of consultancy not only that the relationship between the parties is short-term but also that the information to be discovered by the consultant is required in a hurry—major management decisions are held up until the consultancy is complete—there can be nothing wrong with doing business in this way by exchange of letters, provided all the essential points are covered.

But then it can equally cogently be argued that almost all contracts can be replaced by an exchange of letters. Why have formal contracts at all? The answer must of course be that to cover all essential points the letter would need to be inordinately long, that much of what needs to be included is standard to other types of contract (eg [A28, A29]) and—most important of all—the structure of a good contract provides a checklist and discipline to ensure that all essentials have indeed been covered.

However, if a reader wishes to use this chapter and Precedent S simply as a checklist for an exchange of letters there is nothing to prevent him from doing so.

11.1   Services to be performed [S2, S4, S5]

The very first requirement is for the client employing the consultant to define precisely what he wants the consultant to do. A clear statement of the terms of reference will help the consultant to use his time efficiently and should also assist the client in setting realistic objectives for the consultant and not expecting the impossible.

All that was said in Chapters 1 and 3 [1.3, 3.1; D2, D4] about the need for a functional specification is relevant here.

The first thing therefore to decide is the end-result of the consultancy. In the example we consider primarily in this chapter, it is the acquisition of a computer system, though it is essential to say what the system is to do. Computers are not an end in themselves for business, but a tool to enable an organisation to achieve particular objectives of speed, efficiency, comprehensiveness, and so forth [S1, Schedule 1].

An alternative type of consultancy is the feasibility study to decide whether a computer is of value at all for a particular application, and such a study usually goes on to ask the consultant to say in general terms what the characteristics of such a system should be if the answer to the first question is yes.

Such terms of reference might therefore include:

> To report on the value of a computer to the Client in carrying out its functions of mail order (or distribution, or production of proposals for clients, or making up to date financial information available to its branch offices, or whatever it may be) as set out in. . . .

Again the end objective in computerising must be clearly identified, and it will be almost essential to set this out in more detail either in a Schedule or by reference to an identified existing document. In this document all the questions the client needs answers to should be fully set out. The main way of deciding whether the consultant has done his job will be to see whether he has given full answers to all such questions [11.3].

11.2   Payment [S9]

The options for payment are likely to be the same as we have already considered in Chapter 3: time and materials, fixed price, or estimated maximum price [3.0.3]—and for the same reasons. It is the nature of consultancy as for software that there is uncertainty as to the amount of work involved. The consultant therefore normally quotes for his time at so much per hour or per day. The contrary pressure will also be felt, of a company wishing to be sure that the consultancy will not end up costing more than the system it is designed to help procure.

Again the same point must be made that if a client insists on a fixed price contract it must not be surprised if the consultant protects himself against underestimating by putting a fairly substantial 'contingency' into his quotation.

Again, like the commissioned software contract, the consultancy contract may, if the work is at all lengthy, require milestones [3.2.1; D5(1)] giving both sides a chance to assess how the work is going before proceeding to a later phase.

At such milestones it may be that the nature of the work will change and that different skills or expertise will be required with some consequential change in the size and composition of the consultancy team. Separate phases will need to be identified in the contract—possibly in a Schedule or by reference to a separate document.

It can also be that at the outset the precise nature of the skills or expertise required for later phases cannot be known, in which case the consultant will need to make provision for a change in the future hourly charge-out rates to cover this.

There may equally be an opportunity for the client to redefine, at least in part, the objectives or terms of reference for future phases [11.5].

In the unlikely event that the parties forget to deal with payment, the law will imply an obligation on the client to pay a reasonable charge to the consultant (Supply of Goods and Services Act 1982, s 15).

11.3   Completion of the consultancy [S1]

In some instances a consultancy will be indefinite in time, continuing until such time as either of the parties chooses to give notice of termination, but it is usually preferable for the project to have a definite completion. The correct definition of the service to be performed [11.1] should assist in deciding this.

If the contract is a feasibility one alone, it will terminate on the delivery by the consultant to the client of a report or rather on the presentation of the report with an opportunity for the client to question the consultant on the report—see 11.7.1. The importance (mentioned in 11.1) of listing all the questions to which the client needs answers will be apparent here, and it must be the case that the more detail the client can go into in defining them, the better will be the result. Woolly terms of reference all too often result in a woolly report.

In the case of consultancy leading to the acquisition of a system it may be rather easier to test the finished result, provided that the consultant is retained until full acceptance of the system [2.3, 3.3; A11, A12; D10]. This will also have the further advantages of encouraging the consultants to get on with the procurement and also taking the burden of procurement and even testing of the system off the client's shoulders. However, such a lengthy consultancy may well require milestone payments [11.2; D5(1)] and also a lengthy period of cancellation.

Another technique for the consultant which may be used in addition to or instead of this is some system of retainer or refresher payments to continue during the life of the contract even though the client is not actually obtaining consultancy advice from the consultant all the time. This in effect means that the consultant is on hand to give such advice at once when requested and obviously he cannot then be full-time engaged in other work.

The obvious danger to the client is that the project may drag on indefinitely, through circumstances beyond his control (eg a supplier's late delivery), and he must ensure that he himself acts promptly on such matters as preparing his machine room, which are within his own control [2.3.7; A15].

If the parties do not fix a time for performing the consultancy services in the contract, there is an implied term that the consultant will, if acting in the course of a business, carry out the services within a reasonable time (Supply of Goods and Services Act 1982, s 14).

11.4   Termination [S3]

The usual types of termination clause considered for other contracts will be applicable here.

Like most professionals, the consultant will not usually expect to be able to terminate the contract before it is completed unless there is good cause. On the other hand, consultants will recognise that any professional relationship is based on the trust of the client and once that trust is gone there is little to be gained from insisting on any period of notice from the client; the relationship is only likely to get worse rather than better. However, in a long consultancy, or one involving many consultancy staff, or both, there may be a period of notice for termination sufficient to allow the consultant time to redeploy productively what may be a significant proportion of his staff [3.4.2].

In the event of termination it will be desirable for the client to ensure that all working papers of the consultant and any draft report pass to him and that he has full rights over these.

11.5   Alterations [D7]

The fact that consultancy from its nature deals with matters which contain an element of the unknown (at least for the client) means that the probability of future alteration of the terms of reference must often be allowed for—particularly in larger consultancy tasks. It helps both parties considerably not only to insist that all such changes are properly defined and agreed in writing with full consideration of the effect in terms of cost and duration of the project as a whole [3.5.2; D7], but also to limit the times when they can take place to completion of defined phases or milestones [11.2]. This in turn means that the timetable for the various phases must allow sufficient time between one phase and the next for an adequate review by both sides before the next phase can commence.

11.6   Client's duties [S6]

These must draw largely on those appropriate for commissioned software [3.6].

11.7   Consultant's duties

11.7.1   The report

Chapter 3 is again relevant [3.7], but in addition the consultant will probably be required to deliver up any report in a particular form and in a specified number of copies. The need for clarity in defining the matters the consultant should address has been stressed more than once [11.1, 11.3, 11.4]. Such points are probably best dealt with in a Schedule.

SCHEDULE X

The Consultant shall upon Completion of the Project provide five (5) copies of the Report to the Client.

The Report shall be divided into sections as follows:
Introduction
Terms of Reference
Statement of present system
Summary of areas where information technology may help
Consideration in detail of each such area
Description of proposed system
Proposed system suppliers
Proposed system environmental considerations
Proposed system training needs
Timetable of proposed system implementation
Costs of proposed system
Summary of recommendations

It will almost certainly be necessary for the consultant to attend at least one meeting following the completion of his report so as to present the report and answer questions about it.

If necessary this also can be incorporated into a definition of completion of the project:

217

'Completion of the Project' means the acceptance by the Client of the Report following the attendance by the Consultant's Team at the Client's premises to present the Report and reply to questions from the Client's directors and staff about it.

11.7.2 Confidentiality [S5, S10, S11]

In addition to the points made in 3.7.2, it is perhaps worth stating that any report produced by the consultant must itself remain confidential. Copyright in the report should pass on acceptance and payment to the client, and this may also go for a draft report on premature termination of the contract [11.4].

In certain cases a client may insist that the consultant does no similar work for rival companies. Such a condition would amount to a restraint of trade and will be enforceable if it is reasonable in its scope and necessary to protect the legitimate interests of the client. Clearly, a consultant advising on the implementation of an accounts package is not nearly so likely to be asked to agree to such a restriction as one who has advised on a specialist program which only the client's direct competitors could benefit from. There is an analogy with 'poaching' [3.6.2].

11.7.3 Quality of service

The quality of the service which the consultant is to provide is obviously a key concern for the client. It is perhaps therefore at first sight alarming to find out how many consultancy contracts avoid the issue altogether. The reason for this may often lie in the fact that where a consultant acts in the course of a business, s 13 of the Supply of Goods and Services Act 1982 implies a term that the consultant will carry out his services with reasonable skill and care.

In many cases, this may be perfectly adequate and nothing more is required. What is reasonable in this context will depend on the circumstances and, in particular, upon the standards generally observed in the industry as good practice. The codes of practice of bodies in the industry representing consultants may therefore become relevant—see Chapter 13. The type of work undertaken will also be relevant. For instance, one would expect the standards of skill and care to be applied by a surgeon to be somewhat higher than those of a car mechanic. This somewhat obvious and stark comparison may be applied in a more refined way when considering different types of consultancy. A client who is concerned that his consultant should provide a particular quality of service would be well advised to specify this in the contract. A consultant who sells his services on the basis that he abides by a particular code of practice may expect to have to restate this as a term of the contract.

PART IV PUBLIC SECTOR CONTRACTS

Chapter 12

Public sector contracts

12.1 Cultural differences

12.2 EU/GATT Rules
12.2.1 Supplies
12.2.2 Services
12.2.3 Utilities
12.2.4 Compliance and remedies

Chapter 12

Public sector contracts

Public sector contracts differ from private sector contracts in three main respects. First there is the cultural difference between the two. For example, liquidated damages pose particular problems for public sector bodies who cannot point to any loss in profits in the event of their contractor failing to supply what is required. Secondly there are clauses in contracts which are appropriate only to the public sector, such as those dealing with the Official Secrets Act. Thirdly there is a large amount of law and procedure enjoined on public sector bodies by the EU/GATT Rules, which increasingly replace the old Compulsory Competitive Tender (CCT) Rules.

12.1 Cultural differences

It is difficult to be exhaustive about the cultural differences. The following is therefore a selection of points.

One area in which public sector contracts are likely to differ from private sector contracts is in the overall *timescale for implementation.* The EU/GATT Rules will be considered in detail below, but the time which must elapse between each stage means that inevitably contracts above a certain size will take anything from six months to one year to implement. Several results flow from this. In the first case, it is more likely that a contract with such a long gestation will probably result in a change in the requirement during the course of the negotiation. Such a change may come about as a result of technical advances, or as a result of better understanding of the requirement, or both. This means that the contractor will need to be prepared to negotiate for the whole of this period and recognise that it will be expensive for him to do so. Inevitably this tends to rule out the smaller contractors for the larger jobs. It also means that the change control procedure [3.5.2] must be rigorous and that the clear mechanism for documenting any possible changes to the requirement since it was first defined and ensuring that the implications of such changes in terms not only of cost but also of timescale and performance must be fully clarified and agreed by both sides.

One possible solution is to have some sort of technical design stage to be let as a sort of pre-contract to a number of interested suppliers before the main contract is proceeded with. For a contract with a good deal of development work this may be appropriate, but for other contracts it may be less useful.

A lengthy timescale also implies a lengthy *acceptance* procedure [3.3.1]. There is nothing to prevent private sector contracts from having a full acceptance procedure though in many cases this is curtailed simply because the purchaser of the goods or services is in a hurry to obtain the benefits they represent. The dangers of this are obvious. However, with a full acceptance procedure lasting at least a month or longer, it inevitably means that the contractor must wait longer for his money. Early part payment of the value of the contract is a possibility but it must be made clear that these payments do not pre-empt the acceptance process and in particular do not imply an acceptance that has not yet been completed. Thus, if a system fails the acceptance tests, any moneys paid in advance should be recoverable.

Public sector contracts are also usually let following a *competition*. The rules for this for the larger contracts are set out below in discussion of the EU/GATT Rules, but even for small contracts it is typical for there to be several competitors. A short list of three is often considered the optimum. This protects the officers letting the contract from any suspicion of favouritism and enables them to show a clear understanding of competitive costs for the goods or services. Each supplier has to be held at arm's length during the negotiation process, and the exact selection process has to be well documented showing, at least for the senior officers in the public sector body, the criteria used for selection, any weighting given to those criteria, and the relative performances of the various suppliers against this.

Another effect of the sheer difficulty in putting in place public sector contracts is that they tend to last for longer. Once everyone has gone through the gruelling process of acquiring a system, it is inevitable that neither the public sector body nor contractors themselves can face a rerun. There is therefore a reluctance to terminate such contracts early. The length of time a public sector contract may run obviously varies but five or even seven years are not untypical. It follows from this that a public sector body may be held to ransom by a contractor who has managed to find some inequitable clause in the contract since he knows that the public sector body cannot easily switch to an alternate supplier, or if they do it will take them at least six months to a year to complete that switch.

To amplify the matter of *liquidated damages*, the point here is that such damages should be easily calculable and represent a clear estimate of the loss to the organisation in question. For a commercial company a loss in profits would be an obvious criterion. For a public sector body there may be a loss in some cash saving which was to have been realised and if this is the case calculation may not be too difficult. It may be that additional staff will need to be brought in on a contract basis and their exact cost can again be calculated. Or it may be some diminution in a service to the public. For example, the failure of the library system run by a local authority may result in an extreme case in the borrowers being unable to take any books out at all or in a less extreme case that there are excessive queues for borrowers taking books out and that the tracking of books and collecting fines may not be up to standard. Here the calculation of liquidated damages is virtually impossible.

Another area is *publicity*. Whereas most commercial organisations may be perfectly content that both they and others with whom they do business should be entitled to publicity and their only concern is likely to be how factual it is and what if any effect it has on them, for a public sector body there is usually no particular advantage in publicity of this kind. Indeed on occasion it may be positively harmful. The public sector body is therefore likely to require strict control on publicity and even ban it altogether.

Arbitration is another area where public sector bodies may differ from private sector bodies. If a contract goes wrong, and bearing in mind the difficulties mentioned above about liquidated damages, it may well be that the most powerful weapon the public sector body holds over the defaulting contractor is that of publicity. Inevitably any failure in a public sector contract receives far more publicity than would a corresponding failure in a private sector contract. This is not to suggest that public sector bodies welcome the publicity so generated, especially as some sections of the press particularly delight in investigating public sector bodies in these circumstances. Nevertheless, it must be recognised that the failure is likely to be even more damaging to the contractor and may well result in a considerable loss in business once the failure of the system is known. This may be so even when the case is first set down for hearing. It is thus in the interests of the contractor to avoid this state of affairs and arbitration may be one way in which he is tempted to do this. Arbitration will at the very least buy time and no publicity about the failure can be possible during this time. It is therefore usually in the interests of the public sector body not to have an arbitration clause in the contract but to use the threat of adverse publicity as an aid to enforcement.

We propose to say nothing in detail about the clauses specific to public sector contracts such as the Official Secrets Act, certain clauses about corrupt gifts or the right to use land. Such clauses are typical of all public sector contracts and not just of ones involving computers and information technology and the wording is purely 'boiler plate'.

12.2 EU/GATT Rules

Strictly speaking these are two separate sets of rules, though in practice they tend to be grouped together since they apply to the same bodies and their provisions are fairly close. The general philosophy behind these rules is the encouragement of open tendering and the prohibition of protectionist policies in the public sector.

The rules are binding on public sector bodies seeking to let contracts, rather than on the contractors themselves, though the contractors will need to be aware of the rules which affect both the procurement process and the contract itself. It is also the case that the rules allow the public sector body to take into account its understanding of certain characteristics of the contractor such as his record on health and safety (*London Borough of Greenwich v General Building and Maintenance PLC The Times*, 9 March, Legal Studies Publishing Ltd 1993 p 200) and financial status (*Ballast Nedam Group NV v Belgium* Case C–389/92).

It is probably simplest to consider the various EU directives individually, and then bring together the conclusions which arise from their application. The public contracts directives, and their implementing regulations, divide into the following main classes:

(*a*) goods and supplies;
(*b*) services;
(*c*) works;
(*d*) utilities;
(*e*) compliance and remedies

'Works' is concerned with building works (the Public Works Contracts Regulations 1991, Sched 1 (SI 1991 No 2680)) and can be ignored from the point of view of IT.

12.2.1 Supplies

The Supplies Directive goes back to 1976/77 (77/62/EEC) which was embodied in the Public Supply Contracts Regulations 1991 (SI 1991 No 2679), but the 1993 Directive (93/36/EEC) embodied in the Public Supply Contracts Regulations 1995 (SI 1995 No 201) supersedes this. Title 1, art 1 contains the definitions and in particular defines a contracting authority. The same article also defines supplies simply as 'products' but goes on to note that 'The delivery of such products may in addition include siting and installation operations'. The exemptions in art 2 in particular include contracts involving security where secrecy is important.

On a *de minimis* basis, the regulations do not apply to small contracts. Different types of regulations have different thresholds below which the rules will not apply though the thresholds are constantly being revised and brought into line. The threshold for supply contracts is set at 200,000 Ecu which equates to £149,728 though this threshold is in fact superseded by the threshold of Special Drawing Rights (SDRs) which is set out in Annex 1 of the Marrakesh 1994 GATT Agreement on Government Procurement and is contained in Cm 2575, where this threshold is set at 130,000 Special Drawing Rights (SDRs) which equal £96,403. The thresholds are revised every two years and come into force on 1 January in even-numbered years. Thus the next such revision is likely to be for 1 January 1996. However, the method of calculation is to be reviewed two years after the initial application that is to say from August 1995 onwards (art 5(1)(c)).

Article 5(1)(d) lays down that the thresholds should be fixed by the GATT agreement with publication in ecu in the *Official Journal* at the beginning of the month of November which follows the revision laid down in para (c).

The value of the contract is calculated for a contract that lasts less than 12 months simply on the value of the contract itself. Where, however, the contract exceeds 12 months the residual value of any goods supplied must be taken into account. Where a contract is for an indefinite period, it is assumed to last at least four years and thus the annual cost must be multiplied by four (art 5(2)). Where there are regular contracts or contracts which are renewed within a given time the value is either the actual aggregate value of similar contracts concluded over the previous physical year of 12 months or an estimated aggregated value during the 12 months following the first delivery or during the term of the contract where this is greater than 12 months (art 5(3)). Where the procurement is for a series of contracts in different parts, these must be aggregated (art 5(4))—in other words it is not possible to split a contract in order to avoid the thresholds.

Article 6 specifies occasions when contracts may be negotiated without prior publication of a tender notice. The most important of these are perhaps research or technical or artistic reasons or extreme urgency. The difficulty with this last one is it is necessary to show clearly what the extreme urgency is, and this in itself takes time and makes it extremely hard for any procuring body to fulfil whatever it was that had to be done urgently.

Article 7 concerns the debriefing of unsuccessful candidates and the publication of the result of the competition.

Article 8 raises the question of standards. There is a reference to Annex III which mentions various bodies who might produce standards, but the general point is that where a European standard exists, it should normally be specified and adhered to in a contract. If no European standard exists then an international standard should be used. The CCTA [13.4.1] has established a series of interlocking standards which were originally known as GOSIP (Government Open Systems Implementation Profile). Subsequently these have been superseded, after negotiation with other European countries by the EPHOS (European Procurement Handbook for Open Systems) Standards. EPHOS operates over the whole of the European Union, whereas GOSIP is purely within the UK. GOSIP is very much more detailed and the CCTA published an *Open Systems Handbook* in 1994 which is the most recent statement on standards. For GOSIP they have produced two encyclopaedic copies of the *GOSIP Handbook*, one for purchasers (ie public sector bodies) and one for suppliers. The *GOSIP Handbooks* were produced in 1992 and although they have been revised, they are starting to show their age. A detailed discussion of open systems standards is out of place in a book of this type, but in general it may be said that the history of open systems is one of lofty ideals and practical disappointments. Time and again there is either no standard appropriate and competing commercial offerings are the only way of performing some particular function, or there is a standard which is then superseded or bypassed by commercial considerations. The production of standards which are seriously likely to be adopted is primarily a question of timing. An appropriate standard that comes at the right time has a much better chance of being accepted than a far better standard whose time is wrong. The rejection of the 7 ft gauge for railways pioneered by the Great Western Railway Company in favour of the 4 ft 6 in gauge which is now standard in Britain and elsewhere was not a question of whether the 4 ft 6 in gauge was the better of the two. The received wisdom seems to suggest that it was the worse of the two. It was simply that it is not really sensible for one railway, however grand, to have a standard totally at variance with that of everybody else. Much of open systems is concerned with precisely this point and a less satisfactory standard that really is a standard is often far more practical than a superb standard which is adopted by nobody.

Title iii gives the timetable for advertising contracts. For contracts in excess of 750,000 Ecu (£561,480) an indicative notice is also required at the beginning of the budgetary year.

There are three types of procedure available: open, restricted or negotiated. An open procedure is one whereby all interested suppliers may submit tenders. A restricted procedure limits tenders to those suppliers who have actually been invited to submit. A negotiated procedure allows the contracting authority to consult with suppliers of their choice and then negotiate the terms of the contract with one or more of them. Above the thresholds only open procedure is generally possible.

The notice has to be drawn up in a form set out in Annex 4 so that it can be published in the *Official Journal* of the European Communities 12 days after despatch or four days in the case of accelerated procedure (see art 12). It cannot be published elsewhere until the *Official Journal* has published it. At least 50 days from despatch of notice must elapse between the advertisement and the receipt of tenders. Where the negotiated or restricted procedures are appropriate, at least 37 days must be allowed from date of despatch for the receipt of requests to participate (art 11). In no less than 40 days, the procuring body may request those who have asked to participate to produce their tenders. In practice a sifting process is usually necessary to ensure that everyone is agreed who the contractors are.

Criteria for selection are set out in Chapter 2 (art 20 and following) and for award of contracts in Chapter 3 of Title iv (art 26 and following). The general purpose behind these is to prevent the award of a contract on frivolous grounds. An important provision in art 27 allows the contracting body to enquire more closely into an abnormally low tender. A very low tender may be a loss leader by the company who is anxious to do business with the contracting authority; it is more likely because the company has totally failed to understand the scope, size or complexity of what is required.

12.2.2   Services

Services are defined in Schedule 1 of the Public Services Contracts Regulations 1993 (SI 1993 No 3328) which implements Directive 92/50/EEC. Services include (Part A, Category 7) computers and related services.

We have gone into the supply contract regulations in some detail since they provide the most complete and up-to-date statement of how these things are to be done. So we shall deal with services in rather less detail. The threshold (reg 7 of the Regulations and art 7 of the Directive) is set at 200,000 Ecu which equates to £149,728 though on 1 January 1996 the threshold will be reduced to the same as that for the supplies contract, namely 130,000 SDRs which is roughly equivalent to £96,403.

The aggregation rule whereby like contracts can be considered jointly to see whether they have reached the threshold is particularly important with the services contract, since it seems that contracts for broadly similar services must be so aggregated. The most likely candidate here is consultancy and public sector bodies are being advised to lump together all IT consultancy contracts for aggregation purposes. A threshold of £149,728 is easily reached and one of £96,403 even more so. The way to deal with this must be for the public sector body to procure by full open tender one or more contractors who can provide the services after a competition. It will then be possible for the public sector body to call off days or weeks for particular projects for consultancy from these contractors as required. A framework arrangement which falls well short of a contract may be equally valid provided it had been procured by full open tender in this way. The effect of this is to procure letters of intent which can then be converted into contracts at a later stage.

In addition to the open procedures, restricted procedures and negotiated procedures used in the supplies contracts, the services contract also has design contests (reg 24 and arts 1(g) and 13). This enables a jury to select a particular design (typically in the field of architecture but it could also apply to IT) following a full open procedure which has selected a number of candidates.

Where contracts are for a mixture of goods and services the rule is basically that the contract is treated as a services or as a supply contract depending solely on which of the two components is the larger. In practice, since service contracts tend to have a longer life than supply contracts, it is often the case that the balance is more easily tipped towards service contracts than supply contracts.

12.2.3   Utilities

A utility is a public sector body in such fields as water, energy, transport and telecommunications performing its relevant activity. For example, a public rail network procuring a traffic control system for itself would be a utility.

The original Utilities Directive 90/531/EEC which was implemented by the Utilities Supply and Works Contracts Regulations 1992 (SI 1992 No 3279) was amended by the Utilities Supply and Works Contracts (Amendment) Regulations 1993 (SI 1993 No 3227) only to the extent that certain exemptions for utilities operating in the oil and gas, and other solid fuel sectors were considered. However, the original directive and the regulations are now superseded by Directive 93/38/EEC, which lists in its annexes the various utilities affected in the UK and elsewhere in Europe. The thresholds were set in art 14 and are set at 400,000

Ecu for all utilities except public telecommunications utilities where the threshold is set at 600,000 Ecu (there is also a threshold of 5 million Ecu in the case of works contracts, which we can ignore for the purposes of this book). These thresholds correspond to £299,656 and £449,184 respectively. In other respects, the directive is broadly similar to the Supplies and Services Directives, at least so far as IT contracts are likely to be concerned.

12.2.4 Compliance and remedies

Under Directive 89/665/EEC which was implemented as reg 26 of the Public Supply Contracts Regulations 1991 (SI 1991 No 268), reg 31 of the Public Works Contracts Regulations 1991 (SI 1991 No 2680), reg 30 of the Utilities Supply and Works Contracts Regulations 1992 (SI 1992 No 3279), reg 32 of the Public Services Contracts Regulations 1993 (SI 1993 No 3328) and reg 29 of the Public Supply Contracts Regulations 1995 (SI 1995 No 201), remedies are available in the UK courts. Remedies are also available before the European Court of Justice. An action in either of these, if successful, may result in an injunction or damages. However, for an injunction to be successful the contract will need not yet to have been let. In practice there is usually insufficient time for this. Damages also are time limited to within three months of the contract being let.

An alternative strategy is for the company not to raise an action itself but simply to notify the Commission and under Directive art 3, the Commission itself may take the necessary action against the defaulting country. The problem here is that the Commission have acquired the reputation of being reluctant to take action unless the case is a particularly gross one. It is also the case that there will be considerable delay. A further point is that it is unlikely to result in any useful result for the aggrieved company beyond seeing humiliation of their rival.

PART V   SOURCES OF ADVICE

Chapter 13

Professional, trade and special interest associations

13.1 Professional bodies
13.1.1 British Computer Society
13.1.2 Institute of Data Processing Management

13.2 Trade associations
13.2.1 Computing Services and Software Association
13.2.2 Federation Against Software Theft (FAST)

13.3 Other bodies
13.3.1 The Office of Telecommunications (Oftel)
13.3.2 National Computing Centre (NCC)

13.4 Public sector bodies
13.4.1 CCTA
13.4.2 HM Treasury (CUP and Public Sector Procurement)
13.4.3 SOCITM
13.4.4 The Audit Commission

13.5 Special interest groups
13.5.1 Society for Computers and Law
13.5.2 BCS Specialist Groups
13.5.3 NCC Legal Group
13.5.4 LAMUG

13.6 User groups

Chapter 13

Professional, trade and special interest associations

Computing in all its forms is an open profession in the sense that anyone can call himself a programmer or analyst, or run a bureau service, without requiring any particular qualifications for the task. There is not even an agreed word to describe someone who makes his living by computers, though we personally rather like 'computerist'[1]. Nevertheless, 'computerists' have from the outset been anxious to police their own profession (or trade or industry, if you prefer it) and have established professional bodies to institute standards of conduct and expertise in the hope that the lay public in time may come to rely on the qualifications of these bodies as a guarantee of excellence. A guarantee implies an indemnity in the sense that any falling short of the professional standards must be subject to a sanction.

This section considers two purely professional bodies—the British Computer Society and the Institute of Data Processing Management—some trade associations, and two other bodies (Oftel and NCC). It also considers special interest groups, particularly the Society for Computers and Law which provides a forum for those further interested in computer law.

The heads of these various organisations might be considered as suitable persons to be named in an arbitration clause for the purpose of nominating an arbitrator in the event that the parties cannot agree on the appointment of an appropriate person.

Finally a brief word is included about user groups, as a possible forum for dealing with complaints and common problems.

---

[1] It is believed that this word is the invention of the late Mr Alan Woods, a solicitor in London and the first Chairman of the Society for Computers and Law.

13.1 Professional bodies

There are two principal professional bodies for computer personnel in Britain: the British Computer Society, and the Institute of Data Processing Management.

13.1.1 British Computer Society

This is the oldest professional body for computer people in Britain, and one of the oldest in the world, being founded in 1957. The Society's entrance is now by examination. It has 34,000 members which probably represents between one- and two-thirds of the profession (depending on definitions of the profession: is a manager whose job includes computer responsibilities but with no day-to-day involvement, a member of the profession?).

The British Computer Society has two codes for its members—a Code of Practice, and a Code of Conduct. The Code of Practice is a document far too little known and used. It takes a step-by-step approach to computer operations and provides a valuable checklist of points to look for. Unfortunately it is a little abbreviated in its attempt to cover a very wide field, and it may be said that the information will not always be easily understood by the non-expert. So far as the previous (1972) version of the Code of Good Practice's legal status is concerned, article 9 (p 15) was explicit:

> Relevance to Law: The Code has no relevance to law. But the Code may be quoted by an expert witness giving his assessment of whether certain conduct was good practice. Or a supplier may be asked to comment if, in his view, his product is in accordance with the Code. There is no way in which the Code as at present written can be quoted in a contract and enforced.

See also *Johnson v Bingley & Others* (1995) *The Times*, 28 February, where it was held that breach of a professional code of conduct was not *ipso facto* negligence.

However, a new BCS code of practice has been published which no longer incorporates this limitation and it is the hope of the Professional Panel of the BCS that the Code may be incorporated by reference into contracts as providing a standard to be invoked in case of dispute.

The Code of Conduct is a much shorter document, but more immediately comprehensible. It is binding on all members of the British Computer Society.

Copies of up-to-date versions of both codes are available from:

The Chief Executive
The British Computer Society
1 Sanford Street
Swindon SN1 1HJ

Tel: 01793–417417
Fax: 01793–480270

If anyone having work done for them by a member of the BCS feels that the work does not measure up to this Code of Conduct, they should immediately contact the BCS.

It must be emphasised that in the past there has not been extensive use of this disciplinary procedure—a fact which may reflect either the probity of BCS members or the ignorance of the public. However, it is the case that the BCS has been successful in encouraging members to resign whose activity is liable to bring the Society into disrepute.

The BCS also keeps a register of expert witnesses for the benefit of solicitors and others who need advice in disputes involving computer contracts and technology.

Finally, arbitration clauses in computer contracts have not been discussed in detail in this book since their format is indistinguishable from any other arbitration clauses. However, it is worth pointing out that the President of The Law Society may be thought, without being unkind or patronising, to be a less appropriate appointor of an arbitrator in computer contracts than the President of the British Computer Society. Anyone wishing to do this is requested to use the BCS's approved clause which is as follows:

In the event of any dispute or difference under or arising out of this Agreement either party may give notice thereof in writing to the other and the same shall be referred to the Arbitration of a person agreed upon or failing agreement within 14 days of the date of such notice of some person appointed by the President for the time being of the British Computer Society. Such Arbitration shall be in accordance with the provision of the Arbitration Act 1950 or any statutory modification or re-enactment thereof.

Anyone wishing to make use of this facility should contact either the Registrar or the Chief Executive of the BCS first.

13.1.2   Institute of Data Processing Management

This body is an amalgamation of two professional bodies—the Data Processing Management Association (founded in 1966) and the Institute for Data Processing (founded in 1967). It now numbers 6,500 members and 3,000 students.

The IDPM introduced in July 1989 a Code of Professional Conduct. The IDPM's present address is:

> Institute of Data Processing Management Limited
> IDPM House
> Edgington Way
> Ruxley Corner
> Sidcup
> Kent
> DA14 5HR
>
> Tel: 0181–308 0747
> Fax: 0181–308 0604

The President of the Institute of Data Processing Management could also be suggested as a potential nominator of an arbitrator in the appropriate clauses of computer contracts. He would, of course, be an alternative to the President of the British Computer Society.

13.2   Trade associations

13.2.1   Computing Services and Software Association

The Computing Services and Software Association was formed in 1975 as an amalgamation of two older associations. It has only corporate members (unlike the BCS and IDPM, both of which have personal membership). A condition of membership is adherence to a Code of Conduct (the newest edition is August 1980). Complaints of any infringement by a CSSA member should be addressed to:

> The Director General
> Computing Services and Software Association Ltd
> Hanover House
> 73/74 High Holborn
> London
> WC1V 6LE
>
> Tel: 0171–405 2171
> Fax: 0171–404 4119

The Association has powers to invoke sanctions against any member found to be infringing the code, though to date all fully investigated complaints have been more or less contractual misunderstandings.

The Association's consultancy, facilities management, contingency planning, education and training, bureau, and marketing groups have Codes of Practice and the third-party maintenance group is in the process of producing one.

13.2.2 Federation Against Software Theft (FAST)

The Federation Against Software Theft was formed in 1984. Its members are generally companies who produce or market software. It was a major lobbyist for the Copyright (Computer Software) Amendment Act 1985, and since then it has spearheaded prosecutions against those infringing software copyright and publicised methods of software protection.

Further information is available from:

Mr Geoffrey Webster, Chief Executive
Federation Against Software Theft
2 Lake End Court
Taplow
Maidenhead
Berks
SL6 0JQ

Tel: 01628–660377
Fax: 01628–660348

13.3 Other bodies

13.3.1 Office of Telecommunications (Oftel)

Under the Telecommunications Act of 1984, the Office of Telecommunications (Oftel) was established under a Director General of Telecommunications and Parts II and III of the Act describe his functions. These include in particular:

(1) Investigating complaints about the provision of telecommunications services and the supply of apparatus (s 49).
(2) Exercising powers under the Fair Trading Act 1973 and the Competition Act 1980 concurrently with the Director of Fair Trading in relation to monopoly situations and anti-competitive practices in telecommunications (s 50).
(3) Monitoring and enforcing conditions in telecommunications licences (s 16).

The majority of Oftel's functions are concerned with competition in the telecommunications industry, but obviously at least the three functions listed above and possibly others also have consumer aspects. Anyone with grievances on telecommunications matters should first try to resolve their complaint with the supplier of the service. However, if this does not produce a satisfactory solution, customers may well think it worthwhile contacting Oftel. They should note that the Director General has no responsibilities for any other aspects of computing except telecommunications. There are separate Advisory Committees on telecommunications for England, Scotland, Wales and Northern Ireland, but Oftel's Headquarters are to be found at:

> Office of Telecommunications (Oftel)
> Export House
> 50 Ludgate Hill
> London
> EC4M 7JJ
>
> Tel: 0171–634 8700
> Fax: 0171–634 8943

13.3.2   National Computing Centre (NCC)

The National Computing Centre was established in 1966, with the primary objective of 'promoting an increased and more effective use of computers in every field of national and commercial activity'.

The Centre is a non-profit-distributing organisation with revenue derived from members' subscriptions, government contracts for projects and sales of products and services. Many of the NCC's activities lie outside the scope of this book but readers may wish to be aware of three: a conciliation service, the escrow service and the NCC Legal Group. These are all run by NCC Services Ltd which is the trading subsidiary of the NCC.

Conciliation: The staff of the NCC will, when invited to do so, see both sides in a dispute, all on a without-prejudice basis, and consider the legal, commercial and technical issues. It is an informal procedure, leading to pragmatic solutions.

Escrow: The NCC provides what is probably the largest escrow arrangement in the world with about 1,800 software products in their safekeeping—see 3.3.1, 9, N.

For the NCC Legal Group see 13.5.3 below.

Anyone interested in any of these activities can contact the NCC at:

The National Computing Centre Ltd
Oxford Road
Manchester
M1 7ED

Tel: 0161–228 6333
Fax: 0161–228 2579

13.4   Public sector bodies

13.4.1   CCTA

The CCTA is the Government Centre for Information Systems responsible for stimulating and promoting the effective use of information systems in support of the efficient delivery of business objectives and improved quality of services by the public sector. It is part of the Office of Public Service under the Chancellor of the Duchy of Lancaster. Its customers are government departments, executive agencies and certain non-Crown bodies and for these organisations it provides a number of services including model agreements, assistance in procurement and legal advice including advice on contracts. It also has a commercial intelligence service and another of its roles is advice on standards.
Its address is:

CCTA
Rosebery Court
St Andrews Business Park
Norwich
NR7 OHS

Tel: 01603–704704
Fax: 01603–704817

13.4.2   HM Treasury (CUP and Public Sector Procurement)

The Central Unit on Procurement (formerly the Central Unit on Purchasing) is part of the HM Treasury's Procurement Group and provides advice and help to government departments to improve their procurement practice, and monitoring and reporting on their achievements. It also gives advice on capital works projects and promotion of quality standards.
CUP issues a number of guidance notes and No 42 'Contracting for the Provision of Services' is particularly relevant. It provides a menu of contract conditions, examples of letters and other supporting documentation.
Their address is:

> Central Unit on Procurement
> HM Treasury
> Allington Towers
> Allington Street
> London
> SW1E 5EB
>
> Tel: 0171–270 1638

The other half of HM Treasury's Procurement Group, called the Public Sector Procurement division, are the experts on public procurement policy, including international obligations (EC, GATT, EEA). Their address is also at Allington Towers and their telephone number is:

> 0171–270 1645 or 1647

13.4.3 SOCITM

Two organisations particularly serving the needs of local government may also be mentioned. The first is the Society of Information Technology Management. As its title suggests the organisation is not confined to local authority needs but much of its original focus was on public utilities and with liberalisation/privatisation it has increasingly turned its attention to local government. It is a professional organisation for officers responsible for recommending corporate IT policy and it serves 'to provide a focal point for IT and related issues, share experiences, promote the recognition of IT and influence legislation'. The society operates through regional branches co-ordinated by a national committee. It has local meetings on IT and a twice-yearly conference. It can be contacted at:

> Mr R P Griffith
> Secretary, SOCITM Office,
> PO Box 121
> Northampton
> NN4 6TG
>
> Tel and fax: 01604–674800

13.4.4 The Audit Commission

The Audit Commission for Local Authorities and the National Health Service in England and Wales is charged under s 26 of the Local Government Finance Act 1982 with carrying out studies designed to improve the economy, efficiency and effectiveness of local government. It can provide informal advice on contracts and it has produced a number of reports some of which deal with contractual issues. It can be contacted at:

Director of Audit Support
The Audit Commission
1 Vincent Square
London
SW1P 2PN

Tel: 0171–828 1212
Fax: 0171–976 6187

13.5   Special interest groups

13.5.1   Society for Computers and Law

This Society was founded in 1973 and now has nearly 2,000 members. It exists to encourage and develop both IT for lawyers and IT-related law. Hence it is interested in such topics as data protection and software ownership as well as computer contracts. It publishes a journal *Computers and Law* which includes articles on contracts as well as reports of leading IT cases and it sponsors talks and seminars (including branch meetings) on these topics. Those interested in the Society should contact:

The Administrative Secretary
Society for Computers and Law
10 Hurle Crescent
Clifton
Bristol
BS8 2TA

Tel: 0117–923 7393
Fax: 0117–923 9305

13.5.2   BCS Special Interest Groups

An aspect of the British Computer Society we have not touched on is its special interest groups. These bodies vary in size, scope and vigour, but usually provide a forum for talks and discussion. These groups include a word processing group, data protection group and a law group. Details of their activities are available from the British Computer Society [13.1.1]

245

13.5.3   NCC Legal Group

This is part of the NCC [13.3.2]. It provides informed comment to NCC members and issues a useful series of guidance notes on a number of IT contractual issues. It also provides first-line support on legal issues to its members, as well as briefings and seminars on legal matters.

13.5.4   LAMUG

The Local Authority Microcomputer User Group is a national organisation of local authorities using PCs and aims to share common experience. The group meets quarterly and issues a magazine, also quarterly. It can be contacted at:

> Mr J New
> Secretary, LAMUG
> Weymouth and Portland Borough Council
> 2a Spring Gardens
> Fortuneswell
> Portland
> Dorset
> DT5 1JG
>
> Tel: 01305–206272
> Fax: 01305–206276

13.6   User groups

All the main manufacturers of hardware, many of the smaller ones, many specialised bureaux and even some of the package software suppliers, have user groups. Their purpose is twofold: first, to provide a common front to the manufacturer/supplier when joint action is required, and generally to safeguard their members' interests; secondly, to act as a forum for the manufacturer/supplier when he wishes to announce improvements, new ranges of equipment or software, and so forth. It will be seen that these two activities can easily be in conflict, and it must be said that some user groups incline more to one aspect than the other. Some, for instance, are, in effect, the manufacturer's poodle, having an annual beano at the manufacturer's expense when they receive a pep-talk as to why their manufacturer's equipment is the best. Others have been formed from a common sense of frustration at the dilatoriness or inability of the manufacturer to put right genuine grievances. But even at their most docile they provide an insurance to their users. If you have equipment that is faulty, or package software which is unreliable (even though hitherto your supplier's record has been good), the user group gives you an opportunity to compare your experiences with others and, if you think the supplier is at fault, to present a common front.

Again, if you are looking for mutual back-up facilities [8.1.2], your first requirement will be another user of the same equipment or package as near as possible to you geographically. A user group meeting will enable you to canvass a number of possible firms (though, to be fair, manufacturers are usually very willing to put their users in touch with each other for this purpose anyway).

Enhancements are also often fostered through user groups. You may wish for some particular additional feature in a software package; you cannot put it in yourself either because you have no source language form of the package or because you are debarred from doing so contractually. But if you can find other like-minded users, your chances of persuading the supplier to include that feature as a standard option in the package are greatly enhanced.

Or perhaps it isn't a question of software, but rather some hardware enhancement. Your manufacturer A, forces all his users to have disks of a certain size, or printers of a certain speed, and you are aware that manufacturer B (whose hardware is comparable and compatible) has equipment of the type you need. Your hardware maintenance contract debars you from attaching B's disks or printers to A's processor. But a joint simultaneous revolt by all A's users might force A either to introduce peripherals of the type required, or even to sanction direct interfacing of B's peripherals. Users contemplating a mixed shop [8.5.1] would do well to consider this possibility and make discreet enquiries among their fellow users before going off on their own.

And finally there is the opportunity of banding together in the face of disaster. Hardware manufacturers and suppliers of packaged software have gone out of business before now. This is not a common event, but when it does happen their wretched users are in an unenviable position because they are virtually stripped of all maintenance cover. Individually, there is usually little they can do, but as a group they may be able to find someone to take over at least the maintenance aspects, and possibly even part of the manufacturing or software function. In extreme cases they may even raise the finance to take over some of the sinking company themselves.

If the disaster is solely on the software side, it may be possible to identify the individual programmers who worked on the programs for the now defunct software house and offer them the business of software maintenance. Again such an offer from a user group will be very much more effective than an individual user trying this on his own.

This situation, involving the total collapse of a supplier or manufacturer, is mercifully rare. But the user group can still find itself faced with very similar problems without such a dramatic failure. This can arise when a manufacturer decides he no longer wishes to support (ie maintain) a particular piece of hardware or software. This usually goes through a number of stages, of which the first is likely to be an announcement by the manufacturer that he is no longer making or supplying the particular piece of hardware or software, though he has no plans to phase out its maintenance. Nevertheless, in this situation, no manufacturer wishes to keep large numbers of staff working on obsolete equipment—indeed, the staff themselves do not like it and, in a highly mobile industry, this will be sufficient to cause some of them to seek employment elsewhere. Since the user base of the equipment is being reduced, the manufacturer will be under pressure to redeploy his staff, both for financial and personnel reasons.

A user faced with this situation usually has about a couple of years before facing the total loss of manufacturer's support. His first question must be to see what the manufacturer is offering instead; perhaps this is the right moment for him to change to a new machine—or even another manufacturer. Perhaps what is being withdrawn is software and the supplier is offering a very much better alternative. The user must see whether this better alternative is compatible with his requirement and his other software; if it is, he will probably be well advised to change. Users who have changes of this nature forced upon them by the manufacturer will be in a good bargaining position (if they can present a united front through their user group) to negotiate special terms for existing users—perhaps a healthy discount, or some other hardware or software provided or maintained free—since it will very much suit the manufacturer to have all his users abandon the obsolete equipment at the same time as he does. If, on the other hand, the alternatives offered do not look attractive, the user group can either try to force the manufacturer to make them more attractive (perhaps by keeping some aspect of compatibility), or can even, in extreme cases, refuse to change and at the same time obtain a good deal of publicity for their case.

The power that user groups wield should not be exaggerated. No manufacturer will automatically fulfil all user group demands. But equally, manufacturers are highly sensitive to criticism from their user groups, if only because such criticism is likely, if well publicised, to impair their future sales. The situation produces an uneasy ambivalent relationship between manufacturers and their user groups which must be exploited by both sides with care, reserving confrontation for really important issues, and proceeding in a spirit of give-and-take on smaller issues.

With this in mind, it is recommended that all purchasers of hardware and package software (and bureau users)—particularly those using specialised services—enquire from their manufacturer/supplier about the relevant user group, and join at the first opportunity. If there is no user group, they should think seriously of forming one—neither so as to be the manufacturer's poodle nor his hornet (for both extremes are to be avoided) but so as to exchange ideas and provide mutual assistance.

Precedents

Introduction to precedents

Introduction to precedents

The drafting of a good precedent is comparable to the writing of good software. We have endeavoured to think through all the error conditions likely and unlikely, but cannot guarantee to have eliminated all bugs any more than a software house can.

The precedents follow the general structure of the book, except that PCs seem not to merit separate treatment (Chapter 4) and (as we point out in Chapter 7) new finance leases are less frequent than before and while the points in Chapter 7 may prove helpful in interpreting finance leases, a precedent for such a lease is lengthy and likely to be of limited value.

The rest of the precedents are, we hope, straightforward though we should point out that we have included a set of hardware maintenance clauses in the Rental Agreement (B) since in our experience separate maintenance agreements on rental are rare.

At the risk of repeating what was said in the preface, we must point out that readers should study the relevant sections of the text of this book before using any precedent. To assist the reader we have in many instances provided cross-reference numbers in square brackets after the clause titles to identify the sections of the text. Readers should also bear in mind that any attempt to be exhaustive would have tripled the length of this book. We have therefore been selective in the circumstances covered by the precedents. In many cases more than one precedent is required and the Turnkey Precedent (O) is an attempt to show how in one instance this might be done and when the reader is referred back to clauses in earlier precedents he may have to alter the titles of the parties and make some other minor amendments in order to apply the clause.

We have used square brackets to indicate alternatives [either this clause] [or that] or to indicate material which may be omitted.

Notes and commentary on the precedents are contained within square brackets and can be recognised by the smaller type size. Words or numbers which are examples, and which the user will doubtless wish to vary, eg 'within *14* days', have been indicated with the use of italics.

Precedent A

Hardware sale and installation agreement

THIS AGREEMENT is made the   day of   19

PARTIES:

(1) COMPUTER COMPANY [LIMITED] [PLC] whose registered office is at

('the Supplier')

(2) CUSTOMER [LIMITED] [PLC] whose registered office is at

('the Customer')

RECITAL:

The Supplier has agreed to supply and install certain computer equipment for the Customer upon the terms and conditions hereinafter contained

NOW IT IS HEREBY AGREED as follows:

1 Definitions

In this Agreement, unless the context otherwise requires, the following expressions have the following meanings:

1	'the Equipment' [2.1.1]	means the computer equipment specified in the Schedule and any replacement equipment and/or parts provided pursuant to Clause 18 [and the Integral Software] as the context admits or the case may require
	['the Integral Software' [2.8.3]	means the computer software embedded in or forming an integral part of the Equipment as specified in the Schedule]

255

'the Price'	means the price for the Equipment and the services to be provided hereunder as specified in the Schedule
['the Equipment Price'	means that part of the Price payable in respect of the Equipment as specified in the Schedule]

[**Note:** The definition of 'the Equipment Price' will only be required if clause 3(2) is used (currency rate fluctuation).]

'the Off-Loading Point'	means the Customer's off-loading point specified in the Schedule
'the Location' [2.1.2]	means the Customer's computer room in which the Equipment is to be installed as specified in the Schedule
'the Delivery Date' [2.3.7]	means the delivery date specified in the Schedule or such extended date as may be granted pursuant to Clause 15
'the Commissioning Date' [2.3.4]	means the date on which the Equipment is accepted by the Customer pursuant to Clause 12 or one month after operational use by the Customer of the Equipment has begun, whichever shall be the earlier

[**Note:** The definition of 'the Commissioning Date' is designed to protect the supplier from the situation where the customer unreasonably refuses to accept the equipment yet brings it into operational use. In those circumstances the balance of the price will be payable after the expiry of one month—see clause 3(1).]

'business day'	means a day other than a Saturday, Sunday or a public holiday

2   Products and services to be provided [2.1.1]

(1) The Supplier hereby agrees to:

(a) sell the Equipment to the Customer free from any encumbrances;

(b) deliver the Equipment to and install it at the Location on the Delivery Date;

(c) provide the other services hereinafter described

upon the terms and conditions hereinafter contained

[(2) The Supplier reserves the right prior to delivery of the Equipment to substitute an alternative item of equipment for any item of equipment agreed to be supplied hereunder provided that such substitution will not materially affect the performance of such equipment and will not result in any increase in the Price]

> [**Note:** If the customer is unhappy about allowing substitutions he should delete this sub-clause. Any substitutions will then have to be agreed to in writing by the customer—see clause 29.]

(3) Operating supplies such as disk packs, stationery, printing cartridges and similar accessories are not supplied as part of the Equipment

3 Price and payment [2.2.1]

(1) The Price shall be paid by the Customer as to *15* per cent upon the signing of this Agreement [(by way of a deposit)] [(by way of a part payment)] and as to the balance upon the Commissioning Date

[Currency rate [2.2.4]

(2)(a) The Equipment Price is based on an exchange rate between the United States dollar and the United Kingdom pound sterling of $*1.61* to £*1* ('the Contract Rate'). If on the date on which the Supplier pays its supplier for the Equipment ('the Payment Date') the dollar value of the pound shall have fallen by *2* cents or more below the Contract Rate then the Supplier shall be entitled to increase the Equipment Price to compensate the Supplier for such fall in the dollar value of the pound but not further or otherwise. The amount of such increase shall be paid by the Customer on the Commissioning Date

(b) For the purposes of paragraph (a) above the value of the pound on the Payment Date shall be taken as [the arithmetic average of the buying and selling dollar prices of the pound quoted by *ABC* Bank plc as their closing prices on the business day immediately preceding the Payment Date]

> [**Notes:** The use of sub-clause (2) should be examined critically by the customer who should consider the following:
>   (1) The clause assumes that the supplier will be purchasing with dollars and selling in pounds. If the supplier is purchasing in pounds then the clause is unnecessary.
>   (2) Strictly speaking, any adjustment to the price should be crystallised on the date on which the supplier buys his dollars not when he pays for the equipment. However, if a supplier is constantly purchasing dollars this date might be difficult to establish. It is

therefore suggested that the date of payment be used; although this does to some extent leave the situation open to manipulation by the supplier who could choose a payment date (within the constraints of its contractual arrangements with its own supplier) when the dollar value of the pound is low and then pay with dollars already purchased at a more favourable rate.

(3) It should be noted that the clause does not provide for the price to be reduced in the event of a rise in the value of the pound. Also, some of the equipment may not be purchased in the US (or not in dollars) in which case any increase should only apply to the equipment which is.

(4) There may be more than one US manufacturer delivering to the Supplier on different dates.]

[Price adjustment on long deliveries [2.2.4]

(3) The Price and any additional charges payable under this Agreement are in accordance with the Supplier's standard scale of charges in force on the date of this Agreement. The Supplier shall be entitled at any time before the period of *30* days immediately preceding the Delivery Date to vary the Price and any additional charges payable under this Agreement to accord with any changes in the Supplier's standard scale of charges and to give written notice of such variation to the Customer. This Agreement shall be deemed to be varied accordingly by such notice of variation unless the Customer shall within *14* days of the receipt of such notice terminate this Agreement by giving notice in writing to the Supplier in which event neither party shall have any liability to the other in respect of such termination]

(4) The Price and any additional charges payable under this Agreement are exclusive of Value Added Tax which shall be paid by the Customer at the rate and in the manner for the time being prescribed by law

(5) Any charges payable by the Customer under this Agreement in addition to the Price shall be paid on the Commissioning Date

(6) If any sum payable under this Agreement is not paid within *7* days after the due date then (without prejudice to the Supplier's other rights and remedies) the Supplier reserves the right to charge interest on such sum on a day to day basis (as well after as before any judgment) from the date or last date for payment thereof to the date of actual payment (both dates inclusive) at the rate of *2* per cent above the base rate of *ABC* Bank plc (or such other London Clearing Bank as the Supplier may nominate) from time to time in force compounded quarterly. Such interest shall be paid on demand by the Supplier.

4 Title and risk [2.8.1, 2.8.3]

(1) The legal and beneficial ownership of the Equipment shall pass to the Customer on payment in full and in cleared funds of the Price and any other sums which may then be due under this Agreement

(2) Risk in the Equipment shall pass to the Customer on delivery of the Equipment to [the Off-Loading Point] [the Location] and accordingly the Customer shall be responsible for insuring the Equipment against all normal risks with effect from the time risk passes

[(3) In relation to each item of Integral Software the copyright, design right or other intellectual property rights in which are owned by a third party ('the software owner') as identified in the Schedule:

(a) the performance by the Supplier of its obligations under this Agreement is in all respects conditional upon the Customer entering into on the date of this Agreement an end-user licence agreement with the software owner or (as the case may be) a sub-licence agreement with the Supplier (in either case a 'Licence Agreement') governing the use by the Customer of that item of Integral Software as may be required by the software owner in the form annexed to this Agreement; and

(b) the Customer agrees with the Supplier as a term of this Agreement to be bound and abide by the terms and conditions of each such Licence Agreement.]

[(4) In relation to each item of Integral Software the copyright, design right or other intellectual property rights in which are owned by the Supplier as identified in the Schedule:

(a) the Customer is purchasing the media on which such Integral Software is recorded or embedded only;

(b) nothing contained in this Agreement shall be construed as an assignment or transfer of any copyright, design right or other intellectual property rights in such Integral Software, all of which rights are reserved by the Supplier;

(c) the Supplier hereby grants to the Customer a non-exclusive and (except as provided in paragraph (e) below) non-transferable licence to use such Integral Software in the form in which it is embedded in or integrated into the Equipment at the time of delivery to the Customer as an integral part of the Equipment for use in conjunction with the remainder of the Equipment but subject to the condition that the Equipment is used only for its intended purpose and for the Customer's internal business purposes only;

(d) except as expressly permitted by this sub-clause (4) and save to the extent and in the circumstances expressly required to be permitted

259

by law, the Customer shall not rent, lease, sub-license, loan, copy, modify, adapt, merge, translate, reverse engineer, decompile, disassemble or create derivative works based on the whole or any part of such Integral Software or use, reproduce or deal in such Integral Software or any part thereof in any way;

(e) the Customer shall be entitled to transfer the benefit of the licence granted pursuant to paragraph (c) ('the Licence') and the right to transfer the Licence in terms of this paragraph (e) to any purchaser of the Equipment provided the purchaser agrees before making such purchase to be bound by the terms of this sub-clause (4) including the provisions of this paragraph (e). If the purchaser does not accept such terms then the Licence shall automatically and immediately terminate;

(f) the Licence shall remain effective without limit in time until it is terminated in accordance with paragraph (e) or until the Customer shall terminate it by erasing or destroying such Integral Software. The Licence shall also terminate automatically and immediately if the Customer shall fail to abide by the terms of this sub-clause (4). Upon termination of the Licence, for whatever reason, the Customer shall deliver up to the Supplier the media on which such Integral Software is recorded or embedded (and all copies thereof (if any) in the Customer's possession) or, at the Supplier's option, shall erase or otherwise destroy such Integral Software (and all copies thereof (if any) in the Customer's possession) and shall certify to the Supplier that the same has been done.]

[(5)   The Price includes the right for the Customer to use the Integral Software in terms of sub-clauses (3) and (4).]

5   Location preparation [2.6.3]

The Supplier shall supply to the Customer in reasonable time before delivery of the Equipment such information and assistance as may be necessary to enable the Customer to prepare the Location for the installation of the Equipment and to provide proper environmental and operational conditions for the efficient working and maintenance of the Equipment and for this purpose the Supplier will make available to the Customer free of charge the advice of a suitably qualified engineer. The Customer shall at its own expense prepare the Location and provide such environmental and operational conditions prior to delivery

[**Note:** It will be in the interests of the customer to require the supplier to provide the necessary advice in writing. This may avoid arguments at a later stage if it is alleged that the customer failed to prepare the location properly.]

6   Information and access [2.6.1]

(1) The Customer undertakes to provide the Supplier promptly with any information which the Supplier may reasonably require from time to time to enable the Supplier to proceed uninterruptedly with the performance of this Agreement

(2) The Customer shall, for the purposes of this Agreement, afford to the authorised personnel of the Supplier during normal working hours full and safe access to the Location and shall provide adequate free working space and such other facilities as may be necessary for the installation of the Equipment

> [**Note:** If the proposed location is particularly sensitive then the customer may wish to restrict access to the supplier's named personnel only. The customer may also wish to reserve a right to refuse to admit persons who are in its reasonable opinion unfit to be on its premises.]

[7   Pre-delivery tests [2.3.2]

(1) The Supplier shall submit the Equipment to its standard works tests ('the Works Tests') before delivery to the Customer. The Supplier shall promptly supply to the Customer on request copies of the specification of the Works Tests and a certificate that the Equipment has passed the same

(2) The Customer or its authorised representative may attend the Works Tests. If the Works Tests are held in the presence of the Customer or its authorised representative, the Supplier will charge the Customer its standard fee therefor. The Supplier shall give the Customer at least 7 days' written notice of the date and time at which the Supplier proposes to carry out the Works Tests. In the event of any delay or failure by the Customer or its authorised representative in attending the Works Tests at such time, the Supplier reserves the right to proceed with the Works Tests without the Customer]

8   Delivery [2.3.3]

either:

[(1) On the Delivery Date the Supplier shall deliver the Equipment to the Off-Loading Point but shall not be responsible for off-loading the Equipment or moving it to the Location which shall be undertaken by the Customer at its own expense]

or:

[(1)(a) On the Delivery Date the Supplier shall deliver the Equipment to the Off-Loading Point and then move it to the Location

(b) The Supplier shall not carry out or be responsible for the removal of doors, widening of entrances or any other structural work of any description for the purpose of moving the Equipment from the Off-Loading Point to the Location, which work shall be undertaken by the Customer at its own expense prior to delivery

(c) The Customer shall be responsible for all reasonable costs incurred by the Supplier in providing special equipment, personnel or works necessary to move the Equipment from the Off-Loading Point to the Location. Such costs shall be paid by the Customer in addition to the Price]

either:

[(2) [Save for the special delivery costs referred to in sub-clause (1)(c)] the Price includes the cost of delivery of the Equipment to the [Off-Loading Point] [the Location] by any method of transport selected by the Supplier]

or:

[(2) The Price does not include the cost of transportation of the Equipment [from the Supplier's premises] [within the United Kingdom] or any other delivery costs, which shall be paid by the Customer in addition to the Price]

[(3) All packing cases, skids, drums and other packing materials used for delivery of the Equipment to the Location must be returned by the Customer to the Supplier in good condition and at the Customer's expense. The Supplier reserves the right to charge for any such cases and materials not so returned]

9   Installation [2.3.3]

(1) The Supplier shall install the Equipment at the Location on the Delivery Date

(2) If in the reasonable opinion of the Supplier it is necessary to remove or otherwise disconnect any of the Customer's existing equipment at the Location in order to carry out the installation of the Equipment, then the Customer shall permit, and obtain all necessary consents for, such removal and/or disconnection and shall give the Supplier all necessary assistance to enable such work to be carried out

10   Time [not] of the essence [2.3.7]

The time of delivery and installation of the Equipment shall [not] be of the essence of this Agreement

[Notes:

(1) Time of delivery and installation will be of the essence in this agreement by virtue of the fact that a delivery date is specified (although it avoids argument to incorporate an express provision to that effect). If the supplier wishes to avoid the consequences of this he should incorporate this clause specifying that time will not be of the essence. Where time is not of the essence and the supplier does not deliver by the delivery date then, unless the supplier quickly remedies its default, the customer should serve notice on the supplier requiring him to complete within a reasonable time:

'The time for delivery and installation of the equipment under the above-mentioned agreement has passed. We now require you to deliver and install the equipment no later than *31 December 1995*. Failure to do this will entitle us to terminate the agreement and, whether or not we terminate, to recover from you all damages and costs resulting from such failure.'

One means of stipulating a revised delivery date would be to obtain a new estimate from the supplier. It would then be difficult for the supplier to argue that the time allowed was unreasonable.

(2) It should be remembered that even if time is made of the essence, the supplier will be allowed an extension of time for performance in the circumstances specified in clause 15.

(3) The supplier may only agree to a specific delivery date if its liability for delay is confined to liquidated damages—see 2.3.7.]

11   Post-delivery tests [2.3.4]

(1) The Supplier shall, within *14* days after the Equipment has been installed, submit the Equipment to the Supplier's standard installation tests ('the Installation Tests') to ensure that the Equipment and every part thereof is in full working order. The Supplier shall supply to the Customer copies of the specification and results of the Installation Tests

(2) If any part of the Equipment fails to pass the Installation Tests then, if required by the Customer, the Installation Tests shall be repeated on such part of the Equipment within a reasonable time thereafter

(3) The Customer or its authorised representative may attend the Installation Tests. The Supplier shall give the Customer at least *3* days' written notice of the date and time at which the Supplier proposes to carry out the Installation Tests. In the event of any delay or failure by the Customer or its authorised representative in attending the Installation Tests at such time the Supplier reserves the right to proceed with the Installation Tests which will then be deemed to have been carried out in the presence of the Customer and the results thereof accepted by the Customer

[Note: Three days' notice is probably sufficient, as the tests will be carried out on the customer's premises. However, if the customer requires the tests to be carried out in the presence of his consultant a longer period of notice may have to be negotiated. In practice, it will be difficult for the supplier to carry out tests in the absence of the customer as they will have to be carried out on the customer's premises.]

12   Acceptance [2.3.6]

Once the Equipment and every part thereof has successfully passed the Installation Tests the Equipment shall be accepted by the Customer and the Customer shall, if required by the Supplier, sign a commissioning certificate in the form annexed hereto acknowledging such acceptance

[13   Electromagnetic compatibility [2.7.3]

(1) In this Clause the expression 'Electromagnetic Equipment' means any part or parts of the Equipment which are electric or electronic and covered by the Electromagnetic Compatibility Regulations 1992

(2) The Supplier warrants to the Customer that at the date hereof all the Electromagnetic Equipment complies fully with the Electromagnetic Compatibility Regulations 1992

(3) The Customer undertakes to the Supplier that it will not make any modification to the Electromagnetic Equipment without the prior written consent of the Supplier]

[14   Telecommunications [2.7.4]

(1) In this Clause the expression 'Relevant Equipment' means any part of the Equipment which is intended to be connected to any telecommunication system which is, or is to be connected to, a public telecommunication system

(2) The Supplier warrants to the Customer that at the date hereof the Relevant Equipment is approved by the Secretary of State for Trade and Industry for connection to the telecommunication systems specified in the instructions for use of the Relevant Equipment subject to the conditions set out therein but does not warrant the continuance of any such approval

(3) If after the date hereof the Secretary of State or any person to whom he has delegated his powers requires the Relevant Equipment or any part thereof to be modified as a condition of the continuance of any

such approval the Supplier reserves the right to make such modification at the Customer's expense

(4) If the Customer connects the Relevant Equipment to any telecommunication system the Customer shall be responsible for obtaining the consent of the owner of that system (if necessary) to such connection and for complying with all conditions relating thereto

(5) The Customer undertakes to the Supplier that it will not make any modification to the Relevant Equipment without the prior written consent of the Supplier

(6) Where any data transmission speeds are given by the Supplier in relation to the Equipment, such speeds are at all times subject to any conditions attached to the use of the relevant modem or telecommunication equipment at the speeds indicated and to the capability of such modem or other telecommunication equipment to achieve such speeds]

15   Force majeure

Notwithstanding anything else contained in this Agreement, neither party shall be liable for any delay in performing its obligations hereunder if such delay is caused by circumstances beyond its reasonable control (including without limitation any delay caused by any act or omission of the other party) provided however that any delay by a sub-contractor or supplier of the party so delaying shall not relieve that party from liability for delay except where such delay is beyond the reasonable control of the sub-contractor or supplier concerned. Subject to the party so delaying promptly notifying the other party in writing of the reasons for the delay (and the likely duration of the delay), the performance of such party's obligations shall be suspended during the period that the said circumstances persist and such party shall be granted an extension of time for performance equal to the period of the delay. Save where such delay is caused by the act or omission of the other party (in which event the rights, remedies and liabilities of the parties shall be those conferred and imposed by the other terms of this Agreement and by law):

(1) any costs arising from such delay shall be borne by the party incurring the same;

(2) either party may, if such delay continues for more than 5 weeks, terminate this Agreement forthwith on giving notice in writing to the other in which event neither party shall be liable to the other by reason of such termination [save that the Customer shall pay the Supplier a reasonable sum in respect of any work carried out by it prior to such termination and for that purpose the Supplier

may deduct such sum from any amounts previously paid by the Customer under this Agreement (the balance (if any) of which shall be refunded to the Customer whether paid by way of a deposit or otherwise)]

[Notes:

(1) Even if time is made of the essence in relation to a particular obligation this clause will override that provision to give the delaying party an extension of time for performance without incurring any liability for the delay.

(2) A frequent problem with a clause of this nature is that the delaying party is inclined to seek its protection even if the delay is due to its own default. This can be avoided to some extent by requiring the delaying party promptly to notify the reason for the delay (which can then be investigated) and by providing the other party with an opportunity to terminate the agreement if the delay continues for an unreasonable period.

(3) Many customers will refuse to entertain a clause of this nature if it excuses defaults by sub-contractors or suppliers. Customers will argue, perhaps rightly so, that it is up to the supplier to ensure that his sub-contractors and suppliers are reliable.

(4) Where a delay does occur it will be in the interests of both parties to ensure that a proper record of the period of the delay is kept and that the extended date for performance is confirmed in writing.]

16   Customer's default [2.3.7]

If the Supplier is prevented or delayed from performing its obligations under this Agreement by reason of any act or omission of the Customer (other than a delay by the Customer for which the Customer is excused under Clause 15) then the Customer will pay to the Supplier all reasonable costs, charges and losses sustained or incurred by the Supplier as a result (including without limitation the cost of storage and insurance of the Equipment). The Supplier shall promptly notify the Customer in writing of any claim which it may have under this Clause giving such particulars thereof as it is then able to provide

17   Cancellation [2.4.1]

(1) If the Customer wishes to cancel this Agreement in respect of all or any part of the Equipment (other than for any breach of this Agreement by the Supplier as would entitle the Customer to terminate) then the Customer shall be entitled so to do at any time up to *14* days prior to the Delivery Date upon giving written notice to the Supplier and upon paying to the Supplier as agreed and liquidated cancellation charges:

(a) a sum equal to *6* per cent of the price of the equipment cancelled; and

(b) a sum equal to *12* per cent of such price reduced by *1* per cent in respect of each complete calendar month unexpired between the date of cancellation and the Delivery Date

[(2) The amount of the Customer's deposit paid under Clause 3(1), if forfeited to the Supplier, shall be deducted from the cancellation charges payable under sub-clause (1)

(3) Until the Supplier shall have received such payment, the Customer's notice of termination shall be of no effect and the Supplier may treat this Agreement as subsisting]

[**Note:** If a deposit has been taken, the supplier may be content simply to keep that sum on a cancellation, in which case this clause will be unnecessary.]

18 Termination [2.4.1]

(1) This Agreement may be terminated forthwith by either party on giving notice in writing to the other if the other party shall have a receiver or administrative receiver appointed or shall pass a resolution for winding-up (otherwise than for the purpose of a bona fide scheme of solvent amalgamation or reconstruction) or a court of competent jurisdiction shall make an order to that effect or if the other party shall become subject to an administration order or shall enter into any voluntary arrangement with its creditors or shall cease or threaten to cease to carry on business

(2) Any termination under sub-clause (1) shall discharge the parties from any liability for further performance of this Agreement and in the case of a termination by the Supplier shall entitle the Supplier to enter any of the Customer's premises and recover any equipment and materials the property of the Supplier (and so that the Customer hereby irrevocably licenses the Supplier, its employees and agents to enter any such premises for that purpose) and also to be paid a reasonable sum for any work carried out by it prior to such termination and in the case of a termination by the Customer shall entitle the Customer to be repaid forthwith any sums previously paid under this Agreement (whether paid by way of a deposit or otherwise) and to recover from the Supplier the amount of any [direct] loss or damage sustained or incurred by the Customer as a consequence of such termination

(3) Any termination of this Agreement (howsoever occasioned) shall not affect any accrued rights or liabilities of either party nor shall it affect the coming into force or the continuance in force of any provision hereof

which is expressly or by implication intended to come into or continue in force on or after such termination

19   Warranties [and performance] [2.3.8]

(1)(a) The Supplier warrants that the Equipment will be free from defects in materials, workmanship and installation for a period of *12* months after the Commissioning Date ('the Warranty Period')

(b) If the Supplier receives written notice from the Customer of any breach of the said warranty then the Supplier shall at its own expense and within a reasonable time after receiving such notice, repair or, at its option, replace the Equipment or such parts of it as are defective or otherwise remedy such defect provided that the Supplier shall have no liability or obligations under the said warranty unless it shall have received written notice of the defect in question no later than the expiry of the Warranty Period. The legal and beneficial ownership of the Equipment or any defective parts shall revert to the Supplier upon the replacement of the Equipment or such defective parts whereupon the legal and beneficial ownership of the replacement equipment or parts shall vest in the Customer

> [Note: Some warranty provisions provide that replacement parts will themselves be subject to a 12 months' warranty period with effect from the date of replacement.]

(c) The Supplier shall have no liability or obligations under the said warranty other than to remedy breaches thereof by the provision of materials and services within a reasonable time and without charge to the Customer. If the Supplier shall fail to comply with such obligations its liability for such failure shall be limited to a sum equal to the Price. The foregoing states the entire liability of the Supplier, whether in contract or tort, for defects in the Equipment notified to it after the Commissioning Date other than liability assumed under Clause 27

(d) The said warranty is contingent upon the proper use of the Equipment by the Customer and does not cover any part of the Equipment which has been modified without the Supplier's prior written consent or which has been subjected to unusual physical or electrical stress or on which the original identification marks have been removed or altered. Nor will such warranty apply if repair or parts replacement is required as a result of causes other than ordinary use including without limitation accident, hazard, misuse or failure or fluctuation of electric power, air conditioning, humidity control or other environmental conditions

> [Note: A warranty of this nature will be of less importance if the customer immediately takes out a maintenance contract with the supplier. However,

where the supplier has built a contingency element into the price to cover his warranty obligations the customer will wish to ensure that such contingency is taken into account when assessing the first year's maintenance charges.]

(2) The Supplier warrants to the Customer that the Equipment complies fully as to noise heat radiation and all other characteristics with the requirements in the Annex to EC Council Directive 90/270/EEC and in particular that the display screens and keyboards comply fully with the said Annex

(3) The Supplier does not give any warranty that the Equipment is fit for any particular purpose unless that purpose is specifically advised to the Supplier in writing by the Customer and the Supplier confirms in writing that the Equipment can fulfil that particular purpose

[(4) The Supplier does not warrant that the Equipment will achieve any particular performance criteria unless:

(a) the Supplier has specifically guaranteed such criteria in writing subject to specified tolerances in an agreed sum as liquidated damages; and

(b) the environmental conditions specified by the Supplier are maintained

The payment by the Supplier of such liquidated damages shall be in full satisfaction of any liability of the Supplier in respect of the Equipment failing to achieve such performance criteria]

(5) The express terms of this Agreement are in lieu of all warranties, conditions, terms, undertakings and obligations implied by statute, common law, custom, trade usage, course of dealing or otherwise, all of which are hereby excluded to the fullest extent permitted by law.

20 Customer's Warranty

The Customer hereby warrants to the Supplier that the Customer has not been induced to enter into this Agreement by any prior representations or warranties, whether oral or in writing, except as specifically contained in this Agreement and the Customer hereby irrevocably and unconditionally waives any right it may have to claim damages for any misrepresentation not contained in this Agreement or for breach of any warranty not contained herein (unless such misrepresentation or warranty was made fraudulently) and/or to rescind this Agreement.

[Note: At first sight this may appear harsh on the customer, but it will be in the best interests of the customer to incorporate important representations into the agreement by specific reference, rather than rely on oral promises or general descriptions. It will probably not be

possible to bind the customer to waive damages for fraudulent
misrepresentation.]

21   Confidentiality [2.6.2, 2.7.1]

Each party shall treat as confidential all information obtained from the
other pursuant to this Agreement and shall not divulge such information
to any person (except to such party's own employees and then only
to those employees who need to know the same) without the other party's
prior written consent provided that this Clause shall not extend to
information which was rightfully in the possession of such party prior
to the commencement of the negotiations leading to this Agreement,
which is already public knowledge or becomes so at at a future date
(otherwise than as a result of a breach of this Clause) or which is trivial
or obvious. Each party shall ensure that its employees are aware of
and comply with the provisions of this Clause. If the Supplier shall
appoint any sub-contractor then the Supplier may disclose confidential
information to such sub-contractor subject to such sub-contractor giving
the Customer an undertaking in similar terms to the provisions of this
Clause. The foregoing obligations as to confidentiality shall survive any
termination of this Agreement

> [**Note:** Pre-contract disclosures should, of course, be covered by a separate
> confidentiality undertaking — see Precedent U.]

22   Operating manuals and training

(1) The Supplier shall provide the Customer with *2* copies of a set of
operating manuals containing sufficient information for the proper
operation of the Equipment. If the Customer requires further copies
of such operating manuals then these will be provided by the Supplier
in accordance with its standard scale of charges from time to time in
force

(2) The Supplier shall provide training in the use of the Equipment for
the Customer's staff as set out in the Schedule. Any additional training
required by the Customer shall be provided by the Supplier in accordance
with its standard scale of charges from time to time in force

23   Removal of labels [2.6.5]

The Customer shall not change, remove or obscure any labels, plates,
insignia, lettering or other markings which are on the Equipment at
the time of installation thereof

[24 Maintenance [2.6.4]

The parties undertake to enter into a maintenance agreement on the Commissioning Date in respect of the Equipment in the form of the draft annexed hereto]

> [**Note:** Alternatively, the parties could enter into a maintenance agreement at the same time as this agreement, such agreement to commence on the Commissioning Date or perhaps on the expiry of the warranty period under clause 19.]

[25 Export Control [2.9.1]

The Equipment is subject to Export Control imposed by the Department of Commerce of the United States of America and is restricted to resale in the United Kingdom]

> [**Note:** This clause will apply only to equipment of United States origin.]

26 Intellectual property rights indemnity [2.8.1]

(1) The Supplier will indemnify the Customer and keep the Customer fully and effectively indemnified on demand against all costs, claims, demands, expenses and liabilities of whatsoever nature arising out of or in connection with any claim that the normal use or possession of the Equipment infringes the intellectual property rights (including without limitation any patent, copyright, registered design, design right or trademark) of any third party, subject to the following conditions:

(a) the Customer shall promptly notify the Supplier in writing of any allegations of infringement of which it has notice and will not make any admissions without the Supplier's prior written consent;

(b) the Customer, at the Supplier's request and expense, shall allow the Supplier [(subject to paragraph (c) below)] to conduct and/or settle all negotiations and litigation resulting from any such claim;

[(c) the conduct by the Supplier of any such negotiations or litigation shall be conditional upon the Supplier:

(i) giving to the Customer such reasonable security as shall from time to time be required by the Customer to cover the amount ascertained or agreed or estimated, as the case may be, of any compensation, damages, expenses and costs for which the Customer may become liable; and

(ii) taking over such conduct within a reasonable time after being notified of the claim in question]

271

(d) the Customer shall, at the request of the Supplier, afford all reasonable assistance with such negotiations or litigation, and shall be reimbursed by the Supplier for any out of pocket expenses incurred in so doing

(2) The indemnity given under sub-clause (1) above will not apply to infringement arising out of the use of the Equipment or any part thereof in combination with any equipment and/or computer programs not supplied or approved by the Supplier for use with the Equipment

(3) If the Customer's normal use or possession of the Equipment is held by a court of competent jurisdiction to constitute an infringement of a third party's intellectual property rights or if the Supplier is advised by legal counsel that such use or possession is likely to constitute such an infringement then the Supplier shall promptly and at its own expense:

(a) procure for the Customer the right to continue using and possessing the Equipment; or

(b) modify or replace the Equipment (without detracting from its overall performance) so as to avoid the infringement (in which event the Supplier shall compensate the Customer for the amount of any direct loss and/or damage sustained or incurred by the Customer during such modification or replacement); or

(c) if (a) or (b) cannot be accomplished on reasonable terms, remove the Equipment from the Location and refund the Price to the Customer

[**Note:** Some contracts provide for the price to be refunded less depreciation. This may be inadequate if the customer has to purchase new equipment at much greater cost.]

(4) The foregoing states the Supplier's entire liability to the Customer in respect of the infringement of the intellectual property rights of any third party

27   Liability

(1) The Supplier shall indemnify the Customer and keep the Customer fully and effectively indemnified on demand against any loss of or damage to any property or injury to or death of any person caused by any negligent act or omission or wilful misconduct of the Supplier, its employees, agents or sub-contractors or by any defect in the design or workmanship of the Equipment

(2) The Customer shall indemnify the Supplier and keep the Supplier fully and effectively indemnified on demand against any loss of or damage to any property or injury to or death of any person caused by any

negligent act or omission or wilful misconduct of the Customer, its employees, agents or sub-contractors

(3) Except in respect of injury to or death of any person (for which no limit applies) the respective liability of the Supplier and the Customer under sub-clauses (1) and (2) in respect of each event or series of connected events shall not exceed £500,000

[Note: Some contracts specifically require the parties to back up their indemnities with insurance.]

[(4) Notwithstanding anything else contained in this Agreement the Supplier shall not be liable to the Customer for loss of profits or contracts or other indirect or consequential loss whether arising from negligence, breach of contract or howsoever]

(5) The Supplier shall not be liable to the Customer for any loss arising out of any failure by the Customer to keep full and up-to-date security copies of the computer programs and data it uses in accordance with best computing practice

28 Waiver of remedies

No forbearance, delay or indulgence by either party in enforcing the provisions of this Agreement shall prejudice or restrict the rights of that party nor shall any waiver of its rights operate as a waiver of any subsequent breach and no right, power or remedy herein conferred upon or reserved for either party is exclusive of any other right, power or remedy available to that party and each such right, power or remedy shall be cumulative

29 Entire agreement

This Agreement supersedes all prior agreements, arrangements and understandings between the parties and constitutes the entire agreement between the parties relating to the subject matter hereof. No addition to or modification of any provision of this Agreement shall be binding upon the parties unless made by a written instrument signed by a duly authorised representative of each of the parties

[Note: This clause may have to be amended in the light of any side letters or collateral agreements.]

30   Assignment [2.6.5]

Save as expressly provided in this Agreement, neither party shall assign or otherwise transfer this Agreement or any of its rights and obligations hereunder whether in whole or in part without the prior written consent of the other

31   Sub-contracts

The Supplier shall not, without the prior written consent of the Customer (which shall not be unreasonably withheld), enter into any sub-contract with any person for the performance of any part of this Agreement provided that this provision shall not apply to:

(a) the purchase by the Supplier of equipment and materials; and

(b) the sub-contract(s) (if any) specified in the Schedule

The Supplier shall not be relieved from any of its obligations hereunder by entering into any sub-contract for the performance of any part of this Agreement. If requested by the Customer, the Supplier shall promptly provide the Customer with copies of any sub-contracts

32   Notices

All notices which are required to be given hereunder shall be in writing and shall be sent to the address of the recipient set out in this Agreement or such other address in England as the recipient may designate by notice given in accordance with the provisions of this Clause. Any such notice may be delivered personally or by first class pre-paid letter or facsimile transmission and shall be deemed to have been served if by hand when delivered, if by first class post 48 hours after posting and if by facsimile transmission when despatched

33   Interpretation

In this Agreement:

[(1) reference to any statute or statutory provision includes a reference to that statute or statutory provision as from time to time amended, extended or re-enacted;]

(2) words importing the singular include the plural, words importing any gender include every gender and words importing persons include bodies corporate and unincorporate; and (in each case) vice versa;

(3) any reference to a party to this Agreement includes a reference to his successors in title and permitted assigns;

(4) the headings to the Clauses are for ease of reference only and shall not affect the interpretation or construction of this Agreement.

34   Law

This Agreement shall be governed by and construed in accordance with the laws of England

35   Disputes

Any dispute which may arise between the parties concerning this Agreement shall be determined by the English Courts and the parties hereby submit to the exclusive jurisdiction of the English Courts for such purpose

[**Note:** An alternative is to provide for an expert or an arbitrator to resolve disputes—see Clause 37 of Precedent D—or use the British Computer Society Clause [13.1.1].]

36   Severability

Notwithstanding that the whole or any part of any provision of this Agreement may prove to be illegal or unenforceable the other provisions of this Agreement and the remainder of the provision in question shall remain in full force and effect.

EXECUTED under hand in two originals the day and year first before written

SIGNED for and on behalf of
COMPUTER COMPANY [LIMITED] [PLC]

By   ....
Signature   ....
Title   ....
Witness   ....

SIGNED for and on behalf of
CUSTOMER [LIMITED] [PLC]

By   ....
Signature   ....
Title   ....
Witness   ....

THE SCHEDULE

A THE EQUIPMENT [2.1.1]

[**Note:** The Schedule should show a full description of each item, the number of such items and the price per item. The description should have both the manufacturer's reference number and enough English narrative to define the equipment uniquely from other equipment from the same manufacturer—eg 'Disk drive' is not enough. It should state the capacity of the disks—'149 Gbyte Disk Drive'.]

[B THE INTEGRAL SOFTWARE

Owned by third parties:

Owned by the Supplier:]

C THE PRICE [2.2.4]
[THE EQUIPMENT PRICE]

D THE OFF-LOADING POINT

E THE LOCATION

F THE DELIVERY DATE

G TRAINING

H SUB-CONTRACTS

COMMISSIONING CERTIFICATE

TO: COMPUTER COMPANY [LIMITED] [PLC]
FROM: CUSTOMER [LIMITED] [PLC]

Date: 19

Dear Sirs,

We refer to the agreement between our respective companies dated
            19   ('the Agreement') relating to the sale and
installation of certain computer equipment ('the Equipment') and confirm
the following:

1   We have today accepted the Equipment.

2   We have inspected the Equipment and confirm that the same
      conforms to the description contained in the Agreement and that
      the same has been installed and set up to our satisfaction at the
      Location (as defined in the Agreement).

3   The Equipment has passed the Installation Tests (as defined in
      the Agreement), the results of which are annexed hereto and signed
      by us for the purpose of identification.

SIGNED for and on behalf of
CUSTOMER [LIMITED] [PLC]

By   ....
Signature   ....
Title   ....
Witness   ....

Precedent B

Rental maintenance agreement

[**Note:** At the risk of repeating material from Precedent K we have included maintenance obligations in this agreement since this is a common practice.]

THIS AGREEMENT is made the   day of   19

PARTIES:

(1) RENTAL COMPANY [LIMITED] [PLC] whose registered office is at

('the Supplier')

(2) CUSTOMER [LIMITED] [PLC] whose registered office is at

('the Hirer')

RECITAL:

The Supplier has agreed to install and let on hire to the Hirer certain computer equipment and to maintain the same upon the terms and conditions hereinafter contained

NOW IT IS HEREBY AGREED as follows:

1   Definitions

In this Agreement, unless the context otherwise requires, the following expressions have the following meanings:

'the Equipment' [2.1.1]	means the computer equipment specified in the Schedule and any replacements or renewals of the whole or any part thereof provided by the Supplier from time to time

'the Delivery Charge'	means the charge for the delivery and installation of the Equipment as specified in the Schedule
'the Off-Loading Point'	means the Hirer's off-loading point specified in the Schedule
'the Location' [2.1.2]	means the Hirer's computer room in which the Equipment is to be installed as specified in the Schedule
'the Delivery Date' [2.3.7]	means the delivery date specified in the Schedule or such extended date as may be granted pursuant to Clause 37
'the Acceptance Date'	means the date on which the Equipment is accepted by the Hirer pursuant to Clause 9
'the Rental Period' [2.2.2]	means the period during which the letting and hiring of the Equipment under this Agreement shall continue and during which the Maintenance Services shall be provided
'the Initial Period'	means the initial period of the Rental Period as specified in the Schedule
'the Scheduled Maintenance Services'	means the maintenance services to be provided by the Supplier pursuant to Clause 20
'the Emergency Maintenance Services'	means the emergency maintenance services to be provided by the Supplier pursuant to Clause 21
'the Maintenance Services'	means the Scheduled Maintenance Services and the Emergency Maintenance Services
'Maintenance Hours'	means the hours between 9.00 am and 5.00 pm each day excluding Saturdays, Sundays and public holidays

2 Products and services to be provided [2.2.2]

(1) The Supplier hereby agrees to:

(a) deliver the Equipment and install it at the Location on the Delivery Date;

(b) let the Equipment on hire to the Hirer;

(c) provide the Maintenance Services;

upon the terms and conditions hereinafter contained

[(2) Substitutions—*see Clause 2(2) of Precedent A*]

[**Note:** For 'the Price' substitute 'the rentals or the charges for the Scheduled Maintenance Services'.]

(3) Operating supplies excluded—*see Clause 2(3) of Precedent A*

3 Location preparation [2.6.3]

See Clause 5 of Precedent A

4 Information and access [2.6.1]

See Clause 6 of Precedent A

5 Delivery [2.3.3]

(1) On the Delivery Date the Supplier shall deliver the Equipment to the Off-Loading Point and then move it to the Location

(2) The Supplier shall not carry out or be responsible for the removal of doors, widening of entrances or any other structural work of any description for the purpose of moving the Equipment from the Off-Loading Point to the Location, which work shall be undertaken by the Hirer at its own expense prior to delivery

(3) The Hirer shall be responsible for all reasonable costs incurred by the Supplier in providing special equipment, personnel or works necessary to move the Equipment from the Off-Loading Point to the Location. Such costs shall be paid by the Hirer in addition to the Delivery Charge

[(4) All packing cases, skids, drums and other packing materials used for delivery of the Equipment must be returned by the Hirer to the Supplier in good condition and at the Hirer's expense. The Supplier reserves the right to charge for any such cases and materials not so returned]

[**Note:** In the case of a rental agreement where title to the equipment remains with the supplier, the supplier will usually wish to assume full control over the delivery and installation of the equipment.]

6   Installation [2.3.3]

See Clause 9 of Precedent A

7   Time [not] of the essence [2.3.7]

See Clause 10 of Precedent A

8   Acceptance tests [2.3.4]

See Clause 11 of Precedent A

9   Acceptance [2.3.6]

See Clause 12 of Precedent A

10   Hirer's default [2.3.7]

See Clause 16 of Precedent A

[11   Supplier's warranties [2.3.8]

If required adapt Clauses 19(2)–(5) of Precedent A]

12   Hirer's warranty

See Clause 20 of Precedent A

13   Letting and hiring [2.2.2]

The Supplier shall let and the Hirer shall take on hire the Equipment for the Rental Period upon the terms and conditions hereinafter contained

14   Rental Period [2.2.2]

The Rental Period shall commence on the Acceptance Date, shall continue for the Initial Period and shall remain in force thereafter [unless and] until terminated by either party giving to the other not less than 6 months' written notice of termination [given on] [expiring on] the last day of the Initial Period or at any time thereafter but shall be subject to earlier termination as hereinafter provided

[**Note:** Delete the first and third bracketed phrases if the agreement is to be for a minimum period equal to the Initial Period plus the notice period. Delete the second bracketed phrase if the agreement is to be for a minimum period equal to the Initial Period.]

15   Charges and payment [2.2; 8.2]

(1) The Delivery Charge and any additional charges payable by the Hirer under Clause 5(3) shall be paid on the Acceptance Date

(2) During the Rental Period the Hirer shall pay to the Supplier the rentals and the charges for the Scheduled Maintenance Services specified in the Schedule periodically in advance as stated therein. Such rentals and charges shall be paid without prior demand and no payment shall be considered made until it is received by the Supplier. All such payments shall be made in the manner specified in the Schedule

(3) Any charges payable by the Hirer under this Agreement in addition to those specified in sub-clauses (1) and (2) above shall be paid within *14* days after the receipt by the Hirer of the Supplier's invoice therefor

(4) The Supplier shall be entitled at any time and from time to time after the expiry of the [Initial Period] [the period of *one* year after the Acceptance Date] to vary the rentals and/or charges for the Scheduled Maintenance Services to accord with any change in the Supplier's standard scale of charges by giving to the Hirer not less than *90* days' prior written notice. Where and whenever such notice is given, the Hirer shall have the right to terminate this Agreement as from the date on which such notice expires by giving to the Supplier written notice of termination not less than *30* days before such date

[**Note:** For a clause limiting the increase by reference to the Retail Prices Index—see the second alternative clause 3(4) of Precedent K.]

(5) Rentals and other charges exclusive of VAT—*see Clause 3(4) of Precedent A*

(6) Interest on overdue amounts—*see Clause 3(6) of Precedent A*

[**Note:** Where reliability is an important factor for the customer the downtime clause (clause 13 of Precedent K) may be appropriate.]

16   Ownership

The Equipment shall at all times remain the sole and exclusive property of the Supplier and the Hirer shall have no right or interest in the

Equipment except for quiet possession and the right to use the Equipment upon the terms and conditions contained in this Agreement

17   Replacements and renewals

The provisions of this Agreement shall apply to all replacements and renewals of the Equipment or any part thereof made by the Supplier during the continuance of this Agreement

18   Insurance [2.6.5]

(1) The Hirer shall from (and including) the date on which the Equipment is delivered to the Location effect (if not previously effected) and maintain thereafter until the Equipment has been re-delivered to the Supplier with insurers acceptable to the Supplier:

> (a) insurance covering the Equipment against all usual risks relating to loss or damage from whatever cause arising (other than exclusions agreed in writing by the Supplier). Such insurance shall:

>> (i) be in the joint names of the Supplier and the Hirer;

>> (ii) cover the Equipment for its full replacement value;

>> (iii) specify the Supplier as loss payee;

>> (iv) contain a provision that the insurers shall waive any breach of warranty under the policy as against the Supplier;

>> (v) be free from restriction or excess (save as may be agreed in writing by the Supplier);

>> (vi) not be capable of cancellation or variation other than by the insurers giving to the Supplier not less than *30* days' prior written notice

> (b) insurance for an amount not less than £*500,000* against claims from any persons whatsoever (including, without limitation, employees, agents and sub-contractors of the Hirer) who may suffer damage to or loss of property on death or bodily injury arising directly or indirectly out of the presence, control or use of the Equipment. Such insurance shall:

>> (i) be in the joint names of the Supplier and the Hirer;

>> (ii) provide that any payment made thereunder pursuant to any claim shall be applied directly in or towards satisfaction of the claim in respect of which such payment is made;

(iii) contain a provision that the insurers shall waive any breach of warranty under the policy as against the Supplier;

(iv) not be capable of cancellation or variation other than by the insurers giving to the Supplier not less than *30* days' prior written notice

(2) The Hirer shall:

(a) prior to the delivery of the Equipment and thereafter on demand produce to the Supplier the policies relating to the aforesaid insurances and the receipts for premiums;

(b) forthwith notify the Supplier in writing in the event of any loss of or damage to the Equipment;

(c) punctually pay all premiums payable under the said insurance policies, do everything necessary to maintain the said insurance policies in full force and effect and not do anything whereby they will or may be vitiated either in whole or in part;

(d) not effect any other insurance relating to the Equipment if a claim under such insurance would result in the operation of any average clause in the policies maintained in compliance with sub-clause (1)

(3) The Hirer shall be responsible for and shall indemnify the Supplier against any loss or damage to the Equipment insofar as such loss or damage is not covered by insurance (other than loss or damage caused by the negligence or wilful misconduct of the Supplier, its employees, agents or sub-contractors)

[**Note:** The alternative is for the supplier to insure and recover the premiums by way of increased rentals.]

19 Application of insurance moneys

(1) If the Equipment shall be damaged and in the opinion of the insurers it is economic that such damage be made good then all insurance moneys payable under the insurance policy mentioned in Clause 18(1)(a) shall be applied in making good such damage

(2) If the Equipment shall be lost, stolen, destroyed or damaged to such an extent as to be in the opinion of the insurers incapable of economic repair then the said insurance moneys shall at the option of the Supplier:

(a) be applied in replacing the Equipment with equipment having capabilities at least equivalent to that of the Equipment in which event the replacement equipment shall be held by the Hirer upon the terms of this Agreement and the Hirer shall continue to be liable to pay the rental and maintenance charges hereunder as if such loss had not taken place; or

(b) be paid to the Supplier to the extent necessary to discharge the Hirer's liability to the Supplier at the date of such payment and to compensate the Supplier for the loss, theft or destruction of or damage to the Equipment, any surplus to be paid to the Hirer. If the insurance moneys paid to the Supplier are insufficient to discharge such liability and to compensate the Supplier as aforesaid the amount of the deficiency shall be paid by the Hirer to the Supplier forthwith. Upon all payments being made as aforesaid this Agreement shall automatically terminate

(3) The Hirer shall be liable to pay to the Supplier a sum equivalent to any amount deducted by the insurers by way of excess or in respect of damage caused to the Equipment prior to the date of total loss

20   Scheduled Maintenance Services [8.1.2]

During the Rental Period the Supplier shall provide the following maintenance services in respect of the Equipment:

See Clause 2 of Precedent K

21   Emergency Maintenance Services [8.3.2]

See Clause 4 of Precedent K

22   Exceptions to the Maintenance Services [8.3]

See Clause 5 of Precedent K

> [Note: Where damage is occasioned to the equipment as a result of an excepted cause the supplier will wish (because it owns the equipment) to impose an obligation on the hirer to permit, and pay for, that damage to be repaired. Clause 5(2) of Precedent K will therefore have to be appropriately modified.]

23   Replacement parts [8.6.5]

Any replacement parts provided by the Supplier hereunder and any parts removed from the Equipment shall remain the property of the Supplier

24 Service visits outside the Maintenance Services

See Clause 7 of Precedent K

[25 Replacement equipment [2.1.1]

The Supplier shall on giving to the Hirer *30* days' prior written notice be entitled if it considers it necessary or desirable to replace the Equipment with equipment having capabilities at least equivalent to that of the Equipment. Where the Supplier avails itself of this right, it shall be responsible for all the costs of replacing the Equipment, but the Hirer shall provide the Supplier with all facilities and assistance reasonably required by the Supplier for the purpose of effecting such replacement]

[26 Additional equipment [2.5]

The Hirer may hire additional equipment (subject to the availability thereof) from the Supplier by the Hirer's written order to the Supplier referring to this Agreement, and by receipt of a written acceptance of such order from the Supplier. The period of hire for such additional equipment shall continue unless otherwise agreed until the expiry of the Rental Period. Periodical rentals initially payable for such additional equipment shall be those in effect when such additional equipment is accepted. Subject to the foregoing such additional equipment shall be hired on the same terms and conditions as provided in this Agreement (insofar as the same are applicable)]

27 Hirer's obligations [2.6]

Rental

(1) The Hirer shall:

    (a) not sell, assign, sub-let, pledge or part with possession or control of or otherwise deal with the Equipment or any interest therein nor purport to do any of such things nor create or allow to be created any mortgage, charge, lien or other encumbrance on the Equipment;

    (b) not change, remove or obscure any labels, plates, insignia, lettering or other markings which are on the Equipment at the time of installation thereof or which may thereafter be placed on the Equipment by the Supplier or by any person authorised by the Supplier;

    (c) protect and defend the Supplier's title to the Equipment against all persons claiming against or through the Hirer and shall keep the Equipment free from distress, execution or any other legal process, and shall forthwith give to the Supplier notice of any claim or threatened claim to the Equipment by any third party;

(d) not cause or permit the Equipment or any part thereof to be attached or affixed to any land or building so as to become a fixture;

(e) not move the Equipment from the Location without the Supplier's prior written consent;

(f) permit the Supplier and any person authorised by it at all reasonable times to have access to the Location (or such other place where the Equipment may be situated) for the purpose of inspecting and examining the condition of the Equipment;

(g) not sell, assign, demise, sub-let, mortgage, charge or otherwise dispose of any land or building on or in which the Equipment is kept or enter into any contract to do any of such things without giving the Supplier at least 2 months' prior written notice. The Hirer shall in any event procure that any such sale, assignment, demise, sub-lease, mortgage, charge or other disposition is made subject to the right of the Supplier to repossess the Equipment at any time and for that purpose to enter upon any such land or building;

(h) pay to the Supplier all costs and expenses (including legal costs on a full indemnity basis) incurred by or on behalf of the Supplier in ascertaining the whereabouts of the Equipment or repossessing it by reason of a breach by the Hirer of any term of this Agreement and of any legal proceedings taken by or on behalf of the Supplier to enforce any provision of this Agreement;

(i) obtain all necessary licences, permits and permissions for the use of the Equipment and not use the Equipment or permit the same to be used contrary to any law or any regulation or bye-law in force from time to time;

(j) indemnify the Supplier against all claims and demands made upon the Supplier (so far as the same are not covered by insurance) by reason of any loss, injury or damage suffered by any person arising directly or indirectly out of the presence, control or use of the Equipment save where such damage loss or injury arises from the negligence or wilful misconduct of the Supplier, its employees, agents or sub-contractors;

(k) at all times keep a record of the use of the Equipment in a form to be approved by the Supplier and shall at the Supplier's request provide the Supplier with copies of the entries and allow the Supplier to inspect such record at all reasonable times

Maintenance [2.6.4]

(2) The Hirer shall:

See Clause 9 of Precedent K for maintenance obligations

28 Electromagnetic compatibility [2.7.3]

See Clause 13 of Precedent A

29 Telecommunications [2.7.4]

See Clause 14 of Precedent A and Clause 12 of Precedent K

30 Operating manuals and training

See Clause 22 of Precedent A

31 Termination [2.4.2]

(1) Notwithstanding anything else contained in this Agreement (and without prejudice to the right of either party to terminate this Agreement prior to the Acceptance Date pursuant to any such right conferred upon it by law), this Agreement may be terminated at any time on or after the Acceptance Date:

> (a) by the Supplier forthwith on giving notice in writing to the Hirer if the Hirer shall fail to pay any sum due under the terms of this Agreement (otherwise than as a consequence of any default on the part of the Supplier) and such sum remains unpaid for *14* days after written notice from the Supplier that such sum has not been paid (such notice to contain a warning of the Supplier's intention to terminate); or

> (b) by either party forthwith on giving notice in writing to the other if:

>> (i) the other commits any [material] [serious] breach of any term of this Agreement (other than any failure by the Hirer to make any payment in which event the provisions of paragraph (a) above shall apply) and (in the case of a breach capable of being remedied) shall have failed, within *30* days after the receipt of a request in writing from the other party so to do, to remedy the breach (such request to contain a warning of such party's intention to terminate);

>> (ii) the other party shall have a receiver or administrative receiver appointed of it or over any part of its undertaking or assets

or shall pass a resolution for winding-up (otherwise than for the purpose of a bona fide scheme of solvent amalgamation or reconstruction) or a court of competent jurisdiction shall make an order to that effect or if the other party shall become subject to an administration order or shall enter into any voluntary arrangement with its creditors or shall cease or threaten to cease to carry on business

[**Note:** This agreement can be separated into two distinct stages; the first being the period up to the Acceptance Date (dealing with delivery, installation, acceptance etc) and the second being the period after acceptance (dealing with rental and maintenance). The parties should always make it clear to which stage any express termination provisions apply. For example, if sub-clause (1)(b) applied to the first period it would, in effect, make time of the essence by giving the innocent party an immediate right to terminate in the event of a breach incapable of remedy.]

(2) The Supplier shall be entitled to terminate this Agreement in any of the events mentioned in sub-clause (1) notwithstanding any subsequent acceptance of rentals

(3) In the event of a termination by the Supplier pursuant to sub-clause (1):

(a) the Hirer shall no longer be in possession of the Equipment with the Supplier's consent who may without notice repossess the Equipment and may for that purpose without notice enter any of the Hirer's premises in which the Equipment or any part thereof is or is reasonably believed by the Supplier to be situated (and so that the Hirer hereby irrevocably licenses the Supplier, its employees and agents to enter upon any such premises for such purpose);

(b) the Hirer shall not be entitled to the repayment of any sums previously paid by it to the Supplier under the terms of this Agreement nor to any credit or allowance in respect of any such payments

(4) Any termination of this Agreement (howsoever occasioned) shall not affect any accrued rights or liabilities of either party nor shall it affect the coming into force or the continuance in force of any provision hereof which is expressly or by implication intended to come into or continue in force on or after such termination

(5) Without prejudice to the provisions of Clause 32, as from the date of termination of this Agreement until such time as the Equipment shall be returned to the Supplier the Hirer will pay by way of compensation for the continued use of the Equipment a monthly sum (payable in arrear) at the same rate as the rental charges previously due in respect thereof.

This sub-clause shall not confer on the Hirer any right to the continued use or possession of the Equipment.

32 Return of the Equipment

(1) Upon termination of the Hirer's right to hire the Equipment (for any reason), the Hirer shall forthwith re-deliver possession of the Equipment in good order, repair and condition to the Supplier who shall for the purpose have access to the Location (or any other place where the Equipment may be situated)

(2) Except in the case of a termination by the Supplier pursuant to Clause 31(1) (in which case the costs of removal and re-delivery shall be borne by the Hirer), normal costs of removal of the Equipment and of re-delivery shall be borne by the Supplier provided that all reasonable costs incurred by the Supplier in providing special equipment, personnel or works necessary to transport the Equipment from the Location (or such other place where the Equipment may be situated) to the Supplier's vehicle shall be borne by the Hirer. The Hirer shall reimburse such costs to the Supplier within *30* days after the receipt of an invoice from the Supplier

33 Intervention by the Supplier

If the Hirer fails to comply with any of its obligations hereunder, the Supplier may, without being obliged to do so, or responsible for so doing, and without prejudice to its other rights and remedies, effect compliance on behalf of the Hirer, whereupon the Hirer shall become liable to pay forthwith any moneys expended by the Supplier together with all costs and expenses (including legal costs on a full indemnity basis) in connection therewith

[34 Option to purchase [2.2.3]

On termination of the hiring of the Equipment (other than by termination by the Supplier pursuant to Clause 31(1)) the Hirer shall have the option to buy the Equipment at a price to be agreed with the Supplier and on the Supplier's standard terms and conditions of sale in force from time to time]

[**Note:** We have included this clause as an example of the type of provision commonly encountered in rental agreements. It should be noted that it is merely an agreement to agree and is not therefore binding on the supplier. In order for the option to have contractual force the price must be ascertainable in advance and not be left to the parties to negotiate at a later stage.]

35 Intellectual property rights indemnity

See Clause 26 of Precedent A or Clause 12 of Precedent C

36 Confidentiality

See Clause 21 of Precedent A

37 Force majeure

See Clause 16 of Precedent K

38 Liability

See Clause 18 of Precedent K

39 Waiver of remedies

See Clause 28 of Precedent A

40 Entire agreement

See Clause 29 of Precedent A

41 Assignment [2.6.5]

See Clause 30 of Precedent A

42 Sub-contracts

See Clause 31 of Precedent A

43 Notices

See Clause 32 of Precedent A

44 Interpretation

See Clause 33 of Precedent A

45   Law

See Clause 34 of Precedent A

46   Disputes

See Clause 35 of Precedent A

47   Severability

See Clause 36 of Precedent A

EXECUTED etc

THE SCHEDULE

A   THE EQUIPMENT

B   THE DELIVERY CHARGE

C   THE OFF-LOADING POINT

D   THE LOCATION

E   THE DELIVERY DATE

F   THE INITIAL PERIOD

G   CHARGES AND METHOD OF PAYMENT

Rentals

£[   ] for each [month] [quarter] [year], payable in advance

First rental payable on: [the Acceptance Date]

Subsequent rentals payable on the first working day of each [month] [quarter] [year] thereafter

Charges for the Scheduled Maintenance Services

£[   ] for each [month] [quarter] [year], payable in advance

First charge payable on: [the Acceptance Date]

Subsequent charges payable on the first working day of each [month] [quarter] [year] thereafter

Method of payment

By standing order to [   ] Bank PLC

(Rental Company's Account No   )

H   TRAINING

Precedent C

Software licence agreement

[**Note:** This agreement covers not only the use of computer programs but also associated documentation such as user manuals. Such agreements frequently include software maintenance—see Precedent L. Alternative Software Licence and Support Agreements for end-users are set out in Schedule 1 of Precedent H and Schedule 1 of Precedent I.]

THIS AGREEMENT is made the   day of   19

PARTIES:

(1) SOFTWARE HOUSE [LIMITED] [PLC] whose registered office is at

('the Licensor')

(2) CUSTOMER [LIMITED] [PLC] whose registered office is at

('the Licensee')

RECITAL:

The Licensor has agreed to deliver to the Licensee and install on the Licensee's computer certain computer programs and to grant the Licensee a non-exclusive licence to use such programs and their associated documentation upon the terms and conditions hereinafter contained

NOW IT IS HEREBY AGREED as follows:

1   Definitions

In this Agreement, unless the context otherwise requires, the following expressions have the following meanings:

'the Licence'   means the licence granted by the Licensor pursuant to Clause 9(1) 'the Equipment'   means the Licensee's computer in respect of which the Licence is granted, specified by type and serial number in the Schedule [and using the *XYZ* operating system]

'the Licensed Programs' means the [systems] [and] [applications] computer programs of the Licensor specified in the Schedule

'the Specification'   means the specification of the Licensed Programs describing the facilities and functions thereof, a copy of which is annexed hereto

[**Note:** Where the Licensed Programs are applications programs intended for use with the licensee's existing systems programs then this should be made clear in the specification. It should also be made clear that such use will not affect the licensor's obligations and liabilities under this agreement.]

'the Program Documentation' means the operating manuals, user instructions, technical literature and all other related materials in eye-readable form supplied to the Licensee by the Licensor for aiding the use of the Licensed Programs

'the Media'   means the media on which the Licensed Programs and the Program Documentation are recorded or printed as provided to the Licensee by the Licensor

'the Licensed Program Materials' means the Licensed Programs, the Program Documentation and the Media

'Use the Licensed Programs' means to load the Licensed Programs into and store and run them on the Equipment in accordance with the terms of this Agreement

'Use the Licensed Program Materials'	means to Use the Licensed Programs, to read and possess the Program Documentation in conjunction with the use of the Licensed Programs and to possess the Media
'the Licence Fee'	means the fee for the Licence and the services to be provided under this Agreement as specified in the Schedule
'the Delivery Date'	means the delivery date specified in the Schedule or such extended date as may be granted pursuant to Clause 23
'the Location'	means the Licensee's computer room where the Equipment is [located] [to be installed] as specified in the Schedule
'the Acceptance Date'	means the date on which the Licensed Programs are accepted (or deemed to be accepted) by the Licensee pursuant to Clause 6

2   Products and services to be provided [3.0.2]

The Licensor hereby agrees to:

(1) grant to the Licensee a non-exclusive licence to Use the Licensed Program Materials;

(2) deliver the Licensed Programs to the Licensee and install them on the Equipment;

(3) provide training and operating manuals to the Licensee;

(4) provide the other services hereinafter described;

upon the terms and conditions hereinafter contained

3   Payment [3.2]

(1) The Licence Fee shall be paid by the Licensee on the Acceptance Date

(2) Licence Fee and other charges exclusive of VAT—*see Clause 3(4) of Precedent A*

(3) Any charges payable by the Licensee hereunder in addition to the Licence Fee shall be paid within *30* days after the receipt by the Licensee of the Licensor's invoice therefor

(4) Interest on overdue amounts—*see Clause 3(6) of Precedent A*

4   Delivery and installation [3.3]

On the Delivery Date the Licensor shall deliver the Licensed Programs to the Licensee and install the same on the Equipment at the Location [but time shall not be of the essence in relation to such obligations]. The Licensed Programs shall consist of one copy of the object code of the Licensed Programs in machine-readable form only, on the storage media specified in the Schedule

5   Risk

Risk in the Media shall pass to the Licensee on delivery. If any part of the Media shall thereafter be lost, destroyed or damaged the Licensor shall at the request of the Licensee replace the same promptly (embodying the relevant part of the Licensed Programs or Program Documentation) subject to the Licensee paying the cost of such replacement. The Licensor shall not make any further or additional charge for such replacement

6   Testing and acceptance [3.3.1]

(1) The Licensee shall supply to the Licensor [immediately after installation of the Licensed Programs] test data which in the reasonable opinion of the Licensee is suitable to test whether the Licensed Programs are in accordance with the Specification together with the results expected to be achieved by processing such test data using the Licensed Programs. The Licensor shall not be entitled to object to such test data or expected results unless the Licensor can demonstrate to the Licensee that they are not suitable for testing the Licensed Programs as aforesaid, in which event the Licensee shall make any reasonable amendments to such test data and expected results as the Licensor may request. Subject to the receipt of such test data and expected results, the Licensor shall process such data, in the presence of the Licensee or its authorised representative, on the Equipment using the Licensed Programs by way of acceptance testing within *7* days after such receipt at a time mutually convenient to both parties

(2) The Licensee shall accept the Licensed Programs immediately after the Licensor has demonstrated that the Licensed Programs have correctly processed the test data by achieving the expected results. The Licensee

shall, if required by the Licensor, sign an acceptance certificate in the form annexed hereto acknowledging such acceptance

(3) If the Licensee shall not supply any test data as aforesaid or shall fail to make itself available to attend acceptance tests within the said period of 7 days then the Licensee shall be deemed to have accepted the Licensed Programs

(4) The Licensed Programs shall not be deemed to have incorrectly processed such test data by reason of any failure to provide any facility or function not specified in the Specification

[7 The Equipment

The Licensee shall be responsible for ensuring that the Equipment is installed and fully operational at the Location on the Delivery Date. If the Licensor is delayed from performing its obligations under Clauses 4 and 6 by reason of any failure by the Licensee to ensure the same, then the Licensee will pay to the Licensor all reasonable costs, charges and losses attributable to such delay]

[Note: This clause will be appropriate where the equipment has not yet been installed and is to be supplied by a third party.]

8 Warranty [3.3.3]

(1)(a) The Licensor warrants that the Licensed Programs will after acceptance by the Licensee provide the facilities and functions set out in the Specification when properly used on the Equipment and that the Program Documentation [and the Licensed Programs] will provide adequate instruction to enable the Licensee to make proper use of such facilities and functions

[Note: The Licensed Programs may also contain 'help' functions to assist the user.]

(b) If the Licensor receives written notice from the Licensee after the Acceptance Date of any breach of the said warranty then the Licensor shall at its own expense and within a reasonable time after receiving such notice remedy the defect or error in question provided that the Licensor shall have no liability or obligations under the said warranty unless it shall have received written notice of the defect or error in question no later than the expiry of 6 months after the Acceptance Date

(c) The said warranty shall be subject to the Licensee complying with its obligations hereunder and to there having been made no alterations to the Licensed Programs by any person other than the Licensor. When notifying a defect or error the Licensee shall (so far as it is able) provide the Licensor with a documented example of such defect or error

(d) The Licensor shall have no liability or obligations under the said warranty other than to remedy breaches thereof by the provision of materials and services within a reasonable time and without charge to the Licensee. If the Licensor shall fail to comply with such obligations its liability for such failure shall be limited to a sum equal to the Licence Fee. The foregoing states the entire liability of the Licensor, whether in contract or tort, for defects and errors in the Licensed Program Materials which are notified to the Licensor after the Acceptance Date

[Note: Where a maintenance agreement is entered into (see clause 17) sub-clause (1) will need to be amended—follow clause 24 of Precedent 2.]

(2) The Licensee acknowledges that the Licensed Programs have not been prepared to meet the Licensee's individual requirements and that it is therefore the responsibility of the Licensee to ensure that the facilities and functions described in the Specification meet its requirements. The Licensor shall not be liable for any failure of the Licensed Programs to provide any facility or function not specified in the Specification

[Note: This is reasonable, of course, in the case of a package. If the licensee requires modifications to the package to meet its individual requirements then these would have to be paid for in addition and this clause will not then be appropriate in this form.]

(3) *See Clause 19(5) of Precedent A*

9   Licence [3.8]

(1) The Licensor hereby grants to the Licensee a non-exclusive licence to Use the Licensed Program Materials subject to the terms and conditions hereinafter contained

(2) The Licensee shall Use the Licensed Program Materials for processing its own data for its own internal business purposes only. The Licensee shall not permit any third party to use the Licensed Program Materials nor use the Licensed Program Materials on behalf of or for the benefit of any third party in any way whatever (including, without limitation, using the Licensed Program Materials for the purpose of operating a bureau service)

[Note: Sub-clause (2) will have to be altered if mutual back-up arrangements with another user are envisaged.]

(3) The use of the Licensed Program Materials is restricted to use on and in conjunction with the Equipment save that:

(a) if the Licensed Program Materials cannot be used with the Equipment because it is inoperable for any reason then the Licence shall be temporarily extended without additional charge to use with any other equipment until such failure has been remedied provided that such equipment is under the direct control of the Licensee. The Licensee shall promptly notify the Licensor of such temporary use and of the commencement and cessation thereof;

(b) the Licensee may with the prior written consent of the Licensor (such consent not to be unreasonably withheld) Use the Licensed Program Materials on and in conjunction with any suitable replacement equipment (to be specified by type and serial number) if the use of the Licensed Program Materials on and in conjunction with the Equipment is permanently discontinued. Upon such consent being given the replacement equipment shall become the Equipment for the purposes of the Licence

The use of the Licensed Program Materials on and in conjunction with such temporary or replacement equipment shall be at the sole risk and responsibility of the Licensee who shall indemnify the Licensor against any loss or damage sustained or incurred by the Licensor as a result. Without prejudice to the generality of the foregoing the Licensor shall not (unless otherwise agreed in writing by the Licensor) have any liability under Clauses 8 and 12 hereof in connection with such use

[(4) The Licensee shall not without the prior written consent of the Licensor Use the Licensed Program Materials in any country except the countries specified in the Schedule]

[**Note:** Some licences restrict use to a designated location.]

(5) The Licence shall not be deemed to extend to any programs or materials of the Licensor other than the Licensed Program Materials unless specifically agreed to in writing by the Licensor

(6) The Licensee hereby acknowledges that it is licensed to use the Licensed Program Materials only in accordance with the express terms of this Agreement and not further or otherwise

10   Duration of Licence

The Licence shall commence on the Acceptance Date and shall continue until terminated in accordance with Clause 21 or as otherwise provided in this Agreement

11   Proprietary rights [3.8]

(1) The Licensed Program Materials and the copyright and other intellectual property rights of whatever nature in the Licensed Program Materials are and shall remain the property of the Licensor and the Licensor reserves the right to grant licences to use the Licensed Program Materials to third parties

(2) The Licensee shall notify the Licensor immediately if the Licensee becomes aware of any unauthorised use of the whole or any part of the Licensed Program Materials by any person

(3) The Licensee will permit the Licensor to check the use of the Licensed Program Materials by the Licensee at all reasonable times and for that purpose the Licensor shall be entitled to enter any of the Licensee's premises (and so that the Licensee hereby irrevocably licenses the Licensor, its employees and agents to enter any such premises for such purpose)

12   Intellectual property rights indemnity

The Licensor shall indemnify the Licensee against any claim that the normal use or possession of the Licensed Program Materials infringes the intellectual property rights of any third party provided that the Licensor is given immediate and complete control of such claim, that the Licensee does not prejudice the Licensor's defence of such claim, that the Licensee gives the Licensor all reasonable assistance with such claim and that the claim does not arise as a result of the use of the Licensed Program Materials in combination with any equipment (other than the Equipment) [or programs] not supplied or approved by the Licensor. The Licensor shall have the right to replace or change all or any part of the Licensed Program Materials in order to avoid any infringement. The foregoing states the entire liability of the Licensor to the Licensee in respect of the infringement of the intellectual property rights of any third party

> [**Note:** Alternatively, use Clause 26 of Precedent A appropriately amended. Sub-clause (3)(c) will read:
>
> > '(c) if (a) or (b) cannot be accomplished on reasonable terms, refund the Licence Fee whereupon the Licence shall terminate'.]

13   Confidentiality of Licensed Program Materials [3.8.1]

(1) The Licensee undertakes to treat as confidential and keep secret all information contained or embodied in the Licensed Program Materials

and the Specification and all information conveyed to the Licensee by training (hereinafter collectively referred to as 'the Information')

(2) The Licensee shall not without the prior written consent of the Licensor divulge any part of the Information to any person except:

(a) the Licensee's own employees and then only to those employees who need to know the same;

(b) the Licensee's auditors, HM Inspector of Taxes, HM Customs & Excise and any other persons or bodies having a right duty or obligation to know the business of the Licensee and then only in pursuance of such right duty or obligation;

(c) any person who is from time to time appointed by the Licensee to maintain any equipment on which the Licensed Programs are being used (in accordance with the terms of the Licence) and then only to the extent necessary to enable such person properly to maintain such equipment

(3) The Licensee undertakes to ensure that the persons and bodies mentioned in paragraphs (a), (b) and (c) of sub-clause (2) are made aware prior to the disclosure of any part of the Information that the same is confidential and that they owe a duty of confidence to the Licensor. The Licensee shall indemnify the Licensor against any loss or damage which the Licensor may sustain or incur as a result of the Licensee failing to comply with such undertaking

[Note: In practice the licensee should obtain written acknowledgements from such persons. The licensee will then be able to demonstrate that he has complied with his undertaking.]

(4) The Licensee shall promptly notify the Licensor if it becomes aware of any breach of confidence by any person to whom the Licensee divulges all or any part of the Information and shall give the Licensor all reasonable assistance in connection with any proceedings which the Licensor may institute against such person for breach of confidence

(5) The foregoing obligations as to confidentiality shall remain in full force and effect notwithstanding any termination of the Licence or this Agreement

14   Copying [3.8.1]

(1) The Licensee may make only so many copies of the Licensed Programs as are reasonably necessary for operational security and use. Such copies

and the media on which they are stored shall be the property of the Licensor and the Licensee shall ensure that all such copies bear the Licensor's proprietary notices. The Licence shall apply to all such copies as it applies to the Licensed Programs

(2) No copies may be made of the Program Documentation without the prior written consent of the Licensor

15 Security and control

The Licensee shall during the continuance of the Licence:

(1) effect and maintain adequate security measures to safeguard the Licensed Program Materials from access or use by any unauthorised person

(2) retain the Licensed Program Materials and all copies thereof under the Licensee's effective control

(3) maintain a full and accurate record of the Licensee's copying and disclosure of the Licensed Program Materials and shall produce such record to the Licensor on request from time to time

16 Alterations [3.5.1, 3.8.1]

either:

[(1) Except to the extent and in the circumstances expressly required to be permitted by the Licensor by law, the Licensee shall not alter, modify, adapt or translate the whole or any part of the Licensed Program Materials in any way whatever nor permit the whole or any part of the Licensed Programs to be combined with or become incorporated in any other computer programs nor decompile, disassemble or reverse engineer the same nor attempt to do any of such things

(2) To the extent that [the law in the Licensee's jurisdiction] [local law] grants the Licensee the right to decompile the Licensed Programs in order to obtain information necessary to render the Licensed Programs interoperable with other computer programs used by the Licensee, the Licensor hereby undertakes to make that information readily available to the Licensee. The Licensor shall have the right to impose reasonable conditions such as a reasonable fee for doing so. In order to ensure that the Licensee receives the appropriate information, the Licensee must first give the Licensor sufficient details of the Licensee's objectives and the other software concerned. Requests for the appropriate information should be given by notice to the Licensor in accordance with this Agreement]

or:

[(1)(a) The Licensee may modify the Licensed Program Materials at its own expense and responsibility. The Licensee shall indemnify the Licensor against any claim that such modifications infringe the intellectual property rights of any third party

(b) The copyright and other intellectual property rights of whatever nature in such modifications shall vest in the Licensor and the Licensee shall ensure that all such modifications bear the Licensor's proprietary notice. The Licensee hereby assigns (by way of future assignment) all such rights to the Licensor. The Licensee shall be entitled without further charge to use such modifications upon the same terms and conditions as the Licensed Program Materials but not further or otherwise. The Licence shall be extended accordingly

(c) The Licensee shall promptly notify the Licensor of all such modifications and shall supply to the Licensor without charge copies of all documentation relating to such modifications including specifications and source codes

(2) The Licensee may combine, at its own expense and responsibility, the Licensed Programs with other programs to form a combined work. Any of the Licensed Programs included in the combined work shall continue to be subject to the terms and conditions contained herein. Where such other programs are the property of a third party the Licensee shall be responsible for obtaining all necessary consents to their use with the Licensed Programs. The Licensee shall indemnify the Licensor against any claim that the use of the Licensed Programs in combination with such other programs infringes the intellectual property rights of any third party. Upon termination of the Licence the Licensee shall completely remove the Licensed Programs from such combined work before returning or destroying the same in accordance with Clause 21(4)

(3) The Licensor shall not be responsible for any error in the Licensed Programs or failure of the Licensed Programs to fulfil the Specification insofar as such error or failure occurs in or is caused by any part of the Licensed Programs modified or combined by the Licensee as aforesaid]

17   Software maintenance [9.1]

The parties undertake to enter into a maintenance agreement on the Acceptance Date in respect of the Licensed Program Materials in the form of the draft annexed hereto

[**Note:** See Precedent L.]

alternatively:

[Unless the Licensee enters into a software maintenance agreement with the Licensor on or before the Acceptance Date (on terms to be agreed between the parties) the Licensor will not provide any maintenance in respect of the Licensed Program Materials. If at a later date the Licensee wishes to receive the then current release of the Licensed Program Materials or maintenance therefor then the Licensor may at its option provide the same subject to the Licensee entering into a new licence agreement in respect of such release (and paying the Licensor's then current charge therefor) and (if applicable) entering into the Licensor's standard software maintenance agreement then in force]

18   Operating manuals [3.7.3]

The Licensor shall provide the Licensee with *2* copies of a set of operating manuals for the Licensed Programs containing sufficient information to enable proper use of all the facilities and functions set out in the Specification. If the Licensee requires further copies of such operating manuals then these may be obtained under licence from the Licensor in accordance with its standard scale of charges from time to time in force

19   Training [3.7.3]

(1) The Licensor undertakes to provide training in the use of the Licensed Programs for the staff of the Licensee as set out in the Schedule

(2) Any additional training required by the Licensee shall be provided by the Licensor in accordance with its standard scale of charges from time to time in force

20   Licensee's confidential information [3.7.2]

The Licensor shall treat as confidential all information supplied by the Licensee under this Agreement which is designated as confidential by the Licensee or which is by its nature clearly confidential provided that this Clause shall not extend to any information which was rightfully in the possession of the Licensor prior to the commencement of the negotiations leading to this Agreement or which is already public knowledge or becomes so at a future date (otherwise than as a result of a breach of this Clause). The Licensor shall not divulge any confidential information to any person except to its own employees and then only to those employees who need to know the same. The Licensor shall ensure that its employees are aware of and comply with the provisions of this Clause. The foregoing obligations shall survive any termination of the Licence or this Agreement

[**Note:** If real personal data is involved the bureau Data Protection Clause [P15] may also be relevant [3.7.2].]

21 Termination [3.4]

(1) The Licensee may terminate the Licence at any time by giving at least *30* days' prior written notice to the Licensor

(2) The Licensor may terminate the Licence forthwith on giving notice in writing to the Licensee if:

(a) the Licensee commits any material breach of any term of this Agreement and (in the case of a breach capable of being remedied) shall have failed, within *30* days after the receipt of a request in writing from the Licensor so to do, to remedy the breach (such request to contain a warning of the Licensor's intention to terminate);

(b) the Licensee permanently discontinues the use of the Licensed Program Materials; or

[**Note:** Evidence for this might be that the licensee no longer uses a computer capable of running the licensed programs.]

(c) the Licensee shall have a receiver or administrative receiver appointed of it or over any part of its undertaking or assets or shall pass a resolution for winding up (otherwise than for the purpose of a bona fide scheme of solvent amalgamation or reconstruction) or a court of competent jurisdiction shall make an order to that effect or if the Licensee shall enter into any voluntary arrangement with its creditors or shall become subject to an administration order or shall cease to carry on business

(3) Save as expressly provided in sub-clause (2) or elsewhere in this Agreement the Licence may not be terminated

(4) Forthwith upon the termination of the Licence the Licensee shall return to the Licensor the Licensed Program Materials [including any modifications thereof made by the Licensee] and all copies of the whole or any part thereof or, if requested by the Licensor, shall destroy the same (in the case of the Licensed Programs by erasing them from the magnetic media on which they are stored) and certify in writing to the Licensor that they have been destroyed. The Licensee shall also cause the Licensed Programs to be erased from the Equipment and shall certify to the Licensor that the same has been done

(5) Any termination of the Licence or this Agreement (howsoever occasioned) shall not affect any accrued rights or liabilities of either party nor shall it affect the coming into force or the continuance in force of any provision hereof which is expressly or by implication intended to come into or continue in force on or after such termination

22   Assignment

The Licensee shall not be entitled to assign, sub-license or otherwise transfer the Licence whether in whole or in part [save that the Licensee shall be entitled to assign the entire benefit of the Licence (but not part thereof) to any company which is from time to time a holding company or a subsidiary of the Licensee or a subsidiary of any such holding company (as those expressions are defined in s 736 Companies Act 1985) subject to such company first entering into a legally binding covenant with the Licensor undertaking to comply with the terms and conditions hereof and provided that at the time of such assignment such company shall be entitled to the exclusive possession of the Equipment (or such substituted equipment as is permitted under Clause 9(3)(b)) for its own use and benefit]

> [**Note:** The exception in brackets is designed to facilitate group reconstructions. The licensee may also wish to negotiate a right to assign to a purchaser of its business. The purchase of a corporate licensee's shares will not cause a problem as the identity of the licensee will not change.]

23   Force majeure

See Clause 15 of Precedent A

24   Licensee's warranty

See Clause 20 of Precedent A

25   Liability

See Clause 27 of Precedent A

26   Waiver of remedies

See Clause 28 of Precedent A

27 Entire agreement

See Clause 29 of Precedent A

28 Notices

See Clause 32 of Precedent A

29 Interpretation

See Clause 33 of Precedent A

30 Law

See Clause 34 of Precedent A

31 Disputes

See Clause 35 of Precedent A or Clause 37 of Precedent D

32 Severability

See Clause 36 of Precedent A

EXECUTED etc

THE SCHEDULE

A   THE EQUIPMENT

B   LICENSED PROGRAMS

C   LICENCE FEE

D   DELIVERY DATE

E   LOCATION

F   STORAGE MEDIA

G   COUNTRIES

H   TRAINING

[**Note:** This section should identify for each operational function:
   (i) how many staff are to be trained in total;
   (ii) how many can be trained at one time;
   (iii) how many days' training is required for each person and function;
   (iv) where and when training is to take place;
   (v) who is to be responsible for subsistence and travelling expenses.]

ACCEPTANCE CERTIFICATE

TO: SOFTWARE HOUSE [LIMITED] [PLC]
FROM: CUSTOMER [LIMITED] [PLC]

Date: 19

Dear Sirs,

We refer to the agreement between our respective companies dated
19   ('the Agreement') relating to the installation
and licensing of certain computer programs ('the Licensed Programs')
and confirm the following:

1   We have today accepted the Licensed Programs
2   We have inspected the Licensed Programs and confirm that the
      same conform to the description contained in the Agreement and
      that the same have been installed on the Equipment (as defined
      in the Agreement) to our satisfaction
3   The Licensed Programs have correctly processed the test data
      referred to in Clause 6 of the Agreement. Copies of such data
      and the results of such tests are annexed hereto and signed by
      us for the purpose of identification

SIGNED for and on behalf of
CUSTOMER [LIMITED] [PLC]

By   . . . .
Signature   . . . .
Title   . . . .
Witness   . . . .

Precedent D

Commissioned software agreement

[**Note:** This agreement assumes that the client has commissioned and paid for a feasibility study by the software house and that a detailed functional specification has been prepared and agreed.]

THIS AGREEMENT is made the   day of   19

PARTIES:

(1) SOFTWARE HOUSE [LIMITED] [PLC] whose registered office is at

('the Software House')

(2) CLIENT [LIMITED] [PLC] whose registered office is at

('the Client')

RECITAL:

The Software House has agreed to write certain computer programs for the Client and to provide the other services hereinafter described upon the terms and conditions hereinafter contained

NOW IT IS HEREBY AGREED as follows:

1 Definitions

In this Agreement, unless the context otherwise requires, the following expressions have the following meanings:

'the Programs'	means the [applications] computer programs to be written by the Software House pursuant to Clause 4

'the Functional Specification'	means the functional specification [dated *31 July 1995*] in accordance with which the Programs are to be written [a copy of which is annexed hereto]

[Note: For a document such as a functional specification which goes through several drafts the date may serve to identify the relevant version.]

'the Equipment'	means the Client's computer equipment specified in Schedule 1 or such other equipment as may be agreed between the parties

[Note: If performance criteria are relevant then any change in the configuration of the equipment ought to be agreed between the parties.]

'the Operating Manuals'	means the operating manuals to be prepared by the Software House pursuant to Clause 12
'the Services'	means the services to be provided by the Software House under this Agreement
'the Implementation Plan'	means the time schedule for the completion of the stages of preparation and delivery of the Programs as specified in Schedule 2
'Stage'	means a stage of the Implementation Plan
'the Staff'	has the meaning attributed thereto in Clause 20
['the Price'	means the price to be paid by the Client for the Services as specified in Schedule 4]

[Note: The definition of 'the Price' will only be required in the case of a fixed price contract.]

['the Maximum Cost'	means the sum specified in Schedule 4]

[Note: The definition of 'the Maximum Cost' will only be required in the case of a time and materials contract.]

'the Acceptance Date'	means the date on which the Programs are accepted (or deemed to be accepted) by the Client pursuant to Clause 10
'Ready for Use'	means fully installed, and tested and accepted in accordance with Clause 10
'the Completion Date'	means the date specified in the Implementation Plan by which the Software House is to provide the Programs Ready for Use or such extended date as may be granted pursuant to any provision of this Agreement

[**Note:** When fixing the Completion Date the parties should allow sufficient time for acceptance testing.]

['the Performance Criteria'	means the performance criteria which it is intended the Programs shall fulfil as specified in the Functional Specification subject to the tolerances, limitations and exceptions stated therein]

[**Note:** See 3.3.2 for suggested performance criteria.]

'the Training Plan'	means the training in the use of the Programs to be provided by the Software House for the Client's staff the details of which are set out in Schedule 5

2   Services to be provided [3.0.3; 3.1]

The Software House hereby agrees to:

(1) write the Programs;

(2) install the Programs on the Equipment;

(3) provide the Programs Ready for Use by the Completion Date;

(4) provide operating manuals and training;

upon the terms and conditions hereinafter contained

315

3   Software House's acknowledgement

The Software House acknowledges that the Programs are to be used by the Client in conjunction with the Equipment and the Client's existing *XYZ* operating system. The Software House also acknowledges that it has been supplied with sufficient information about the Equipment and the said operating system to enable it to write the Programs in accordance with the Functional Specification for use with the Equipment and the said operating system. The Software House shall not be entitled to any additional payment nor excused from any liability under this Agreement as a consequence of any misinterpretation by the Software House of any matter or fact relating to the functions, facilities and capabilities of the Equipment or the said operating system

4   Writing of programs [3.1]

The Software House shall write a series of applications programs in *C* language which shall provide the facilities and functions set out in the Functional Specification [and shall fulfil the Performance Criteria]

> [**Note:** It will be a sensible precaution to specify the language in which the programs are to be written; otherwise they may be written in an esoteric language which may be difficult for anyone else to understand.]

5   Payment and expenses [3.0.3; 3.2]

either:

[Fixed price—payment by milestones [3.0.3; 3.2.1]

(1) The Price shall be paid as to *10* per cent upon the signing of this Agreement [(by way of a deposit)] [(by way of a part payment)] as to *x* per cent upon the completion of each Stage (by way of part payments) and as to *10* per cent on the Acceptance Date]

> [**Note:** Where payment is linked to stages the criteria for deciding when each stage is completed should be made clear in the Implementation Plan.]

or:

[Time and materials—subject to a maximum and a retention] [3.0.3]

(1)(a) The Client shall pay the Software House for the time properly spent (which for the purposes of this Agreement shall include any travelling time spent necessarily by the Staff in the course of providing the Services) and the materials and computer time properly used by the Staff in providing the Services on the terms and conditions set out below provided that the total amount payable to the Software House for the Services shall not (save as expressly provided elsewhere in this Agreement) exceed the Maximum Cost

(b) The time spent by the Staff in providing the Services shall be charged at the hourly rates specified in Schedule 6. Parts of an hour shall be charged on a pro-rata basis. [The Software House shall ensure that those Staff engaged in providing any part of the Services shall not be unduly over-qualified or under-qualified to provide the same]

[**Note:** This clause assumes that the hourly charge out rates for the Staff include the cost of ancillary staff and overheads and a profit element.]

(c) The rates of charge for materials and computer time shall be those specified in Schedule 6

[(d) The Software House shall be entitled at any time and from time to time to vary any or all of the rates referred to in paragraphs (b) and (c) above to accord with any change in its standard scale rates by giving to the Client not less than *30* days' prior written notice]

[**Note:** The software house may also wish to reserve a right to adjust the Maximum Cost accordingly.]

(e) The Software House shall maintain full and accurate records of the time spent and materials and computer time used by the Staff in providing the Services in a form to be approved in writing by the Client. The Software House shall produce such records to the Client for inspection at all reasonable times on request

(f) The Software House shall render itemised invoices to the Client in respect of the said charges monthly in arrears. Each invoice shall specify the time spent by each member of the Staff and shall give a breakdown of the charges for materials and computer time

(g) Each invoice will be subject to a *10* per cent retention by the Client up to a maximum cumulative retention amount equal to *10* per cent of the Maximum Cost. The cumulative retention moneys shall be paid to the Software House on the Acceptance Date

(2) If it shall be necessary for any of the Staff to visit the Client's premises or make any other journeys in the course of providing the Services then the Client shall reimburse the Software House for all reasonable travelling and subsistence expenses properly incurred in so doing. Apart from minor out-of-pocket expenses, claims for reimbursement of expenses shall be paid by the Client only if accompanied by the relevant receipts

[(3) The Software House advises the Client that at the Completion Date the Programs will contain special software which will deny the Client the use of the Programs or part of the Programs in the event that the Client fails fully to comply with sub-clause (1) of this Clause. The Software House undertakes to the Client immediately and completely to disable and remove such special software as soon as the Client complies fully with sub-clause (1) of this Clause]

[**Note:** For the validity of so-called logic bombs for non-payment see 3.2.2.]

(4) All charges payable by the Client under this Agreement [other than the payments mentioned in sub-clause (1)] shall be paid within *30* days after the receipt by the Client of the Software House's invoice therefor

[**Note:** Delete the bracketed phrase in sub-clause (4) if the time and materials basis is used.]

(5) Payments exclusive of VAT—*see Clause 3(4) of Precedent A*

(6) Interest on overdue amounts—*see Clause 3(6) of Precedent A*

6   Implementation Plan and delays [3.2.1]

[**Note:**

(1) If a delay arises due to the fault of the software house then the client should consider the payment terms of the agreement carefully. Where a fixed sum is payable in instalments linked to milestones, the client will not have to make any payment until the relevant milestone is reached. Where, however, payment is to be made on a time and materials basis the software house will be entitled to payment for services performed during the period of the delay unless the agreement provides otherwise. If the software house does cause a delay in breach of the agreement then the client will in any event be entitled to damages.

(2) If a delay arises due to the fault of the client then in the case of a fixed price contract payable in instalments linked to milestones the software house should seek a provision that payments should be made on the scheduled dates for completion even though actual completion is delayed. The software house should also seek compensation for any other costs and losses arising out of the client's default including any additional time spent on rectifying errors caused by the client. Where payment is on a time and materials basis, work performed during the period of the delay will automatically be rewarded (subject to any maximum) but the software house should make it clear that payment will be made for additional time spent on rectifying errors caused by the client.

(3) Where a delay is caused by force majeure, clause 28 will be brought into operation. In the event of force majeure the parties must decide whether payment is still to be linked to milestones or whether any additional or accelerated payment should be made or, if

payment is on a time and materials basis what payment, if any, should be made for idle time. This is a difficult area of course because neither party is at fault. Clause 28 is drawn on the assumption that both parties will incur costs as a result of the delay and therefore provides that each party will bear its own costs. However, clause 28 gives either party a right to terminate in the event of a prolonged delay; the possibility of a termination should encourage the parties to reach a sensible compromise if they wish to continue with the contract.]

Version A (Fixed Price)

[(1) The Software House undertakes to use its reasonable endeavours to complete each Stage by the date specified in the Implementation Plan but time shall not be of the essence in relation to such obligations

[**Note:** The client will, of course, be primarily interested in the date on which the programs are finally completed and ready for operational use. However, a timetable for each stage of preparation will give the client an indication of how matters are progressing during the course of the contract.]

Software House's default

(2)(a) The Software House shall provide the Programs Ready for Use on or before the Completion Date

(b) If the Software House shall fail to provide the Programs Ready for Use by the Completion Date then the Software House shall pay to the Client as and by way of liquidated damages for any loss or damage sustained by the Client resulting from delay during the period from the Completion Date to the date on which the Software House provides the Programs Ready for Use the sum of £*500* for each week of such delay and pro rata for parts of a week up to a total maximum of £*5,000*. Subject to the provisions of paragraph (c) below, the payment of such sums shall be in full satisfaction of the Software House's liability for such delay. The payment of liquidated damages shall not relieve the Software House from its obligation to provide the Programs Ready for Use or from any other liability or obligation under this Agreement

(c) If the Software House shall fail to provide the Programs Ready for Use within *10* weeks after the Completion Date then notwithstanding anything else contained in this Agreement the Client shall be entitled to terminate this Agreement forthwith on giving written notice to the Software House and to recover from the Software House the amount of all [direct] damages and loss suffered by the Client resulting from such failure. Upon such termination the Software House shall (without prejudice to the Client's right to recover the amount of such damages and loss as aforesaid) forthwith refund to the Client all moneys previously paid to the Software House under this Agreement

Client's default

(3) If the Software House shall be prevented or delayed from performing any of its obligations under this Agreement by reason of any act or omission of the Client (other than a delay by the Client for which the Client is excused under Clause 28) then, notwithstanding anything else contained in this Agreement:

> (a) if as a result any Stage is not completed by the date specified in the Implementation Plan (or by any extended date granted pursuant to any provision of this Agreement) then the part payment due to be paid on the completion of that Stage shall be paid on the scheduled date for such completion (taking into account any extension of time granted pursuant to any provision of this Agreement) as distinct from the actual date of completion;

> (b) the Client shall pay to the Software House a reasonable sum in respect of any additional time spent and materials and computer time used by the Staff in rectifying any errors in the Programs or the Operating manuals caused by such act or omission of the Client including without limitation the provision of any incorrect or inadequate information or data by the Client; and

> (c) the Client shall pay to the Software House all other reasonable costs, charges and losses sustained or incurred by the Software House as a result of such act or omission (and for which the Software House is not compensated pursuant to paragraph (a) and (b) above)

The Software House shall promptly notify the Client in writing of any claim which it may have under this sub-clause giving such particulars thereof as it is then able to provide]

Version B (Time and materials)

[(1) *See sub-clause (1) of Version A*

Software House's default

(2) *See sub-clause (2) of Version A*

(3) If the Software House shall fail to provide the Programs Ready for Use by the Completion Date then notwithstanding anything else contained in this Agreement the Software House shall not be entitled to any payment for the time spent and materials and computer time used by the Staff in providing any part of the Services after the Completion Date

Client's default

(4) If the Software House shall be prevented or delayed from performing any of its obligations under this Agreement by reason of any act or

omission of the Client (other than a delay by the Client for which the Client is excused under Clause 28) then, notwithstanding anything else contained in this Agreement:

(a) the Client shall pay the Software House (at the rates specified in Schedule 6) for any additional time spent and materials and computer time used by the Staff in rectifying any errors in the Programs or the Operating Manuals caused by such act or omission of the Client including without limitation the provision of any incorrect or inadequate information or data by the Client; and

(b) the Client shall pay to the Software House all other reasonable costs, charges and losses sustained or incurred by the Software House which are attributable to such act or omission

Any payments due under paragraphs (a) and (b) shall be paid notwithstanding that when added to the other payments due under this Agreement the resultant sum exceeds the Maximum Cost

The Software House shall promptly notify the Client in writing of any claim which it may have under this sub-clause giving such particulars thereof as it is then able to provide]

7 Alterations [3.5.2]

(1) If at any time [before the completion of Stage X] the Client wishes to alter all or any part of the Programs then the Client shall provide the Software House with full written particulars of such alterations and with such further information as the Software House may reasonably require

[**Note:** Alterations which result in a significant reduction in the price may not be acceptable to the software house which may require some control over such reductions.]

(2) The Software House shall then submit to the Client as soon as reasonably practicable a full written quotation for such alterations specifying what changes (if any) will be required to [the Price] [the Maximum Cost] and the Implementation Plan and what adjustments will be required to the Functional Specification, the Operating Manuals and the Training Plan

(3) Upon receipt of such quotation the Client may elect either:

(a) to accept such quotation in which case this Agreement shall be amended in accordance therewith; or

(b) to withdraw the proposed alterations in which case this Agreement shall continue in force unchanged (subject to sub-clause (4) below)

(4) The Software House shall be entitled to make a reasonable charge for considering such alterations and preparing the said quotation and if the Client's request for such alterations is subsequently withdrawn but results in a delay in the performance of the Services then the Software House shall not be liable for such delay and shall be entitled to an extension of time for performing its obligations equal to the period of the delay

(5) The Software House shall not be obliged to consider or make any alterations to the Programs save in accordance with the aforesaid procedure

8   Changes to the Functional Specification and Operating Manuals

If any alterations are made to the Programs pursuant to Clause 7 then the Software House shall make appropriate modifications to the Functional Specification the Operating Manuals and the Training Plan to reflect such alterations. The provisions of this Agreement shall then apply to the Functional Specification the Operating Manuals and the Training Plan as so modified. The cost of such modifications shall be included in the quotation given under Clause 7

9   Delivery and installation [3.3]

The Software House shall at the agreed Stage:

(1) deliver to the Client:

(a) one copy of the object code of the Programs in machine-readable form on the storage media specified in Schedule 7;

(b) certified copies of the test data and results of tests carried out by the Software House on all parts of the Programs prior to delivery;

(c) the Operating Manuals

(2) install the Programs on the Equipment

10   Testing and acceptance [3.3.1]

(1) On or before the completion of Stage *P* the Client shall submit to the Software House test data which in the reasonable opinion of the Client is suitable to test whether the Programs are in accordance with the Functional Specification [and the Performance Criteria] together with the results expected to be achieved by processing such test data on the Equipment using the Programs and the Client's *XYZ* operating system. The Software House shall not be entitled to object to such test data or expected results unless the Software House can demonstrate to the

Client that they are not in accordance with the Functional Specification [and/or the Performance Criteria], in which event the Client shall make such amendments to such test data and expected results as may be necessary for them to conform to the Functional Specification [and the Performance Criteria]

(2) After the Programs have been fully installed on the Equipment, the Software House shall give to the Client at least *7* days' prior written notice (or such shorter notice as may be agreed between the parties) of the date ('the Testing Date') on which the Software House will be ready to attend acceptance tests at the Client's premises. The Client and the Software House shall attend such tests on the Testing Date and shall provide all necessary facilities to enable such tests to be carried out

(3) On the Testing Date the Client shall process, in the presence of the authorised representatives of the Software House, the said test data on the Equipment using the Programs and the said *XYZ* operating system. The Software House shall if required by the Client give the Client's personnel all reasonable assistance in processing such test data

(4) The Client shall accept the Programs immediately after the Programs have correctly processed such test data by achieving the expected results

(5) The Programs shall not be deemed to have incorrectly processed such test data by reason of any failure to provide any facility or function not specified in the Functional Specification

(6) If the Programs shall fail to process such test data correctly then repeat tests shall be carried out on the same terms and conditions within a reasonable time thereafter but in any event no later than *14* days thereafter. [The Software House shall not be entitled to make any charge for attending such repeat tests]

[**Note:** The words in brackets will be needed only in the case of a time and materials contract.]

(7) If such repeat tests demonstrate that the Programs are not in accordance with the Functional Specification [or the Performance Criteria] then the Client may by written notice to the Software House elect at its sole option:

(a) to fix (without prejudice to its other rights and remedies) a new date for carrying out further tests on the Programs on the same terms and conditions as the repeat tests (save that all costs which the Client may incur as a result of carrying out such tests shall be reimbursed by the Software House). If the Programs shall fail such further tests then the Client shall be entitled to proceed under paragraph (b) or (c) below;

(b) to accept the Programs subject to an abatement of [the Price] [the total consideration payable hereunder] such abatement to be such amount as, taking into account the circumstances, is reasonable. In the absence of written agreement as to abatement within *14* days after the date of such notice the Client shall be entitled to reject the Programs in accordance with paragraph (c) below; or

(c) to reject the Programs as not being in conformity with this Agreement in which event this Agreement shall automatically terminate and the Software House shall (without prejudice to the Client's other rights and remedies) forthwith refund to the Client all sums previously paid to the Software House under this Agreement

(8) Notwithstanding anything else contained in this Clause the Software House shall be entitled (provided it has complied with its obligations under this Clause) at any time and from time to time after the Testing Date to serve written notice on the Client requiring the Client to identify any part of the Functional Specification [or the Performance Criteria] which the Programs do not fulfil. If the Client shall fail to identify in writing to the Software House within *14* days after the receipt of such notice any part of the Functional Specification [or the Performance Criteria] which the Programs do not fulfil then the Client shall be deemed to have accepted the Programs

(9) If at any time the Client shall commence live running of the whole or any part of the Programs (as distinct from acceptance testing) then the Client shall be deemed to have accepted the Programs

[**Notes:** (1) Sub-clauses (8) and (9) are designed to protect the software house in the event that the customer unreasonably refuses to accept the Programs.

(2) In a complicated development, testing and acceptance will be undertaken in stages with a final contractual acceptance at the end.]

11   Warranty [3.3.3]

(1)(a) The Software House warrants that the Programs will after acceptance by the Client provide the facilities and functions set out in the Functional Specification [and will fulfil the Performance Criteria] when properly used with the Equipment and the Client's *XYZ* operating system and that the Operating Manuals and the Training Plan will provide adequate instruction to enable the Client to make full and proper use of the Programs in conjunction with the Equipment and the said operating system without reference to any other person or document

(b) If the Software House receives written notice from the Client after the Acceptance Date of any breach of the said warranty then the Software House shall at its own expense and within a reasonable time after receiving such notice remedy the defect or error in question provided that the Software House shall have no liability or obligations under the said warranty unless it shall have received written notice of the defect or error in question no later than the expiry of *12* months after the Acceptance Date

(c) The Software House shall have no liability or obligations under the said warranty other than to remedy breaches thereof by the provision of materials and services within a reasonable time and without charge to the Client. If the Software House shall fail to comply with such obligations its liability for such failure shall be limited to [a sum equal to the Price] [£   ]. The foregoing states the entire liability of the Software House, whether in contract, tort or howsoever for defects and errors in the Programs and the Operating Manuals which are notified to the Software House after the Acceptance Date

[**Note:** Where a maintenance agreement is entered into (see clause 16) sub-clause (1) will need to be amended—follow clause 24 of Precedent O.]

(2) See Clause 19(5) of Precedent A

12   Operating Manuals [3.7.3]

The Software House shall prepare and provide the Client with *2* copies of a set of operating manuals containing sufficient information to enable the Client to make full and proper use of the Programs in conjunction with the Equipment and the Client's *XYZ* operating system. [If the Client requires further copies of the Operating Manuals then these will be supplied by the Software House under licence at a reasonable charge]

[**Note:** If copyright in the operating manuals is to pass to the client then the bracketed sentence will not be required.]

13   Training [3.7.3]

(1) The Software House undertakes to provide training in the use of the Programs for the Client's staff in accordance with the Training Plan

(2) Any additional training required by the Client shall be provided by the Software House in accordance with its standard scale of charges from time to time in force

14   Proprietary rights [3.8.2]

Version A (Rights retained by the Software House)

[(1) The copyright and all other intellectual property rights of whatever nature in the Programs, the Operating Manuals, the Functional Specification and in all other specifications and documentation relating to the Programs (other than in any material provided by the Client) shall be and shall remain vested in the Software House

(2) The Software House hereby grants to the Client with effect from the Acceptance Date a perpetual non-exclusive and non-transferable licence to use and copy the Programs and the Operating Manuals for its own internal business purposes but for no other purpose whatsoever. The Client shall not be entitled to sub-license the use of the whole or any part of the Programs or the Operating Manuals

[Notes:

  (1) The client may wish to reserve a right to assign the licence to another member of its group of companies—see clause 22 of Precedent C.
  (2) The software house may wish to impose a more restricted right to use the programs in which case incorporate all relevant clauses of Precedent C.
  (3) The client may accept a non-exclusive licence in return for the software house undertaking to refrain from making the programs available to any of the client's competitors.]

(3) The Software House and the Client shall enter into a source code deposit agreement on the Acceptance Date in respect of the Programs in the form of the draft annexed hereto and the Software House shall procure that the third party named therein shall enter into such agreement

[Notes:

  (1) Adapt Precedent N for use with a single user.
  (2) The alternative would be for the source codes to be made available to the Client immediately against an undertaking only to use them for the purposes of maintenance.]

(4) Client to treat the Programs, the Operating Manuals and the Functional Specification as confidential—*See Clause 13 of Precedent C*]

Version B (Rights to vest in the Client)

[(1) The copyright and all other intellectual property rights of whatever nature in the Programs, the Operating Manuals, the Functional Specification and in all other specifications and documentation relating to the Programs shall pass to the Client on the Acceptance Date

[Note: The effect of sub-clause (1) will be to make this agreement an agreement for the sale of copyright thereby attracting ad valorem stamp duty under section 59 of the Stamp Act 1891. Where appropriate a certificate of value should be incorporated.]

[(2) Notwithstanding sub-clause (1), the Software House reserves the right to use in any way it thinks fit any programming tools, skills and techniques acquired or used by the Software House in the performance of this Agreement]

(3) The Software House shall treat as confidential all information contained or embodied in the Programs (and in any documentation relating thereto, including source code), the Operating Manuals and the Functional Specification and shall not disclose the whole or any part of such information to any third party without the prior written consent of the Client. The Software House shall ensure that its employees comply with the provisions of this sub-clause. The foregoing obligations shall survive any termination of this Agreement

(4) The Software House shall deliver to the Client on the Acceptance Date:

(a) the source code of the Programs in the form both of printed listings and magnetic [tape] [disk];

(b) the Operating Manuals;

(c) all other materials necessary to enable a reasonably skilled programmer to correct, modify and enhance the Programs without reference to any other person or document]

[**Note:** If the software house is to maintain the programs then it will need to retain copies of the source code for maintenance purposes.]

15   Indemnity

The Client will indemnify the Software House and keep the Software House fully and effectively indemnified against all costs, claims, demands, expenses and liabilities of whatsoever nature arising out of or in connection with any claim that the use by the Software House of any information or material supplied by the Client for the purpose of enabling the Software House to prepare and write the Programs and/or the Operating Manuals infringes the intellectual property rights (of whatever nature) of any third party

[16   Maintenance [9.1]

The parties undertake to enter into a maintenance agreement on the Acceptance Date in respect of the Programs and the Operating Manuals in the form of the draft annexed hereto]

[**Note:** See Precedent M.]

17   Representatives [3.6.1; 3.7.1]

Each party shall nominate in writing upon the signing of this Agreement the person who will act as its representative for the purposes of this Agreement and who will be responsible for providing any information which may be required by the other party to perform its obligations hereunder

18   Progress meetings

The parties shall procure that their respective representatives will meet at least once a month between the date hereof and the Acceptance Date to discuss and minute the progress of the Services

> [Note: Minute taking is a laborious but useful exercise especially if a dispute arises.]

19   Information [3.6.1]

Without prejudice to the provisions of Clause 3 the Client shall provide all information and documentation reasonably requested by the Software House to enable the Software House to prepare and write the Programs and the Operating Manuals. Such information and documentation shall be subject to the provisions of confidentiality contained in Clause 21

20   The Staff [3.7.1]

The Services shall be provided by the employees of the Software House named in Schedule 3 or such other persons as may be approved by the Client in writing from time to time ('the Staff'), such approval not to be unreasonably withheld or delayed

21   Confidentiality [3.7.2]

(1) *See Clause 21 of Precedent A*

(2) The Software House will establish and maintain such security measures and procedures as are reasonably practicable to provide for the safe custody of the Client's information and data in its possession and to prevent unauthorised access thereto or use thereof

> [Note: If real personal data is involved, the bureau Data Protection Clause [P15] may also be relevant [3.7.2].]

[22   Computer facilities [3.6.1]

The Client agrees to provide the Software House free of charge during the Client's normal working hours (or during such other times as the Client may agree in writing) with such computer facilities (including computer consumables, storage and data preparation facilities) and time on the Equipment as may be necessary to enable the Software House to prepare, write, test and install the Programs]

> [Notes:
>
> (1) This will be an alternative to the software house using its own facilities.
> (2) The client may wish to insure against the possibility of failure of its equipment giving rise to a delay in completing the work.]

[23   Office facilities [3.6.1]

The Client undertakes to provide the Staff with such desks, word processing, copying and other office facilities at the Client's premises as may be necessary to enable the Software House to fulfil its obligations under this Agreement]

[24   Dress and conformity [3.7.1]

While the Staff attend at the Client's premises they will conform to the Client's normal codes of staff and security practice]

[25   Poaching staff [3.6.2]

The Client shall not without the prior written consent of the Software House (and so that each of sub-clauses (1) and (2) below shall be deemed to constitute a separate agreement and shall be construed independently of the other):

> (1) at any time during the period from the date hereof to the expiry of six months after the Acceptance Date or the date of termination of this Agreement (as the case may be) solicit or endeavour to entice away from or discourage from being employed by the Software House any person who is, or shall at any time between the date hereof and the Acceptance Date or the date of such termination be, one of the Software House's employees engaged in providing the Services provided however that this provision shall not apply to any person employed by the Software House whose rate of gross basic contractual remuneration payable by the Software House as at the date of this Agreement (or as at the date of

commencement of such person's employment if such employment shall commence after the date of this Agreement) is less than £25,000 per annum;

(2) at any time during the period from the date hereof to the expiry of six months after the Acceptance Date or the date of termination of this Agreement (as the case may be) employ or attempt to employ any person who is, or shall at any time between the date hereof and the Acceptance Date or the date of such termination be, one of the Software House's employees engaged in providing the Services provided however that this provision shall not apply to any person employed by the Software House whose rate of gross basic contractual remuneration payable by the Software House as at the date of this Agreement (or as at the date of commencement of such person's employment if such employment shall commence after the date of this Agreement) is less than £25,000 per annum]

[26   Termination [3.4]

Notwithstanding anything else contained herein, this Agreement may be terminated:

(1) by the Software House forthwith on giving notice in writing to the Client if the Client shall fail to pay any sum due under the terms of this Agreement (otherwise than as a consequence of any default on the part of the Software House) and such sum remains unpaid for *14* days after written notice from the Software House that such sum has not been paid (such notice to contain a warning of the Software House's intention to terminate); or

(2) by either party forthwith on giving notice in writing to the other if the other commits any [material] [serious] breach of any term of this Agreement (other than any failure by the Client to make any payment hereunder in which event the provisions of sub-clause (1) above shall apply) and (in the case of a breach capable of being remedied) shall have failed, within *30* days after the receipt of a request in writing from the other party so to do, to remedy the breach (such request to contain a warning of such party's intention to terminate); or

(3) by either party forthwith on giving notice in writing to the other if the other party shall have a receiver or administrative receiver appointed of it or over any part of its undertaking or assets or shall pass a resolution for winding-up (otherwise than for the purpose of a bona fide scheme of solvent amalgamation or reconstruction) or a court of competent jurisdiction shall make an order to that effect or if the other party shall become subject

to an administration order or shall enter into any voluntary arrangement with its creditors or shall cease or threaten to cease to carry on business [; or

(4) by the Client by giving to the Software House not less than *30* days' written notice of termination to expire on the scheduled date for completion of any Stage (taking into account any extensions of time granted pursuant to any provision hereof). Upon such termination the Client shall immediately pay to the Software House all sums accrued due to the Software House hereunder]

27   Effects of termination

(1) Any termination of this Agreement (howsoever occasioned) shall not affect any accrued rights or liabilities of either party nor shall it affect the coming into force or the continuance in force of any provision hereof which is expressly or by implication intended to come into or continue in force on or after such termination

(2) Upon any termination of this Agreement by the Client pursuant to Clause 26(2) or 26(3) the Software House shall forthwith deliver to the Client all specifications, programs (including source codes) and other documentation relating to the preparation and writing of the Programs and the Operating Manuals existing at the date of such termination whether or not the same shall be complete. In the event of such termination the copyright and other intellectual property rights in and ownership of all such material shall forthwith automatically pass to the Client who shall be entitled to enter any premises of the Software House for the purpose of taking possession of such material (and so that the Software House hereby irrevocably licenses the Client, its employees and agents to enter any such premises for such purpose)

[**Note:** If the software house defaults or goes into liquidation the client will usually wish to terminate the agreement and appoint another software house to complete the work as quickly as possible. This clause enables the client to obtain all documentation relating to the programs and to hand it to the new software house for the purpose of completing the work.]

(3) Upon any termination of this Agreement (howsoever occasioned) the Software House shall forthwith deliver up to the Client all copies of any information and data supplied to the Software House by the Client for the purposes of this Agreement and shall certify to the Client that no copies of such information or data have been retained

28   Force majeure

(1) *See Clause 15 of Precedent A*

(2) In the event of any extension of time being granted pursuant to sub-clause (1) the Implementation Plan shall be amended accordingly

[29   Further assurance

The parties shall execute and do all such further deeds, documents and things as may be necessary to carry the provisions of this Agreement into full force and effect]

> [**Note:** This clause should be incorporated where Version B of Clause 14(1) is used. The client will then be able to require the Software House to execute any further documents which may be necessary fully to vest the proprietary rights to the programs in the client.]

30   Liability

See Clause 27 of Precedent A

31   Waiver of remedies

See Clause 28 of Precedent A

32   Entire agreement

See Clause 29 of Precedent A

33   Sub-contracts

See Clause 31 of Precedent A

34   Notices

See Clause 32 of Precedent A

35   Interpretation

See Clause 33 of Precedent A

36   Law

See Clause 34 of Precedent A

37   Disputes [13.1.1]

Any dispute which may arise between the parties concerning this Agreement shall be determined as follows:

(1) if the dispute shall be of a technical nature concerning the interpretation of the Functional Specification or relating to the functions or capabilities of the Programs or any similar or related matter then such dispute shall be referred for final settlement to an expert nominated jointly by the parties or, failing such nomination with *14* days after either party's request to the other therefor, nominated at the request of either party by the President from time to time of the British Computer Society. Such expert shall be deemed to act as an expert and not as an arbitrator. His decision shall (in the absence of clerical or manifest error) be final and binding on the parties and his fees for so acting shall be borne by the parties in equal shares unless he determines that the conduct of either party is such that such party should bear all of such fees

(2) in any other case the dispute shall be determined by the High Court of Justice in England and the parties hereby submit to the exclusive jurisdiction of that court for such purpose

38   Severability

See Clause 36 of Precedent A

EXECUTED etc

SCHEDULE 1

THE EQUIPMENT

SCHEDULE 2

IMPLEMENTATION PLAN

[**Note:** This Schedule should show each stage of the preparation of the Programs and the scheduled completion date for each stage. Each stage should be as detailed as possible and should specify what will happen and what will be produced on the completion thereof.]

SCHEDULE 3

SOFTWARE HOUSE'S PERSONNEL

SCHEDULE 4

[THE PRICE][THE MAXIMUM COST]

SCHEDULE 5

TRAINING PLAN

See the Schedule to Precedent C

SCHEDULE 6

CHARGING RATES

[**Note:** The Client should agree the following with the Software House:
    (a) Hourly rate for each individual or staff category
    (b) Rates of charge for materials and computer time.]

SCHEDULE 7

STORAGE MEDIA

Precedent E

'Shrink-wrap' licence [5.3.6.4]

LICENCE AGREEMENT

The copyright in this software ('the Software') and its associated documentation is owned by [   ] ('the Owner'). By opening this package you (an individual or legal entity) agree with the Owner to be bound by the terms of this Agreement which will govern your use of the Software. If you do not accept these terms you may within *14* days of purchase return the Software, its packaging and documentation unused and intact to your supplier together with proof of purchase for a full refund.

Licence

You are permitted to:

(1) load the Software into and use it on a single computer which is under your control;

(2) transfer the Software from one computer to another provided it is used on only one computer at any one time;

(3) use the Software on a computer network provided you have purchased such number of copies of the Software equal to the maximum number of copies of the Software in use on that network at any one time;

(4) make up to *3* copies of the Software for back-up purposes only in support of the permitted use. The copies must reproduce and include the Owner's copyright notice;

[**Note:** This may not be possible if the software is 'copy protected'.]

(5) transfer the Software (complete with all its associated documentation) and the benefit of this Agreement to another person provided he has agreed to accept the terms of this Agreement and you contemporaneously transfer all copies of the Software you have made to that person or destroy all copies not transferred. If any transferee does not accept such terms then this Agreement shall automatically terminate. The transferor

335

does not retain any rights under this Agreement in respect of the transferred Software.

You are not permitted:

(a) to load the Software on to a network server for the purposes of distribution to one or more other computer(s) on that network or to effect such distribution (such use requiring a separate licence);

(b) except as expressly permitted by this Agreement and save to the extent and in the circumstances expressly required to be permitted by law, to rent, lease, sub-license, loan, copy, modify, adapt, merge, translate, reverse engineer, decompile, disassemble or create derivative works based on the whole or any part of the Software or its associated documentation or use, reproduce or deal in the Software or any part thereof in any way.

[To the extent that local law gives you the right to decompile the Software in order to obtain information necessary to render the Software interoperable with other computer programs, the Owner hereby undertakes to make that information readily available to you. The Owner shall have the right to impose reasonable conditions such as a reasonable fee for doing so. In order to ensure that you receive the appropriate information, you must first give the Owner sufficient details of your objectives and the other software concerned. Requests for the appropriate information should be made to [   ].]

Term

This Agreement is effective until you terminate it by destroying the Software and its documentation together with all copies. It will also terminate if you fail to abide by its terms. Upon termination you agree to destroy all copies of the Software and its documentation including any Software stored on the hard disk of any computer under your control.

Ownership

You own only the diskette (or authorised replacement) on which the Software is recorded. You may retain the diskette on termination of this Agreement provided the Software has been erased. The Owner shall at all times retain ownership of the Software as recorded on the original diskette and all subsequent copies thereof regardless of form. This Agreement applies to the grant of the licence contained herein only and not to the contract of sale of the diskette. The Owner's warranties and telephone support service under this Agreement are available only to the original registered user (being the person who has signed and returned duly completed the enclosed Licence Registration Form to the Owner within *30* days after the date of original purchase).

Warranties

The Owner warrants that the diskette on which the Software is supplied will be free from defects in materials and workmanship under normal use for a period of *90* days after the date of original purchase ('the Warranty Period'). If a defect in the diskette shall occur during the Warranty Period it may be returned with proof of purchase to the Owner who will replace it free of charge.

The Owner warrants that the Software will perform substantially in accordance with its accompanying documentation (provided that the Software is properly used on the computer and with the operating system for which it was designed) and that the documentation correctly describes the operation of the Software in all material respects. If the Owner is notified of significant errors during the Warranty Period it will correct any such demonstrable errors in the Software or its documentation within a reasonable time or (at its option) provide or authorise a refund (against return of the Software and its documentation).

> [Note: The computer (minimum configuration) and operating system (version) must be specified and visible in either the licence agreement or on the packaging before the diskette package is opened.]

The above represent your sole remedies for any breach of the Owner's warranties, which are given only to the original registered user.

The express terms of this Agreement are in lieu of all warranties, conditions, undertakings, terms and obligations implied by statute, common law, trade usage, course of dealing or otherwise all of which are hereby excluded to the fullest extent permitted by law.

The Owner does not warrant that the Software will meet your requirements or that the operation of the Software will be uninterrupted or error-free or that defects in the Software will be corrected. You shall load and use the Software at your own risk and in no event will the Owner be liable to you for any loss or damage of any kind (except personal injury or death resulting from the Owner's negligence) including lost profits or other consequential loss arising from your use of or inability to use the Software or from errors or deficiencies in it whether caused by negligence or otherwise except as expressly provided herein. In no event shall the Owner's liability exceed the amount paid by you for the Software.

Support

The Owner's technical support staff will endeavour to answer by telephone any queries the original registered user may have regarding the use of the Software or its application for a period of *60* days after the first support service call, which must be made within the Warranty Period. For telephone support please call [   ] between the hours of [   ] and [   ] [Monday] to [Friday] inclusive.

Law

This Agreement shall be governed by English law.

If you have any questions concerning this Agreement please write to [   ].

[**Notes:** It is recommended that in conjunction with the Licence Agreement you observe the following guidelines:

(1) The usual copyright notice should appear prominently on the diskette, the packaging and the user manual as well as being encoded in the Software:

© [Owner] *1995*

(2) The following notice should appear on the front of the packaging:

IMPORTANT NOTICE: This software and its associated documentation is the copyright of [   ]. The use of this software is governed by the Licence Agreement accompanying this package.

This package requires an [ABC] computer with a minimum of [YM] of memory and the [XYZ] operating system version [4.1].

(3) A copy of the Licence Agreement should appear in the user manual.

(4) The following first screen display should be encoded in the Software to appear each time the Software is loaded:

© [Owner] **1991**

IMPORTANT NOTICE: This software is the copyright of [   ] and its use is governed by the terms of the Licence Agreement accompanying this package a copy of which is set out in the user manual. If you cannot locate the Licence Agreement please write to the owner at [ADDRESS] for a copy. If you accept the terms of the Licence Agreement, enter 'AGREED'.

(5) The accompanying Licence Registration Form entitling the original registered user to technical support should contain a form of confirmation for signature to the effect that the user agrees to be bound by the Licence Agreement.

(6) As well as describing the use of the software the user manual should:

(a) identify the software;

(b) describe its purpose;

(c) say what equipment (minimum configuration) and operating system (version) the software is suitable for;

(d) give the name and address of the owner;

(e) describe the software and the documentation as being copyright;

(f) give the telephone number for service calls and say between what hours, and on what days, the lines are open.]

Precedent F

Multiple copy software licence agreement [5.3.6.5]

[**Note:** This agreement is designed for use by a supplier in relation to a large corporate user which wishes to have the freedom to use multiple copies of package software either on a stand alone basis, or distributed via host computers to personal computers or workstations on a network, both for its own use and the use of other companies within its group.]

THIS AGREEMENT is made the   day of   19

PARTIES:

(1) SUPPLIER [LIMITED] [PLC] whose registered office is at
(‘the Supplier’)

(2) CUSTOMER [LIMITED] [PLC] whose registered office is at
(‘the Customer’)

RECITALS:

(A) [The Supplier is the owner of various computer software products and their associated documentation] [The Supplier is authorised by [　　　　　], a company incorporated in　　　　　 (‘the Owner’), to distribute and sub-license various computer software products and their associated documentation which are owned by the Owner]

(B) The Customer wishes to have for its own benefit and for the benefit of its Associates (as hereinafter defined) a non-exclusive licence to possess and reproduce multiple copies of certain of such software products (and any additional software products as may be mutually agreed) for internal use by its employees and those of its Associates on one or more computers owned or lawfully used by the Customer or its Associates and the Supplier has agreed to grant such licence on the terms of this Agreement

NOW IT IS HEREBY AGREED as follows:

1   Definitions

In this Agreement, unless the context otherwise requires, the following expressions have the following meanings:

'Associate'	means, in relation to the Customer, another person, firm or company which directly or indirectly controls, is controlled by or is under common control with the Customer (and the expression 'control' shall mean the power to direct or cause the direction of the general management and policies of the person, firm or company in question) but only (i) so long as such control exists, (ii) if that person, firm or company is approved in writing by the Supplier and (iii) if that person, firm or company has previously entered into a Deed of Adherence
'Authorised Computers'	means (i) the Hosts and (ii) the personal computers and workstations specified in Schedule 2 and/or such other personal computers and workstations as the Customer may notify the Supplier in Customer Reports from time to time and which, in each such case, [are located at the Premises and] are owned or lawfully used by one of the Users, but excluding, in any such case, any Hosts, personal computers or workstations which cease to be Authorised Computers in accordance with Clause 6(6) or Clause 13(3)

[**Note:** If laptops or other PCs are used at home or elsewhere than in the Premises omit the words in square brackets]

'Copies'	means Electronic Copies and Stand Alone Copies
'Credit'	has the meaning ascribed thereto in Clause 6(7)

340

'Customer Report' means a report from the Customer to the Supplier in the form set out in Schedule 4 or in such other form as the Supplier and the Customer may agree in writing from time to time and which is certified as true and complete by a [director] of the Customer

'Deed of Adherence' means a deed of adherence in the form set out in Schedule 5 or in such other form as the Customer and the Supplier may agree in writing from time to time

'Electronic Copies' means copies of the Software which the Users may make from time to time pursuant to Clause 2(1)(c)

'End User Licence Agreement' means, in relation to each item of Software, the latest version of the end-user licence agreement routinely provided with Stand Alone Copies thereof by the [Supplier] [Owner] to end-users in the United Kingdom from time to time (copies of the current versions of those relating to the Original Software being attached as the Appendix hereto) and a copy of which has been supplied to the Customer either in the Appendix hereto or pursuant to Clause 2(2)(e)

'the Hosts' means the mainframe computers, mini computers and/or file servers specified in Schedule 2 and/or such other mainframe computers, mini computers and/or file servers as the customer may notify to the Supplier in Customer Reports from time to time which are located at the Premises and which are, in each such case, owned or lawfully used by one of the Users

'the Master Copies' means the master copies of the Software to be supplied by the Supplier pursuant to this Agreement

341

'the Original Software'	means the computer software which the Supplier has agreed to supply to the Customer hereunder as specified in Schedule 1
['the Premises'	means those premises located in [the United Kingdom] specified in Schedule 2 and/or such other premises located in [the United Kingdom] as the Customer may notify the Supplier in Customer Reports from time to time]
'Products'	means the Software, the Master Copies, the Copies, the Software Documentation and the Stand Alone Products
'Software'	means all or any items of Original Software and/or Supplemental Software as the context admits or the case may require
'the Software Documentation'	means, in relation to each item of Software, the operating manuals and other literature routinely provided from time to time as part of the Stand Alone Product in respect of such Software by the [Supplier] [Owner] or in conjunction with any modification, enhancement or upgrade of such Software
'Stand Alone Copies'	means copies of the Software comprised in Stand Alone Products
'Stand Alone Product'	means, in relation to each item of Software, the boxed software product routinely provided by the [Supplier] [Owner] to end-users in [the United Kingdom] from time to time which is designed for use by an end-user on and in conjunction with a single personal computer or workstation and which comprises, inter alia, a diskette with that Software recorded on it, a copy of the operating manuals and other

	literature, an End User Licence Agreement and its associated packaging
'Supplemental Software'	means any software additional to the Original Software which the Supplier may agree in writing to license pursuant to this Agreement from time to time and which shall be accepted by the Customer and, in relation to the Original Software and such additional software, all modifications, enhancements, upgrades and replacements thereof and additions thereto as may be provided by the Supplier pursuant to this Agreement from time to time and accepted by the Customer
'United Kingdom'	means the United Kingdom of Great Britain and Northern Ireland
'Users'	means the Customer and its Associates

2   Grant of licence

(1) Subject to the terms and conditions of this Agreement, the Supplier hereby grants to each of the Users a non-exclusive right:

(a) for the User's employees to use the Software in accordance with the Software Documentation for the User's own internal business purposes on Authorised Computers;

(b) to install the Software on the Hosts using the Master Copies;

(c) to reproduce the Software for use in accordance with paragraph (a) either by downloading copies of the Software electronically from the Hosts to the hard disks of other Authorised Computers or by installing the Software directly on to the hard disks of such other Authorised Computers using the Master Copies;

(d) to install each Stand Alone Copy which may be supplied pursuant to this Agreement on the hard disk of a single personal computer which is an Authorised Computer for use in accordance with paragraph (a)

(2) For the purposes of this Agreement, the Supplier shall supply to the Customer:

(a) two master copies of the Original Software (in a form suitable for reproduction of multiple copies) on appropriate electronic media within *14* days of the date of this Agreement;

(b) in respect of the Original Software, such number of copies of the Software Documentation and Stand Alone Products as are specified in Schedule 3 within *14* days of the date of this Agreement;

(c) two master copies of any Supplemental Software (in a form suitable for reproduction of multiple copies) on appropriate electronic media at such time or times as may be separately agreed between the Supplier and the Customer;

(d) such new or additional copies of the Software Documentation and Stand Alone Products at such time or times as may be separately agreed between the Supplier and the Customer;

(e) a copy of the latest version of each End User Licence Agreement which may be issued hereafter from time to time

(3) No User shall be entitled to copy or reproduce any Stand Alone Copies (except for back-up copies permitted by the relative End User Licence Agreement or by law) or the Software Documentation either in whole or in part

(4) The use of each of the Copies made available under this Agreement shall be governed by the terms and conditions of the End User Licence Agreement relative to such Copy and the Users shall be subject to the obligations and shall be granted the rights specified therein except insofar as the terms and conditions thereof are inconsistent with the terms and conditions of this Agreement in which case the latter shall prevail. Each of the Users covenants and agrees with the Supplier that during the term of this Agreement such User will observe, perform and be bound by all the terms of such End User Licence Agreements as modified by this Agreement

(5) Save as expressly provided in this Agreement or in the relative End User Licence Agreement as modified by this Agreement and save to the extent and in the circumstances expressly required to be permitted by law, none of the Users shall:

(a) rent, lease, sub-license, loan, copy, modify, adapt, merge, translate, reverse engineer, decompile, disassemble or create derivative works based on the whole or any part of the Products;

(b) use, reproduce or deal in the Products or any part thereof in any way

(6) No User shall be entitled to use the Software on any Authorised Computer which is located at premises outside the United Kingdom

[Note: The territorial restriction should correspond to those jurisdictions in which the governing law of the end user agreements is considered to be effective]

(7) The Supplier will make the Software available to the Customer in object code form only

(8) Each User shall effect and maintain adequate security measures to safeguard the Products from access or use by any unauthorised person and shall retain all copies thereof made available to it under this Agreement under its effective control

(9) Each User shall duplicate the [Supplier's] [Owner's] copyright and other proprietary notices on each copy of the Software within its possession or control both within the program and on any diskette (or other media) labels

(10) The provision of each Stand Alone Product pursuant to this Agreement shall be deemed to be a contract of sale of the physical item (but not the copyright or other intellectual property rights therein) between the Supplier and the User first employing the same. Such User may sell such Stand Alone Products in accordance with the End User Licence Agreement governing that Stand Alone Product. All copies of the other Products are and shall remain the property of the Supplier and are made available under this Agreement by way of a non-exclusive licence to possess the same for use in accordance with this Agreement and may not be sold or otherwise disposed of to any third party

(11) This Agreement, and all or any of the rights or obligations hereunder, shall not be assigned or sub-licensed by any User without the prior written approval of the Supplier

3   Guarantee and indemnity

(1) Each of the Users ('the Guarantor') hereby (1) guarantees to the Supplier the due and punctual performance and observance by each of the other Users of all such other User's obligations under this Agreement (by virtue of its execution of this Agreement or a Deed of Adherence) and (2) undertakes to hold the Supplier fully and completely indemnified on demand against any loss, damage and liability occasioned by any failure of any of the other Users so to perform or observe any of its obligations under this Agreement

(2) The liability of the Guarantor under this Clause 3 shall be as primary obligor and not merely as surety and shall not be affected, impaired or discharged by reason of any act, omission, matter or thing which but for this provision might operate to release or otherwise exonerate the Guarantor from its obligations under this Clause 3 including without

limitation any time or other indulgence granted by the Supplier to any of the other Users or any variation of the terms of this Agreement or any End User Licence Agreement or any new or revised End User Licence Agreement becoming applicable to the use of any Software in terms of this Agreement

(3) Where more than one User is liable under this Clause 3 their liability shall be joint and several

(4) The provisions of this Clause 3 shall survive the termination of this Agreement

4   Duration

This Agreement shall commence on [the date hereof] for an initial period of 2 years and shall continue thereafter unless or until terminated by either the Supplier or the Customer giving to the other not less than 6 months' written notice expiring on the last day of the said initial period or at any time thereafter, but shall be subject to earlier termination as provided in Clause 11

5   Prices and payment

(1) The Customer shall pay the charges specified in Schedule 3 for:

(a) the supply hereunder by the Supplier of the master copies of the Original Software;

(b) the number of Electronic Copies of the Original Software which the Users wish to make immediately after delivery of the master copies of the Original Software as specified in Schedule 3;

(c) in relation to the Original Software, the number of copies of the Software Documentation to be supplied by the Supplier hereunder as specified in Schedule 3;

(d) in relation to the Original Software, the number of Stand Alone Products to be supplied by the Supplier hereunder as specified in Schedule 3;

(e) the number of Electronic Copies of the Software made by Users from time to time (in addition to those mentioned in paragraph (b));

(f) the supply hereunder by the Supplier of the master copies of any Supplemental Software;

(g) any new or additional copies of the Software Documentation and Stand Alone Products supplied hereunder by the Supplier from time to time

(2) The charges for the items mentioned in paragraphs (1)(a) to (d) shall be paid forthwith upon the execution of this Agreement. The charges for the Electronic Copies mentioned in paragraph (1)(e) made in a particular calendar month shall be paid at the same time as the submission of the Customer Report immediately following the making of such Electronic Copies (or, if such submission is late, the date on which such Customer Report should have been submitted in accordance with this Agreement). The charges for each of the items mentioned in paragraphs (1)(f) and 1(g) shall be invoiced to the Customer on delivery of such item to the Customer and shall be paid within *30* days after the delivery of such invoice

(3) Any charges payable by the Customer hereunder in addition to those mentioned in this Clause 5 shall be paid within *30* days after the receipt by the Customer of the Supplier's invoice therefor

(4) All charges payable under this Agreement are exclusive of Value Added Tax which shall be paid by the Customer at the rate and in the manner from time to time prescribed by law

(5) If the Customer fails to make any payment to the Supplier under this Agreement on the due date then, without prejudice to any other right or remedy available to the Supplier, the Supplier shall be entitled to:

(a) suspend (by notice in writing to the Users) the rights granted to the Users pursuant to Clause 2(1) of this Agreement until payment of the unpaid sum is made in full (and the Users shall so comply with such suspension); and/or

(b) charge the Customer interest on the amount outstanding on a day-to-day basis (as well after as before any judgment) from the date or last date for payment thereof to the date of actual payment (both dates inclusive) at the rate of *2* per cent above the base rate of [   ] Bank plc (or such other London Clearing Bank as the Supplier may nominate) from time to time in force compounded quarterly. Such interest shall be paid on demand by the Supplier

(6) The Supplier's standard retail price list in force from time to time as referred to in Schedule 3 shall be made available by the Supplier to the Customer promptly after written request therefor by the Customer at any time during the term of this Agreement

347

6   Customer reports

(1) The Customer agrees to record the exact number of Electronic Copies made by Users during each calendar month of the term of this Agreement and to report that information in Customer Reports together with the other information required by such Customer Reports

(2) The Customer shall provide a Customer Report to the Supplier within *30* days after the end of every calendar month of the term of this Agreement (commencing with the calendar month in which this Agreement is executed) containing the information required thereby in respect of, and accurate as at the last day of, such calendar month

(3) Each Customer Report shall be certified as true and complete by a [director] of the Customer

(4) If no Electronic Copies are made during a calendar month, the Customer shall state this in the Customer Report

(5) References in this Clause 6 to a calendar month shall include, where appropriate, references to the unexpired part of the calendar month in which this Agreement is executed and to the expired part of the calendar month in which this Agreement is terminated

(6) If during any calendar month of the term of this Agreement any Authorised Computer shall no longer be used for the purposes of running any Software then the Customer shall state this in the next Customer Report and shall prior to the submission of such Customer Report procure that all Software is erased from such Authorised Computer. Upon the submission of such Customer Report that Authorised Computer shall cease to be an Authorised Computer for the purposes of this Agreement

(7) If during any calendar month of the term of this Agreement any of the Users shall cease to use any Electronic Copy on an Authorised Computer then the Customer shall state this and specify the Authorised Computer concerned in the next Customer Report and shall prior to the submission of such Customer Report procure that the relevant Software is erased from such Authorised Computer. Upon the submission of such Customer Report the Customer shall be given a credit in respect of that item of Software ('Credit') which shall entitle a User to use one Electronic Copy of that item of Software (but only that item and not any other version thereof) on another Authorised Computer free of any additional charge under this Agreement. Such Credit and, where applicable, such use shall be reported in the relevant Customer Report. A Credit shall not entitle the Customer to any cash refund or any other form of compensation

(8) The Supplier reserves the right at any time to change the name and/or address of the person to whom Customer Reports and the associated

payments should be despatched by the Customer (as appearing in the Customer Report from time to time) by notice in writing to the Customer, and the Customer shall thereafter comply with such instructions

7   Implementation, training and help line services

(1) At the request of the Customer the Supplier agrees to provide:

(a) assistance to all or any of the Users with the installation and implementation of any item of Software;

(b) training in the use of any item of Software for employees of all or any of the Users; and

(c) access for the Users' technical personnel to the Supplier's telephone help line for the purpose of assisting in the resolution of the Users' difficulties and queries in using the Software

(2) The services described in paragraph (1) shall be charged to and paid for by the Customer at the Supplier's standard scale of charges for such services in force from time to time (which shall be supplied to the Customer on request) less a discount of X per cent. Unless otherwise agreed with the Supplier, training shall take place at the premises of the Supplier. Access to the Supplier's help line for assistance in relation to a particular item of Software shall be restricted to those employees of the Users who have first successfully completed a training course in respect of that Software in accordance with the Supplier's current minimum recommendations or who can demonstrate to the Supplier's reasonable satisfaction that they are competent in the use of that Software

8   Audits

(1) The Users shall keep and shall make available to the Supplier on request accurate records to enable the Supplier to verify all payments due to it under this Agreement

(2) During the term of this Agreement and for the period of 6 months after its termination and upon 5 business days' prior written notice to the Customer, the Supplier shall have the right at any time and from time to time (subject as provided in sub-clause (4)), during the Customer's normal business hours, to send an independent accountant (not generally providing services to the Supplier except in respect of payment audits) to audit the records of the Users and the use of the Software by the Users and to verify the payments due to the Supplier under this Agreement. The Users shall give such accountant full access to their premises, computers, employees and relevant records for such purpose. Any such audit shall be conducted in such a manner as not to interfere

with the Users' normal business activities and will not include access to the Users' cost or profit information. Each such audit shall cover the period since the last most recent audit or, if none, the date of this Agreement down to the business day immediately preceding the commencement of the audit ('Audit Period')

(3) The Supplier shall use its reasonable endeavours to procure that such accountant shall keep confidential the information which comes to his knowledge as a consequence of his audit and to enter into any confidentiality undertaking reasonably requested by the Customer in respect thereof prior to any disclosure except that the accountant shall be entitled to reveal to the Supplier any information necessary to provide the Supplier with confirmation of the accuracy of any Customer Reports, the payment remittances made to the Supplier or any deviations therefrom. Upon written request, the Supplier agrees to make available to the Customer, in the event the Supplier makes any claim with respect to an audit, a copy of the records and reports pertaining to the audit

(4) The Supplier agrees not to cause such audits to be carried out more frequently than *twice* a year, except where the Supplier has reasonable cause to believe that correct Customer Reports or payments are not being tendered by the Customer in which case the Supplier may cause any number of audits to be carried out until such time as the Supplier is reasonably satisfied that the position has been corrected

(5) Each such audit shall be carried out at the Supplier's expense unless it reveals a deficiency of 5 per cent or more of the payment remittances for the relevant Audit Period in which event the Customer shall pay the costs thereof. Payment of such costs and any payment deficiency shall be made within 7 days after the Customer shall have received written notice thereof from the Supplier together with a copy of the accountant's report and, if applicable, fee note showing the amount(s) due. Any such deficiency shall carry interest in accordance with Clause 5(5)(b) from the date it was originally due

9   Limited warranty

(1) The Supplier warrants to the Customer that each of the Products provided to the Customer hereunder will, at the time of delivery and for *ninety* days thereafter, be free from defects in materials and will conform to the [Supplier's] [Owner's] applicable standard written specifications. The Customer's remedy and the Supplier's obligations under this limited warranty shall be limited to, at the Supplier's election, return of the Product in question for a refund of amounts paid to the Supplier hereunder for each copy of the Product or replacement of any defective Product. Any replacement shall not extend the original warranty

period. This limited warranty shall not apply to Products which the Supplier reasonably determines have been subject to misuse, neglect, improper installation, repair, alteration or damage by any of the Users

(2) The Supplier does not warrant that the Products will meet the Users' requirements or that the operation of the Products will be uninterrupted or error-free or that defects in the Products will be corrected. The Users shall load and use the Products at their own risk and in no event will the Supplier be liable to any of the Users for any loss or damage of any kind (except personal injury or death resulting from the Supplier's negligence) including lost profits or other consequential loss arising from any User's use of or inability to use the Products or from errors or deficiencies in them whether caused by negligence or otherwise except as expressly provided herein

(3) The express terms of this Agreement are in lieu of all warranties, conditions, terms and obligations implied by statute, common law, custom, trade usage, course of dealing or otherwise, all of which are hereby excluded to the fullest extent permitted by law

(4) Each of the Users hereby warrants to the Supplier that such User has not been induced to enter into this Agreement by any prior representations whether oral or in writing except as specifically mentioned in this Agreement and each of the Users hereby waives any claim for breach of any such representations which are not so specifically mentioned

10   Warranty of authority and indemnity

(1) The Supplier warrants to each of the Users that it has the right to grant the rights and comply with its obligations contained in this Agreement

(2) The Supplier agrees to indemnify, hold harmless and defend each of the Users from and against any and all damages, costs and expenses, including reasonable legal fees, incurred in connection with any claim that the Supplier does not have the necessary authority to enter into this Agreement, or that a Product infringes the intellectual property rights of any third party, provided that the Supplier is notified promptly in writing of any claim, that the Supplier is given immediate and complete control of such claim, that at the Supplier's request and expense each of the Users gives the Supplier all reasonable assistance with such claim and that none of the Users prejudices the Supplier's defence of such claim

(3) Following notice of a claim the Supplier shall at its option and at its expense, either procure for the Users the right to continue to use the alleged infringing Product or replace or modify the Product to make

it non-infringing. If the Supplier elects to replace or modify that Product, such replacement shall meet substantially the [Owner's] [Supplier's] current written specifications for that Product. If the Supplier is unable to replace or modify the Product, the Customer shall be entitled to a refund of amounts paid to the Supplier hereunder for each copy of that Product

(4) The Supplier shall have no liability for any claim under this Clause 10 in respect of the Supplier's lack of authority in respect of a Product or any claim of infringement of any intellectual property rights based on the Customer's (i) use or reproduction of the Product after the Supplier's notice to the Customer that the Users should cease use or reproduction of such Product due to an infringement claim, or of other than the then current release of a Product received from the Supplier if such claim would have been avoided by the use of the then current release, and/or (ii) the combination of a Product with a program or data not supplied by the Supplier if such claim would have been avoided by the exclusive use of the Product

(5) The foregoing states the entire liability of the Supplier to the Users in respect of any lack of authority or any infringement of the intellectual property rights of any third party

11   Termination

Notwithstanding anything else contained herein, this Agreement may be terminated:

(1) by the Supplier forthwith on giving notice in writing to the Customer if:

> (a) the control (as defined for the purposes of Section 416 of the Income and Corporation Taxes Act 1988) of the Customer shall be transferred to any person or persons other than the person or persons in control of the Customer at the date hereof (but the Supplier shall only be entitled to terminate within the period of 60 days after the Customer shall have been notified in writing of the change in control); or

> (b) any audit carried out pursuant to Clause 8 shall reveal a deficiency of 10 per cent or more in the payment remittances which should have been made in the period covered by the audit

(2) by the Customer forthwith on giving notice in writing to the Supplier if any of the Users shall object to any of the terms of the latest version of an End User Licence Agreement which may be supplied by the Supplier pursuant to Clause 2(2)(e) (such notice to identify the User and the objection concerned);

(3) by either the Supplier or the Customer forthwith on giving notice in writing to the other if:

(a) the other (and the Customer shall be deemed to be in breach if any of the Users is in breach) commits any breach of any term of this Agreement and (in the case of a breach capable of being remedied) shall have failed, within *30* days after the receipt of a request in writing from the first party so to do, to remedy the breach (such request to contain a warning of such party's intention to terminate); or

(b) the other (which in the case of the Customer shall mean any of the Users) shall have a receiver or administrative receiver appointed of it or over any part of its undertaking or assets or shall pass a resolution for winding-up (otherwise than for the purpose of a bona fide scheme of solvent amalgamation or reconstruction) or a court of competent jurisdiction shall make an order to that effect or if the other (with the meaning aforesaid) shall enter into any voluntary arrangement with its creditors or shall become subject to an administration order

12 Effect of termination

(1) In the event that this Agreement is terminated by either the Supplier or the Customer pursuant to Clause 4 or is terminated by the Supplier pursuant to Clause 11(1)(a) or by the Customer pursuant to Clause 11(2) or Clause 11(3), the Users may continue to use and possess those copies of the Products which they use and possess on the date of such termination subject to the terms and conditions of the End User Licence Agreements applicable to such Products and subsisting on the date of such termination which shall thereafter apply to such use and possession to the exclusion of this Agreement (and which such Users hereby covenant and agree with the Supplier to observe, perform and be bound by) but no other use may be made of such Products by such Users and, in particular, no copying or reproduction of the Software shall thereafter be permitted (save for back-up copies permitted by law or by the terms of an End User Licence Agreement)

(2) In the event that this Agreement is terminated by the Supplier pursuant to Clause 11(1)(b) or Clause 11(3) the Users shall immediately cease using the Products and copying and reproducing the Software and shall forthwith return the Products and all copies thereof in the possession of the Users to the Supplier or, at the option of the Supplier, shall destroy the same and certify to the Supplier that they have been so destroyed. The Users shall also cause the Software to be erased from all Authorised Computers and all other computers in their possession

or under their control and shall certify to the Supplier that the same has been done

(3) If this Agreement is terminated by the Customer pursuant to Clause 11(2) then the references in sub-clause (1) to an End User Licence Agreement shall, in the case of Users who objected in terms of Clause 11(2), be deemed to be references to the version of the End User Licence Agreement in force immediately prior to the version to which such Users objected and sub-clause (1) shall be construed accordingly

(4) On the termination of this Agreement all the rights and obligations of the parties under this Agreement shall automatically terminate except for such rights of action as shall have accrued prior to such termination and any obligations and rights which expressly or by implication are intended to come into or continue in force on or after such termination

13   Associates

(1) Upon execution of a Deed of Adherence by an Associate and by the Supplier, such Associate shall be deemed to be a User and a party to this Agreement and shall accordingly be bound by and required to comply with the terms of this Agreement as a User and shall be entitled to the rights and benefits conferred on a User by this Agreement

(2) Upon an Associate ceasing to be an Associate because the requisite control described in the definition of 'Associate' in Clause 1 no longer exists, such former Associate shall forthwith and automatically cease to be a party to this Agreement and all its rights and obligations under this Agreement shall automatically terminate save for any provision hereof which in relation to such former Associate is expressly or by implication intended to come into force on or to continue in force after cessation and without prejudice to the due performance by such former Associate of all its obligations up to the date of such cessation and the remedies of any of the other parties hereto in respect of a breach thereof

(3) If an Associate ceases to be a party to this Agreement in the circumstances mentioned in sub-clause (2), such former Associate may continue to use and possess those copies of the Products which it uses and possesses on the date of such cessation subject to the terms and conditions of the End User Licence Agreements applicable to such Products and subsisting on the date of such cessation which shall thereafter apply to such use and possession to the exclusion of this Agreement (and which the former Associate hereby covenants and agrees with the Supplier to observe, perform and be bound by) but no other use may be made of such Products by such former Associate and, in particular, no copying or reproduction of the Software shall thereafter be permitted (save for back-up copies permitted by law or by the terms

of an End User Licence Agreement). Upon such cessation all Authorised Computers owned or lawfully used immediately prior to such cessation by such former Associate shall immediately cease to be Authorised Computers for the purposes of this Agreement. Notwithstanding the foregoing, Clause 2(10) shall continue to apply to such Products such that, except in respect of Stand Alone Products, all copies of such Products shall remain the property of the Supplier and may not be sold or otherwise disposed of by such former Associate to any third party. If such former Associate fails to abide by any of its obligations under this sub-clause (3) the Supplier may by notice in writing to such former Associate terminate forthwith the rights of such former Associate under this subclause (3) whereupon such former Associate shall forthwith return the Products and all copies thereof in its possession to the Supplier or, at the option of the Supplier, shall destroy the same and certify to the Supplier that they have been so destroyed and shall also cause the Software to be erased from all computers in its possession or under its control and shall certify to the Supplier that the same has been done

(4) If an Associate ceases to be a party to this Agreement in the circumstances mentioned in sub-clause (2):

(a) such former Associate shall continue to be liable in respect of any claim made by the Supplier against such former Associate under Clause 3 of this Agreement which is notified to such former Associate prior to such cessation but shall not otherwise have any liability under Clause 3 following such cessation;

(b) the Users shall continue to be liable in respect of any claim made by the Supplier against them or any of them under Clause 3 of this Agreement in relation to any breach by such former Associate of any of its obligations under this Agreement which is notified to them prior to such cessation but shall not otherwise be liable under Clause 3 in relation to any breach by such former Associate of any of its obligations under this Agreement

(5) The Customer undertakes to notify the Supplier in writing immediately upon any of its Associates ceasing to be such for the purposes of this Agreement and also to report that fact in its next Customer Report and to include therein details of the copies of the Products which that former Associate will be entitled to use pursuant to sub-clause (3) and the computers on which they will be used following such cessation

14   Force majeure

None of the parties shall be liable for any delay in performing any of its obligations under this Agreement if such delay is caused by circumstances beyond the reasonable control of the party so delaying and such party shall be entitled (subject to giving the other parties full particulars of the circumstances in question and to using its best endeavours to resume full performance without avoidable delay) to a reasonable extension of time for the performance of such obligations

15   Waiver of remedies

See Clause 28 of Precedent A

16   Entire agreement

See Clause 29 of Precedent A
and add:
Any addition to or modification of this Agreement agreed to by the Customer shall be binding on all the Users

17   Notices

See Clause 32 of Precedent A
and add:
Any notice served on the Customer shall be deemed to have been served simultaneously on all the Users

18   Severability

See Clause 36 of Precedent A

19   Interpretation

See Clause 33 of Precedent A

20   Law

See Clause 34 of Precedent A

21   Disputes

See Clause 35 of Precedent A

EXECUTED etc

SCHEDULE 1

DESCRIPTION OF THE ORIGINAL SOFTWARE

SCHEDULE 2

DESCRIPTION OF THE INITIAL AUTHORISED COMPUTERS AND PREMISES

1   HOSTS:

Item	Serial Number	User	Premises at which item located *(Street, Town, Postcode)*

2   PERSONAL COMPUTERS/WORKSTATIONS ON WHICH ELECTRONIC COPIES WILL BE LOADED

Item	Serial Number	User	[Premises at which item located *(Street, Town, Postcode)*]

3   PERSONAL COMPUTERS ON WHICH STAND
    ALONE COPIES WILL BE LOADED:

| | | | [Premises at which item located *(Street, Town, Postcode)*] |
Item	Serial Number	User	

SCHEDULE 3

CHARGES

1   The total price for the supply of the master copies of the Original
    Software shall be as follows:

Item of Original Software	Price

Total   £ _____

2   It is recorded that the Users wish to make the following numbers
    of Electronic Copies of the Original Software immediately, the total
    price for which shall be as follows:

Item of Original Software	Number of Electronic Copies	Unit Price	Aggregate Price

Total   £ _____

[**Note:** It is assumed that the supplier will wish to offer an extra discount at this stage to encourage the customer to commit to the greatest possible number of copies. If no such incentive is offered, the customer may defer its commitment in order to take advantage of the credit period built into the customer reporting procedure. The customer's initial order may also affect the future discount levels which the supplier is willing to provide.]

3 The Customer requires immediately the following number of copies of the Software Documentation in respect of the Original Software, the total price for which shall be as follows:

Item of Original Software	Number of Copies of Software Documentation	Unit Price	Aggregate Price

Total £ _____

4 The Customer requires immediately the following numbers of copies of the Stand Alone Products in respect of the Original Software, the total price for which shall be as follows:

Item of Original Software	Number of Copies of Stand Alone Products	Unit Price	Aggregate Price

Total £ _____

5 The price for each Electronic Copy made by Users in addition to those mentioned in paragraph 2 above shall be a sum equal to the price of the relative item of Software appearing in the Supplier's standard retail price list in force at the time the Electronic Copy is made less a discount of X per cent

Where the relative Software is Supplemental Software the previous version of which is already used by Users and the Supplier generally offers in its standard retail price list a more favourable price (including nil) to an existing user of the previous version in question then the price of each Electronic Copy thereof (up to an aggregate number equal to the total number of Electronic Copies of such previous version used by Users prior to such Supplemental Software being made available to the Customer) shall be calculated as aforesaid using such more favourable price

6   The price for each of the master copies of any Supplemental Software shall be a sum equal to the price of a single copy of such Supplemental Software appearing in the Supplier's standard retail price list in force from time to time. Where the previous version of such Supplemental Software is already used by Users and the Supplier generally offers in its standard retail price list a more favourable price (including nil) to an existing user of the previous version in question then the price payable by the Customer shall be that more favourable price

7   The price for any new or additional copies of the Software Documentation and Stand Alone Products shall be a sum equal to the price therefor appearing in the Supplier's standard retail price list in force from time to time less a discount of Y per cent

[**Note:** Documentation may be listed separately from the software if (as is increasingly the case) the documentation is not automatically provided with the software but has to be ordered separately. The same may go for such items as templates and even training courses]

8   All prices quoted or referred to above are exclusive of value added tax

SCHEDULE 4

CUSTOMER REPORT

CUSTOMER REPORT

Customer: ....

For the calendar month ending: ....

[Words and expressions defined in the Multiple Copy Software Licence Agreement made between [NAME OF SUPPLIER] and the Customer dated   19   shall have the same meanings in this Customer Report Form]

[If the Customer has no information to report under a particular section of this Customer Report Form then the relevant section should be completed 'none' or 'not applicable' as appropriate]

A   NEW AUTHORISED COMPUTERS BROUGHT INTO USE DURING THE CALENDAR MONTH:

HOSTS:

Item	Serial Number	User	Premises at which item located *(Street, Town, Postcode)*

PERSONAL COMPUTERS/WORKSTATIONS ON WHICH ELECTRONIC COPIES WILL BE LOADED:

Item	Serial Number	User	[Premises at which item located *(Street, Town, Postcode)*]

B   AUTHORISED COMPUTERS NO LONGER USED FOR
    RUNNING ANY SOFTWARE AND FROM WHICH ALL
    SOFTWARE HAS BEEN ERASED DURING THE CALENDAR
    MONTH:

			[Premises at which item located *(Street, Town, Postcode)*]
Item	Serial Number	User	

C   ELECTRONIC COPIES NO LONGER USED ON, AND WHICH
    HAVE BEEN ERASED FROM, AUTHORISED COMPUTERS
    DURING THE CALENDAR MONTH AND FOR WHICH
    CREDITS NOW ARISE:

Item of Software *(Description and version number)*	Authorised Computer on which previously used *(Description and serial number)*	User	Premises at which Authorised Computer located *(Street, Town, Postcode)*

D   NUMBERS OF UNUSED CREDITS CARRIED FORWARD
    FROM PREVIOUS CALENDAR MONTHS:

Item of Software *(Description and version number)*	Number of Credits

E   TOTAL NUMBERS OF UNUSED CREDITS NOW AVAILABLE (ie C + D):

Item of Software
*(Description and
version number)*   Number of Credits

F   NUMBERS OF NEW ELECTRONIC COPIES MADE DURING THE CALENDAR MONTH AND THE CHARGES PAYABLE:

NEW ELECTRONIC COPIES:

Item of Software *(Description and version number)*	Authorised Computer on which loaded *(Description and serial number)*	User	[Premises at which Authorised Computer located *(Street, Town, Postcode)*]

CHARGES:

Item of Software *(Description and version number)*	Number of Electronic Copies made	Number of Credits available *(as per E above)*	Net number of Electronic Copies for which payment is required	Total price payable *(Supplier's retail price per copy less X per cent discount multiplied by number of copies)*

Grand Total   £ _____
Due this month   _____

Remittance attached   £[   ]
(including VAT)

G   NUMBER OF UNUSED CREDITS CARRIED FORWARD TO FUTURE CALENDAR MONTHS (ie E LESS CREDITS UTILISED IN F):

Item of Software *(Description and version number)*	Number of Credits

H IDENTITY OF ANY USER WHICH CEASED TO BE AN ASSOCIATE DURING THE CALENDAR MONTH TOGETHER WITH DETAILS OF THOSE PRODUCTS WHICH IT IS ENTITLED TO CONTINUE TO USE SUBJECT TO THE TERMS AND CONDITIONS OF APPLICABLE END USER LICENCE AGREEMENTS:

User *(Name and address)*	Products which it will continue to use *(Description and version number)*	Number of copies	Computer on which used *(Description and serial number)*

I certify on behalf of [CUSTOMER] that the information set out in this Customer Report is true and complete

. . . .
Name (Please print or type)

. . . .
Title

. . . .
Signature

Date:

This Customer Report and the enclosed payment should be sent to:

[NAME OF SUPPLIER]

[ADDRESS]

Attention: [   ]

SCHEDULE 5

DEED OF ADHERENCE

THIS DEED is made the   day of   19

PARTIES:

(1) *NEW ASSOCIATE* of

('the New Party')

(2)   [LIMITED] [PLC] whose registered office is at

('the Supplier')

RECITALS:

(A) This Deed is supplemental to a Multiple Copy Software Licence Agreement dated   19   made between the Supplier and [CUSTOMER] ('the Customer'), as the same may have been or may be amended (whether before, on or after the date hereof) from time to time ('the Agreement')

(B) The New Party wishes to become a User for the purposes of the Agreement

NOW THIS DEED WITNESSES AS FOLLOWS:

1 The New Party confirms that it has been supplied with a copy of the Agreement and undertakes to each of the other parties from time to time to the Agreement to observe, perform and be bound by all the terms of the Agreement which are capable of applying to the New Party to the intent and effect that the New Party shall be deemed with effect from the date of execution of this Deed to be a party to the Agreement and to be a User (as defined in the Agreement)

2 The New Party hereby warrants to the Supplier that the New Party is an Associate of the Customer

3 The Supplier has joined in this Deed to confirm its approval of the New Party in reliance upon the warranty contained in Clause 2 above

4 Words and expressions defined in the Agreement shall have the same meanings in this Deed

5 This Deed shall be governed by and construed in accordance with English law

EXECUTED as a deed in two originals the day and year first before written

EXECUTED as a deed by *NEW ASSOCIATE* and signed by two duly authorised officers on its behalf } Director:

Director/Secretary:

EXECUTED as a deed by *SUPPLIER* and signed by two duly authorised officers on its behalf } Director:

Director/Secretary:

The Appendix

COPIES OF END USER LICENCE AGREEMENTS
RELATING TO THE ORIGINAL SOFTWARE

Precedent G

Exclusive distributorship agreement

THIS AGREEMENT is made the   day of   19

PARTIES:

(1) COMPANY [LIMITED] [PLC] whose registered office is at
('the Company')

(2) DISTRIBUTOR [LIMITED] [PLC] whose registered office is at
('the Distributor')

RECITALS:

(A) The Company is the manufacturer and producer of various computer products

(B) The Company has agreed to appoint the Distributor as its exclusive distributor in the Territory (as hereinafter defined) for certain of its products on the terms and conditions hereinafter contained

NOW IT IS HEREBY AGREED as follows:

1 Definitions

In this Agreement (which expression shall be deemed to include the Schedules hereto), unless the context otherwise requires, the following expressions have the following meanings:

'the Hardware Products'	means those of the Products which are computer hardware
'Initial Order'	means the Distributor's initial order for the Products [and spare parts] as set out in the Company's invoice delivered to the Distributor on the

execution hereof and signed by the Distributor for the purpose of identification

'intellectual property rights'

means patents, trade marks, service marks, registered designs, applications for any of the foregoing, copyright, design rights, know-how, confidential information, trade and business names and any other similar protected rights in any country

'Invoice Price' [5.2]

means, in relation to the purchase of any of the Products, the amount invoiced by the Company to the Distributor excluding Value Added Tax and any other taxes, duties or levies and any transport and insurance charges included in such invoice

'the Products'

means the computer products described in Schedule 1 and such other products as the parties may agree in writing from time to time

'the Product Documentation' means the operating manuals and other literature accompanying the Products for use by end-users

'Shrink Wrap Licence'

means the licence agreement accompanying each of the Software Products and contained within its packaging expressed to be made between the Company and the end-user of such product

'the Software Products'

means those of the Products which are computer software

'the Territory' [5.3.1]

means *the United Kingdom of Great Britain and Northern Ireland*

'Year'

means any period of 12 months commencing on [the date hereof] or any anniversary of [the date hereof]

2 Appointment [5.0.2, 5.3.2]

(1) The Company hereby appoints the Distributor and the Distributor hereby agrees to act as the exclusive distributor of the Company for the resale of the Products in the Territory

(2) The Company shall not during the continuance of this Agreement appoint any other person to act as its distributor or agent in the Territory for the Products

(3) The Distributor shall perform its obligations hereunder in accordance with all reasonable instructions which the Company may give the Distributor from time to time

(4) The Distributor shall not be entitled to assign or sub-contract any of its rights or obligations under this Agreement or appoint any sub-distributor or agent to perform such obligations

(5) The Distributor shall not be entitled to any priority of supply of the Products over the Company's other customers and the Company may allocate production and delivery among its customers as it sees fit

(6) The Distributor represents and warrants to the Company that it has the necessary ability and experience to carry out the obligations assumed by it under this Agreement and that by virtue of entering into this Agreement it is not and will not be in breach of any express or implied obligation to any third party binding upon it

3 Duration

This Agreement shall commence on the [date hereof] for an initial period of *2* years and shall continue thereafter [unless or] until terminated by either party giving to the other not less than *6* months' written notice [expiring] [given] on the last day of the said initial period or at any time thereafter, but shall be subject to earlier termination as hereinafter provided

4 Sale and purchase of the Products [5.2]

(1) [The provisions of Schedule 2 shall have effect] [The sale and purchase of the Products as between the Company and the Distributor shall be governed by the Company's standard conditions of sale in force at the date hereof, a copy of which is annexed hereto for the purpose of identification]

(2) If there shall be any inconsistency between the provisions of [Schedule 2] [the said conditions of sale] and the [other] provisions of this Agreement then the latter shall prevail

(3) On the execution of this Agreement the Distributor shall deliver a [cheque] [banker's draft] to the Company in payment in full for the Initial Order

5   Demonstration versions [5.3.6.4]

(1) The Company shall provide the Distributor with a reasonable number of demonstration versions of the Products which shall be and shall remain the property of the Company

(2) The Distributor shall not remove or interfere with any notices on such demonstration versions indicating that they are the property of the Company

(3) The Company shall promptly replace such demonstration versions with an equivalent number of any new versions of the Products which the Company may produce from time to time, subject to all previous demonstration versions being delivered up to the Company

(4) The Distributor shall use such demonstration versions for the purpose of demonstrating the Products to bona fide prospective customers only and for no other purpose

(5) The Distributor shall at all times keep such demonstration versions properly stored, protected and insured and under its exclusive control and shall return them to the Company free from any lien, restriction or encumbrance or otherwise dispose of them as the Company may from time to time direct

6   Training [5.3.6.6]

(1) The Company shall provide training in the use, installation and maintenance of the Products for the Distributor's personnel as specified in Schedule 3

(2) Any additional training required by the Distributor shall be provided by the Company in accordance with its standard scale of charges in force from time to time

(3) The Distributor shall offer training in the use of the Products to all its customers on commercially reasonable terms and shall use its reasonable endeavours to persuade them to complete training courses in accordance with the Company's minimum recommendations from time to time in force

7   Distributor's obligations [5.1, 5.6]

The Distributor shall:

(1) use its best endeavours to promote and extend the sale of the Products throughout the Territory;

(2) promptly inform the Company of any facts or opinions of which the Distributor becomes aware likely to be relevant in relation to the commercial exploitation of the Products in the Territory and which are advantageous or disadvantageous to the interests of the Company;

(3) at all times conduct its business in a manner that will reflect favourably on the Products and on the good name and reputation of the Company;

(4) not by itself or with others participate in any illegal, deceptive, misleading or unethical practices including, but not limited to, disparagement of the Products or the Company or other practices which may be detrimental to the Products, the Company or the public interest;

(5) not during the continuance of this Agreement [and for the period of *1 year* after its termination] (whether alone or jointly and whether directly or indirectly) be concerned or interested in the manufacture, marketing, distribution or sale of any products which are similar to or competitive with any of the Products or which perform the same or similar functions;

(6) if any dispute shall arise between the Distributor and any of its customers in respect of the Products (or their installation or maintenance), promptly inform the Company and comply with all reasonable directions of the Company in relation thereto;

(7) at all times employ a sufficient number of full-time technical support and sales staff having sufficient training and expertise properly to display, demonstrate, sell and instruct customers in the installation and use of the Products and capable of addressing customer enquiries and needs regarding the Products;

(8) at all times maintain adequate demonstration facilities for the Products;

(9) supply to the Company such reports, returns and other information relating to orders and projected orders for the Products as the Company may from time to time reasonably require;

(10) provide the Company with quarterly stock reports showing the Distributor's stock of each of the Products at the beginning and end of each quarter [and the movement of stocks during the quarter];

(11) provide the Company with such financial information relating to the Distributor's business as may be necessary for the Company to establish and maintain a credit limit for the Distributor from time to time;

(12) not make any promises or representations or give any warranties or guarantees in respect of the Products except such as are consistent with those which accompany the Products or as expressly authorised by the Company in writing;

(13) use the Company's trade marks and trade names relating to the Products only in the registered or agreed style in connection with the marketing and sale of the Products and shall not use such trade marks or trade names in connection with any other products or services or as part of the corporate or any trade name of the Distributor;

(14) not alter, obscure, remove, interfere with or add to any of the trade marks, trade names, markings or notices affixed to or contained in the Products or the Product Documentation at the time when they are delivered to the Distributor;

(15) not alter or interfere with the Products or the Product Documentation;

(16) keep sufficient stocks of the Products to satisfy customer demand;

(17) be responsible for the proper installation of the Products, save where installation can readily and easily be undertaken by the customer in accordance with the instructions set out in the Product Documentation and the customer indicates that he wishes to undertake installation himself;

(18) offer maintenance contracts in respect of the Hardware Products to its customers on commercially reasonable terms and shall undertake its obligations thereunder to the standards generally observed in the industry;

(19) purchase and maintain an inventory of spare parts for the Hardware Products in accordance with the Company's minimum recommendations from time to time (such spare parts to be purchased on the same terms as the Products (so far as the same are applicable));

(20) not offer or undertake any maintenance services in respect of the Software Products;

(21) provide an efficient after sales service in respect of the Products;

(22) observe all applicable laws and regulations in respect of and obtain all necessary licences, consents and permissions required for the storage, marketing and sale of the Products and for the maintenance of the Hardware Products in the Territory;

(23) provide the Company with all information necessary to enable the Company to ensure that the Products comply with local laws and regulations and promptly advise the Company of any change or proposed change thereto;

(24) co-operate with the Company in the recall of any of the Products for safety checks or modifications;

(25) not at any time represent itself as the agent of the Company;

(26) permit the Company and its authorised agents at all reasonable times to enter any of the Distributor's premises for the purpose of ascertaining that the Distributor is complying with its obligations under this Agreement

8   Company's obligations [5.1, 5.3.6.6]

The Company shall:

(1) provide the Distributor with such marketing and technical assistance as the Company may in its discretion consider necessary to assist the Distributor with the promotion of the Products;

(2) endeavour to answer as soon as possible all technical queries raised by the Distributor or its customers concerning the use or application of the Products;

(3) provide the Distributor with adequate quantities of instruction manuals, technical and promotional literature and other information relating to the Products;

(4) subject to the Distributor complying with its obligations under Clause 7(23), ensure that the Products comply with local laws and regulations relating to their sale and use in the Territory;

(5) give the Distributor reasonable advance written notice of any significant change to any of the Products or of the Company's intention to discontinue selling any of the Products to the Distributor;

(6) offer to the Distributor for inclusion in the Products any product of the Company which can reasonably be regarded as a replacement for or successor to any Product which the Company discontinues selling pursuant to Clause 12(2); and

(7) provide the Distributor promptly with all information and assistance necessary to enable the Distributor properly to perform its obligations hereunder in respect of any modified or enhanced versions of the Products

9 Intellectual property rights [2.8; 3.8]

(1) All intellectual property rights in or relating to the Products and the Product Documentation are and shall remain the property of the Company [or its licensors]

(2) The Distributor shall notify the Company immediately if the Distributor becomes aware of any illegal or unauthorised use of any of the Products or the Product Documentation or any of the intellectual property rights therein or relating thereto and will assist the Company (at the Company's expense) in taking all steps necessary to defend the Company's rights therein

(3) The provisions of this Clause shall survive the termination of this Agreement

10 Software Products [5.3.6, 5.3.6.4; E]

(1) The Distributor shall ensure that all copies of the Software Products which are sold to its customers shall be accompanied by a Shrink-Wrap Licence together with the following sticker (which will appear on the front of the packaging for the Software Products):

> 'IMPORTANT NOTICE: This software and its associated documentation is the copyright of [   ]. The use of this software is governed by the Licence Agreement accompanying this package'

(2) If any of the Distributor's customers shall return any Software Product to the Distributor within the time period permitted by its accompanying Shrink-Wrap Licence on the ground that he does not agree to the terms of such licence, the Distributor shall promptly refund the purchase price to that customer (whereupon the Company will give the Distributor a new copy of the Software Product in exchange for the returned copy)

11 Confidentiality

(1) Neither party shall use or divulge or communicate to any person (other than those whose province it is to know the same or as permitted or contemplated by this Agreement or with the written authority of the other party or as may be required by law):

> (a) any confidential information concerning the products, customers, business, accounts, finance or contractual arrangements or other dealings, transactions or affairs of the other party [and

its subsidiaries] which may come to the first party's knowledge during the continuance of this Agreement; or

(b) any of the terms of this Agreement

and each party shall use its best endeavours (i) to prevent the unauthorised publication or disclosure of any such information or documents and (ii) to ensure that any person to whom such information or documents are disclosed by such party is aware that the same is confidential to the other party

(2) Each party shall ensure that its employees are aware of and comply with the confidentiality and non-disclosure provisions contained in this Clause and shall indemnify the other party against any loss or damage which the other may sustain or incur as a result of any breach of confidence by any of such party's employees

(3) If either party becomes aware of any breach of confidence by any of its employees it shall promptly notify the other party and give the other party all reasonable assistance in connection with any proceedings which the other party may institute against any such employees

(4) The provisions of this Clause shall survive the termination of this Agreement but the restrictions contained in sub-clause (1) shall cease to apply to any information which may come into the public domain otherwise than through unauthorised disclosure by the receiving party or its employees.

12   Reservation of rights

The Company reserves the right:

(1) to make modifications or additions to the Products or the packaging or finish thereof in any way whatsoever as the Company may in its discretion determine;

(2) to discontinue selling any of the Products to the Distributor; and

(3) to require the Distributor either not to use or to cease to use any advertising or promotional materials in respect of the Products which the Company considers not to be in the Company's best interests

13   The Territory [5.3.1]

(1) The Company shall not during the continuance of this Agreement sell or supply any of the Products (including any products which it has discontinued selling to the Distributor pursuant to Clause 12(2)) to any third party situated in the Territory

(2) The Company shall promptly forward to the Distributor any enquiries it may receive for any of the Products from persons situated in the Territory

(3) The Company shall have no liability to the Distributor in the event that any of the Company's distributors appointed in other territories import any of the Products into the Territory for sale therein

(4) The Distributor shall not advertise or maintain stocks of the Products outside the Territory or otherwise actively solicit orders for the Products from persons who are situated outside the Territory but the Distributor shall not be prohibited from fulfilling any unsolicited orders actually placed by such persons

14   Legal relationship [5.0.2]

(1) During the continuance of this Agreement the Distributor shall be entitled to use the title '[   ] AUTHORISED DISTRIBUTOR' but such use shall be in accordance with the Company's policies in effect from time to time and before using such title (whether on the Distributor's business stationery, advertising material or elsewhere) the Distributor shall submit to the Company proof prints and such other details as the Company may require and the Company may in its discretion grant or withhold permission for such proposed use

(2) The relationship of the parties is that of seller and buyer and nothing in this Agreement shall render the Distributor a partner or agent of the Company. The Distributor is an independent contractor buying and selling in its own name and at its own risk. The Distributor shall not bind or purport to bind the Company to any obligation nor expose the Company to any liability nor pledge or purport to pledge the Company's credit

15   Termination [5.4]

(1) Notwithstanding anything else contained herein, this Agreement may be terminated:

(a) by the Company forthwith on giving notice in writing to the Distributor if:

(i) the Distributor shall (or shall threaten to) sell, assign, part with or cease to carry on its business or that part of its business relating to the distribution of the Products; or

(ii) the control (as defined for the purposes of Section 416 of the Income and Corporation Taxes Act 1988) of the Distributor shall be transferred to any person or persons other than the person or persons in control of the Distributor at the date hereof (but the Company shall only be entitled to terminate within the period of *60* days after the Company shall have been notified in writing of the change in control)

(b) by either party forthwith on giving notice in writing to the other if:

(i) the other party commits any material or persistent breach of any term of this Agreement and (in the case of a breach capable of being remedied) shall have failed, within *30* days after the receipt of a request in writing from the other party so to do, to remedy the breach (such request to contain a warning of such party's intention to terminate);

[(ii) diplomatic relations between the respective countries of the parties makes the continuance of this Agreement unduly difficult;]

(iii) the other party shall have been unable to perform its obligations hereunder for a period of *90* consecutive days or for periods aggregating *180* days in any Year (but the party entitled to terminate may only terminate within the period of *60* days after the expiration of the said consecutive period or Year); or

(iv) the other party shall have a receiver or administrative receiver appointed of it or over any part of its undertaking or assets or shall pass a resolution for winding up (otherwise than for the purpose of a bona fide scheme of solvent amalgamation or reconstruction) or a court of competent jurisdiction shall make an order to that effect or if the other party shall enter into any voluntary arrangement with its creditors or shall become subject to an administration order

(2) The Distributor shall not be entitled to any compensation or indemnity (whether for loss of distribution rights, goodwill or otherwise) as a result of the termination of this Agreement in accordance with its terms.

(3) Each delivery of a consignment of the Products shall be regarded as a separate contract of sale and no one default in a delivery shall be cause for terminating this Agreement

16 Sales coverage [5.2]

If the Distributor shall fail to submit orders to the Company for the Products having (or which would have had if fulfilled) an aggregate Invoice Price of *£1,000,000* in any Year the Company may within *60* days after the expiration of such Year forthwith by notice in writing to the Distributor:

(1) vary the extent of the distributorship either by reducing the extent of the Territory or by converting the exclusive distributorship into a non-exclusive distributorship (in which latter event Clauses 2(2), 13(1) and 13(2) hereof shall cease to have effect); or (and whether or not the Company has previously taken any action pursuant to this sub-clause (1) in relation to any prior Year)

(2) terminate this Agreement

[Notes:

(1) A more sophisticated clause might provide for a scale of sales targets in respect of successive years automatically adjusted for inflation against an appropriate index. Such clauses are not without their problems however as it may be difficult to assess in advance what the targets should be and actual sales may dip in any year for a whole number of legitimate reasons (eg the obsolescence of the products coupled with a time lag in introducing a new range).

(2) The stance of the parties on this Clause will depend on its objectives. In some cases it will be a genuine minimum requirement with actual sales expected to be much greater; in others the sales target will be aggressively pitched to ensure maximum sales effort (although in achieving this the distributor may spend less effort on training, maintenance and after sales support).

(3) The Clause attempts to deal with the problem of the company failing to supply due to force majeure, by referring to orders submitted rather than actual sales. However, this does not deal with the force majeure of the distributor; in that case it might be appropriate to take the period of force majeure out of account in the relative year and adjust the sales target for that year pro-rata. Again, it depends whether the sales target is an aggressive one or not.]

17   Effect of termination

On the termination of this Agreement:

(1) all the rights and obligations of the parties under this Agreement shall automatically terminate except:

(a) for such rights of action as shall have accrued prior to such termination and any obligations which expressly or by implication are intended to come into or continue in force on or after such termination;

(b) the Distributor shall be entitled to sell any of its stocks of the Products which have been fully paid for and which are required to fulfil any unperformed contracts of the Distributor outstanding at the date of termination (and to that extent and for that purpose the provisions of this Agreement shall continue in effect)

(2) the Distributor shall immediately eliminate from all its literature, business stationery, publications, notices and advertisements all references to the title '[   ] AUTHORISED DISTRIBUTOR' and all other representations of the Distributor's appointment hereunder;

(3) the Distributor shall at its own expense forthwith return to the Company or otherwise dispose of as the Company may instruct all technical and promotional materials and other documents and papers whatsoever sent to the Distributor and relating to the Products or the business of the Company (other than correspondence between the parties) and all property of the Company being in each case in the Distributor's possession or under its control;

(4) the Distributor shall cause the Software Products to be erased from all computers of or under the control of the Distributor and shall certify to the Company that the same has been done;

(5) all orders for undelivered Products shall be automatically cancelled;

(6) all outstanding unpaid invoices in respect of the Products shall become immediately payable in place of the payment terms previously agreed between the parties;

(7) the Company shall forthwith pay to the Distributor any amount standing to the credit of the Distributor's account with the Company (less any moneys then owed by the Distributor to the Company);

(8) the Company shall be entitled to repossess any of the Products which have not been paid for against cancellation of the relevant invoices (and so that the Distributor hereby irrevocably licenses the Company, its employees and agents to enter any of the premises of the Distributor for such purpose);

(9) the Company shall be entitled (but not obliged) to purchase all or any unsold Products in the possession or under the control of the Distributor which have been paid for by the Distributor (and which are not required to fulfil any unperformed contracts of the Distributor outstanding at the date of termination) at the Invoice Price (or, if lower, the written down value of the Products appearing in the accounting records of the Distributor at the date of termination), subject to the Company paying all necessary Value Added Tax and other taxes, duties or levies, and paying the cost of and arranging transport and insurance and to notifying the Distributor in writing of its requirements within *14* days of the date of termination. The Distributor shall give the Company all necessary assistance and co-operation for the purpose of giving effect to the provisions of this sub-clause and of delivering the Products to the Company but, subject thereto, any Products which are not purchased

by the Company within *30* days of its notice may be sold by the Distributor (the Distributor using its best endeavours to sell the same within *3* months thereafter) in accordance with the terms of this Agreement (and to that extent and for that purpose such terms shall continue in effect); and

(10) the Distributor shall give the Company details of all outstanding maintenance contracts which it has entered into in respect of the Hardware Products and subject thereto and to the Distributor forthwith taking all necessary steps to determine the same at the earliest possible date (without causing the Distributor to incur any additional liability thereby) the Company shall continue to supply the Distributor on the terms of this Agreement (which to that extent and for that purpose shall continue in effect) with all spare parts necessary for the Distributor properly to perform its remaining obligations under such maintenance contracts but for a period of no longer than *2* years after the date of termination; Provided that the provisions of this sub-clause shall apply only where this Agreement has been terminated by notice given in accordance with Clause 3 or by the Distributor under Clause 15 or by the Company under Clause 16

18   Liability [5.8]

(1) The Company warrants to the Distributor that the Products sold to the Distributor hereunder will comply with their published specifications and will be of satisfactory quality

(2) If the Company shall be in breach of the said warranty its liability shall be limited to replacing the Products concerned (at the Company's risk and expense) or, at its option, refunding the price paid by the Distributor (subject to the Distributor returning the defective Products to the Company at the Company's risk and expense) or (if an abatement of the price is agreed with the Distributor) refunding to the Distributor the appropriate part of the price paid

(3) The Company shall have no liability to the Distributor under sub-clauses (1) and (2) above:

> (a) for any damage to or defects in any of the Products caused by fair wear and tear, improper use, maintenance or repair, negligent handling, failure to observe the instructions accompanying the Products or any alterations thereto

> (b) unless, in the case of any damage to or defect in the Products which would have been apparent on reasonable inspection, the Distributor notifies the Company of the same in writing within *14* days after the date of delivery thereof or, in any other case, the Company receives written notice thereof within *2* years after

the date of delivery, and if no such notification is given (in either case) within the requisite period the Distributor shall not be entitled to reject the Products concerned and shall be obliged to pay the price therefor in full

(4) Notwithstanding anything else contained in this Agreement but subject to sub-clause (5) below, the Company shall not be liable to the Distributor for loss of profits or contracts or other indirect or consequential loss or damage whether arising from negligence, breach of contract or any other cause of action arising out of the subject matter of this Agreement

(5) The Company does not exclude liability for death or personal injury caused by the Company's negligence

(6) *See Clause 19(5) of Precedent A*

19 Waiver of remedies

See Clause 28 of Precedent A

20 Indemnities

(1) The Company shall indemnify the Distributor and keep the Distributor fully and effectively indemnified against any and all losses, claims, damages, costs, charges, expenses, liabilities, demands, proceedings and actions which the Distributor may sustain or incur or which may be brought or established against it by any person and which in any case arise out of or in relation to or by reason of:

(a) any claim or allegation that any of the Products infringes any intellectual property rights of any third party;

(b) any claim that the Products do not comply with local laws and regulations relating to their sale and use in the Territory

and which are not due to the Distributor's negligence, recklessness or wilful misconduct or any breach of its obligations under this Agreement

(2) The Distributor shall indemnify the Company and keep the Company fully and effectively indemnified against any and all losses, claims, damages, costs, charges, expenses, liabilities, demands, proceedings and actions which the Company may sustain or incur, or which may be brought or established against it by any person and which in any case arise out of or in relation to or by reason of:

(a) the negligence, recklessness or wilful misconduct of the Distributor in the performance of any of its obligations in connection with the installation and maintenance of the Products;

(b) any unauthorised action or omission of the Distributor or its employees;

(c) the manner in which the Distributor markets and sells the Products;

(d) the independent supply by the Distributor of any products or services for use in conjunction with or in relation to the Products; or

(e) any breach or alleged breach of any applicable laws or regulations relating to the storage, marketing or sale by the Distributor of the Products in the Territory

(3) If any claim is made against either party for which indemnification is sought under this Clause, the indemnified party shall consult with the other and, subject to being secured to its reasonable satisfaction, shall co-operate with the other in relation to any reasonable request made by the other in respect of such claim

21   Force majeure

Subject as provided in Clause 15, neither party shall be liable for any delay in performing any of its obligations under this Agreement if such delay is caused by circumstances beyond the reasonable control of the party so delaying and such party shall be entitled (subject to giving the other party full particulars of the circumstances in question and to using its best endeavours to resume full performance without avoidable delay) to a reasonable extension of time for the performance of such obligations

22   Notices

See Clause 32 of Precedent A

[**Note:** This clause will require modification if the parties are situated in different countries.]

23   Interpretation

See Clause 33 of Precedent A

[24   Registration

Notwithstanding any other provision of this Agreement, no provision hereof which is of such a nature as to make this Agreement liable to registration under the Restrictive Trade Practices Act 1976 shall take effect until the day after that on which particulars thereof shall have been furnished to the Director General of Fair Trading pursuant to the said Act. The parties shall use their best endeavours to procure the furnishing of such particulars as soon as possible after the signing of this Agreement]

[**Note:** The parties may also wish to notify the agreement to the EU Commission.]

25 General

This Agreement constitutes the entire understanding between the parties concerning the subject matter of this Agreement and shall be governed by and construed in accordance with the laws of England. No waiver or amendment of any provision of this Agreement shall be effective unless made by a written instrument signed by both parties. Each provision of this Agreement shall be construed separately and notwithstanding that the whole or any part of any such provision may prove to be illegal or unenforceable the other provisions of this Agreement and the remainder of the provision in question shall continue in full force and effect. The parties submit to the exclusive jurisdiction of the English Courts [but without prejudice to either party's rights to bring proceedings in any other jurisdiction where the other party is incorporated or has assets]

EXECUTED etc

SCHEDULE 1

PRODUCTS

SCHEDULE 2

SALES TERMS

1 Orders

(1) Each order for the Products submitted by the Distributor to the Company shall be in writing and shall stipulate the type and quantity of the Products ordered and the requested delivery date and delivery destination

(2) The Distributor may cancel any order [(whether or not accepted)] or reduce the quantity of any of the Products ordered by submitting to the Company a written notice that specifically refers to the relevant order, stipulates the change and is actually received by the Company not less than *14* days prior to the requested delivery date or, if later, the estimated delivery date notified to the Distributor pursuant to paragraph 3(2) below

[**Note:** delete the square-bracketed phase if sub-paragraph (4) is omitted.]

(3) The Distributor shall be responsible for ensuring the accuracy of its orders

[(4) Each order shall be subject to acceptance by the Company which may be made either by depositing an acknowledgment card in the [United Kingdom] mail, postage prepaid and addressed to the Distributor or by delivering the Products ordered or any part thereof]

[**Note:** If the Company reserves the right to refuse to accept orders the Distributor will be less inclined to agree to sales targets or any other obligation which could be affected by the Company's refusal to supply.]

2   Price and payment

(1) Subject as hereinafter provided, the price for each of the Products (including packaging) to be paid by the Distributor shall be the Company's published ex-factory price (in *pounds sterling*) in effect on the date of delivery ('the Ex-Factory Price') less a discount of *15* per cent ('the Basic Price')

(2) The Company reserves the right to change the Ex-Factory Price at any time and from time to time but shall give the Distributor not less than *60* days' prior written notice ('Price Change Notice Period') of the effective date of any change

(3) In the case of an increase in the Ex-Factory Price, the price for any of the Products ordered under a purchase order submitted to the Company prior to the commencement of a Price Change Notice Period requesting delivery during the Price Change Notice Period shall be based on the Ex-Factory Price in effect prior to the effective date of such price increase whether or not delivered prior to that effective date

(4) In the case of a decrease in the Ex-Factory Price, the price for any of the Products delivered within the Price Change Notice Period shall be based on the Ex-Factory Price as decreased

(5) All prices for the Products are exclusive of Value Added Tax or other applicable sales tax which shall be paid by the Distributor at the appropriate rate

(6) Payment for the Products shall be made no later than the last day of the calendar month next following the date of the Company's invoice therefor

(7) The Company may sue for the price of the Products notwithstanding that delivery has not occurred or property in them not passed to the Distributor

(8) The Distributor shall be entitled to a pre-payment discount of *3* per cent of the Ex-Factory Price in addition to the discount referred to in sub-paragraph (1) above. To take advantage of the pre-payment discount the Distributor must remit the price for the Products (less the pre-payment discount) to the Company at the same time as it submits its order therefor and contemporaneously notify the Company in writing of its decision. If payment is not received by the Company in cleared funds within 7 days after receiving the Distributor's order, the Distributor shall not be entitled to the pre-payment discount and sub-paragraph (6) above shall apply

(9) The Distributor shall be entitled to an additional volume discount on the Ex-Factory Price (before the discounts referred to in sub-paragraphs (1) and (8) above are applied) calculated by reference to its purchase of the Products in any Year in accordance with the following table:

[*Sterling*] *Volume Purchased in Year* (calculated on the Basic Price before any pre-payment discount)	*Discount*
Up to £299,999	Nil
£300,000 to £499,999	%
£500,000 to £699,999	%
£700,000 to £899,999	%
£900,000 and above	%

If the Distributor is entitled to any such additional discount in respect of its purchase of the Products in any Year the Company shall within *30* days after the end of that Year credit to the Distributor's account the amount of the additional discount to which it is entitled. Purchases in a Year shall be calculated by reference to the date on which the Company receives payment in cleared funds.

(10) Payment for the Products shall be made in *pounds sterling* and by bank transfer to such bank account(s) as the Company shall notify in writing to the Distributor from time to time

(11) If payment for any of the Products is not received by the due date then (without prejudice to the Company's other rights and remedies) the Company shall be entitled to:

(a) suspend all further deliveries of the Products until payment is received; and

(b) charge the Distributor interest on the unpaid sum on a day to day basis (as well after as before judgment) from the date or last date for payment thereof to the date of actual payment (both dates inclusive) at the rate of 3 per cent above the base rate of [   ] Bank plc (or such other London Clearing Bank as the Company may nominate) from time to time in force compounded quarterly. Such interest shall be paid on demand by the Company.

(12) The Company reserves the right to suspend deliveries of the Products while the aggregate amount of outstanding unpaid invoices exceeds the Company's credit limit for the Distributor from time to time as notified to the Distributor in writing

3   Deliveries

(1) The Company shall use all reasonable endeavours to meet the delivery dates requested by the Distributor [(subject to acceptance of the relative order)], but time of delivery shall not be of the essence and the Company shall have no liability to the Distributor if it fails to meet any requested or estimated date for delivery

[**Note:** delete the square bracketed phrase if paragraph 1(4) is omitted.]

(2) If the Company is unable to meet any requested delivery date it shall as soon as practicable notify the Distributor of its estimated date for delivery

(3) Appropriation of the Products to any order of the Distributor shall occur when the Products are delivered to the Distributor

(4) Delivery of the Products will be ex the Company's main distribution centre at [   ] [or such other place in *the United Kingdom* as the Company shall notify the Distributor from time to time] ('the Delivery Point')

(5) The Company shall bear the expense of putting the Products in the possession of the carrier at the Delivery Point but the Distributor shall pay all other costs of transport and insurance

(6) If requested in the Distributor's order, the Company shall arrange (as agent for the Distributor) transport and insurance of the Products to the destination designated in the Distributor's order and shall obtain and promptly deliver to the Distributor the documents, if any, necessary for the Distributor or the Distributor's customer (as the case may be) to obtain possession of the Products. The Distributor shall reimburse

the Company for all costs incurred by the Company in respect of the foregoing and all applicable provisions of this Schedule shall apply, mutatis mutandis, to the payment of such costs as they apply to the payment of the price for the Products

(7) The Company reserves the right to make partial deliveries of any consignment of the Products ordered but, unless otherwise agreed, no delivery of the whole or any part of a consignment shall be made before the delivery date requested by the Distributor

(8) The Company will pack the Products suitably for delivery to the destinations requested by the Distributor and each consignment shall be accompanied by a delivery note in such form as may be agreed between the parties

[(9) The Distributor shall be responsible for obtaining, prior to delivery, all necessary licences, certificates of origin and other documents for the importation of the Products into the Territory and for paying all applicable import duties and other levies]

(10) The Distributor shall notify the Company in writing of any Products delivered in excess of the quantities ordered within *14* days after delivery. The Distributor reserves the right to return such surpluses to the Company at the Company's risk and expense. Alternatively, the Distributor shall have the right to retain such surpluses upon payment therefor at the price which the Distributor would have paid if it had ordered the same

(11) The Distributor shall notify the Company within *14* days after the delivery of any consignment of the Products of any shortage in the quantity ordered. The Company shall make good any such shortage as soon as reasonably practicable after written notice is received from the Distributor in compliance with this paragraph but otherwise the Company shall have no liability to make good such shortage

4   Risk and property

(1) Risk in each consignment of the Products shall pass to the Distributor at the Delivery Point upon placement of that consignment into the carrier's possession by the Company

(2) Legal and beneficial ownership of any consignment of the Products shall not pass to the Distributor until payment in full and in cleared funds has been received by the Company in respect of the price for that consignment and for all other consignments of the Products for which payment is then due.

SCHEDULE 3

TRAINING

[**Note:** This Schedule should identify:

(1) How many staff are to be trained in total.
(2) How many can be trained at one time.
(3) How many days' training is required for each person.
(4) Where and when training is to take place.
(5) Who is to be responsible for subsistence and travelling expenses.]

Precedent H

Software marketing agreement

[**Note:** Schedule 1 contains a software licence agreement to be used by the dealer in procuring contracts with end-users (licensees)]

THIS AGREEMENT is made the   day of   19

PARTIES:

(1)   COMPANY [LIMITED] [PLC] whose registered office is at
('the Company')

(2)   DEALER [LIMITED] [PLC] whose registered office is at
('the Dealer')

RECITALS:

(A)   The Company is the proprietor of certain computer software known as ['   ']

> [**Note:** If the agreement relates to all software from the Company rather than a particular package then the agreement will need to be modified accordingly.]

(B)   The Company has agreed to appoint the Dealer as its non-exclusive marketing agent for the purpose of securing licence and support agreements for such software with end-users situated in the Territory (as hereinafter defined) on the terms and conditions hereinafter contained

NOW IT IS HEREBY AGREED as follows:

1   Definitions

In this Agreement, unless the context otherwise requires, the following expressions shall have the following meanings:

'End-User Agreement'	means a software licence and support agreement in the form set out in Schedule 1 or in such other form as the Company may from time to time direct or approve in writing and as the same may be amended from time to time
'intellectual property rights'	means patents, trade marks, service marks, registered designs, applications for any of the foregoing, copyright, design rights, know-how, confidential information, trade and business names and any other similar protected rights in any country
'licensee'	means a person situated in the Territory who is a party to an End-User Agreement with the Company in respect of the Software and who was introduced (or deemed to be introduced) by the Dealer pursuant to this Agreement
'Net Licence Fee' [5.2]	means the fee paid by a licensee to use the Software excluding (i) support charges, (ii) any charges payable in respect of modifications, additions, installation or training made or provided by the Company in respect of the Software and (iii) Value Added Tax
'the Product Description'	means the product description of the Software describing the facilities and functions thereof as supplied to the Dealer by the Company from time to time
'the Software'	means the Company's [' '] software and all modifications, enhancements and replacements thereof and additions thereto produced by the Company from time to time
'the Software Documentation'	means the operating manuals and other literature provided by the

	Company from time to time to end-users for use in conjunction with the Software
'the Software Materials'	means the Software, the Product Description and the Software Documentation
'the Territory' [5.3.1]	means *the United Kingdom of Great Britain and Northern Ireland*
'Year'	means any period of 12 months commencing on [the date hereof] or any anniversary of [the date hereof]

2   Appointment [5.0.2, 5.3.3]

(1) The Company hereby appoints the Dealer and the Dealer hereby agrees to act as the non-exclusive marketing agent of the Company for the purpose of securing End-User Agreements with prospective licensees situated in the Territory

(2) The Dealer shall secure End-User Agreements in accordance with the licence and support fees specified by the Company from time to time and in accordance with the terms of this Agreement and otherwise in accordance with any instructions which the Company may give the Dealer from time to time

(3) The Dealer shall not be entitled to assign or sub-contract any of its rights or obligations under this Agreement or appoint any agent to perform such obligations

(4) The Dealer represents and warrants to the Company that it has the ability and experience to carry out the obligations assumed by it under this Agreement and that by virtue of entering into this Agreement it is not and will not be in breach of any express or implied obligation to any third party binding upon it

3   Duration

See Clause 3 of Precedent G

4   Licensing [5.3.6]

(1) The Dealer shall ensure that any prospective licensee who wishes to obtain a licence of and support for the Software shall execute an End-User Agreement in duplicate which shall then be submitted to the Company for approval

(2) The Dealer shall invite bona fide prospective licensees only to enter into End-User Agreements

(3) The Dealer shall be responsible for ensuring that all particulars required by each End-User Agreement are fully completed prior to its submission to the Company (except the agreement number which shall be allocated by the Company) and for remitting to the Company the licence and support charges payable by the licensee on signature of the End-User Agreement

(4) The Company shall not be bound to enter into any End-User Agreement, but in the event of a refusal shall notify the Dealer of such refusal promptly

(5) No End-User Agreement shall become effective unless and until it is executed by the Company

(6) The Dealer shall have no authority to enter into any End-User Agreement on behalf of the Company

(7) The Dealer shall use its reasonable endeavours to persuade each prospective licensee to pay the full licence fee and the first year's support charge immediately upon the prospective licensee's signature of an End-User Agreement but if this is not acceptable the Dealer shall be entitled to invite the prospective licensee to agree to instalment payments no less favourable to the Company than the following:

> (a) *30* per cent of the licence fee (by way of a deposit) on the prospective licensee's signature of the End-User Agreement;
>
> (b) *50* per cent of the licence fee at the time of installation of the Software at the licensee's site; and
>
> (c) *20* per cent of the licence fee and the full amount of the first year's support charge within *30* days after installation at the licensee's site

(8) After the Company's acceptance of an End-User Agreement, the Company shall deliver to the Dealer, as soon as reasonably practicable, one copy of the current version of the Software and the Software Documentation together with an original of the End-User Agreement duly executed by the Company, whereupon the Dealer shall be responsible for the following (which shall be undertaken as soon as reasonably possible):

> (a) delivery of the Software Materials and the executed End-User Agreement to the licensee;
>
> (b) successful installation and implementation of the Software on the licensee's computer;

(c) demonstrating to the licensee that the Software is in accordance with the Product Description and the Software Documentation by the use of appropriate test data;

(d) obtaining the licensee's acceptance of the Software by returning to the Company a completed acceptance certificate in a form approved by the Company and signed by the licensee;

(e) where applicable, obtaining the balance of the licence fee and the full amount of the first year's support charge in accordance with the payment dates agreed with the licensee

(9) If the Dealer fails to comply with any of its obligations under sub-clause (8) the Company may effect compliance on behalf of the Dealer whereupon the Dealer shall forthwith become liable to pay to the Company all reasonable costs and expenses incurred by the Company as a result

(10) The Dealer shall ensure that only the current versions of the Software and the Software Documentation supplied to the Dealer from time to time are delivered to licensees

(11) All copies of the Software and the Software Documentation shall remain at the risk of the Company until delivered to a licensee but the Dealer shall at all times take proper care of any copies which are from time to time in its possession or under its control

(12) The Dealer shall be entitled in its discretion to negotiate and to charge a licensee for reasonable additional fees for delivery, implementation and training in respect of the Software, but such additional fees shall be charged only after payment in full of the licence fee and the first year's support charge due to the Company and until payment is made in full as aforesaid any additional fees received by the Dealer shall be held in trust for the Company and may be appropriated by the Company in payment of all outstanding charges due to the Company from the licensee

5   Demonstration copies [5.3.6.4]

(1) The Company shall provide the Dealer with *10* demonstration copies of the Software and the Software Documentation which shall be and shall remain the property of the Company

[Note:

(1) It is quite common for a demonstration version of the package to be produced which lacks many of the main features but enables a prospective customer to get an idea of it. If that is the case this clause would need to be adapted to permit demonstrations

395

of the demonstration version only with an appropriate definition in clause 1
(2)   See chapter 6 for discussion of demonstration copies.]

(2) Such demonstration copies shall be promptly replaced with an equivalent number of any new versions of the Software and the Software Documentation which the Company may produce from time to time, subject to all copies of the previous versions being delivered up to the Company

(3) The Dealer shall use such demonstration copies for the purpose of demonstrating the Software to bona fide prospective licensees only and for no other purpose

(4) The Dealer shall at all times keep such demonstration copies properly stored and protected and under its exclusive control

6   Training [5.3.6.6]

(1) The Company shall provide training in the installation, implementation and use of the Software for the Dealer's personnel as specified in Schedule 2

(2) Any additional training required by the Dealer shall be provided by the Company in accordance with its standard scale of charges in force from time to time

(3) The Company shall offer training courses for licensees at its standard rates in force from time to time and the Dealer shall use its reasonable endeavours to persuade all licensees to complete training courses in accordance with the Company's minimum recommendations from time to time

(4) The Dealer may apply to the Company to become an authorised trainer for the Software and if so appointed shall be entitled during such appointment to train licensees at the Company's standard rates in force from time to time

(5) The Dealer's appointment as an authorised trainer may be revoked at any time or in a particular case by notice in writing given by the Company and shall automatically be revoked by the termination (for whatever reason) of this Agreement

7   Dealer's obligations [5.1, 5.6]

The Dealer shall:

(1) use its best endeavours to secure End-User Agreements with prospective licensees situated in the Territory and to promote and extend the licensing of the Software throughout the Territory

(2) promptly inform the Company of any facts or opinions of which the Dealer becomes aware likely to be relevant in relation to the commercial exploitation of the Software and which are advantageous or disadvantageous to the interests of the Company

(3) at all times conduct its business in a manner that will reflect favourably on the Software and on the good name and reputation of the Company

(4) not by itself or with others participate in any illegal, deceptive, misleading or unethical practices including, but not limited to, disparagement of the Software or the Company or other practices which may be detrimental to the Software, the Company or the public interest

either:

[(5) not during the continuance of this Agreement (whether alone or jointly and whether directly or indirectly) be concerned or interested in the marketing, distribution or sale of any software products which are similar to or competitive with the Software or which perform the same or similar functions]

> [**Note:** Consider whether any restriction makes the agreement registrable under the Restrictive Trade Practices Act 1976]

or:

[(5) at all times display, demonstrate and otherwise represent the Software fairly in comparison with competitive products from other suppliers]

(6) at all times employ a sufficient number of full-time staff who are capable of competently demonstrating the Software to prospective licensees

(7) at all times maintain adequate demonstration facilities for the Software

(8) supply to the Company such reports, returns and other information relating to orders and projected orders for the Software and regarding prospective licensees as the Company may from time to time reasonably require

(9) not make any promises or representations or give any warranties or guarantees in respect of the Software except such as are contained in the Product Specification or the Software Documentation or as expressly authorised by the Company in writing

(10) use the Company's trade marks and trade names relating to the Software only in the registered or agreed style in connection with the marketing of the Software and shall not use such trade marks or trade

names in connection with any other products or services or as part of the corporate or any trade name of the Dealer

(11) deliver copies of the Product Description to bona fide prospective licensees only

(12) not alter, obscure, remove, interfere with or add to any of the trade marks, trade names, markings or notices affixed to or contained in the Software Materials at the time when they are delivered to the Dealer

(13) not supply or recommend any computer equipment to a licensee for use in conjunction with the Software save for that equipment which is contained in the Company's current Recommended Compatible Hardware List supplied to the Dealer from time to time

(14) permit the Company and its authorised agents at all reasonable times to enter any of the Dealer's premises for the purpose of ascertaining that the Dealer is complying with its obligations under this Agreement (and so that the Dealer hereby irrevocably licenses the Company, its employees and agents to enter any such premises for such purpose)

8   Company's obligations [5.1, 5.3.6.6, 5.5, 5.7]

The Company shall:

(1) provide the Dealer with such marketing and technical assistance as the Company may in its discretion consider necessary to assist the Dealer with the promotion of the Software

(2) provide the Dealer with a reasonable number of copies of the Product Description and such other promotional literature relating to the Software which the Company may produce from time to time

(3) notify the Dealer from time to time of any change in the Net Licence Fee or in the Company's charges for the support of the Software

(4) give the Dealer reasonable advance written notice of any change in the Software or of the Company's intention to discontinue licensing the Software in the Territory

(5) provide the Dealer promptly with all information and assistance necessary to enable the Dealer properly to perform its obligations hereunder in respect of any modified, enhanced or replacement version of or addition to the Software

9   Commission [5.2]

(1) The Company shall pay the Dealer a commission at the rate of *30* per cent on the Net Licence Fee for copies of the Software licensed to and paid for by licensees

(2) The said rate of commission shall be exclusive of Value Added Tax which shall be paid by the Company at the appropriate rate and the Dealer shall be responsible for delivering a VAT invoice to the Company at the same time as its commission accrues. No commission shall be paid except against receipt of such invoice

(3) No commission shall be payable in respect of an End-User Agreement submitted by the Dealer and not accepted by the Company

(4) The Dealer's commission shall accrue on the execution by the Company of an End-User Agreement but, where the Net Licence Fee is payable in instalments, commission on the first instalment shall accrue as aforesaid and on each subsequent instalment shall accrue when the instalment is received by the Company

(5) Within 7 days of receipt by the Company of the Net Licence Fee (or an instalment thereof) the Company shall send to the Dealer a remittance advice showing particulars of the amount due to the Dealer by way of commission accompanied by a remittance for the commission due

(6) The Dealer shall receive all payments of licence fees and support charges as agent for the Company, shall hold such payments separate from its own moneys and shall remit such payments to the Company within 7 days of the receipt of such payments from prospective licensees

10 Property rights [5.3.6.2]

(1) The Software Materials and the intellectual property rights therein or relating thereto are and shall remain the property of the Company and all copies thereof in the Dealer's possession, custody or control shall (to the extent that they are not exhausted by proper use) be returned to the Company or otherwise disposed of by the Dealer as the Company may from time to time direct

(2) The Dealer shall notify the Company immediately if the Dealer becomes aware of any unauthorised use of any of the Software Materials or any of the intellectual property rights therein or relating thereto and will assist the Company (at the Company's expense) in taking all steps to defend the Company's rights therein

(3) The Dealer shall not use, reproduce or deal in the Software Materials or any copies thereof except as expressly permitted by the terms of this Agreement

(4) The provisions of this Clause shall survive the termination of this Agreement

11   Confidentiality

(1) The Dealer shall not use or divulge or communicate to any person (other than as permitted by this Agreement or with the written authority of the Company):

(a) any confidential information concerning the products, customers, business, accounts, finance or contractual arrangements or other dealings, transactions or affairs of the Company [and its subsidiaries] which may come to the Dealer's knowledge during the continuance of this Agreement;

(b) the Software Materials or any information concerning the same; or

(c) any of the terms of this Agreement

and the Dealer shall use its best endeavours to prevent the unauthorised publication or disclosure of any such information, materials or documents

(2) The Dealer shall ensure that its employees are aware of and comply with the confidentiality and non-disclosure provisions contained in this Clause and the Dealer shall indemnify the Company against any loss or damage which the Company may sustain or incur as a result of any breach of confidence by any of its employees

(3) If the Dealer becomes aware of any breach of confidence by any of its employees it shall promptly notify the Company and give the Company all reasonable assistance in connection with any proceedings which the Company may institute against any such employees

(4) The provisions of this Clause shall survive the termination of this Agreement but the restrictions contained in sub-clause (1) shall cease to apply to any information which may come into the public domain otherwise than through unauthorised disclosure by the Dealer or its employees

12   Reservation of rights [5.3.1]

The Company reserves the right:

(1) to exploit the Software itself in the Territory by such means as it may think fit including, without limitation, by the appointment of other agents, distributors and dealers;

(2) to modify, enhance, replace or make additions to the Software in any way whatsoever as the Company may in its discretion determine (whether for a particular licensee or generally) and to charge additional fees therefor;

(3) to discontinue licensing the Software in the Territory (whereupon this Agreement shall automatically terminate); and

(4) to require the Dealer either not to use or to cease to use any advertising or promotional materials in respect of the Software which the Company considers not to be in the Company's best interests

13   Customer enquiries [5.3.1]

(1) The Dealer shall promptly forward to the Company any enquiries it may receive for the Software from persons situated outside the Territory

(2) The Company shall not enter into any agreement for the licensing and support of the Software with any prospective licensee situated in the Territory in which the Dealer has established and recorded his interest unless the Dealer fails to secure an End-User Agreement with that prospective licensee within a reasonable time thereafter

(3) The Company may if it wishes (but without being under any obligation so to do) refer to the Dealer any enquiry for the Software it may receive direct from a potential licensee situated in the Territory and if the Dealer shall secure an End-User Agreement with that person the Dealer shall be deemed to have introduced that person pursuant to this Agreement and shall be entitled to its commission in the usual way

14   Legal relationship [5.0.2]

(1) During the continuance of this Agreement the Dealer shall be entitled to use the title 'AUTHORISED [   ] DEALER' but such use shall be in accordance with the Company's policies in effect from time to time and before using such title (whether on the Dealer's business stationery, advertising material or elsewhere) the Dealer shall submit to the Company proof prints and such other details as the Company may require and the Company may in its discretion grant or withhold permission for such proposed use

(2) Nothing in this Agreement shall render the Dealer a partner or (except for the purpose of securing End-User Agreements in the manner permitted by this Agreement) an agent of the Company and the Dealer shall not (except as expressly permitted or contemplated by this Agreement) purport to undertake any obligation on the Company's behalf nor expose the Company to any liability nor pledge or purport to pledge the Company's credit

15   Termination

(1) Notwithstanding anything else contained herein, this Agreement may be terminated:

(a) by the Company forthwith on giving notice in writing to the Dealer if:

(i) the Dealer shall (or shall threaten to) sell, assign, part with or cease to carry on its business or that part of its business relating to the marketing of the Software; or

(ii) the control (as defined for the purposes of Section 416 of the Income and Corporation Taxes Act 1988) of the Dealer shall be transferred to any person or persons other than the person or persons in control of the Dealer at the date hereof (but the Company shall only be entitled to terminate within the period of *60* days after the Company shall have been notified in writing of the change in control) [; or

(iii) the Dealer shall fail to submit *10* End-User Agreements to the Company in any Year]

(b) by either party forthwith on giving notice in writing to the other if:

(i) the other commits any material or persistent breach of any term of this Agreement and (in the case of a breach capable of being remedied) shall have failed, within *30* days after the receipt of a request in writing from the other party so to do, to remedy the breach (such request to contain a warning of such party's intention to terminate);

(ii) the other party shall have been unable to perform its obligations hereunder for a period of *90* consecutive days or for periods aggregating *180* days in any Year (but the party entitled to terminate may only terminate within the period of *60* days after the expiration of the said consecutive period or Year); or

(iii) the other party shall have a receiver or administrative receiver appointed of it or over any part of its undertaking or assets or shall pass a resolution for winding up (otherwise than for the purpose of a bona fide scheme of solvent amalgamation or reconstruction) or a court of competent jurisdiction shall make an order to that effect or if the other party shall enter into any voluntary arrangement with its creditors or shall become subject to an administration order

(2) The Dealer shall not be entitled to any compensation or indemnity (whether for loss of agency rights, goodwill or otherwise) as a result of the termination of this Agreement in accordance with its terms

16 Effect of termination

On the termination of this Agreement:

(1) all rights and obligations of the parties under this Agreement shall automatically terminate except:

(a) for such rights of action as shall have accrued prior to such termination and any obligations which expressly or by implication are intended to come into or continue in force on or after such termination;

(b) that the terms of this Agreement shall remain in full force and effect in respect of any obligations to be performed hereunder by the parties in respect of an End-user Agreement which remain unperformed at the time of termination (and the Dealer's obligations under sub-clauses (3) and (4) below shall be deferred insofar as may be necessary for the Dealer to perform its outstanding obligations but only until they are so performed)

(2) the Dealer shall immediately eliminate from all its literature, business stationery, publications, notices and advertisements all references to the title 'AUTHORISED [   ] DEALER' and all other representations of the Dealer's appointment hereunder;

(3) the Dealer shall at its own expense forthwith return to the Company or otherwise dispose of as the Company may instruct all promotional materials and other documents and papers whatsoever sent to the Dealer and relating to the business of the Company (other than correspondence between the parties), all property of the Company and all copies of the Software Materials, being in each case in the Dealer's possession or under its control; and

(4) the Dealer shall cause the Software to be erased from all computers of or under the control of the Dealer and shall certify to the Company that the same has been done

17 Waiver of remedies

See Clause 28 of Precedent A

18 Indemnities

(1) The Company shall indemnify the Dealer and keep the Dealer fully and effectively indemnified against any and all losses, claims, damages, costs, charges, expenses, liabilities, demands, proceedings and actions which the Dealer may sustain or incur or which may be brought or established against it by any person and which in any case arise out of or in relation to or by reason of:

(a) any claim or allegation that any of the Software Materials infringes any intellectual property rights of any third party;

(b) any breach or alleged breach by the Company of any of the terms (whether express or implied) of any End-User Agreement; or

(c) any breach or alleged breach by the Company of any applicable laws or regulations relating to the licensing or support of the Software in the Territory

and which are not in any such case due to the Dealer's negligence, recklessness or wilful misconduct or any breach of its obligations under this Agreement

(2) The Dealer shall indemnify the Company and keep the Company fully and effectively indemnified against any and all losses, claims, damages, costs, charges, expenses, liabilities, demands, proceedings and actions which the Company may sustain or incur, or which may be brought or established against it by any person and which in any case arise out of or in relation to or by reason of:

(a) any breach by the Dealer of its obligations under this Agreement;

(b) the negligence, recklessness or wilful misconduct of the Dealer in the performance of its obligations under Clause 4(8);

(c) any unauthorised act or omission of the Dealer or its employees;

(d) the manner in which the Dealer markets the Software; or

(e) the independent supply by the Dealer of any products or services for use in conjunction with or in relation to the Software

(3) If any claim is made against either party for which indemnification is sought under this Clause, the indemnified party shall consult with the other and, subject to being secured to its reasonable satisfaction, shall co-operate with the other in relation to any reasonable request made by the other in respect of such claim

19   Force majeure

See Clause 17 of Precedent S

20   Notices

See Clause 32 of Precedent A

21   Interpretation

See Clause 33 of Precedent A

22   General

This Agreement constitutes the entire understanding between the parties concerning the subject matter of this Agreement and shall be governed by and construed in accordance with the laws of England. No waiver or amendment of any provision of this Agreement shall be effective unless made by a written instrument signed by both parties. Each provision of this Agreement shall be construed separately and notwithstanding that the whole or any part of any such provision may prove to be illegal or unenforceable the other provisions of this Agreement and the remainder of the provision in question shall continue in full force and effect.

EXECUTED etc

SCHEDULE 1

SOFTWARE LICENCE AND SUPPORT AGREEMENT

Agreement No:
(to be completed
by [*Insert the name of the company*])

Dealer's Name and Address:

Licensee's Name and Address:

Licensee's business:

Designated Equipment:
(to be specified by
type and serial number)

Installation Address:

We request the grant of a licence and the provision of support services
in accordance with the above particulars and on the terms and conditions
of this Agreement, which we undertake to observe.

Date: . . . .
                                         for and on behalf of the
                                         prospective licensee ('the
                                         Licensee')

                                         Name and Title of signatory:

We approve the above prospective licensee and agree to grant and provide
the requested licence and support services on the terms and conditions
of this Agreement.

Date: . . . .
                                         for and on behalf of
                                         Company [Limited] [plc]
                                         ('the Company')

                                         Name and Title of signatory:

1   Definitions

In this Agreement, unless the context otherwise requires, the following expressions have the following meanings:

(1) '*Acceptance*' means the Licensee's acceptance of the Licensed Programs pursuant to Clause 5(2)

(2) '*CPU*' means the central processing unit of a computer system

(3) '*the Designated Equipment*' means the Licensee's computer equipment in respect of which the Licence is granted, specified by type and serial number on the face page of this Agreement or in a notice given to the Company in accordance with Clause 4 (12)(b)

(4) '*intellectual property rights*' means patents, trade marks, service marks, registered designs, applications for any of the foregoing, copyright, design rights, know-how, confidential information, trade and business names and other similar protected rights in any country

(5) '*the Licensed Programs*' means the applications computer programs known as [*insert a description of the programs*] in object code form including any modified or enhanced versions thereof which may be supplied by the Company to the Licensee from time to time

(6) '*the Licensed Program Materials*' means the Licensed Programs, the Program Documentation and the Media

(7) '*the Licence*' means the licence to Use the Licensed Program Materials granted hereunder

(8) '*the Media*' means the media on which the Licensed Programs and the Program Documentation are recorded or printed as provided to the Licensee by the Company

(9) '*the Product Description*' means the product description of the Licensed Programs describing the functions and facilities thereof as supplied to the Licensee by the Company

(10) '*the Program Documentation*' means the operating manuals, user instructions, technical literature and other related materials supplied to the Licensee by the Company for aiding the use and application of the Licensed Programs

(11) '*Recommended Equipment*' means any computer equipment which the Company may recommend for use with the Licensed Programs from time to time

(12) '*the Support Period*' means the period during which the Support Services shall be provided determined in accordance with Clause 8(5)

(13) '*the Support Services*' means the software support services to be provided by the Company pursuant to Clause 8(1)

(14) *'Use the Licensed Programs'* means to load the Licensed Programs into and store and run them on the Designated Equipment in accordance with the terms of this Agreement

(15) *'Use the Licensed Program Materials'* means to Use the Licensed Programs, to read and possess the Program Documentation in conjunction with the use of the Licensed Programs and to possess the Media

2 Effective date

This Agreement shall come into effect on the date on which it is executed by the Company but unless so executed shall never become effective

3 Services to be provided

The Company hereby agrees to:

[(1) make the agreed modifications to the Licensed Programs;]

(2) deliver the Licensed Programs to the Licensee and to install them on the Designated Equipment;

(3) license the Licensee to Use the Licensed Program Materials;

(4) provide training in the use of the Licensed Programs for the staff of the Licensee; and

(5) provide software support services in respect of the Licensed Programs

upon the terms and conditions hereinafter contained

4 Licence

(1) The Company hereby grants to the Licensee (with effect from the date of Acceptance) a non-exclusive and non-transferable licence to Use the Licensed Program Materials subject to the terms and conditions hereinafter contained

(2) The Licensee hereby acknowledges that it is licensed to Use the Licensed Program Materials in accordance with the express terms of this Agreement but not further or otherwise

(3) In consideration of the grant of the Licence, the Licensee shall pay to the Company the single licence fee specified in the Schedule hereto in accordance with the payment terms set out therein

(4) The Licensed Program Materials (and the intellectual property rights therein or relating thereto) are and shall remain the property of the Company

(5) The Licensee shall Use the Licensed Program Materials for processing its own data for its own internal purposes only. The Licensee shall not permit any third party to use the Licensed Program Materials in any way whatever nor use the Licensed Program Materials on behalf of or for the benefit of any third party in any way whatever (including, without limitation, using the Licensed Program Materials for the purpose of operating a bureau service)

(6) The Licensee shall treat the Licensed Program Materials as strictly confidential and shall not divulge the whole or any part thereof to any third party. The Licensee shall ensure that its employees comply with such confidentiality and non-disclosure obligations

(7) The Licensee shall keep exclusive possession of and control over the copies of the Licensed Program Materials in its possession and shall effect and maintain adequate security measures to safeguard the Licensed Program Materials from access or use by any unauthorised person

[(8) The Licensee shall not without the prior written consent of the Company use the Licensed Program Materials at any location other than the installation address specified on the face page of this Agreement]

(9) Except to the extent and in the circumstances expressly required to be permitted by law, the Licensee shall not alter, modify, adapt or translate the whole or any part of the Licensed Program Materials in any way whatever nor permit the whole or any part of the Licensed Programs to be combined with or to become incorporated in any other programs nor to decompile, disassemble or reverse engineer the Licensed programs or any part thereof nor attempt to do any of such things. To the extent that local law grants to the Licensee the right to decompile the Licensed Programs in order to obtain information necessary to render the Licensed Programs interoperable with other computer programs used by the Licensee, the Company hereby undertakes to make that information readily available to the licensee. The Company shall have the right to impose reasonable conditions such as a reasonable fee for doing so. In order to ensure that the Licensee receives the appropriate information, the Licensee must first give the Company sufficient details of the Licensee's objectives and the other software concerned. Requests for the appropriate information should be made to [*contact name and address*]

(10) The Licensee may make up to *3* copies of the Licensed Programs for operational security and back-up purposes but shall make no other copies thereof. Such copies and the media on which they are stored shall be the property of the Company and the Licensee shall ensure that all such copies bear the same proprietary notices as the original. The provisions of this Agreement shall apply to all such copies as they

apply to the Licensed Programs. No copies may be made of the Program Documentation without the prior written consent of the Company

(11) The Company shall be entitled to terminate the Licence forthwith by notice in writing to the Licensee if the Licensee shall commit any [material] breach of the terms of this Agreement or shall become insolvent or shall have a liquidator, receiver, administrator or administrative receiver appointed or if the Licensee permanently ceases to use the Licensed Programs Materials. Upon such termination the Licensee will return the Licensed Program Materials and all copies thereof to the Company or, at the option of the Company, shall destroy the same and certify to the Company that they have been so destroyed. The Licensee shall also cause the Licensed Programs to be erased from the Designated Equipment and shall certify to the Company that the same has been done.

(12) The use of the Licensed Program Materials is restricted to use on and in conjunction with the Designated Equipment save that:

(a) if the Licensed Program Materials cannot be used with the Designated Equipment because it is inoperable for any reason then the Licence shall be temporarily extended without additional charge to use with any other item of Recommended Equipment at any one time until such failure has been remedied, provided such item is under the direct control of the Licensee;

(b) the Licensee may use the Licensed Program Materials on and in conjunction with any replacement equipment (which is Recommended Equipment) if the use of the Licensed Program Materials on and in conjunction with the Designated Equipment is permanently discontinued and provided such replacement equipment does not comprise more than one CPU. Upon such discontinuance the Licensee shall forthwith give the Company written notice of the type and serial number of the replacement equipment whereupon the replacement equipment shall become the Designated Equipment for all the purposes of the Licence

(13) The Licensee hereby acknowledges that the Licence is limited to the use of the Licensed Program Materials with Designated Equipment which comprises one CPU only and that an additional licence fee is payable for each additional CPU which the Licensee wishes to use with the Licensed Program Materials

(14) Risk in the Media shall pass to the Licensee on delivery of the same to the Licensee. If any part of the Media shall thereafter be lost, destroyed or damaged the Company shall replace the same (embodying the relevant part of the Licensed Programs or Program Documentation)

subject to the Licensee paying the Company's standard charge for replacement

(15) In the event that any enhancement or modification of the Licensed Program Materials is made or evolves in the performance of or as a result of this Agreement the Licensee agrees that the same (and all intellectual property rights therein) shall be the exclusive property of the Company unless otherwise agreed in writing by the Company

(16) (a) The Company warrants to the Licensee that the Licensed Programs, when delivered to the Licensee, shall provide the facilities and functions described in the Product Description and the Program Documentation. The Licensee acknowledges that the Licensed Programs are of such complexity that they may have certain defects when delivered, and the Licensee agrees that the Company's sole liability and the Licensee's sole remedy in respect of a defect shall be for the Company to provide correction of documented program errors which the Company's investigation indicates are caused by a defect in an unaltered version of the Licensed Programs, and are not due to a defect or deficiency in, or a failure of, the equipment upon which the Licensed Programs are operated or hardware or software not recommended or approved by the Company, or incorrect handling or employment of the Licensed Programs by the Licensee. All warranties hereunder extend only to and are for the benefit only of the Licensee. The Company's obligation to correct any such program errors shall cease at the end of the Support Period.

(b) The Company makes no warranties or representations concerning the computer equipment used in conjunction with the Licensed Program Materials

(17) The Company shall indemnify the Licensee against any claim that the normal use or possession of the Licensed Program Materials infringes the intellectual property rights of any third party provided that the Company is given immediate and complete control of such claim, that the Licensee does not prejudice the Company's defence of such claim, that the Licensee gives the Company all reasonable assistance with such claim and that the claim does not arise as a result of the use of the Licensed Program Materials otherwise than in accordance with the terms of this Agreement or in combination with any equipment (other than the Designated Equipment) or programs not supplied or approved by the Company. The Company shall have the right to replace or change all or any part of the Licensed Program Materials in order to avoid any infringement. The foregoing states the entire liability of the Company to the Licensee in respect of the infringement of the intellectual property rights of any third party

(18) The Licensee shall notify the Company if the Licensee becomes aware of any unauthorised use of the whole or any part of the Licensed Program Materials by any person

(19) The Licensee will permit the Company to check the use of the Licensed Program Materials by the Licensee at all reasonable times and for that purpose and the purpose of verifying the discharge of the Licensee's obligations under sub-clause (11) the Company shall be entitled to enter any of the Licensee's premises (and so that the Licensee hereby irrevocably licenses the Company, its employees and agents to enter any such premises for such purpose)

5   Installation and acceptance

(1) The Company shall deliver the Licensed Programs to the Licensee and install them on the Designated Equipment at a time mutually convenient to both parties

(2) The Licensed Programs shall be deemed to be accepted when they have been installed and the Company has successfully carried out appropriate acceptance tests and the Licensee has accepted the same. Such acceptance shall not be unreasonably withheld by the Licensee

6   Training

Upon request, the Company undertakes to provide training in the use of the Licensed Programs for the staff of the Licensee in accordance with the Company's standard scale of charges in force from time to time. Such training shall take place at the premises of the Company or its appointed agent

[7   Modifications

(1) Before delivery of the Licensed Programs, the Company shall make the modifications thereto described in the Schedule hereto

(2) An additional charge shall be made for such modifications at the hourly rate(s) specified in the Schedule hereto. Such additional charge shall be paid to the Company on the date of Acceptance

(3) The Licensee shall indemnify the Company against all liabilities, costs and expenses which the Company may incur as a result of any such modifications which are made in accordance with the Licensee's requirements or specifications and which give rise to an infringement of any intellectual property rights of any third party]

8   Support services

(1) Subject to compliance by the Licensee with its responsibilities as specified in sub-clause (2), the Company shall during the Support Period:

(a) use its reasonable endeavours to correct any faults in the Licensed Programs notified to it by the Licensee (but not to recover or reconstruct the Licensee's own computer records corrupted or lost as a result of such faults)

(b) deliver to the Licensee from time to time such enhanced versions of the Licensed Programs as the Company shall release to its licensees generally and which are compatible with the version installed for the Licensee

(c) provide the Licensee with all documentation which the Company reasonably deems necessary for the utilisation of any modified, enhanced or replacement versions of or additions to the Licensed Programs delivered to the Licensee by the Company from time to time

(d) provide the Licensee with such technical advice by telephone, facsimile transmission or mail as shall be necessary to resolve the Licensee's difficulties and queries in using the current version of the Licensed Programs; Provided that the provision of this service shall be conditional upon the Licensee having first successfully completed a training course in accordance with the Company's current minimum recommendations

(e) make visits to the Licensee's premises at the request of the Licensee to test the functions of the Licensed Programs and make such adjustments and modifications as shall be necessary to ensure that the Licensed Programs continue to operate correctly

(2) The Licensee shall:

(a) use only the current version of the Licensed Programs made available to it from time to time by the Company;

(b) ensure that the Licensed Programs are used on the Designated Equipment in a proper manner by competent trained employees only or by persons under their supervision;

(c) notify each software fault to the Company as it arises and shall supply the Company with a documented example of such fault;

(d) co-operate fully with the Company in diagnosing any software fault;

(e) make available to the Company free of charge all reasonable facilities and services which are required by the Company to enable it to provide the Support Services including, without limitation, computer runs, memory dumps, telecommunications facilities, printouts, data preparation, office accommodation, typing and photocopying;

(f) not request, permit or authorise anyone other than the Company to provide any support services in respect of the Licensed Programs; and

(g) keep full security copies of the Licensed Programs and of the Licensee's data bases and other computer programs it uses in accordance with best computing practice

(3) The Support Services do not include:

(a) attendance to faults caused by using the Licensed Programs otherwise than in accordance with the Program Documentation;

(b) support or maintenance of software, accessories, attachments, computer hardware, systems or other devices not supplied by the Company;

(c) diagnosis and/or rectification of problems not attributable to the Licensed Programs; or

(d) loss or damage caused directly or indirectly by operator error or omission

and any service which is provided by the Company as a result of any of the foregoing shall be charged extra at the Company's standard rates from time to time in force

(4)   (a) In consideration of the Support Services the Licensee shall pay the annual support charge specified in the Schedule hereto. The first such charge shall be paid on the date specified in the Schedule and then annually in advance on each subsequent anniversary. No support services shall be provided while the Licensee is in default of its payment obligations

(b) The Company shall be entitled at any time and from time to time after the payment of the first support charge to make reasonable increases thereto to accord with any change in the Company's standard scale of charges by giving to the Licensee not less than *30* days' written notice expiring on the date for payment of the next support charge from time to time

(5) The Support Period shall commence on the date of Acceptance, shall continue for an initial period of *1* year and shall remain in force thereafter unless and until terminated by either party giving to the other not less than *3* months' written notice of termination expiring on the last day of the said initial period or on any subsequent anniversary of such day, but shall automatically terminate on the termination of the Licence.

No refund of any part of the support charge shall be made on the termination of the Licence

9   Assignment

This Agreement is personal to the Licensee and the Licensee shall not assign, sub-license or otherwise transfer this Agreement or any of its rights or obligations hereunder whether in whole or in part without the prior written consent of the Company

10   Force majeure

Neither party shall be liable for any delay in performing any of its obligations hereunder if such delay is caused by circumstances beyond the reasonable control of the party so delaying and such party shall be entitled to a reasonable extension of time for the performance of such obligations

11   Liability

(1) The Company shall not be liable for any loss or damage sustained or incurred by the Licensee or any third party resulting from any defect or error in the Licensed Programs except to the extent that such loss or damage arises from any unreasonable delay by the Company in providing the Support Services

(2) The Company shall not be responsible for the maintenance, accuracy or good running of any version of the Licensed Programs except the latest version thereof supplied to the Licensee for the time being

(3) Notwithstanding anything else contained in this Agreement but subject to sub-clause (4) below, the Company shall not be liable to the Licensee for loss (whether direct or indirect) of profits, business or anticipated savings or for any indirect or consequential loss or damage whatsoever even if the Company shall have been advised of the possibility thereof and whether arising from negligence, breach of contract or howsoever

(4) The Company does not exclude liability for death or personal injury caused by the Company's negligence

(5) Where the Company is liable to the Licensee for negligence, breach of contract or any other cause of action arising out of this Agreement such liability shall not exceed a sum equal to the licence fee (exclusive of VAT) referred to in Clause 4(3).

(6) The Company will not be liable for any loss arising out of any failure by the Licensee to keep full and up-to-date security copies of its data and the computer programs it uses in accordance with best computing practice

(7) The express terms of this Agreement are in lieu of all warranties, conditions, terms, undertakings and obligations implied by statute, common law, custom, trade usage, course of dealing or otherwise all of which are hereby excluded to the fullest extent permitted by law

12   General

(1) This Agreement constitutes the entire understanding between the parties concerning the subject matter of this Agreement and the Licensee warrants to the Company that in entering into this Agreement it has not relied on any warranty, representation or undertaking save as expressly set out in this Agreement. No waiver or amendment of any provision of this Agreement shall be effective unless made by a written instrument signed by both parties. Each provision of this Agreement shall be construed separately and notwithstanding that the whole or any part of any such provision may prove to be illegal or unenforceable the other provisions of this Agreement and the remainder of the provision in question shall continue in full force and effect

(2) Waiver of remedies — *See Clause 28 of Precedent A*

(3) Notices — *See Clause 32 of Precedent A*

(4) Interest on late payment — *see Clause 3(6) of Precedent A*

(5) Save as expressly provided herein, all payments shall be made within *30* days after the date of the Company's invoice therefor

(6) All sums payable under this Agreement are exclusive of Value Added Tax which the Licensee shall be additionally liable to pay to the Company

(7) Interpretation — *See Clause 33 of Precedent A*

(8) Law — *See Clause 34 of Precedent A*

(9) The Company shall be entitled to engage the services of sub-contractors or agents to perform any of its obligations hereunder

[(10) This Agreement is subject to the special conditions (if any) contained in the Schedule hereto. In the event of any inconsistency between such special conditions and the other terms of this Agreement such special conditions shall prevail]

SCHEDULE 1

(to the Software Licence and Support Agreement)

A LICENCE FEE: £[   ] plus VAT

   PAYMENT TERMS:

B MODIFICATIONS

   1 [*insert a description of the modifications*]

   2 [*insert hourly charge out rates*] plus VAT

C SUPPORT CHARGE

   £[   ] plus VAT payable on [   ]

   and then annually on each subsequent anniversary

D SPECIAL CONDITIONS

SCHEDULE 2

TRAINING

[**Note:** This Schedule should identify:

   (1) How many staff are to be trained in total.
   (2) How many can be trained at one time.
   (3) How many days' training is required for each person.
   (4) Where and when training is to take place.
   (5) Who is to be responsible for subsistence and travelling expenses.]

Precedent I

Software distribution agreement

[**Note:** Schedule 1 contains a software licence and support agreement to be used by the distributor in entering into contracts with end-users (licensees).]

THIS AGREEMENT is made the   day of   19

PARTIES:

(1)   COMPANY [LIMITED] [PLC] whose registered office is at
                                      ('the Company')
(2)   DISTRIBUTOR [LIMITED] [PLC] whose registered office is at
                                    ('the Distributor')

RECITALS:

(A)   The Company is the proprietor of certain computer software known as ['   ']

[**Note:** If the agreement relates to all software from the company rather than a particular package then the agreement will need to be modified accordingly.]

(B)   The Company has agreed to appoint the Distributor as its non-exclusive distributor to distribute and sub-license such software and its associated documentation in the Territory (as hereinafter defined) on the terms and conditions hereinafter contained

NOW IT IS HEREBY AGREED as follows:

1   Definitions

In this Agreement, unless the context otherwise requires, the following expressions have the following meanings:

'business day'	means a day other than a Saturday, Sunday or a public holiday
['Distributor Modifications'	means all modifications and enhancements of the Software made by the Distributor pursuant to Clause 7(4) but excluding any such modifications or enhancements which are adopted by the Company and embodied in the Software from time to time]
'End-User Agreement'	means a software licence and support agreement in the form set out in Schedule 1 or in such other form as the Company may from time to time direct or approve in writing and as the same may be amended from time to time
'intellectual property rights'	means patents, trademarks, service marks, registered designs, applications for any of the foregoing, copyright, design rights, know-how, confidential information, trade and business names and any other similar protected rights in any country
'licensee'	means a person situated in the Territory who is a party to an End-User Agreement with the Distributor and the Company in respect of the Software
'the Product Description'	means the product description of the Software describing the facilities and functions thereof as supplied to the Distributor by the Company from time to time
'the Software'	means the Company's [' '] software and all modifications, enhancements and replacements thereof and additions thereto

provided by the Company and made available to the Distributor from time to time pursuant to this Agreement [but excluding Distributor Modifications]

'the Software Documentation'

means the operating manuals and other literature provided by the Company to the Distributor from time to time for use by end-users in conjunction with the Software

'the Software Materials'

means the Software, the Product Description and the Software Documentation

'the Source Materials'

means all logic, logic diagrams, flowcharts, orthographic represent-ations, algorithms, routines, sub-routines, utilities, modules, file structures, coding sheets, coding, source codes listings, functional specifications, program specifica-tions and all other materials and documents necessary to enable a reasonably skilled programmer to maintain, amend and enhance the software in question without reference to any other person or documentation and whether in eye-readable or machine-readable form

'the Support Services'

means the software support services provided or to be provided by the Distributor pursuant to each End-User Agreement

'the Territory' [5.3.1]

means *the United Kingdom of Great Britain and Northern Ireland*

'Year'

means any period of 12 months commencing on [the date hereof] or any anniversary of [the date hereof]

2   Appointment [5.0.2, 5.3.3]

(1) The Company hereby appoints the Distributor and the Distributor hereby agrees to act as the non-exclusive distributor of the Company to distribute and sub-license the Software Materials in the Territory

(2) The Distributor shall not be entitled to assign or sub-contract any of its rights or obligations under this Agreement or appoint any agent to perform such obligations

(3) The Distributor represents and warrants to the Company that it has the ability and experience to carry out the obligations assumed by it under this Agreement and that by virtue of entering into this Agreement it is not and will not be in breach of any express or implied obligation to any third party binding upon it

3   Duration

See Clause 3 of Precedent G

4   Distribution and sub-licensing [5.3.6]

(1) The Company hereby grants to the Distributor a non-exclusive licence to reproduce, distribute and sub-license the Software and the Software Documentation and provide the Support Services on the terms and conditions set out in this Agreement

(2) Save as contemplated by Clause 6(2)(c), the Distributor will make the Software available to licensees in object code form only

(3) The Software and the Software Documentation shall not be made available without the Support Services and both shall be made available to end-users by the Distributor only on the terms of an End-User Agreement which all parties thereto have executed

(4) Except as provided in Clause 5(2), the Distributor shall not deliver possession of any copies of the Software or the Software Documentation to any third party unless that person has first executed an End-User Agreement

(5) The Distributor shall enter into End-User Agreements only with persons situated in the Territory and whereby the Software is to be used only in the Territory

(6) Within *14* days after the execution of this Agreement, the Company shall provide the Distributor with a master copy of the Software (in machine-readable form), the Software Documentation and the Product Description suitable for reproduction of multiple copies by the Distributor. Thereafter, the Company will provide the Distributor

promptly with master copies, suitable for reproduction, of any new versions of the Software Materials in the event that the Company releases any modifications, enhancements or replacements of or additions to any of the Software Materials

(7) The Distributor shall reproduce the Software Materials only in identical form to the master copies provided by the Company (and in particular shall reproduce the Company's copyright and proprietary notices on every such reproduction) and shall only make such number of copies as are necessary to satisfy the Distributor's obligations pursuant to End-User Agreements together with a reasonable number of copies for demonstration, support and training purposes

(8) The Distributor shall enter into End-User Agreements only with prospective licensees whom the Distributor reasonably believes are responsible and likely to comply with their obligations under an End-User Agreement

(9) The Distributor undertakes to the Company to comply with and perform its obligations under each End-User Agreement fully and promptly

(10) If the Distributor fails to comply with any of its obligations under an End-User Agreement the Company may effect compliance on behalf of the Distributor whereupon the Distributor shall forthwith become liable to pay to the Company all reasonable costs and expenses incurred by the Company as a result

(11) The Distributor shall ensure that only the current versions of the Software and the Software Documentation supplied to the Distributor from time to time are delivered to licensees and shall make any new or modified versions available to licensees promptly

(12) The Distributor shall at all times take proper care of any copies of the Software and the Software Documentation which are from time to time in its possession or under its control

(13) The Distributor shall deliver copies of the Product Description to bona fide prospective licensees only

(14) If any licensee breaches the terms of his End-User Agreement the Distributor shall use all reasonable endeavours to procure that the breach is remedied but if the Distributor is unsuccessful or the breach is incapable of remedy the Distributor shall (if it is entitled so to do) terminate the End-User Agreement in accordance with its terms and exercise its rights to recover the Software Materials from the licensee or procure that they are destroyed

5   Demonstrations

(1) The Distributor shall be entitled to demonstrate the Software and the Software Documentation to any bona fide prospective licensee but (subject as provided in Clause 5(2)) shall always retain the Software and the Software Documentation in its possession and under its control and shall not allow any such person to retain any copies of the whole or any part thereof

> [**Note:** It is quite common for a demonstration version of the package to be produced which lacks many of the main features but enables a prospective customer to get an idea of it. If that is the case this Clause would need to be adapted to permit demonstrations of the demonstration version only with an appropriate definition in Clause 1.]

(2) With the prior written approval of the Company, the Distributor may deliver a copy of any new or enhanced version of the Software and the Software Documentation to a bona fide prospective licensee or an existing licensee for evaluation purposes subject to the prospective licensee or existing licensee entering into the Company's standard Beta Test Agreement in force from time to time

> [**Note:** See Precedent J for a suitable precedent of a Beta Test Agreement.]

6   Source Materials [5.3.6.6]

(1) Within *14* days after the execution of this Agreement, the Company shall provide the Distributor with one copy of the Source Materials relating to the Software. At the same time as any modified, enhanced or replacement version of or addition to the Software is delivered to the Distributor pursuant to Clause 4(6) the Company shall provide the Distributor with one copy of the Source Materials relating thereto

(2) The Distributor shall use the Source Materials relating to the Software solely for the purposes of:

(a) providing the Support Services;

[(b) analysis to determine the correct interfaces between any other programs supplied by the Distributor and the Software;] and

(c) depositing copies of the same pursuant to source code escrow arrangements requested by licensees

and shall only make such number of copies as is reasonably necessary for those purposes

(3) Any source code escrow arrangements to be entered into by the Distributor with licensees shall be subject to the prior written approval of the Company and no copies of the Source Materials relating to the Software shall be delivered to any escrow agent without such approval

> [**Note:** The company may wish to set up an escrow scheme for the whole territory and negotiate a standard agreement to be used by the distributor. In particular, it may wish to be a party to the agreement and provide that if the distributor becomes insolvent or defaults but the company assumes its support obligations or cures the default the source codes will not be released.]

(4) Save as permitted by Clauses 6(2)(c) and 6(3), no copy of the Source Materials or any part thereof shall be made available to any third party by the Distributor

7   Corrections [and modifications] [5.3.6.6, 5.5]

(1) The Distributor shall promptly notify the Company of any error or defect in the Software Materials of which it becomes aware and give the Company documented examples of such faults

(2) The Company shall within 5 business days of receipt of such notification evaluate the notified fault and provide to the Distributor an estimate of the length of time it will take to issue a master copy of a correction under Clause 4(5). The Company will use its reasonable endeavours to provide such master copy within the estimated timescale

(3) Pending the delivery of the said master copy the Distributor shall be entitled to take, with the prior approval of the Company (such approval not to be unreasonably withheld or delayed), such measures and give such advice as may be necessary to provide a temporary solution to the fault for licensees

[(4) The Distributor may modify or enhance the Software for a particular purpose as it deems fit. The Distributor shall promptly provide the Company with a copy of all such modifications and enhancements and the Source Materials relating thereto and details of any licensees to whom such modifications or enhancements have been provided. The Distributor Modifications and the Source Materials relating thereto and the intellectual property rights therein or relating thereto shall be the absolute property of the Company and the Distributor hereby, as beneficial owner, assigns (by way of present and future assignment) to the Company all such property and intellectual property rights free from any encumbrance. The Distributor shall assume full responsibility for Distributor Modifications. The Company may but shall have no obligation to make any corrections to Distributor Modifications pursuant to Clause 7(2) and any warranties, indemnities and other obligations given or assumed by the Company in respect of the Software shall be void as to Distributor Modifications. In the event that the Company agrees to support any Distributor Modifications such support shall be provided to the Distributor on a time and materials basis at the Company's standard rates in force from time to time. Save as provided above, all the provisions of this Agreement shall apply to Distributor Modifications and the Source Materials relating thereto, mutatis mutandis, as they apply to the Software and the Source materials relating to the Software]

or:

[(4) Save as permitted by sub-clause (3), the Distributor shall not alter or modify the whole or any part of the Software in any way whatever nor permit the whole or any part of the Software to be combined with, or become incorporated in, any other programs]

8 Training

(1) The Company shall provide training in the installation, implementation and use of the Software for the Distributor's personnel as specified in Schedule 2

(2) Any additional training required by the Distributor shall be provided by the Company in accordance with its standard scale of charges in force from time to time

(3) The Distributor shall offer training courses for licensees at its standard rates in force from time to time and the Distributor shall use its reasonable endeavours to persuade all licensees to complete training courses in accordance with the Company's minimum recommendations from time to time

9 Distributor's obligations [5.1, 5.6]

The Distributor shall:

(1) use its best endeavours to promote and extend the licensing of the Software throughout the Territory

(2) promptly inform the Company of any facts or opinions of which the Distributor becomes aware likely to be relevant in relation to the commercial exploitation of the Software and which are advantageous or disadvantageous to the interests of the Company

(3) at all times conduct its business in a manner that will reflect favourably on the Software and on the good name and reputation of the Company

(4) not by itself or with others participate in any illegal, deceptive, misleading or unethical practices including, but not limited to, disparagement of the Software or the Company or other practices which may be detrimental to the Software, the Company or the public interest

either:

[(5) not during the continuance of this Agreement (whether alone or jointly and whether directly or indirectly) be concerned or interested in the marketing, distribution, licensing or sale of any software products which are similar to or competitive with the Software or which perform the same or similar functions]

> [**Note:** Consider whether any restriction makes the Agreement registerable under the Restrictive Trade Practices Act 1976.]

or:

[(5) at all times display, demonstrate and otherwise represent the Software fairly in comparison with competitive products from other suppliers]

(6) at all times employ a sufficient number of full-time staff who are capable of competently demonstrating the Software to prospective licensees

(7) at all times maintain adequate demonstration facilities for the Software

(8) supply to the Company such reports, returns and other information relating to orders and projected orders for the Software and regarding licensees as the Company may from time to time reasonably require

(9) not make any promises or representations or give any warranties, guarantees or indemnities in respect of the Software Materials except such as are contained in an End-User Agreement or as expressly authorised by the Company in writing and shall not supply the Software to any person knowing that it does not meet that person's specified requirements

(10) use the Company's trade marks and trade names relating to the Software only in the registered or agreed style in connection with the distribution and sub-licensing of the Software and shall not use such trade marks or trade names in connection with any other products or services or as part of the corporate or any trade name of the Distributor

(11) not alter, obscure, remove, interfere with or add to any of the trade marks, trade names, markings or notices affixed to or contained in the Software Materials delivered to the Distributor

(12) not supply or recommend any computer equipment to a licensee for use in conjunction with the Software save for that equipment which is contained in the Company's current Recommended Compatible Hardware List supplied to the Distributor from time to time

(13) permit the Company and its authorised agents at all reasonable times to enter any of the Distributor's premises for the purpose of ascertaining that the Distributor is complying with its obligations under this Agreement (and so that the Distributor hereby irrevocably licenses the Company, its employees and agents to enter any such premises for such purpose)

10   Company's obligations [5.1, 5.7]

The Company shall:

(1) provide the Distributor with such marketing and technical assistance as the Company may in its discretion consider necessary to assist the Distributor with the promotion of the Software

(2) endeavour to answer as soon as possible all technical queries raised by the Distributor or licensees concerning the use or application of the Software

(3) provide the Distributor with a reasonable number of copies of any promotional literature relating to the Software which the Company may produce from time to time

(4) give the Distributor reasonable advance written notice of any change in or modification of the Software or of the Company's intention to discontinue licensing or sub-licensing the Software in the Territory

(5) provide the Distributor promptly with all information and assistance necessary to enable the Distributor properly to perform its obligations hereunder in respect of any modified, enhanced or replacement version of or addition to the Software

11   Royalties and payments [5.2]

(1) The Distributor agrees to pay to the Company royalties in respect of each End-User Agreement entered into by the Distributor

(2) The royalty amount shall be *50* per cent of the Company's standard price for the Software ('Licence Royalty') for each licence fee levied by the Distributor under an End-User Agreement and *30* per cent of the Company's standard annual support charge for the Software ('Support Royalty') for each annual support charge levied by the Distributor under an End-User Agreement, both as shown on the Company's [United Kingdom] domestic price list in force from time to time. The Company

shall give the Distributor at least *60* days' advance notice of any change to such price list. The current price list is set out in Schedule 3

[**Note:** If the domestic price list is in a currency different from that charged by the distributor an appropriate clause to fix the exchange rate should be included.]

(3) The Licence Royalty and the Support Royalty shall be payable by the Distributor to the Company in cleared funds not later than the *14th* day of the calendar month following receipt of the relevant licence fee or annual support charge from a licensee by the Distributor. If for any reason the Distributor receives payment in part only then part payment proportional thereto shall likewise be made by the Distributor to the Company. All payments shall be made in *pounds sterling*

(4) The Distributor shall be free to fix its own licence fees and annual support charges with licensees in respect of each End-User Agreement and any additional delivery, implementation and training fees

(5) At the time of each payment of the Licence Royalty the Distributor shall supply the Company with one executed original of each of the End-User Agreements to which the payment relates

(6) The Distributor shall keep and shall make available to the Company on request accurate records to enable the Company to verify all royalty payments due to it

(7) During the term of this Agreement and for any period thereafter during which royalties shall continue to accrue and upon 5 business days' prior written notice to the Distributor, the Company shall have the right at any time and from time to time (subject as provided below), during the Distributor's normal business hours, to send an independent accountant (not generally providing services to the Company except in respect of other royalty audits) to audit the records of the Distributor relating to the sub-licensing and support of the Software and to verify the royalty payments due to the Company under this Agreement. The Distributor shall give such accountant full access to its premises, computers, employees and relevant records for such purpose. Any such audit shall be conducted in such a manner as not to interfere with the Distributor's normal business activities and will not include access to the Distributor's cost or profit information. Each such audit shall cover the period since the last most recent audit or, if none, the date of this Agreement down to the business day immediately preceding the commencement of the audit ('Audit Period'). The Company shall use its reasonable endeavours to procure that such accountant shall keep confidential the information which comes to his knowledge as a consequence of his audit (and to enter into any confidentiality undertaking reasonably requested by the Distributor in respect thereof prior to any

disclosure) except that the accountant shall be entitled to reveal to the Company any information necessary to provide the Company with confirmation of the accuracy of the Distributor's royalty remittances or any deviations therefrom. Upon written request, the Company agrees to make available to the Distributor, in the event the Company makes any claim with respect to an audit, a copy of the records and reports pertaining to the audit. The Company agrees not to cause such audits to be carried out more frequently than *twice* a year, except where the Company has reasonable cause to believe that correct payments are not being tendered by the Distributor in which case the Company may cause any number of audits to be carried out until such time as the Company is reasonably satisfied that the position has been corrected. Each such audit shall be carried out at the Company's expense unless it reveals a deficiency of 5 per cent or more of the royalties remitted for the relevant Audit Period in which event the Distributor shall pay the costs thereof. Payment of such costs and any royalty deficiency shall be made by the Distributor within 7 days after the Distributor shall have received written notice thereof from the Company together with a copy of the accountant's report and, if applicable, fee note showing the amount(s) due. Any such deficiency shall carry interest in accordance with sub-clause 8(c) from the date it was originally due

(8) If the Distributor fails to make any payment to the Company under this Agreement on the due date then, without prejudice to any other right or remedy available to the Company, the Company shall be entitled to:

> (a) suspend the performance or further performance of its obligations under this Agreement without liability to the Distributor;

> (b) suspend (by notice in writing) the Distributor's right to enter into any further End-User Agreements until payment in full is made (and the Distributor shall so comply with such suspension); and

> (c) charge the Distributor interest (both before and after any judgment) on the amount outstanding on a daily basis at the rate of 2 per cent per annum above the base rate of [   ] Bank plc (or such other London Clearing Bank as the Company may nominate) from time to time in force, such interest to be calculated from the date or last date for payment thereof to the date of actual payment (both dates inclusive) compounded quarterly. Such interest shall be payable on demand by the Company

(9) All royalties payable under this Agreement are exclusive of any Value Added Tax and other applicable sales taxes, which the Customer shall be additionally liable to pay to the Company

(10) The provisions of this Clause shall survive the termination of this Agreement

12   Property rights [5.3.6.2]

(1) The Software Materials and the Source Materials relating to the Software and the intellectual property rights therein or relating thereto are and shall remain the property of the Company and all copies thereof in the Distributor's possession, custody or control shall (to the extent that they are not exhausted by proper use) be returned to the Company or otherwise disposed of by the Distributor as the Company may from time to time direct

(2) The Distributor shall notify the Company immediately if the Distributor becomes aware of any unauthorised use of any of the Software Materials or the Source Materials relating to the Software or any of the intellectual property rights therein or relating thereto and will assist the Company (at the Company's expense) in taking all steps to defend the Company's rights therein

(3) The Distributor shall not use, reproduce or deal in the Software Materials or the Source Materials relating to the Software or any copies thereof except as expressly permitted by this Agreement

(4) The provisions of this Clause shall survive the termination of this Agreement

13   Confidentiality

(1) The Distributor shall not use or divulge or communicate to any person (other than as permitted by this Agreement or with the written authority of the Company):

(a) any confidential information concerning the products, customers, business, accounts, finance or contractual arrangements or other dealings, transactions or affairs of the Company [and its subsidiaries] which may come to the Distributor's knowledge during the continuance of this Agreement;

(b) the Software Materials or any information concerning the same;

(c) the Source Materials relating to the Software; or

(d) any of the terms of this Agreement

and the Distributor shall use its best endeavours to prevent the unauthorised publication or disclosure of any such information, materials or documents

(2) The Distributor shall ensure that its employees are aware of and comply with the confidentiality and non-disclosure provisions contained in this Clause and the Distributor shall indemnify the Company against any loss or damage which the Company may sustain or incur as a result of any breach of confidence by any of its employees

(3) If the Distributor becomes aware of any breach of confidence by any of its employees it shall promptly notify the Company and give the Company all reasonable assistance in connection with any proceedings which the Company may institute against any such employees

(4) The provisions of this Clause shall survive the termination of this Agreement but the restrictions contained in sub-clause (1) shall cease to apply to any information which may come into the public domain otherwise than through unauthorised disclosure by the Distributor or its employees

14   Reservation of rights [5.3.1]

The Company reserves the right:

(1) to exploit the Software itself in the Territory by such means as it may think fit including, without limitation, by the appointment of other distributors

(2) to modify, enhance, replace or make additions to the Software in any way whatsoever as the Company may in its discretion determine

(3) to discontinue licensing or sub-licensing the Software in the Territory (whereupon this Agreement shall automatically terminate) and

(4) to require the Distributor either not to use or to cease to use any advertising or promotional materials in respect of the Software which the Company considers not to be in the Company's best interests

15   Customer enquiries [5.3.1]

(1) The Distributor shall promptly forward to the Company any enquiries it may receive for the Software from persons situated outside the Territory

(2) The Company shall not enter into any agreement for the licensing and support of the Software with any prospective licensee situated in the Territory in which the Distributor has established and recorded its interest unless the Distributor fails to enter into an End-User Agreement with that prospective licensee within a reasonable time thereafter

(3) The Company may if it wishes (but without being under any obligation so to do) refer to the Distributor any enquiry for the Software it may receive direct from a potential licensee situated in the Territory

16 Legal relationship

(1) During the continuance of this Agreement the Distributor shall be entitled to use the title 'AUTHORISED [   ] SOFTWARE DISTRIBUTOR' but such use shall be in accordance with the Company's policies in effect from time to time and before using such title (whether on the Distributor's business stationery, advertising material or elsewhere) the Distributor shall submit to the Company proof prints and such other details as the Company may require and the Company may in its discretion grant or withhold permission for such proposed use

(2) Nothing in this Agreement shall render the Distributor a partner or (except as expressly permitted by this Agreement) an agent of the Company and the Distributor shall not (except as expressly permitted or contemplated by this Agreement) purport to undertake any obligation on the Company's behalf nor expose the Company to any liability nor pledge or purport to pledge the Company's credit

(3) The Distributor is hereby authorised to act as the Company's agent to execute on the Company's behalf each End-User Agreement which the Distributor is permitted to enter into pursuant to this Agreement and shall so execute each such End-User Agreement

17 Termination [5.4]

(1) Notwithstanding anything else contained herein, this Agreement may be terminated:

(a) by the Company forthwith on giving notice in writing to the Distributor if:

(i) the Distributor shall (or shall threaten to) sell, assign, part with or cease to carry on its business or that part of its business relating to the distribution of the Software;

(ii) the control (as defined for the purposes of Section 416 of the Income and Corporation Taxes Act 1988) of the Distributor shall be transferred to any person or persons other than the person or persons in control of the Distributor at the date hereof (but the Company shall only be entitled to terminate within the period of *60* days after the Company shall have been notified in writing of the change in control);

(iii) the Distributor shall fail to remit to the Company in any Year royalties equal to or in excess of the royalty targets set out in Schedule 4 or such other targets as may be agreed between the Company and the Distributor from time to time; or

(iv) any audit carried out pursuant to Clause 11(7) shall reveal a deficiency of *10* per cent or more in the relevant period

(b) by either party forthwith on giving notice in writing to the other if:

(i) the other commits any material or persistent breach of any term of this Agreement and (in the case of a breach capable of being remedied) shall have failed, within *30* days after the receipt of a request in writing from the other party so to do, to remedy the breach (such request to contain a warning of such party's intention to terminate);

(ii) the other party shall have been unable to perform its obligations hereunder for a period of *90* consecutive days or for periods aggregating *180* days in any Year (but the party entitled to terminate may only terminate within the period of *60* days after the expiration of the said consecutive period or Year); or

(iii) the other party shall have a receiver or administrative receiver appointed of it or over any part of its undertaking or assets or shall pass a resolution for winding up (otherwise than for the purpose of a bona fide scheme of solvent amalgamation or reconstruction) or a court of competent jurisdiction shall make an order to that effect or if the other party shall enter into any voluntary arrangement with its creditors or shall become subject to an administration order

(2) The Distributor shall not be entitled to any compensation or indemnity (whether for loss of distribution rights, goodwill or otherwise) as a result of the termination of this Agreement in accordance with its terms

18   Effect of termination

On the termination of this Agreement:

(1) all rights and obligations of the parties under this Agreement shall automatically terminate except:

(a) for such rights of action as shall have accrued prior to such termination and any obligations which expressly or by implication are intended to come into or continue in force on or after such termination;

(b) that the terms of this Agreement shall remain in full force and effect to the extent and for the period necessary to permit the Distributor properly to perform its continuing obligations under each End-User Agreement subsisting at the date of termination (and the Distributor's obligations under sub-clauses (3) and (4) below shall be deferred during such period as those continuing obligations subsist);

(c) that the obligations of the parties contained in Clauses 4(9), 4(10) and 4(14) shall continue in respect of each End-User Agreement subsisting at the date of termination

(2) the Distributor shall immediately eliminate from all its literature, business stationery, publications, notices and advertisements all references to the title 'AUTHORISED [   ] SOFTWARE DISTRIBUTOR' and all other representations of the Distributor's appointment hereunder

(3) the Distributor shall at its own expense forthwith return to the Company or otherwise dispose of as the Company may instruct all promotional materials and other documents and papers whatsoever sent to the Distributor and relating to the business of the Company (other than correspondence between the parties), all property of the Company and all copies of the Software Materials and the Source Materials relating to the Software, being in each case in the Distributor's possession or under its control

(4) the Distributor shall cause the Software to be erased from all computers of or under the control of the Distributor and shall certify to the Company that the same has been done; and

(5) each End-User Agreement then subsisting shall continue in effect and shall survive the termination of this Agreement

19 Novation of End-User Agreements

If the Company novates an End-User Agreement in favour of itself or another distributor in accordance with its entitlement thereunder, the Distributor shall:

(1) give the Company or such distributor, at the Company's request, all reasonable cooperation in transferring the Distributor's obligations under such End-User Agreement to the Company or such distributor; and

(2) forthwith pay to the Company or as it shall direct a proportionate part of any annual support fee (including VAT) paid in advance by the licensee thereunder apportioned from the effective date of the novation down to the expiry of the year to which the payment relates

20   Waiver of remedies

See Clause 28 of Precedent A

21   Indemnities

(1) The Company shall indemnify the Distributor against any claim (or claim for indemnity from any licensee against a claim) that the normal use or possession of the Software Materials infringes the intellectual property rights of any third party provided that the Company is given immediate and complete control of such claim, that the Distributor does not prejudice the Company's defence of such claim, that the Distributor gives the Company all reasonable assistance with such claim and that the claim does not arise as a result of the use of the Software Materials otherwise than in accordance with the terms of this Agreement or an End-User Agreement or with any equipment or programs not approved by the Company. The Company shall have the right to replace or change all or any part of the Software Materials in order to avoid any infringement. The foregoing states the entire liability of the Company to the Distributor in respect of the infringement of the intellectual property rights of any third party

(2) The Company shall indemnify the Distributor against any claim, loss, liability, damage or expense resulting from or due to a claim for breach of warranty, design defect, negligence or product liability or any similar claim directly attributable to the Software Materials save to the extent that such claim arises as a result of the Distributor's negligence, recklessness or wilful misconduct or any breach of its obligations under this Agreement or any End-User Agreement and provided that the Company is given immediate and complete control of such claim, that the Distributor does not prejudice the Company's defence of such claim and that the Distributor gives the Company all reasonable assistance with such claim

(3) The Distributor shall indemnify the Company and keep the Company fully and effectively indemnified on demand from and against any and all losses, claims, damages, costs, charges, expenses, liabilities, demands, proceedings and actions which the Company may sustain or incur, or which may be brought or established against it by any person and which in any case arise out of or in relation to or by reason of:

(a) any breach by the Distributor of its obligations under this Agreement; or

(b) any unauthorised action or omission of the Distributor or its employees; or

(c) the manner in which the Distributor markets the Software; or

(d) the independent supply by the Distributor of any products or services for use in conjunction with or in relation to the Software; [or

(e) any Distributor Modifications]

If any claim is made against the Company for which indemnification is sought under this sub-clause, the Company shall consult with the Distributor and, subject to being secured to its reasonable satisfaction, shall co-operate with the Distributor in relation to any reasonable request made by the Distributor in respect of such claim

22   Warranties and liability [5.8]

(1) The Company warrants to the Distributor that the Software, when delivered to the Distributor, shall provide, if properly used by the Distributor and licensees, the facilities and functions described in the Product Description and the Program Documentation. The Distributor acknowledges that the Software is of such complexity that it may have certain defects when delivered, and the Distributor agrees that the Company's sole liability and the Distributor's sole remedy in respect of any breach of the said warranty shall be for the Company to provide corrections of documented program errors in accordance with Clause 7(2). If the Company fails (other than through the act or default of the Distributor) within a reasonable time to correct non-conforming Software as aforesaid its liability therefor shall be limited to a sum equal to the total royalties received by the Company from the Distributor pursuant to this Agreement

(2) The express terms of this Agreement are in lieu of all warranties, conditions, terms, undertakings and obligations implied by statute, common law, custom, trade usage, course of dealing or otherwise, all of which are hereby excluded to the fullest extent permitted by law

(3) Notwithstanding anything else contained in this Agreement but subject to sub-clause (4), the Company shall not be liable to the Distributor for loss (whether direct or indirect) of profits, business or anticipated savings or for any indirect or consequential loss or damage whatsoever even if the Company shall have been advised of the possibility thereof and whether arising from negligence, breach of contract or howsoever

(4) The Company does not exclude liability for death or personal injury caused by the Company's negligence

[(5) The Company shall have no liability or responsibility whatsoever under Clauses 21(1) or 21(2) or sub-clause (1) or otherwise under this Agreement for any Distributor Modifications]

23   Force majeure

See Clause 17 of Precedent S

24   Notices

See Clause 32 of Precedent A

25   Interpretation

See Clause 33 of Precedent A

26   General

See Clause 12 of Precedent H

EXECUTED etc

SCHEDULE 1

SOFTWARE LICENCE AND SUPPORT AGREEMENT [5.3.6.5]

THIS AGREEMENT is made the   day of   19

PARTIES:

(1) DISTRIBUTOR [LIMITED] [PLC] whose registered office is at
('the Distributor')

(2) LICENSEE [LIMITED] [PLC] whose registered office is at
('the Licensee')

(3) COMPANY [LIMITED] [PLC] whose registered office is at
('the Owner')

RECITALS:

(A) The Owner is the proprietor of certain computer software known
as ['   ']

(B) By a distribution agreement made between the Distributor and the
Owner, the Distributor has been appointed as a distributor of the Owner
to distribute and sub-license such software and its associated
documentation in the Territory (as hereinafter defined) and to provide
support services therefor on the terms and conditions of agreements
in the form of this Agreement

(C) The Distributor has agreed to sub-license such software and
documentation and provide support services to the Licensee on the terms
and conditions hereinafter contained

NOW IT IS HEREBY AGREED as follows:

1   Definitions

In this Agreement, unless the context otherwise requires, the following
expressions have the following meanings:

(1) '*Acceptance*' means the Licensee's acceptance of the Licensed
Programs pursuant to Clause 4(2)

(2) '*CPU*' means a central processing unit of a computer system

(3) '*Designated CPUs*' means the CPUs designated by type and serial
number in the Schedule hereto

(4) '*the Designated System*' means the Licensee's computer system comprising the Designated CPUs and the peripheral equipment listed in the Schedule

(5) '*the Distributor*' includes any successor to the Distributor pursuant to a novation under Clause 11(3)

(6) '*the Distribution Agreement*' means the distribution agreement in force between the Owner and the Distributor from time to time relating to the Licensed Programs

(7) '*intellectual property rights*' means patents, trade marks, service marks, registered designs, applications for any of the foregoing, copyright, design rights, know-how, confidential information, trade and business names and other similar protected rights in any country

(8) '*the Licensed Programs*' means the applications computer programs known as [*insert a description of the programs*] in object code form including any modified, enhanced or replacement versions thereof or additions thereto which may be supplied by the Distributor to the Licensee from time to time

(9) '*the Licensed Program Materials*' means the Licensed Programs, the Program Documentation and the Media

(10) '*the Licence*' means the licence to Use the Licensed Program Materials granted hereunder

[Note: The licence is drafted as a site licence for a computer network.]

(11) '*the Media*' means the media on which the Licensed Programs and the Program Documentation are recorded or printed as provided to the Licensee by the Distributor

(12) '*the Product Description*' means the product description of the Licensed Programs describing the functions and facilities thereof as supplied to the Licensee by the Distributor

(13) '*the Program Documentation*' means the operating manuals, user instructions, technical literature and other related materials supplied to the Licensee by the Distributor for aiding the use and application of the Licensed Programs

(14) '*Recommended Equipment*' means any computer equipment which the Distributor may recommend for use with the Licensed Programs from time to time

[Note: Both the owner and the distributor will wish to guard against degradation of performance of the software because of undersized equipment. The recommendations from the distributor should therefore include recommendations as to size and capacity.]

(15) '*the Support Period*' means the period during which the Support Services shall be provided determined in accordance with Clause 7(5)

(16) '*the Support Services*' means the software support services to be provided by the Distributor pursuant to Clause 7(1)

(17) '*the Territory*' means *the United Kingdom of Great Britain and Northern Ireland*

(18) '*User*' means any employee of the Licensee accessing the Licensed Programs from a single processor keyboard terminal or peripheral device

(19) '*Use the Licensed Programs*' means to load the object code form of the Licensed Programs into and store and run them on the Designated CPUs in accordance with the terms of this Agreement

(20) '*Use the Licensed Program Materials*' means to Use the Licensed Programs, to read and possess the Program Documentation in conjunction with the use of the Licensed Programs and to possess the Media

2   Services to be provided

The Distributor hereby agrees to:

[(1) make the agreed modifications to the Licensed Programs]

(2) deliver the Licensed Programs to the Licensee and to install them on the Designated CPUs

(3) license the Licensee to Use the Licensed Program Materials

(4) provide training in the use of the Licensed Programs for the staff of the Licensee and

(5) provide software support services to the Licensee in respect of the Licensed Programs

upon the terms and conditions hereinafter contained

3   Licence

(1) The Distributor hereby grants to the Licensee a non-exclusive and non-transferable licence to Use the Licensed Program Materials subject to the terms and conditions hereinafter contained

(2) The Licensee hereby acknowledges that it is licensed to Use the Licensed Program Materials in accordance with the express terms of this Agreement but not further or otherwise

(3) In consideration of the grant of the Licence, the Licensee shall pay to the Distributor the single licence fee specified in the Schedule in accordance with the payment terms set out therein

(4) The Licensed Program Materials (and the intellectual property rights therein or relating thereto) are and shall remain the property of the Owner

(5) The Licensee shall Use the Licensed Program Materials for processing its own data for its own internal purposes only. The Licensee shall not permit any third party to use the Licensed Program Materials in any way whatever nor use the Licensed Program Materials on behalf of or for the benefit of any third party in any way whatever (including, without limitation, using the Licensed Program Materials for the purpose of operating a bureau service)

(6) The Licensee shall treat the Licensed Program Materials as strictly confidential and shall not divulge the whole or any part thereof to any third party. The Licensee shall ensure that its employees comply with such confidentiality and non-disclosure obligations

(7) The Licensee shall keep exclusive possession of and control over the copies of the Licensed Program Materials in its possession and shall effect and maintain adequate security measures to safeguard the Licensed Program Materials from access or use by any unauthorised person

(8) The Licensee shall not without the prior written consent of the Distributor use the Licensed Program Materials at any location other than the installation address specified in the Schedule. In any event, the use of the Licensed Program Materials is limited to use in the Territory only

(9) Except to the extent and in the circumstances expressly required to be permitted by law, the Licensee shall not alter, modify, adapt or translate the whole or any part of the Licensed Program Materials in any way whatever nor permit the whole or any part of the Licensed Programs to be combined with or to become incorporated in any other programs nor to decompile, disassemble or reverse engineer the Licensed Programs or any part thereof nor attempt to do any of such things. To the extent that local law grants to the Licensee the right to decompile the Licensed Programs in order to obtain information necessary to render the Licensed Programs interoperable with other computer programs used by the Licensee, the Owner hereby undertakes to make that information readily available to the Licensee. The Owner shall have the right to impose reasonable conditions such as a reasonable fee for doing so. In order to ensure that the Licensee receives the appropriate information, the Licensee must first give the Owner sufficient details of the Licensee's objectives and the other software concerned. Requests for the appropriate information should be made to [*contact name and address*]

(10) The Distributor shall supply the number of copies of the Licensed Programs and Program Documentation specified in the Schedule. In

addition, the Licensee may make up to 3 copies of the Licensed Programs for operational security and back-up purposes but shall make no other copies thereof. All copies and the media on which they are stored shall be the property of the Owner and the Licensee shall ensure that all such copies bear the same proprietary notices as the original. The provisions of this Agreement shall apply to all such copies as they apply to the originals. No copies may be made of the Program Documentation without the prior written consent of the Owner

(11) The Distributor shall be entitled to terminate the Licence forthwith by notice in writing to the Licensee if the Licensee shall commit any [material] breach of the terms of this Agreement or shall become insolvent or shall have a liquidator, receiver, administrator or administrative receiver appointed or if the Licensee permanently ceases to use the Licensed Program Materials. Upon such termination the Licensee shall return the Licensed Program Materials and all copies thereof to the Distributor or, at the option of the Distributor, shall destroy the same and certify to the Distributor that they have been so destroyed. The Licensee shall also cause the Licensed Programs to be erased from the Designated CPUs and shall certify to the Distributor that the same has been done

(12) The use of the Licensed Program Materials is restricted to use on the Designated CPUs save that:

(a) if the Licensed Program Materials cannot be used on any one Designated CPU because it is inoperable for any reason then the Licence shall be temporarily extended without additional charge to use on a single back-up or substitute CPU (which is Recommended Equipment) until the Designated CPU is operable again, provided such substitute CPU is under the direct control of the Licensee

(b) the Licensee may use the Licensed Program Materials on and in conjunction with a single replacement CPU (which is Recommended Equipment) if the use of the Licensed Program Materials on and in conjunction with any one Designated CPU is permanently discontinued. Upon such discontinuance the Licensee shall forthwith give the Distributor written notice of the type and serial number of the replacement CPU whereupon the replacement CPU shall become a Designated CPU for all the purposes of the Licence

(13) The Licence is limited to the use of the Licensed Program Materials with the Designated System and by the maximum number of concurrent Users specified in the Schedule. The Licensee acknowledges that an additional licence fee is payable for each additional CPU on which the

Licensed Programs are to be used or additional concurrent User which is to have access to the Licensed Programs

(14) Risk in the Media shall pass to the Licensee on delivery of the same to the Licensee. If any part of the Media shall thereafter be lost, destroyed or damaged the Distributor shall replace the same (embodying the relevant part of the Licensed Programs or Program Documentation) subject to the Licensee paying the Distributor's standard charge for replacement

(15) In the event that any enhancement or modification of the Licensed Program Materials is made or evolves in the performance of or as a result of this Agreement the Licensee agrees that the same (and all intellectual property rights therein) shall be the exclusive property of the Owner unless otherwise agreed in writing by the Owner

(16) (a) The Distributor warrants to the Licensee that the Licensed Programs, when delivered to the Licensee, shall provide the facilities and functions described in the Product Description and the Program Documentation. The Licensee acknowledges that the Licensed Programs are of such complexity that they may have certain defects when delivered, and the Licensee agrees that the Distributor's sole liability and the Licensee's sole remedy in respect of a defect shall be for the Distributor to provide correction of documented program errors which the Distributor's investigation indicates are caused by a defect in an unaltered version of the Licensed Programs, and are not due to a defect or deficiency in, or a failure of, the equipment upon which the Licensed programs are operated or hardware or software not recommended or approved by the Distributor, or incorrect handling or employment of the Licensed Programs by the Licensee. All warranties hereunder extend only to the Licensee and are for the benefit only of the Licensee. The Distributor's obligation to correct any such program errors shall cease at the end of the Support Period

(b) The Distributor makes no warranties or representations concerning the computer equipment used in conjunction with the Licensed Program Materials

(17) The Distributor shall indemnify the Licensee against any claim that the normal use or possession of the Licensed Program Materials infringes the intellectual property rights of any third party provided that the Distributor is given immediate and complete control of such claim, that the Licensee does not prejudice the Distributor's defence of such claim, that the Licensee gives the Distributor all reasonable assistance with such claim and that the claim does not arise as a result of the use of the Licensed Program Materials otherwise than in accordance with the

terms of this Agreement or in combination with any equipment (other than the Designated System) or programs not supplied or approved by the Distributor. The Distributor shall have the right to replace or change all or any part of the Licensed Program Materials in order to avoid any infringement. The foregoing states the entire liability of the Distributor to the Licensee in respect of the infringement of the intellectual property rights of any third party

(18) The Licensee shall notify the Distributor if the Licensee becomes aware of any unauthorised use of the whole or any part of the Licensed Program Materials by any person

(19) The Licensee will permit the Distributor to check the use of the Licensed Program Materials by the Licensee at all reasonable times and for that purpose and the purpose of verifying the discharge of the Licensee's obligations under sub-clause (11) the Distributor shall be entitled to enter any of the Licensee's premises (and so that the Licensee hereby irrevocably licenses the Distributor, its employees and agents to enter any such premises for any such purpose)

4   Installation and acceptance

(1) The Distributor shall deliver the Licensed Programs to the Licensee and install them on the Designated CPUs at a time mutually convenient to both parties. The Licensee shall pay to the Distributor the delivery and installation charge specified in the Schedule on the payment terms set out therein

(2) The Licensed Programs shall be deemed to be accepted when they have been installed and the Distributor has successfully carried out appropriate acceptance tests and the Licensee has accepted the same. Such acceptance shall not be unreasonably withheld by the Licensee

5   Training

Upon request, the Distributor undertakes to provide training in the use of the Licensed Programs for the staff of the Licensee in accordance with the Distributor's standard scale of charges in force from time to time. Such training shall take place at the premises of the Distributor

[6   Modifications

(1) Before delivery of the Licensed Programs, the Distributor shall make the modifications thereto described in the Schedule

[(2) An additional charge shall be made for such modifications at the hourly rate(s) specified in the Schedule. Such additional charge shall be paid to the Distributor on the date of Acceptance]

(3) The Licensee shall indemnify the Distributor against all liabilities, costs and expenses which the Distributor may incur as a result of any such modifications which are made in accordance with the Licensee's requirements or specifications and which give rise to an infringement of any intellectual property rights of any third party]

7   Support Services

(1) Subject to compliance by the Licensee with its obligations under Clause 7(2), the Distributor shall during the Support Period:

(a) use its reasonable endeavours to correct any faults in the Licensed Programs notified to it by the Licensee (but not to recover or reconstruct the Licensee's own computer records corrupted or lost as a result of such faults);

(b) deliver to the Licensee from time to time and install such new versions of the Licensed Programs as the Owner shall deliver to its distributors for general release to licensees from time to time which are compatible with the Licensee's version;

(c) provide the Licensee with all documentation which the Distributor reasonably deems necessary for the utilisation of any modified, enhanced or replacement versions of or additions to the Licensed Programs delivered to the Licensee by the Distributor from time to time;

(d) provide the Licensee with remote telephone diagnostic assistance during the hours specified in the Schedule to help resolve the Licensee's difficulties and queries in using the current version of the Licensed Programs; Provided that the Licensee has first successfully completed a training course in accordance with the Distributor's current minimum recommendations; and

(e) make visits to the Licensee's premises at the request of the Licensee to test the functions of the Licensed Programs and make such adjustments and modifications as shall be necessary to ensure that the Licensed Programs continue to operate correctly

(2) The Licensee shall:

(a) use only the current version of the Licensed Programs made available to it from time to time by the Distributor;

(b) ensure that the Licensed Programs are used on the Designated Equipment in a proper manner by competent trained employees only or by persons under their supervision;

(c) notify each software fault to the Distributor as it arises and shall supply the Distributor with a documented example of such fault;

(d) co-operate fully with the Distributor in diagnosing any software fault;

(e) make available to the Distributor free of charge all reasonable facilities and services which are required by the Distributor to enable it to provide the Support Services including, without limitation, computer runs, memory dumps, telecommunications facilities, printouts, data preparation, office accommodation, typing and photocopying;

(f) not request, permit or authorise anyone other than the Distributor or the Owner or the Owner's authorised representatives to provide any support services in respect of the Licensed Programs; and

(g) keep full security copies of the Licensed Programs and of the Licensee's data and other computer programs it uses in accordance with best computing practice

(3) The Support Services do not include:

(a) attendance to faults caused by using the Licensed Programs otherwise than in accordance with the Program Documentation;

(b) support or maintenance of software, accessories, attachments, computer hardware, systems or other devices not supplied by the Distributor;

(c) diagnosis or rectification of problems not attributable to the Licensed Programs; or

(d) loss or damage caused directly or indirectly by operator error or omission

and any service which is provided by the Distributor as a result of any of the foregoing shall be charged extra at the Distributor's standard rates in force from time to time

(4) (a) In consideration of the Support Services the Licensee shall pay the annual support charge specified in the Schedule. The first such charge shall be paid on the date specified in the Schedule and then annually in advance on each subsequent anniversary. No support services shall be provided while the Licensee is in default of its payment obligations

(b) The Distributor shall be entitled at any time and from time to time after the payment of the first support charge to make reasonable increases thereto to accord with any change in the Distributor's standard scale of charges by giving to the Licensee not less than *30* days' written notice expiring on the date for payment of the next annual support charge

(5) The Support Period shall commence on the date of Acceptance, shall continue for an initial period of *one year* and shall remain in force thereafter unless and until terminated by either party giving to the other not less than *3* months' written notice of termination expiring on the last day of the said initial period or on any subsequent anniversary of such day, but shall automatically terminate on the termination of the Licence. No refund of any part of the annual support charge shall be made on termination of the Support Services

8   Assignment

This Agreement is personal to the Licensee and the Licensee shall not assign, sub-license or otherwise transfer this Agreement or any of its rights or obligations hereunder whether in whole or in part

9   Force majeure

No party shall be liable for any delay in performing any of its obligations hereunder if such delay is caused by circumstances beyond the reasonable control of the party so delaying and such party shall be entitled to a reasonable extension of time for the performance of such obligations

10   Liability

(1) The Distributor shall not be liable for any loss or damage sustained or incurred by the Licensee or any third party resulting from any defect or error in the Licensed Programs except to the extent that such loss or damage arises from any unreasonable delay by the Distributor in providing the Support Services

(2) The Distributor shall not be responsible for the maintenance, accuracy or good running of any version of the Licensed Programs except the latest version thereof supplied to the Licensee from time to time

(3) Notwithstanding anything else contained in this Agreement but subject to sub-clause (4) below, the Distributor shall not be liable to the Licensee for loss (whether direct or indirect) of profits, business or anticipated savings or for any indirect or consequential loss or damage whatsoever even if the Distributor shall have been advised of the

possibility thereof and whether arising from negligence, breach of contract or howsoever

(4) The Distributor does not exclude liability for death or personal injury caused by the Distributor's negligence

(5) Where the Distributor is liable to the Licensee for negligence, breach of contract or any other cause of action arising out of this Agreement such liability shall not exceed a sum equal to the licence fee (exclusive of VAT) referred to in Clause 3(3)

(6) The Distributor will not be liable for any loss arising out of any failure by the Licensee to keep full and up-to-date security copies of its data and the computer programs it uses in accordance with best computing practice

(7) The express terms of this Agreement are in lieu of all warranties, conditions, terms, undertakings and obligations implied by statute, common law, custom, trade usage, course of dealing or otherwise all of which are hereby excluded to the fullest extent permitted by law

11   The Owner

(1) The Distributor enters into this Agreement both for itself and as agent on behalf of the Owner and warrants to the Licensee that it has the necessary authority so to do

(2) The Licensee undertakes with the Owner to comply with and perform its obligations under this Agreement fully and promptly

(3) This Agreement shall continue in effect notwithstanding any termination of the Distribution Agreement but at any time after such termination the Owner shall be entitled to serve notice ('Novation Notice') on the Licensee (with a copy to the Distributor) requesting the Licensee to convert this Agreement into a direct agreement between the Owner or another distributor of the Owner as specified in such notice who has entered into a direct covenant with the Licensee to be bound by the terms of this Agreement (the Owner or such distributor being hereinafter referred to as 'the Replacement') (1) and the Licensee (2). The Licensee shall have a period of *30* days from the date of service of the Novation Notice to serve notice ('Acceptance Notice') on the Owner accepting such novation

(4) If an Acceptance Notice is served on the Owner within the said period of *30* days then this Agreement shall be novated as follows:

(a) the Licence shall thereby take effect on the date of such service ('the Transfer Date') as a licence from the Replacement to the Licensee

(b) this Agreement shall thereby be novated on the Transfer Date by the substitution of the Replacement for the Distributor as the Distributor under this Agreement

(c) the Replacement shall thereby undertake, and shall be deemed to have so undertaken with effect from the Transfer Date, to observe and perform all the terms and conditions of this Agreement as if it had been a party hereto and named herein instead of the Distributor but the Replacement shall not be liable for any antecedent breach of this Agreement by the Distributor

(d) the Licensee and the Distributor shall thereby release and discharge each other with effect from the Transfer Date from all obligations, responsibilities and liabilities in respect of this Agreement but not in respect of any liabilities arising out of any antecedent breach of this Agreement

(e) the Licensee shall thereby undertake, and shall be deemed to have undertaken with effect from the Transfer Date, to observe and perform all the terms and conditions of this Agreement as if the Replacement were a party hereto and named herein instead of the Distributor

[(f) the Owner may exclude from the scope of the Support Services and from any warranties and any other liability hereunder such part of the Licensed Programs as it may specify in this Novation Notice (not being any part of the Licensed Programs which the Owner has released generally to end-users) and any such exclusion shall thereby take effect]

[Note: The owner may wish to exclude responsibility for distributor modifications.]

(g) this Agreement shall be deemed thereby to be amended on the Transfer Date in accordance with the terms of this sub-clause (4) and shall otherwise remain in full force and effect

(h) the parties hereto and the Replacement shall execute and do and/or procure the execution and doing of all such further deeds, documents and acts as may be necessary to carry the provisions of this sub-clause (4) into full force and effect

(5) If an Acceptance Notice is not served by the Licensee within the said period of *30* days then the provisons of sub-clause (4) shall have effect on the day following the expiry of the said period of *30* days save that:

(a) the Support Period shall be deemed to have terminated by mutual agreement at the expiry of the said period of *30* days; and

(b) the Owner shall be deemed to be the Replacement

(6) The Owner does not warrant to the Licensee that the Licensed Programs will meet the requirements of the Licensee or that the operation of the Licensed Programs will be uninterrupted or error-free or that defects in the Licensed Software will be corrected. In no event will the Owner be liable to the Licensee for any loss or damage of any kind (except personal injury or death resulting from the Owner's negligence) including lost profits or other consequential loss arising from the Licensee's use of or inability to use the Licensed Programs or from errors or deficiencies in it whether caused by negligence or otherwise howsoever. Nothing in this sub-clause shall affect any obligations assumed by the Owner pursuant to a novation of this Agreement under sub-clause (3)

12   General

(1) This Agreement constitutes the entire understanding between the parties concerning the subject matter of this Agreement and the Licensee warrants to the Distributor and the Owner that in entering into this Agreement it has not relied on any warranty, representation or undertaking save as expressly set out in this Agreement. No waiver or amendment of any provision of this Agreement shall be effective unless made by a written instrument signed by all the parties. Each provision of this Agreement shall be construed separately and notwithstanding that the whole or any part of any such provision may prove to be illegal or unenforceable the other provisions of this Agreement and the remainder of the provision in question shall continue in full force and effect

(2) Waiver of remedies—*See Clause 28 of Precedent A*

(3) Notices—*See Clause 32 of Precedent A*

(4) Interest on late payment—*see Clause 3(6) of Precedent A*

(5) Save as expressly provided herein, all payments shall be made within *30* days after the date of the Distributor's invoice therefor

(6) All sums payable under this Agreement are exclusive of Value Added Tax which the Licensee shall be additionally liable to pay to the Distributor

(7) Interpretation—*See Clause 33 of Precedent A*

(8) Law—*See Clause 34 of Precedent A*

EXECUTED under hand in three originals the day and year first before written

SIGNED by a duly authorised
officer on behalf of THE
DISTRIBUTOR in the presence
of:—

SIGNED by a duly authorised
officer on behalf of THE
LICENSEE in the presence
of:—

SIGNED by a duly authorised
officer on behalf of the
Distributor as agent for THE
OWNER in the presence of:—

SCHEDULE 1

(to the Software Licence and Support Agreement)

A DESIGNATED CPUs

[Type:]

[Serial No.:]

B PERIPHERAL EQUIPMENT

C INSTALLATION ADDRESS

D LICENCE FEE

£[   ] plus VAT

Payment Terms:

E NUMBER OF COPIES TO BE SUPPLIED

Licensed Programs:

Program Documentation:

F MAXIMUM NUMBER OF CONCURRENT USERS

G DELIVERY AND INSTALLATION CHARGE

£[   ] plus VAT

Payment Terms:

[H   MODIFICATIONS

(1) [insert a description of the modifications]

(2) [insert hourly charge-out rates] plus VAT]

I   HOURS FOR REMOTE TELEPHONE DIAGNOSTIC ASSISTANCE

J   SUPPORT CHARGE

£[   ] plus VAT payable on [   ]

and then annually on each subsequent anniversary

SCHEDULE 2

TRAINING

[**Note:** This Schedule should identify:

(1) How many staff are to be trained in total.
(2) How many can be trained at one time.
(3) How many days' training is required for each person.
(4) Where and when training is to take place.
(4) Who is to be responsible for subsistence and travelling expenses.]

SCHEDULE 3

CURRENT [UNITED KINGDOM] DOMESTIC PRICE LIST OF THE COMPANY

SCHEDULE 4

ROYALTY TARGETS

Precedent J

Beta test agreement [6]

THIS AGREEMENT is made the   day of   19

PARTIES:

(1) COMPUTER COMPANY [LIMITED] [PLC] whose registered office is at

('the Supplier')

(2) COMPANY [LIMITED] [PLC] whose registered office is at

('the Company')

RECITALS:

(A) The Supplier has developed the computer [hardware] [software] product specified in the Schedule hereto in a pre-production form ('the Product')

(B) The Supplier has agreed to deliver the Product and its associated documentation ('the Documentation') to the Company and to grant the Company a licence to evaluate the Product and the Documentation upon the terms and conditions hereinafter contained

NOW IT IS HEREBY AGREED as follows:

1 Consideration [6.2]

In consideration of the agreements and undertakings herein set out the parties to this Agreement have granted the rights and accepted the obligations hereinafter appearing

2 Delivery and installation [6.3, 6.7]

(1) The Supplier shall deliver and install the Product in accordance with the delivery instructions and at the installation site ('the Installation Site') specified in the Schedule

(2) Such delivery and installation shall take place at a time and on a date mutually convenient to both parties [but in any event before
[19   ]]

3   Evaluation [6.2]

(1) The Supplier hereby grants to the Company a licence to evaluate the Product and the Documentation on the terms and subject to the conditions of this Agreement

(2) During the term of this Agreement the Company shall evaluate the Product and the Documentation diligently, shall report promptly to the Supplier's evaluation personnel all faults and problems with the Product and the Documentation which it discovers and shall co-operate with such personnel in diagnosing and correcting such faults and problems

(3) The Product and the Documentation shall be used by the Company solely to perform an internal evaluation of the Product and the Documentation and for no other purpose whatsoever. In the course of such evaluation the Company may process its own data and retain the benefit of such processing but the Supplier shall have no liability whatsoever for any errors or defects therein

[(4) The Company shall be entitled to a discount of *20* per cent from the Supplier's standard list price of the Product from time to time after it has first been made available on the [United Kingdom] market in the first contract between the Supplier and the Company for the supply of the Product or a multiple thereof. The Company's entitlement to such discount shall be subject to the Company carefully and diligently completing and returning to the Supplier the evaluation forms which will accompany the Product when it is delivered to the Company by the date specified in such evaluation forms, to the Company complying with its obligations under this Agreement and to the Company entering into such contract within *one year* after the Product has been so first made available. The Supplier shall not unreasonably refuse to enter into or delay entering into any such contract for this purpose]

4   Title and risk [6.3]

(1) The Product and the Documentation are confidential and proprietary to the Supplier and title to both shall remain with the Supplier at all times

(2) Risk in the Product and the Documentation shall remain with the Supplier but the Company shall take all reasonable steps to safeguard the Product and the Documentation from loss or damage

5   The Company's obligations [6.6]

The Company shall:

(1) keep the Product and the Documentation at the Installation Site unless the Supplier consents in writing to the Company moving the Product and the Documentation to alternative premises;

(2) keep confidential and not disclose the existence, features, capabilities or contents of the Product or the Documentation or the results of the Company's evaluation thereof or this Agreement to any third party except to the Company's employees who are directly involved in the evaluation and have a specific need to know the information concerned (such confidentiality and non-disclosure obligations to survive the termination of this Agreement);

(3) ensure that its employees observe the confidentiality and non-disclosure obligations contained in Clause 5(2);

(4) allow the Supplier access to the Installation Site to inspect and make modifications to the Product and the Documentation at all convenient times during the continuance of this Agreement;

[(5) indemnify the Supplier against any loss of or damage to the Product arising as a result of the wilful misconduct, recklessness or gross negligence of the Company or its employees;]

(6) except as expressly provided in this Agreement, not use, reproduce, dispose of, deal with, rent, lease, [sub-license], loan, modify, adapt, [reverse engineer, decompile] or disassemble the whole or any part of the Product or the Documentation;

(7) keep the Product and the Documentation in its exclusive possession and control and safeguard them from access by any unauthorised person;

(8) not incorporate the Product or the Documentation or allow them to be incorporated in any other product or documentation; and

(9) not change, remove or obscure any labels, plates, notices, insignia, lettering or other markings which are on or embodied in the Product or the Documentation at the time of delivery thereof to the Company

6   Term and termination [6.4]

(1) This Agreement shall continue for an initial period of *3* months and shall remain in force thereafter unless or until terminated by either party giving to the other not less than *14* days' notice in writing expiring at the end of the said initial period or at any time thereafter, but shall be subject to earlier termination as hereinafter provided

(2) This Agreement may be terminated forthwith by either party on giving notice in writing to the other if the other shall have a receiver or administrative receiver appointed or shall pass a resolution for winding-up (otherwise than for the purpose of a bona fide scheme of solvent amalgamation or reconstruction) or a court of competent jurisdiction shall make an order to that effect or if the other party shall become subject to an administration order or shall enter into any voluntary arrangement with its creditors or shall cease or threaten to cease to carry on business or shall commit any breach of this Agreement

(3) Any termination of this Agreement (howsoever occasioned) shall not affect any accrued rights or liabilities of either party nor shall it affect the coming into force or the continuance in force of any provision hereof which is expressly or by implication intended to come into or continue in force on or after such termination

either:

[(4) Upon termination of this Agreement the Company shall surrender up to the Supplier the Product and the Documentation and for that purpose the Company hereby irrevocably licenses the Supplier, its employees and agents to enter the Company's premises to repossess the same]

or:

[(4) The Supplier advises the Company that at the time of delivery the Product will contain special software which will deny the Company the use of the Product after *3* months from the date hereof. In the event that this Agreement continues in force for more than *3* months from the date hereof and the Company is not in breach of any of the provisions of this Agreement the Supplier undertakes to amend or remove the said special software so as to allow the Company to continue to use the Product under the terms of this Agreement]

[**Note:** for the validity of so-called logic bombs for non-payment see 3.2.2.]

7   Reservation of rights [6.5]

The Supplier reserves the right to:

(1) recall the Product and the Documentation forthwith (by notice in writing to the Company) up to *60* days before the release by the Supplier of the Product for supply to the [United Kingdom] market, whereupon this Agreement shall automatically terminate; and

(2) recall the Product or the Documentation and replace it with another version at any time during the term of this Agreement

8   Intellectual property rights indemnity [6.7]

The Supplier shall indemnify the Company against any claim that the Company's use or possession of the Product and the Documentation infringes the intellectual property rights of any third party provided that the Supplier is given immediate and complete control of such claim, that the Company does not prejudice the Supplier's defence of such claim, that the Company gives the Supplier all reasonable assistance with such claim and that the claim does not arise as a result of the use of the Product or the Documentation otherwise than in accordance with the terms of this Agreement or in combination with any equipment or programs not supplied or approved by the Supplier. The Supplier shall have the right to replace or change all or any part of the Product or the Documentation or to terminate this Agreement forthwith by notice in writing to the Company in order to avoid any infringement. The foregoing states the entire liability of the Supplier to the Company in respect of the infringement of the intellectual property rights of any third party

9   Liability [6.3]

(1) Because of the experimental nature of the Product and the Documentation, the Supplier does not warrant to the Company that either is free from faults or defects

(2) The Company shall use the Product and the Documentation at its own risk and in no event shall the Supplier be liable to the Company for any loss or damage of any kind (except personal injury or death resulting from the Supplier's negligence) arising from the Company's use of or inability to use the Product or the Documentation or from faults or defects in either whether caused by negligence or otherwise

(3) The express terms of this Agreement are in lieu of all warranties, conditions, undertakings, terms and obligations implied by statute, common law, trade usage, course of dealing or otherwise all of which are hereby excluded to the fullest extent permitted by law

10   Interpretation

In this Agreement the expressions 'the Product' and 'the Documentation' include any modified or replacement versions thereof made available pursuant to Clause 5(4) or Clause 7(2) and, where the context so requires, any other version supplied by the Supplier to the [United Kingdom] market from time to time

11 Entire agreement

See Clause 29 of Precedent A

12 Assignment

See Clause 30 of Precedent A

13 Notices

See Clause 32 of Precedent A

14 Headings

The headings to the Clauses of this Agreement are for ease of reference only and shall not affect the interpretation or construction of this Agreement

15 Law

See Clause 34 of Precedent A

16 Disputes

See Clause 35 of Precedent A

17 Severability

See Clause 36 of Precedent A

EXECUTED etc

THE SCHEDULE

A   THE PRODUCT

B   DELIVERY AND INSTALLATION INSTRUCTIONS

C   INSTALLATION SITE

Precedent K

Hardware maintenance agreement

THIS AGREEMENT is made the   day of   19

PARTIES:

(1) COMPUTER COMPANY [LIMITED] [PLC] whose registered office is at

('the Supplier')

(2) CUSTOMER [LIMITED] [PLC] whose registered office is at

('the Customer')

RECITAL:

The Supplier has agreed to maintain the Customer's computer equipment hereinafter described upon the terms and conditions hereinafter contained

NOW IT IS HEREBY AGREED as follows:

1 Definitions

In this Agreement, unless the context otherwise requires, the following expressions have the following meanings:

'the Equipment' [8.1.1; 8.5.1]	means the computer equipment specified in the Schedule and the Additional Equipment and such additions and changes thereto as shall from time to time be agreed in writing between the parties
'the Additional Equipment'	has the meaning attributed thereto in Clause 3(3)

'the Location' [8.1.1]	means the Customer's computer room in which the Equipment is installed as specified in the Schedule
'the Commencement Date'	means the date on which this Agreement shall become effective as specified in the Schedule
'the Initial Period'	means the initial period of this Agreement as specified in the Schedule
'the Scheduled Maintenance Services'	means the maintenance services to be provided by the Supplier pursuant to Clause 2
'the Emergency Maintenance Services'	means the emergency maintenance services to be provided by the Supplier pursuant to Clause 4
'the Maintenance Services'	means the Scheduled Maintenance Services and the Emergency Maintenance Services
'the Maintenance Charge'	means the periodic charge for the Scheduled Maintenance Services specified in the Schedule as varied from time to time pursuant to Clause 3 or as shall from time to time be agreed in writing between the parties
'Maintenance Hours'	means the hours between *9.00* am and *5.00* pm each day excluding Saturdays, Sundays and public holidays

2   Scheduled Maintenance Services [8.1.2]

During the continuance of this Agreement the Supplier shall provide the following maintenance services in respect of the Equipment:

(1) *Preventive maintenance*

The Supplier shall make visits to the Location [at such intervals as the Supplier shall reasonably determine to be required for the Equipment] [every *6* months] to test the functions of the Equipment and make such adjustments as shall be necessary to keep the Equipment in good working order. Such visits shall be made during Maintenance Hours by prior appointment with the Customer. If it is expedient in the opinion of the Supplier so to do, such

464

maintenance may be carried out at the same time as corrective maintenance

(2) *Corrective maintenance*

Upon receipt of notification from the Customer that the Equipment has failed or is malfunctioning the Supplier shall during Maintenance Hours make such repairs and adjustments to and replace such parts of the Equipment as may be necessary to restore the Equipment to its proper operating condition

(3) *Response time*

On receipt of a request for corrective maintenance the Supplier undertakes [to use its reasonable endeavours] to despatch a suitably qualified service engineer to the Location within *4* Maintenance Hours [but such response time is an estimate only and shall not be binding on the Supplier]

[Note: The time of arrival of the service engineer at the location will depend upon how far he has to travel.]

3 Charges [8.2]

(1) In consideration of the Scheduled Maintenance Services the Customer shall pay the Maintenance Charge periodically in advance as specified in the Schedule. The Maintenance Charge shall be paid without prior demand and no payment shall be considered made until it is received by the Supplier. All payments shall be made in the manner specified in the Schedule

(2) Any charges payable by the Customer hereunder in addition to the Maintenance Charge shall be paid (unless otherwise provided elsewhere in this Agreement) within *14* days after receipt of the Supplier's invoice therefor

(3) Where the Supplier becomes aware of equipment at the Location which is not included in the Equipment and in respect of which the Customer requests any maintenance services ('Additional Equipment') the Supplier will provide the Maintenance Services in respect of the Additional Equipment in the same way as in respect of the Equipment and charge for it according to the rate set out in the Schedule such charge backdated to the date when the Additional Equipment was installed at the Location and to be added to the Maintenance Charge in respect of future payments

either: [8.5.2]

[(4) The Supplier shall be entitled at any time and from time to time after the expiry of the [Initial Period] [the period of *one year* after the Commencement Date] to increase the Maintenance Charge to accord with any change in the Supplier's standard scale of charges by giving to the Customer not less than *90* days' prior written notice. Where and whenever such notice is given, the Customer shall have the right to terminate this Agreement as from the date on which such notice expires by giving to the Supplier written notice of termination not less than *30* days before such date]

or:

[(4) The Supplier shall be entitled at any time and from time to time (subject as mentioned below) after the expiry of the [Initial Period] [the period of *one* year after the Commencement Date] to increase the Maintenance Charge by giving to the Customer not less than *90* days' prior written notice provided that any such increase shall not exceed a percentage equal to the percentage increase in the Retail Prices Index published by the Central Statistical Office for the period from the Commencement Date (in the case of the first such increase) or the date on which the immediately preceding increase came into effect pursuant to this sub-clause (in the case of the second or subsequent increase) up to the date of such notice plus *2* per cent provided further that no increase may be made pursuant to this sub-clause until a period of at least *one* year has elapsed since the date on which the immediately preceding increase came into effect pursuant to this sub-clause]

(5) Charges exclusive of VAT—*see Clause 3(4) of Precedent A*

(6) Interest on overdue amounts—*see Clause 3(6) of Precedent A*

4   Emergency Maintenance Services [8.3.2]

In addition to the Scheduled Maintenance Services the Supplier shall provide during the continuance of this Agreement an emergency corrective maintenance service outside Maintenance Hours as soon as practicable after the receipt of a request by the Customer therefor [(such request to be made during Maintenance Hours)] at the Supplier's standard scale of charges for such service from time to time in force. Such charges shall run from the first arrival of the Supplier's service engineer at the Location to his final departure therefrom

5   Exceptions [8.3]

(1) The Maintenance Services do not include any maintenance of the Equipment which is necessitated as a result of any cause other than fair wear and tear or the Supplier's neglect or fault including without limitation:

(a) failure or fluctuation of electric power, air conditioning, humidity control or other environmental conditions; or

(b) accident, transportation, neglect, misuse, or default of the Customer, its employees or agents or any third party; or

(c) any fault in any attachments or associated equipment (whether or not supplied by the Supplier) which do not form part of the Equipment; or

(d) act of God, fire, flood, war, act of violence, or any other similar occurrence; or

(e) any attempt by any person other than the Supplier's personnel to adjust, repair or maintain the Equipment; or

(f) any head crash or failure of fixed or removable storage media

(2) The Supplier will (if it is able to do so) at the request and expense of the Customer repair or replace any part of the Equipment which has failed due to a cause other than fair wear and tear or due to the Supplier's neglect or fault subject to the Customer accepting the Supplier's written quotation therefor prior to the commencement of work

(3) The Maintenance Services do not include:

(a) service other than at the Location (or such other location as the Supplier shall have approved in writing);

(b) repair or renewal of tapes, disk packs, printing cartridges or other consumable supplies;

(c) maintenance or support of the operating system of any computer;

(d) electrical or other environmental work external to the Equipment;

(e) maintenance of any attachments or associated equipment (whether or not supplied by the Supplier) which do not form part of the Equipment; or

(f) recovery or reconstruction of any data or programs lost or spoiled as a result of any breakdown of or fault in the Equipment

6   Replacement [8.5.1, 8.6.5]

(1) The Supplier reserves the right to replace the whole of the Equipment or any part or parts thereof which may be found to be faulty or in need of investigation

(2) The Supplier in effecting any such replacement shall not remove the Equipment or any part or parts thereof until he is ready to install equipment to replace it ('the Replacement Equipment')

(3) The Supplier shall at the time of any such replacement notify the Customer in writing of the serial numbers of the Replacement Equipment

(4) If the Replacement Equipment is not equipment which is identical in all respects to that replaced the Supplier shall inform the Customer in writing at the time of replacement

(5) Within *2* weeks of being informed of replacement of non-identical equipment the Customer shall have the right to request that the Replacement Equipment or any part or parts thereof be removed and either the Equipment be put back or other equipment identical to the Equipment be installed and the Supplier shall comply with such request forthwith

(6) The Replacement Equipment shall become the property of the owner of the Equipment. The Equipment or any part or parts thereof removed shall become the property of the Supplier provided always that the owner of the Equipment shall be the owner of equipment identical in value and performance to the Equipment

(7) The provisions of this Agreement shall apply to all replacements and renewals of any part or parts of the Equipment made by the Supplier during the continuance of this Agreement

7   Service visits outside the Maintenance Services [8.3.1, 8.3.2]

The Supplier shall make an additional charge, in accordance with its standard scale of charges from time to time in force, for service visits:

(1) made at the request of the Customer by reason of any fault in the Equipment due to causes not covered by the Maintenance Services; or

(2) made at the request of the Customer but which the Supplier finds are frivolous or not necessary

8   Duration

This Agreement shall commence on the Commencement Date, shall continue for the Initial Period and shall remain in force thereafter [unless or] until terminated by either party giving to the other not less than *6* months' written notice of termination [given on] [expiring on] the last day of the Initial Period or at any time thereafter but shall be subject to earlier termination as provided elsewhere in this Agreement

[**Note:** Delete the first and third bracketed phrases if the agreement is to be for a minimum period equal to the Initial Period plus the notice period. Delete the second bracketed phrase if the agreement is to be for a minimum period equal to the Initial Period.]

9 Customer's obligations [8.5.1; 8.6]

During the continuance of this Agreement the Customer shall:

Use and care of the Equipment [8.6.1]

(1) ensure that proper environmental conditions are maintained for the Equipment and shall maintain in good condition the accommodation of the Equipment, the cables and fittings associated therewith and the electricity supply thereto

(2) not make any modification to the Equipment without the Supplier's prior written consent

(3) keep and operate the Equipment in a proper and prudent manner in accordance with [the manufacturer's] [the Supplier's] operating instructions and ensure that only competent trained employees (or persons under their supervision) are allowed to operate the Equipment

(4) ensure that the external surfaces of the Equipment are kept clean and in good condition and shall carry out any minor maintenance recommended by [the manufacturer] [the Supplier] from time to time

(5) save as aforesaid, not attempt to adjust, repair or maintain the Equipment and shall not request, permit or authorise anyone other than the Supplier to carry out any adjustments, repairs or maintenance of the Equipment

(6) use on the Equipment only such operating supplies as [the manufacturer] [the Supplier] shall recommend in writing

(7) not make any movement of the Equipment nor remove the Equipment from the Location without the Supplier's prior written consent

(8) not use in conjunction with the Equipment any accessory, attachment or additional equipment other than that which has been supplied by or approved in writing by the Supplier

Access [8.6.2]

(9) provide the Supplier with full and safe access to the Equipment for the purposes of this Agreement

(10) provide adequate working space around the Equipment for the use of the Supplier's personnel and shall make available such reasonable facilities as may be requested from time to time by the Supplier for the storage and safekeeping of test equipment and spare parts

(11) provide a suitable vehicle parking facility for use by the Supplier's personnel which is free from any legal restrictions and immediately close to the Location

(12) ensure in the interests of health and safety that the Supplier's personnel, while on the Customer's premises for the purposes of this Agreement, are at all times accompanied by a member of the Customer's staff familiar with the Customer's premises and safety procedures

Notification and information [8.6.3]

(13) promptly notify the Supplier if the Equipment needs maintenance or is not operating correctly. [Failure by the Customer so to notify the Supplier within *2* months of the Customer first becoming aware of such failure or incorrect working shall free the Supplier from all obligations to investigate or correct such failure or incorrect working]

(14) subject to Clause 15(2), make available to the Supplier such programs, operating manuals and information as may be necessary to enable the Supplier to perform its obligations hereunder and shall if requested by the Supplier provide staff familiar with the Customer's programs and operations, which staff shall co-operate fully with the Supplier's personnel in the diagnosis of any malfunction of the Equipment

(15) make available to the Supplier free of charge all facilities and services reasonably required by the Supplier to enable the Supplier to perform the Maintenance Services including without limitation computer runs, mercury dumps, print-outs, [data preparation], [office accommodation], [typing] and photocopying

(16) at all times keep a record of the use of the Equipment in a form to be approved by the Supplier and at the Supplier's request provide the Supplier with copies of the entries and allow the Supplier to inspect such record at all reasonable times

(17) in the event that the Supplier is requested to supply any Maintenance Services in respect of any Additional Equipment, advise the Supplier forthwith of the date of installation of such item of Additional Equipment at the Location

Miscellaneous [8.6.5]

(18) provide such telecommunication facilities as are reasonably required by the Supplier for testing and diagnostic purposes at the Customer's expense

(19) keep full security copies of the Customer's programs, data bases and computer records in accordance with best computing practice

[10   Spare parts [8.6.4]

(1) The Customer shall purchase from the Supplier such spare parts as the Supplier shall recommend, which shall be supplied at the Supplier's list prices from time to time in force

(2) The Customer shall keep such spare parts at the Location or at a place immediately close thereto. The Supplier may draw on this stock of spare parts for the maintenance and repair of the Equipment

(3) The Supplier shall not be liable for any delay in performing its obligations hereunder if any recommended spare parts are not available (otherwise than due to the fault of the Supplier) and shall be entitled to charge the Customer for all additional expenses and costs incurred by the Supplier as a result of such delay

(4) Any spare parts which are not included in the Supplier's recommendations shall be supplied by the Supplier at its list prices from time to time in force]

11   Electromagnetic compatibility [2.7.2]

See Clause 13 of Precedent A

12   Telecommunications [2.7.4]

See sub-clauses (3) and (4) of Clause 14 of Precedent A

[13   Downtime

(1) In this Clause:

'Effectiveness Level'	means in relation to each Month (Available Time less Downtime) divided by Available Time and then multiplied by 100
'Available Time'	means the number of Maintenance Hours in the Month in question
'Downtime'	means those hours of Available Time during which the Equipment is unusable or substantially unusable

471

	other than due to the neglect or fault of the Customer
'Month'	means any complete calendar month during which this Agreement continues

(2) Without prejudice to any of the Customer's other rights and remedies, if the Effectiveness Level for any Month falls below *95* the Customer shall be entitled to a credit against the Maintenance Charge for such Month calculated as follows:

$$\text{Credit} \; = \; \frac{(95 - \text{Effectiveness Level for such Month})}{100} \times M$$

where 'M' is the Maintenance Charge for such Month

(3) The amount of such credit shall be set against the Maintenance Charge for the Month immediately following the Month in respect of which the credit is given]

[**Notes:**

(1) Where reliability is an important factor the customer may ask for a clause such as this to enable him to obtain a credit against maintenance charges if 'downtime' exceeds a certain level. It has to be said that only a customer with exceptional leverage will get a supplier to commit himself to such a provision. The effectiveness of the clause will depend on the customer keeping an accurate record of downtime.

(2) This clause assumes that the maintenance charge is payable monthly.]

14   Termination [8.4]

(1) Notwithstanding anything else contained herein, this Agreement may be terminated:

(a) by the Supplier forthwith on giving notice in writing to the Customer if the Customer shall fail to pay any sum due under the terms of this Agreement (otherwise than as a consequence of any default on the part of the Supplier) and such sum remains unpaid for *14* days after written notice from the Supplier that such sum has not been paid (such notice to contain a warning of the Supplier's intention to terminate); or

(b) by the Customer forthwith on giving notice in writing to the Supplier if the Equipment is lost, stolen or destroyed or damaged beyond economic repair; or

(c) by either party forthwith on giving notice in writing to the other if the other commits any [material] [serious] breach of any term of this Agreement (other than any failure by the Customer to make any payment hereunder in which event the provisions of paragraph (a) above shall apply) and (in the case of a breach capable of being remedied) shall have failed, within *30* days after the receipt of a request in writing from the other party so to do, to remedy the breach (such request to contain a warning of such party's intention to terminate); or

(d) by either party forthwith on giving notice in writing to the other if the other party shall have a receiver or administrative receiver appointed of it or over any part of its undertaking or assets or shall pass a resolution for winding-up (otherwise than for the purpose of a bona fide scheme of solvent amalgamation or reconstruction) or a court of competent jurisdiction shall make an order to that effect or if the other party shall become subject to an administration order or shall enter into any voluntary arrangement with its creditors or shall cease or threaten to cease to carry on business

(2) Any termination of this Agreement howsoever occasioned shall not affect any accrued rights or liabilities of either party nor shall it affect the coming into force or the continuance in force of any provision hereof which is expressly or by implication intended to come into or continue in force on or after such termination

(3) On the termination of this Agreement the Customer shall be entitled to reimbursement of a pro-rata part (calculated on a time basis) of the Maintenance Charge paid in advance

15   Confidentiality

(1) *See Clause 21 of Precedent A*

(2) The Customer's obligations under Clause 9(14) to make available the information therein mentioned shall be subject to the Supplier signing such confidentiality undertakings as may be required by or to protect any third party having rights in such information prior to the same being made available

16   Force majeure

Neither party shall be liable for any delay in performing any of its obligations hereunder if such delay is caused by circumstances beyond the reasonable control of the party so delaying and such party shall be entitled to a reasonable extension of time for the performance of such obligations

17   Customer's warranty

See Clause 20 of Precedent A

18   Liability [8.3.4]

(1) [Subject to the provisions of Clause 13] the Supplier shall not be liable for any loss or damage sustained or incurred by the Customer or any third party (including without limitation any loss of use of the Equipment or loss of or spoiling of the Customer's programs or data) resulting from any breakdown of or fault in the Equipment unless such breakdown or fault is caused by the negligence or wilful misconduct of the Supplier, its employees, agents or sub-contractors or except to the extent that such loss or damage arises from any unreasonable delay by the Supplier in providing the Maintenance Services and then only to the extent not excluded by this Agreement

(2) to (6) *See Clause 27 of Precedent A*

19   Waiver of remedies

See Clause 28 of Precedent A

20   Entire agreement

See Clause 29 of Precedent A

21   Assignment

See Clause 30 of Precedent A

22   Sub-contracts

See Clause 31 of Precedent A

23   Notices

See Clause 32 of Precedent A

24   Interpretation

See Clause 33 of Precedent A

25 Law

See Clause 34 of Precedent A

26 Disputes

See Clause 35 of Precedent A

27 Severability

See Clause 36 of Precedent A

EXECUTED etc

THE SCHEDULE

A THE EQUIPMENT

B THE LOCATION

C THE COMMENCEMENT DATE

either:

(a) The date of this Agreement; or

(b) *31 December 1995*; or

(c) The date on which the Equipment is accepted by the Customer under the terms of a sale agreement made between the Customer and [the Supplier] dated [   ]. If the Equipment is not accepted by the Customer as aforesaid than this Agreement shall never become effective

D THE INITIAL PERIOD

E THE MAINTENANCE CHARGE

£[   ] for each [month] [quarter] [year], payable in advance

First charge payable on: [the Commencement Date]

Subsequent charges payable on the first working day of each [month] [quarter] [year] thereafter

F CHARGING RATE FOR ADDITIONAL EQUIPMENT

G METHOD OF PAYMENT

By standing order to [   ] Bank PLC

(Supplier's Account No   )

Precedent L

Software maintenance agreement: licence

THIS AGREEMENT is made the   day of   19

PARTIES:

(1) COMPUTER COMPANY [LIMITED] [PLC] whose registered office is at

('the Licensor')

(2) CUSTOMER [LIMITED] [PLC] whose registered office is at

('the Licensee')

RECITALS:

(A) By a licence agreement dated   19   made between the Licensor and the Licensee ('the Licence Agreement') the Licensor granted to the Licensee a non-exclusive and non-transferable licence to use the Licensor's computer programs and associated documentation more particularly described therein

(B) [By Clause *17* of the Licence Agreement it was agreed that the parties would enter into a maintenance agreement in respect of the said programs and documentation in the form of this Agreement]. [The Licensor has agreed to maintain the said programs and documentation upon the terms and conditions hereinafter contained]

NOW IT IS HEREBY AGREED as follows:

1 Definitions

In this Agreement, unless the context otherwise requires, the following expressions have the following meanings:

'the Licensed Programs' 'the Licensed Program Materials' and 'the Equipment'	have the meanings respectively given to them in the Licence Agreement
'Release'	means any improved version of the Licensed Programs made available to the Licensee by the Licensor pursuant to Clause 5(2)
'the Current Release'	means the Release from time to time accepted by the Licensee under this Agreement or, if no Release has been accepted, the Licensed Programs
'the Specification'	means the specification of the Current Release describing the facilities and functions thereof
'the Program Documentation'	means the operating manuals, user instructions, technical literature and all other related materials in printed form supplied by the Licensor to the Licensee for aiding the use and application of the Current Release
'the Maintenance Services'	means the maintenance services to be provided by the Licensor pursuant to Clause 5
'the Maintenance Charge'	means the periodic charge for the Maintenance Services specified in the Schedule as increased from time to time pursuant to Clause 3
'the Commencement Date'	means the date on which this Agreement shall become effective as specified in the Schedule
'the Initial Period'	means the initial period of this Agreement as specified in the Schedule

2   Services to be performed [9.1.1, 9.1.2]

The Licensor hereby agrees to provide the Maintenance Services for the Licensee upon the terms and conditions hereinafter contained

3 Charges and payment [9.2]

(1) In consideration of the Maintenance Services the Licensee shall pay the Maintenance Charge periodically in advance as specified in the Schedule. The Maintenance Charge shall be paid without prior demand and no payment shall be considered made until it is received by the Licensor. All payments shall be made in the manner specified in the Schedule

(2) Any charges payable by the Licensee hereunder in addition to the Maintenance Charge shall be paid within *30* days after the receipt of the Licensor's invoice therefor

(3) Right to increase charges—*see Clause 3(4) of Precedent K*

(4) Charges exclusive of VAT—*see Clause 3(4) of Precedent A*

(5) Interest on overdue amounts—*see Clause 3(6) of Precedent A*

4 Duration

This Agreement shall commence on the Commencement Date, shall continue for the Initial Period and shall remain in force thereafter [unless or] until terminated by either party giving to the other not less than *12* months' written notice of termination [given on] [expiring on] the last day of the Initial Period or at any time thereafter but shall be subject to earlier termination as provided elsewhere in this Agreement

[Notes:
(1) See the note to clause 8 of Precedent K.
(2) A short initial period will give the licensee little protection and he should therefore look to the licensor for a realistic initial commitment. In a long term arrangement an index-linked charges review clause will be preferable from the licensee's point of view.]

5 Maintenance services

During the continuance of this Agreement the Licensor shall provide the Licensee with the following maintenance services:

(1) *Error correction* [9.1.3, 9.3.1]

(a) If the Licensee shall discover that the Current Release fails to fulfil any part of the Specification then the Licensee shall within *14* days after such discovery notify the Licensor in writing of the defect or error in question and provide the Licensor (so far as the Licensee is able) with a documented example of such defect or error

479

(b) The Licensor shall thereupon use its reasonable endeavours to correct promptly such defect or error. Forthwith upon such correction being completed the Licensor shall deliver to the Licensee the corrected version of the object code of the Current Release in machine readable form together with appropriate amendments to the Program Documentation specifying the nature of the correction and providing instructions for the proper use of the corrected version of the Current Release. The Licensor shall provide the Licensee with all assistance reasonably required by the Licensee to enable the Licensee to implement the use of the corrected version of the Current Release

(c) The foregoing error correction service shall not include service in respect of:

(i) defects or errors resulting from any modifications of the Current Release made by any person other than the Licensor;

(ii) any version of the Licensed Programs other than the Current Release;

(iii) incorrect use of the Current Release or operator error;

(iv) any fault in the Equipment or in any programs used in conjunction with the Current Release;

(v) defects or errors caused by the use of the Current Release on or with equipment (other than the Equipment) [or programs] not supplied by or approved in writing by the Licensor [provided that for this purpose any programs designated for use with the Current Release in the Specification shall be deemed to have the written approval of the Licensor];

(vi) any modification of the Current Release if such modification would result in a departure from the Specification

(d) The Licensor shall make an additional charge in accordance with its standard scale of charges from time to time in force for any services provided by the Licensor:

(i) at the request of the Licensee but which do not qualify under the aforesaid error correction service by virtue of any of the exclusions referred to in paragraph (c) above; or

(ii) at the request of the Licensee but which the Licensor finds are not necessary

For the avoidance of doubt nothing in this paragraph shall impose any obligation on the Licensor to provide services in respect of any of the exclusions referred to in paragraph (c)

(e) If the Licensee shall discover that the Program Documentation does not provide adequate or correct instruction for the proper use of any facility or function set out in the Specification then the Licensee shall notify the Licensor in writing of the fault in question within *14* days after such discovery. The Licensor shall thereupon promptly correct the fault and provide the Licensee with appropriate amendments to the Program Documentation

(2) *Releases* [9.1.2]

Version A (Licensee's option whether or not to accept new Releases)

[(a) The Licensor shall promptly notify the Licensee of any improved version of the Licensed Programs which the Licensor shall from time to time make available to its licensees. The Licensor shall provide with such notification an explanatory memorandum specifying not only the nature of the improvements but also any adverse effects which the new Release may be expected to have including in particular any expected degradation in performance. While it is acknowledged by the Licensee that the explanatory memorandum may not be equivalent to a detailed specification of the new Release it shall contain sufficient information to enable the Licensee to judge whether the new Release will be appropriate to the Licensee's requirements

[Note: To talk of an improved version having adverse effects may appear to be strange at first sight. However, while an improved version may provide a host of additional facilities and functions (none or all of which may be required by the licensee) it may also (for example) affect memory capacity or response times which would result in a degradation in performance criteria and might outweigh the advantages.]

(b) If the Licensee shall wish to evaluate the new Release then the Licensee shall notify the Licensor in writing accordingly. Upon receipt of such notification, the Licensor shall deliver to the Licensee as soon as reasonably practicable (having regard to the number of other users requiring the new Release) the object code of the new Release in machine-readable form together with any amendments to the Specification and the Program Documentation which shall be necessary to describe and enable proper use of the improved facilities and functions of the new Release

(c) If required by the Licensee, the Licensor shall provide training for the Licensee's staff in the use of the new Release at the Licensor's standard scale of charges from time to time in force as soon as reasonably practicable after the delivery of the new Release

(d) The Licensee shall be responsible for evaluating the new Release during the period of 3 months after its delivery to the Licensee. On the expiry of such period the Licensee shall notify the Licensor whether or not it wishes to accept the new Release. If the Licensor does not receive any such notification then the Licensee shall be deemed to have rejected the new Release in which case the provisions of paragraph (f) below shall apply

(e)   If the Licensee accepts the new Release then such Release shall thereby become the Current Release and the provisions of this Agreement shall apply accordingly. Upon such acceptance the Licensee shall [if requested by the Licensor] return to the Licensor the Licensed Programs or the previous Release (as the case may be) and any part of the Program Documentation or the Specification which has been superseded and all copies of the whole or any part thereof, or, if required by the Licensor, shall destroy the same and certify in writing to the Licensor that they have been destroyed

(f) If the Licensee shall not accept the new Release then the Licensee shall return to the Licensor the new Release and the amendments to the Specification and the Program Documentation and all copies of the whole or any part thereof or, if required by the Licensor, shall destroy the same and certify in writing to the Licensor that they have been destroyed

(g) The Licensor shall not be relieved of its obligations to provide the Maintenance Services for the Current Release during the period of 3 months referred to in paragraph (d) above]

Version B (Licensee contractually bound to accept new Releases—subject to safeguards)

[(a) The Licensor shall deliver to the Licensee any improved version of the Licensed Programs which the Licensor shall from time to time make available to its licensees and the Licensee shall be responsible for using such version subject to the conditions set out below

(b) In reasonable time prior to the delivery of a new Release the Licensor shall make available to the Licensee all amendments to the Specification which shall be necessary properly to describe the facilities and functions of the new Release

(c) Notwithstanding anything else contained herein, the Licensee shall not be obliged to accept or use the new Release if its use would result in any of the facilities and functions set out in the Specification being [materially] diminished or curtailed

(d) The Licensor shall deliver to the Licensee the object code of the new Release in machine-readable form together with any amendments to the Program Documentation which shall be necessary to enable proper use of the improved facilities and functions of the new Release

(e) If required by the Licensee, the Licensor shall provide training for the Licensee's staff in the use of the new Release as soon as reasonably practicable after the delivery of the new Release at the Licensor's standard scale of charges from time to time in force

(f) Within 3 months of the Licensee receiving the new Release the Licensee shall test such Release and shall notify the Licensor of any failure of that Release to fulfil the amended Specification as delivered to the Licensee pursuant to paragraph (b)

(g) If within 3 months after such delivery no such notification shall have been received by the Licensor then, subject to the Licensor having complied with its foregoing obligations, the Licensee shall be deemed to have accepted the new Release which shall then become the Current Release and the provisions of this Agreement shall apply accordingly

(h) If the Licensee shall have notified the Licensor of any failure of the new Release to fulfil any part of the amended Specification within the said period of 3 months then the Licensor shall either correct such Release and re-issue it in accordance with this Clause (as if it were a new Release) or withdraw it

(i) Upon acceptance under paragraph (g) above, the Licensee shall return to the Licensor [if required by the Licensor] the Licensed Programs or the previous Release (as the case may be) and any part of the Program Documentation which has been superseded and all copies of the whole or any part thereof, or, if required by the Licensor, shall destroy the same and certify in writing to the Licensor that they have been destroyed

(j) The Licensor shall not be relieved of its obligations to maintain the Current Release and the Program Documentation under sub-clause (1) during the period of 3 months referred to in paragraph (d) above and any extended period during which corrections are carried out pursuant to paragraph (h) above]

(3) *Advice* [9.1.3]

The Licensor will provide the Licensee with such technical advice by telephone facsimile transmission or mail as shall be necessary to resolve the Licensee's difficulties and queries in using the Current Release

[(4) *Changes in Law* [9.1.2]

The Licensor will from time to time make such modifications to the Current Release as shall ensure that the Current Release conforms to any change of legislation or new legal requirements which affect the application of any function or facility described in the Specification. The Licensor shall promptly notify the Licensee in writing of all such changes and new requirements and shall implement the modifications to the Current Release (and all consequential amendments to the Program Documentation and the Specification which may be necessary to enable proper use of such modifications) as soon as reasonably practicable thereafter]

6   Licensee's obligations [9.6]

During the continuance of this Agreement the Licensee shall:

(1) use only the Current Release

(2) ensure that the Current Release and the Equipment are used in a proper manner by competent trained employees only or by persons under their supervision

(3) keep full security copies of the Current Release and of the Licensee's data bases and computer records in accordance with best computing practice

(4) not alter or modify the Current Release or the Program Documentation in any way whatever nor permit the Current Release to be combined with any other programs to form a combined work

(5) not request, permit or authorise anyone other than the Licensor to provide any maintenance services in respect of the Current Release or the Program Documentation

(6) co-operate fully with the Licensor's personnel in the diagnosis of any error or defect in the Current Release or the Program Documentation

(7) make available to the Licensor free of charge all information facilities and services reasonably required by the Licensor to enable the Licensor to perform the Maintenance Services including without limitation computer runs, memory dumps, printouts, [data preparation], [office accommodation], [typing] and photocopying

(8) provide such telecommunication facilities as are reasonably required by the Licensor for testing and diagnostic purposes at the Licensee's expense

(9) provide a suitable vehicle parking facility for use by the Licensor's personnel when visiting the Licensee's premises which is free from any legal restrictions

(10) ensure in the interests of health and safety that the Licensor's personnel, while on the Licensee's premises for the purposes of this Agreement, are at all times accompanied by a member of the Licensee's staff familiar with the Licensee's premises and safety procedures

7 Proprietary rights and licence [3.8.1]

(1) The Current Release (and all corrected versions thereof and all other Releases), the Program Documentation and the Specification and all parts thereof and the copyright and other intellectual property rights of whatever nature therein are and shall remain the property of the Licensor

(2) The provisions of the Licence Agreement shall apply to the Current Release, the Program Documentation and the Specification as such provisions are expressed to apply to the Licensed Program Materials and to the specification referred to in the Licence Agreement mutatis mutandis and the parties hereby undertake to be bound by and comply with the terms of the Licence Agreement accordingly

8 Confidentiality [9.7; 3.7.2]

See Clause 21 of Precedent D

9 Data Protection [3.7.2; 10.3.3]

See Clause 15 of Precedent P

10 Termination [9.4]

(1) Notwithstanding anything else contained herein, this Agreement may be terminated:

> (a) by the Licensor forthwith on giving notice in writing to the Licensee if the Licensee shall fail to pay any sum due under the terms of this Agreement (otherwise than as a consequence of any default on the part of the Licensor) and such sum remains unpaid for *14* days after written notice from the Licensor that such sum has not been paid (such notice to contain a warning of the Licensor's intention to terminate); or

(b) by either party forthwith on giving notice in writing to the other if the other commits any [material] [serious] breach of any term of this Agreement (other than any failure by the Licensee to make any payment hereunder in which event the provisions of paragraph (a) above shall apply) and (in the case of a breach capable of being remedied) shall have failed, within *30* days after the receipt of a request in writing from the other party so to do, to remedy the breach (such request to contain a warning of such party's intention to terminate); or

(c) by either party forthwith on giving notice in writing to the other if the other party shall have a receiver or administrative receiver appointed of it or over any part of its undertaking or assets or shall pass a resolution for winding-up (otherwise than for the purpose of a bona fide scheme of solvent amalgamation or reconstruction) or a court of competent jurisdiction shall make an order to that effect or if the other party shall become subject to an administration order or shall enter into any voluntary arrangement with its creditors or shall cease or threaten to cease to carry on business

(2) Any termination of this Agreement (howsoever occasioned) shall not affect any accrued rights or liabilities of either party nor shall it affect the coming into force or the continuance in force of any provision hereof which is expressly or by implication intended to come into or continue in force on or after such termination

(3) Any termination of this Agreement (howsoever occasioned) shall not of itself affect the Licensee's right to continue to use the Current Release and the Program Documentation in accordance with the provisions of the Licence Agreement

11   Assignment

See Clause 30 of Precedent A

12   Force majeure

See Clause 16 of Precedent K

13   Licensee's warranty

See Clause 20 of Precedent A

14 Liability [9.3.3]

(1) The Licensor shall not be liable for any loss or damage sustained or incurred by the Licensee or any third party (including without limitation any loss of use of the Current Release or loss of or spoiling of the Licensee's data) resulting from any defect or error in the Current Release or the Program Documentation except to the extent that such loss or damage arises from any unreasonable delay by the Licensor in providing the Maintenance Services and then only to the extent not excluded by this Agreement

(2) The Licensor shall not be responsible for the maintenance, accuracy or good running of any version of the Licensed Programs except the Current Release

(3) to (7) *See Clause 27 of Precedent A*

15 Waiver of remedies

See Clause 28 of Precedent A

16 Entire agreement

This Agreement is made pursuant to the Licence Agreement and supersedes all prior agreements, arrangements and undertakings between the parties other than the Licence Agreement and constitutes with the Licence Agreement the entire agreement between the parties relating to the subject matter of the Licence Agreement and this Agreement. No addition to or modification of any provision of this Agreement shall be binding upon the parties unless made by a written instrument signed by a duly authorised representative of each of the parties

17 Notices

See Clause 32 of Precedent A

18 Interpretation

See Clause 33 of Precedent A

19 Law

See Clause 34 of Precedent A

20   Disputes

See Clause 35 of Precedent A or Clause 37 of Precedent D

21   Severability

See Clause 36 of Precedent A

EXECUTED etc

THE SCHEDULE

A THE COMMENCEMENT DATE

either:

(a) The date of this Agreement; or

(b) *31 December 1995*; or

(c) The date on which the Licensed Programs are accepted by the Licensee under the terms of the Licence Agreement. If the Licensed Programs are not accepted by the Licensee as aforesaid then this Agreement shall never become effective

B THE INITIAL PERIOD

C THE MAINTENANCE CHARGE

£[   ] for each [month] [quarter] [year] payable in advance

First charge payable on: [the Commencement Date]

Subsequent charges payable on the first working day of each [month] [quarter] [year] thereafter

D METHOD OF PAYMENT

By standing order to [   ] Bank PLC

(Supplier's Account No   )

Precedent M

Software maintenance agreement: commissioned

THIS AGREEMENT is made the   day of   19

PARTIES:

(1) SOFTWARE HOUSE [LIMITED] [PLC] whose registered office is at

('the Software House')

(2) CLIENT [LIMITED] [PLC] whose registered office is at

('the Client')

RECITALS:

(A) Pursuant to an agreement dated   19   made between the Software House and the Client ('the Programming Agreement') the Software House prepared and wrote certain computer programs and operating manuals for the Client

(B) [By Clause *16* of the Programming Agreement it was agreed that the parties would enter into a maintenance agreement in respect of the said programs and operating manuals in the form of this Agreement] [The Software House has agreed to maintain the said programs and operating manuals upon the terms and conditions hereinafter contained]

NOW IT IS HEREBY AGREED as follows:

1 Definitions

In this Agreement, unless the context otherwise requires, the following expressions have the following meanings:

    'the Equipment'   has the meaning attributed thereto in the Programming Agreement 'the Programs'   means the computer programs written by the Software House pursuant to the Programming Agreement as corrected or modified from time to time pursuant to this Agreement

'the Functional Specification' means the functional specification of the Programs describing the facilities and functions thereof (a copy of which is annexed hereto) as modified from time to time pursuant to any provision of this Agreement

['the Performance Criteria'   means the performance criteria which the Programs have been designed to fulfil as specified in the Functional Specification subject to the tolerances, limitations and exceptions stated therein]

'the Operating Manuals'   means the operating manuals prepared by the Software House pursuant to the Programming Agreement for aiding the use and application of the Programs as corrected or modified from time to time pursuant to any provision of this Agreement

'the Program Materials'   means the Programs, the Functional Specification and the Operating Manuals

'the Maintenance Services'   means the maintenance services to be provided by the Software House pursuant to Clauses 5 and 6 of this Agreement

'the Maintenance Charge'   means the periodic charge for the Maintenance Services specified in the Schedule as increased from time to time pursuant to Clause 3

'the Commencement Date'   means the date on which this Agreement shall become effective as specified in the Schedule

'the Initial Period'   means the initial period of this Agreement as specified in the Schedule

2   Services to be performed [9.1.3]

The Software House hereby agrees to provide the Maintenance Services upon the terms and conditions hereinafter contained

3   Payment [9.2]

See Clause 3 of Precedent L

4   Duration

See Clause 4 of Precedent L

5   Error correction [9.1.3, 9.3.1]

(1) If the Client shall discover that any of the Programs fails to fulfil any part of the Functional Specification [or the Performance Criteria] then the Client shall within *14* days after such discovery notify the Software House in writing of the defect or error in question and provide the Software House (so far as the Client is able) with a documented example of such defect or error

(2) Upon receipt of such notification from the Client the Software House shall (subject to its then current commitments) normally begin work on correcting such defect or error not later than the first working day thereafter and shall diligently continue the work during normal working hours or at such other times as may be mutually agreed between the parties until the work is accepted by the Client as completed satisfactorily. If the Client requests support in an emergency the Software House shall use all reasonable efforts to fulfil the request as quickly as possible

(3) Forthwith upon such correction being completed the Software House shall deliver to the Client the corrected version of the object code of the Programs in machine-readable form for loading on to the Equipment together with appropriate amendments to the Operating Manuals specifying the nature of the correction and providing instructions for the proper use of the corrected version of the Programs on the Equipment

(4) The Software House shall as soon as reasonably practicable after such delivery provide for the number and category of the Client's staff specified in the Schedule such additional training as shall be necessary to enable the Client to make proper use of the corrected version of the Programs. The Software House shall in addition provide the Client with all other assistance reasonably required by the Client to enable the Client to implement the use of the corrected version of the Programs

(5) The foregoing error correction service shall not include service in respect of:

(a) defects or errors resulting from any modifications of the Programs made by any person other than the Software House;

(b) incorrect use of the Programs or operator error;

(c) any fault in the Equipment or in the *XYZ* operating system referred to in the Functional Specification or in any other programs used by the Client in conjunction with the Programs;

(d) any modification of the Programs if such modification would result in a departure from the Functional Specification

(6) The Software House shall make an additional charge in accordance with its standard scale of charges from time to time in force for any services provided by the Software House:

(a) at the request of the Client but which do not qualify under the aforesaid error correction service by virtue of any of the exclusions referred to in sub-clause (5) above;

(b) at the request of the Client but which the Software House finds are not necessary

For the avoidance of doubt nothing in this sub-clause shall impose any obligation on the Software House to provide services in respect of any of the exclusions referred to in sub-clause (5) above

(7) If the Client shall discover that the Operating Manuals do not provide adequate or correct instruction to enable the Client to make proper use of any facility or function set out in the Functional Specification then the Client shall notify the Software House in writing of the fault in question within *14* days after such discovery. The Software House shall thereupon promptly correct the fault and provide the Client with appropriate amendments to the Operating Manuals

[6   **Changes in law** [9.1.2]

The Software House will from time to time make such modifications to the Programs as shall ensure that the Programs conform to any change of legislation or new legal requirements which affect the application of any function or facility described in the Functional Specification. The Software House shall promptly notify the Client in writing of all such changes and new requirements and shall implement the modifications to the Programs as soon as reasonably practicable thereafter. The Software House shall provide at no further cost to the Client such amendments to the Functional Specification and the Operating Manuals as shall be necessary to describe and enable the Client to make proper use of the corrected version of the Programs]

7 Advice and enhancements [9.1.3]

(1) The Software House shall provide to the Client up to *10* man-days per annum of advice, consultancy, systems analysis and design about the work the subject of the Programming Agreement at no further cost to the Client [save for all reasonable travelling and subsistence expenses incurred by the Software House in so doing]

(2) The Software House shall provide to the Client up to *20* man-days per annum of programming effort in connection with the work the subject of the Programming Agreement at no further cost to the Client [save for all reasonable travelling and subsistence expenses incurred by the Software House in so doing]

(3) The Client shall not be entitled to carry forward any time unused under sub-clauses (1) and (2) in any year to any succeeding year. For these purposes 'year' shall mean any year commencing on the Commencement Date or on any subsequent anniversary of the Commencement Date

(4) All other advice, consultancy, systems analysis, design or programming services shall be provided by the Software House to the Client at the Software House's standard scale of charges from time to time in force

[(5) Apart from minor out-of-pocket expenses all claims by the Software House for reimbursement of expenses shall be accompanied by the relevant receipts]

8 Client's obligations

Adapt Clause 6 of Precedent L

9 Proprietary rights [3.8.2]

Version A (Proprietary Rights vested in the Software House)

[(1) The copyright and all other intellectual property rights of whatever nature in any corrected or modified versions of the Program Materials made pursuant to this Agreement shall be and shall remain vested in the Software House

(2) The provisions of Clauses 14(2) and 14(4) of the Programming Agreement shall apply to all corrected and modified versions of the Program Materials as such provisions are expressed to apply to the

495

Program Materials mutatis mutandis and the parties hereby undertake to be bound by and to comply with the terms thereof accordingly

(3) Any termination of this Agreement (howsoever occasioned) shall not of itself affect the Client's right to continue to use the then current versions of the Program Materials in accordance with the provisions of the licence granted by the Software House pursuant to Clause *14(2)* of the Programming Agreement]

Version B (Proprietary Rights vested in the Client)

[(1) The copyright and all other intellectual property rights of whatever nature in any corrected or modified versions of the Program Materials made pursuant to this Agreement shall belong to the Client and the Software House as beneficial owner hereby assigns (by way of future assignment) all such rights to the Client

(2) Notwithstanding sub-clause (1), the Software House reserves the right to use in any way it thinks fit any programming tools, skills and techniques acquired or used by the Software House in the performance of this Agreement

(3) The provisions of Clause *14(3)* of the Programming Agreement shall apply to all corrected and modified versions of the Program Materials as those provisions are expressed to apply to the Program Materials mutatis mutandis and the Software House hereby undertakes to be bound by and to comply with the terms thereof accordingly

(4) The Software House shall be entitled during the continuance of this Agreement to retain a copy of the Program Materials and of the source code of the Programs and all other materials necessary for the proper maintenance of the Programs. Such copies of the Program Materials and source code and other materials shall be held in confidence, shall only be used by the Software House for the purposes of this Agreement and shall be delivered up (together with all copies thereof) to the Client forthwith upon the termination of this Agreement (howsoever occasioned)

(5) If any corrected or modified version of the Program Materials shall be made by the Software House pursuant to this Agreement then the Software House shall promptly deliver to the Client copies thereof together with:

> (a) the source code of the corrected or modified version of the Programs in the form both of printed listings and magnetic [tape][disk];

> (b) all other materials necessary to enable a reasonably skilled programmer to correct, modify and enhance the corrected or modified version of the Programs without reference to any other person or document]

10   Confidentiality

See Clause 21 of Precedent A

[11   Data protection [3.7.2; 10.3.3]

See Clause 15 of Precedent P]

[12   Poaching staff

See Clause 25 of Precedent D]

13   Termination [9.4]

See Clause 10 of Precedent L

14   Assignment

See Clause 30 of Precedent A

15   Force majeure

See Clause 16 of Precedent K

16   Liability [9.3.3]

(1) The Software House shall not be liable for any loss or damage sustained or incurred by the Client or any third party (including without limitation any loss of use of the Programs or loss of or spoiling of the Client's data) as a result of any defect or error in the Programs or the Operating Manuals except to the extent that such loss or damage arises from any unreasonable delay by the Software House in providing the Maintenance Services and then only to the extent not excluded by this Agreement

(2) to (6) *See Clause 27 of Precedent A*

[17   Minor amendments

The Software House may at its own discretion introduce into the Programs such minor amendments as it shall from time to time consider necessary provided that such amendments shall not result in a departure from the Functional Specification. In such event the Software House shall deliver to the Client the amended version of the object code of the

497

Programs together with any consequential amendments to the Operating
Manuals]

18   Waiver of remedies

See Clause 28 of Precedent A

19   Entire agreement

This Agreement is made pursuant to the Programming Agreement and
supersedes all prior agreements, arrangements and undertakings between
the parties other than the Programming Agreement and constitutes with
the Programming Agreement the entire agreement between the parties
relating to the subject matter of the Programming Agreement and this
Agreement. No addition to or modification of this Agreement shall be
binding upon the parties unless made by a written instrument signed
by a duly authorised representative of each of the parties

20   Client's warranty

See Clause 20 of Precedent A

21   Notices

See Clause 32 of Precedent A

22   Interpretation

See Clause 33 of Precedent A

23   Law

See Clause 34 of Precedent A

24   Disputes

See Clause 35 of Precedent A or Clause 37 of Precedent D

25   Severability

See Clause 36 of Precedent A

EXECUTED etc

THE SCHEDULE

A   THE MAINTENANCE CHARGE

B   THE COMMENCEMENT DATE

C   THE INITIAL PERIOD

D   TRAINING (Client's staff)

Precedent N

Source code deposit agreement

[**Note:** See 3.3.1 and 5.]

THIS AGREEMENT is made the   day of   19

PARTIES:

(1) OWNER [LIMITED] [PLC] whose registered office is at
                                                        ('the Owner')
(2) CUSTODIAN [LIMITED] [PLC] whose registered office is at
                                                    ('the Custodian')

RECITALS:

(A) The Owner [has granted and] is proposing to grant to its customers non-exclusive, non-transferable licences to use the object code version of the Owner's computer programs hereinafter described

(B) The Owner wishes to establish for the benefit of its customers a facility for the safe custody of the source codes of the said programs and for the release of the same to its customers upon the occurrence of certain pre-defined events

(C) The Owner and the Custodian have agreed to enter into this Agreement for the purpose of implementing such a facility

> [**Note:** This agreement envisages that the software is a package to be licensed to a number of end-users. It can be easily adapted where the software is bespoke and there is only one user]

NOW IT IS HEREBY AGREED as follows:

1   Definitions

In this Agreement, unless the context otherwise requires, the following expressions have the following meanings:

'Additional Deposit'	means a deposit of Source Materials pursuant to Clause 4(2)
'business day'	means a day other than a Saturday, Sunday or a public holiday
'the Facility'	means the source code deposit facility hereby established
'Initial Deposit'	means a deposit of the Source Codes pursuant to Clause 4(1)
'the Licensed Programs'	means the Owner's computer programs described in Schedule 1 in object code form and all modifications, enhancements and replacements thereof and additions thereto used by the relevant User from time to time
'Maintenance Agreement'	means any agreement between the Owner and a User for the maintenance of the Licensed Programs
'the Register'	means the register to be kept in compliance with Clause 2
'the Source Codes'	means the Source Materials relating to the Licensed Programs
'Source Materials'	means all logic, logic diagrams, flowcharts, orthographic representations, algorithms, routines, subroutines, utilities, modules, file structures, coding sheets, coding, source codes, listings, functional specifications and program specifications and all other materials and documents necessary to enable a reasonably skilled programmer to maintain, amend and enhance the software in question without reference to any other person or document and whether in eye-readable or machine-readable form
'User'	means any person who is licensed by the Owner to use the Licensed Programs and who is a party to this Agreement from time to time

2   The Register

(1) The Custodian shall forthwith establish and thereafter maintain a full and accurate register of Users

(2) A person shall be entitled to have his name entered in the Register (and the Custodian shall enter it therein promptly) if he has been licensed to use the Licensed Programs by the Owner, has signed an undertaking in the form set out in Schedule 2 which has been countersigned by the Owner and has paid the Owner and the Custodian the currently applicable fees for the use of the Facility

(3) Each User shall become a party to this Agreement on being entered in the Register and shall remain a party until he ceases to be such in accordance with the terms of this Agreement or this Agreement is terminated

(4) The Register shall contain the name and address of each User together with his telephone and facsimile numbers and the name(s) of his representative(s) authorised to act on his behalf for the purposes of this Agreement. The Register shall also contain details of the current version of the Licensed Programs being used by each User

(5) The Owner shall promptly notify the Custodian of all new Users and their particulars

(6) Each User undertakes promptly to notify the Custodian of any change in his registered particulars. The Custodian shall record the same in the Register accordingly

(7) Each User shall be entitled to a copy of the Register free of charge on request to the Custodian at any time

(8) If a User shall cease to be a party to this Agreement the Custodian shall delete his name and other details from the Register forthwith

3   The Custodian's obligations

The Custodian shall:

(1) accept each new User notified to it by the Owner;

(2) provide for the safe custody of the copies of the Source Codes deposited with it;

(3) release the Source Codes in the circumstances hereinafter described;

(4) not itself inspect in detail or use the Source Codes or allow any of its employees to do so; and

(5) not subject the Source Codes or allow them to be subjected to any charge, lien or encumbrance or deal in the Source Codes in any way (whether as a means of satisfying any unpaid charges under this Agreement or otherwise)

4   Deposit of Source Codes

(1) The Owner undertakes with each User that within *10* business days after he has been entered in the Register the Owner will deposit with the Custodian, in a container marked with the User's name, one copy of all the Source Codes relevant to that User

(2) The Owner shall deposit with the Custodian in the manner provided in sub-clause (1) the Source Materials relating to any modification, enhancement or replacement of or addition to the Licensed Programs made available to each User by the Owner from time to time (whether pursuant to a Maintenance Agreement or otherwise) within *10* business days after the same has been made so available and shall at the same time withdraw any Source Materials previously deposited which have been superseded by the new deposit

(3) The Owner shall renew the copy of the Source Codes deposited with the Custodian in respect of each User not less frequently than *one year* after the immediately preceding delivery thereof

> [**Note:** This is to protect against natural degeneration of the source codes on magnetic media. See also Clause 6(2).]

(4) Contemporaneously with the delivery to the Custodian of the Initial Deposit and any Additional Deposit and any deposit pursuant to sub-clause (3) the Owner shall deliver to the User concerned and the Custodian a certificate in the form set out in Schedule 3 signed by a director of the Owner

(5) All items deposited under this Agreement by the Owner shall be packaged in a manner suitable for archive storage

(6) The Custodian will place the items deposited hereunder in a secure place [in a climate-controlled environment] and will be responsible for their safekeeping

(7) The Custodian shall notify the Owner and the relevant User promptly in writing of the receipt of any deposit of Source Materials pursuant to this Agreement

(8) Each User shall be entitled at any time and from time to time while it is a party to this Agreement to require an independent expert to verify whether the items deposited hereunder in the name of that User are the Source Codes in conformity with this Agreement. Such expert shall

be appointed by agreement between the Owner and such User or, failing such agreement within *14* days after the request of such User therefor, nominated at the request of such User by the President from time to time of the *British Computer Society*. Such expert shall act as an expert and not an arbitrator and his decision shall (in the absence of clerical or manifest error) be final and binding on the Owner and such User. For the purpose of his determination the expert shall be given full access to the items deposited in the User's name hereunder and to all other information and facilities which he may reasonably require (which the parties hereby undertake promptly to make available). The expert shall keep all information disclosed to him for the purpose of his determination strictly confidential and will not divulge the same to the User or any third party. It shall be a condition of any disclosure to the expert that he enters into a binding undertaking with the Owner to observe such confidentiality and non-disclosure obligations. If the expert decides that a default has occurred then the Owner shall cure the default to the expert's reasonable satisfaction within *30* days after receiving the expert's determination. The fees and expenses of the expert in supervising the cure of any default by the Owner shall be borne by the Owner. The fees and expenses of the expert in making his determination and of his appointment shall be borne by the User unless the expert determines that the Owner has defaulted to a material extent in its obligations in respect of the Source Codes in which event such fees and expenses shall be paid by the Owner. In the case of default by the Owner in paying any fees or expenses it is liable to pay hereunder the User may pay such sums in its stead and any payment made in so doing shall be recoverable from the Owner as a debt payable on demand

[**Note:** A source code deposit arrangement relies heavily on the integrity of the owner in depositing complete and accurate copies of the source codes. To encourage compliance Clause 4(4) requires a director of the owner to give a personal certificate each time a deposit occurs (which usually concentrates the mind wonderfully) and Clause 4(8) gives each user a right to have an independent expert verify compliance. It is worth verifying the initial deposit as a matter of course as this will give Clause 9(1)(h) teeth in respect of a default in relation to an additional deposit.]

[(9) Each time the Owner deposits a copy of the Source Codes ('the Original') hereunder it will at the same time deposit a duplicate copy thereof ('the Duplicate') with the Custodian. The Duplicate shall be stored by the Custodian in a separate building from the Original [located not less than *1 mile* from the place where the Original is stored] but subject thereto all the provisions of this Agreement shall apply, mutatis mutandis, to the Duplicate as they apply to the Original]

[**Note:** This considerably reduces the risk of total loss of the source codes through fire or other disasters but depends on the custodian being able to offer the facility of separate storage.]

5   Owner's undertakings

The Owner hereby undertakes with and warrants to each User that:

(1) each copy of the Source Codes deposited by the Owner in respect of such User with the Custodian from time to time will contain everything necessary to enable a reasonably skilled programmer to maintain, amend and enhance the Licensed Programs without reference to any other person or document;

(2) it will promptly cure any default under sub-clause (1);

(3) the Owner is the owner of the intellectual property rights in the Source Codes and is legally entitled to enter into this Agreement and to perform its obligations hereunder and that by virtue of entering into this Agreement it is not and will not be in breach of any express or implied obligation to any third party binding upon it; and

(4) it will not assign or otherwise transfer the intellectual property rights in the Source Codes without first procuring a novation of this Agreement with the substitution of the assignee or transferee for the Owner hereunder

6   The Custodian's liability

(1) If any copy of the Source Codes or any part thereof deposited in respect of any User shall be lost, destroyed or damaged then the Owner shall replace promptly the copy or part so lost, destroyed or damaged provided however that if such loss, destruction or damage is caused by the negligence, wilful misconduct or recklessness of the Custodian or any of its employees then the cost of such replacement shall be paid by the Custodian. The foregoing states the entire liability of the Custodian for any loss, destruction or damage of or to any of the Source Codes. The Custodian shall promptly notify the Owner and each relevant User of any such loss, destruction or damage

(2) The Custodian shall have no liability to the Owner or any User for any natural degeneration or loss of quality of any of the Source Codes deposited with it which arises as a result of the passage of time alone

(3) The Custodian shall not be responsible for determining whether any items deposited with it pursuant to this Agreement are in conformity with this Agreement or for ensuring the Owner's compliance with any other of its obligations hereunder

(4) If any dispute shall arise between any of the parties to this Agreement relating to the release or non-release of the Source Codes and the Custodian shall be uncertain of its obligations or rights hereunder then the Custodian shall be entitled, without liability to any other party hereto, to refrain from taking any action to release the Source Codes until the Custodian shall be directed otherwise by a court of competent jurisdiction

(5) The Custodian shall be entitled to take or refrain from taking any action ordered by a court of competent jurisdiction without liability to any of the other parties hereto

(6) Notwithstanding anything else contained in this Agreement, the Custodian shall not be liable to any of the other parties hereto for loss (whether direct or indirect) of profits, business or anticipated savings or for any indirect or consequential loss or damage whatsoever (except in respect of personal injury or death caused by the Custodian's negligence) even if the Custodian shall have been advised of the possibility thereof and whether arising from negligence, breach of contract or howsoever

7 Charges

(1) In consideration of the use of the Facility each User shall pay to the Owner and the Custodian the annual charges in force from time to time hereunder. The annual charges in force at the date hereof are those specified in Schedule 4. Such charges shall be paid in advance on the date on which such User shall be entered in the Register and on each subsequent anniversary of such date

(2) The Owner and the Custodian shall each be entitled to increase the annual charge payable to it by giving to all of the Users not less than *30* days' prior written notice provided that any such increase shall not exceed a percentage equal to the percentage increase in the Retail Prices Index published by the Central Statistical Office for the period from the date of this Agreement (in the case of the first such increase) or the date on which the immediately preceding increase came into effect pursuant to this sub-clause (2) (in the case of the second or subsequent increase) up to the date of such notice plus *2* per cent

(3) Charges exclusive of VAT—*See Clause 3(4) of Precedent A*

(4) Interest on overdue amounts—*See Clause 3(6) of Precedent A*

(5) No refund of any part of the annual charges shall be made upon a User ceasing to be a party to this Agreement or this Agreement being terminated

8   Cessation of a User's participation

A User shall cease to be a party to this Agreement forthwith in the event that:

(1) the licence under which such User is from time to time entitled to use the Licensed Programs is properly terminated in accordance with its terms and is not replaced by a new or novated licence;

(2) such User shall fail to pay any sum due to the Owner or the Custodian under the terms of this Agreement (otherwise than as a consequence of any default on the part of the person entitled to payment) and such sum remains unpaid for *30* days after written notice from the person entitled to payment that such sum has not been paid (such notice to contain a warning of that party's intention to terminate) and while such default continues thereafter the person entitled to payment serves written notice of termination on the User;

(3) such User at any time gives notice in writing to that effect to the Owner and the Custodian; or

(4) such User receives the Source Codes deposited in his name pursuant to one of the events described in Clauses 9(1)(e), 9(1)(f) or 9(1)(i)

The accrued rights and liabilities of a User shall not be affected by his ceasing to be a party to this Agreement

9   Release of the Source Codes

(1) If the Owner shall:

> (a) pass a resolution for winding-up (otherwise than for the purpose of a bona fide scheme of solvent amalgamation or reconstruction) or a court of competent jurisdiction shall make an order to that effect; or

> (b) have a receiver or administrative receiver appointed of it or over the whole or any part of its undertaking or assets; or

> (c) cease to carry on business; or

> (d) enter into any voluntary arrangement with its creditors or become subject to an administration order; or

> (e) fail to remedy a material default in any obligation imposed upon it from time to time to provide corrections to or maintenance or enhancements of the Licensed Programs under any Maintenance Agreement or any other agreement between the Owner and a User from time to time after having been given not less than *30* days' notice in writing from the User concerned requiring such remedy (such notice to contain a warning of the User's intention to invoke this Clause); or

[**Note:** The owner may be required to provide error correction under a licence agreement as well as a maintenance agreement.]

(f) voluntarily terminate a Maintenance Agreement without cause by giving notice in writing to the relevant User; or

[**Note:** This would cover the situation where the owner simply ceases to support the software and terminates the maintenance agreement by notice.]

(g) fail to comply with any of its obligations under Clauses 4(2), 4(3) or 5(2) after having been given not less than *30* days' notice in writing from the User concerned requiring such failure to be remedied (such notice to contain a warning of the User's intention to invoke this Clause); or

(h) fail to cure a default to an expert's reasonable satisfaction within *30* days as required by Clause 4(8); or

(i) be ordered by a court of competent jurisdiction to release the Source Codes to a User or be requested by a direction in writing signed by or on behalf of the Owner and a User to release the Source Codes to that User

then, and in any such event (but not otherwise) each User (or in the case of paragraphs (e) to (i), the User or each User affected) shall be entitled (subject to the terms of sub-clause (2) below) to have delivered to him the copy of the Source Codes deposited in his name with the Custodian free of charge and from any encumbrance (subject to the provisions of Clause 10 below)

[**Note:** Another option would be to provide for a release fee to be paid to the owner. If this is significant it will discourage spurious demands for a release of the source codes.]

(2) The Custodian shall upon receipt from a User of a statutory declaration confirming that one or more of the events set out in sub-clause (1) has or have occurred or, if such be the case, to the best of the User's knowledge, information and belief the same has or have occurred:

(a) forthwith deliver a copy of the statutory declaration to the Owner; and

(b) on the *20th* business day after the Custodian's receipt of the statutory declaration (unless directed otherwise by a court of competent jurisdiction) deliver to that User the copy of the Source Codes deposited in his name

Subject as provided in sub-clause (5), the Custodian shall not deliver to any User (and such User shall not be entitled to delivery of) a copy of the Source Codes unless the Custodian has first received a statutory declaration as aforesaid. The receipt by the Custodian of a statutory declaration shall be conclusive evidence to the Custodian of the facts stated therein and the Custodian shall not be required or entitled to make any enquiry regarding their accuracy. The Custodian shall be under no liability to the Owner for any loss or damage suffered by the Owner as a result of any copy of the Source Codes being released by the Custodian in accordance with the foregoing provisions of this Clause

[**Note:** The custodian will not wish to become embroiled in arguments over whether users are entitled to the source codes; hence the reason for this procedure. The delay of *20* business days should give the owner sufficient time to seek an injunction if it considers that a user's demand is unjustified.]

(3) Upon the termination of this Agreement pursuant to Clause 13(1), 13(2) or 13(3) the Custodian shall deliver to the Owner forthwith all copies of the Source Codes then in its possession

(4) Upon a User ceasing to be party to this Agreement pursuant to Clause 8(1), 8(2) or 8(3) the Custodian shall deliver to the Owner forthwith the copy of the Source Codes deposited with the Custodian in that User's name

(5) If the Source Codes deposited in a User's name shall be released to him by reason of any event mentioned in paragraphs (a) to (d) of sub-clause (1) then the Custodian shall forthwith release to all the other Users the copies of the Source Codes deposited in their names

10   User's undertakings

Each User undertakes with the Owner that if a copy of the Source Codes is delivered to him pursuant to this Agreement he will:

(1) use the Source Codes only for the purpose of correcting, modifying and/or enhancing the Licensed Programs and the Source Codes and for no other purpose whatsoever (and the licence governing the use of the Licensed Programs by the User shall be extended automatically to permit the User to use the object code form of any such corrections, modifications and enhancements in accordance with that licence);

(2) treat the Source Codes as confidential and will not divulge the whole or any part thereof to any third party except any person whom the User has appointed from time to time to maintain the Licensed Programs on the User's behalf but the User shall ensure that such person is aware of and shall comply with these obligations as to confidentiality and non-disclosure;

(3) keep the Source Codes in a secure place and safeguard them from access by any unauthorised person;

(4) not deface or remove any proprietary notices affixed to or contained in the Source Codes;

(5) forthwith upon the proper termination (in accordance with its terms) of the licence under which the User is entitled to use the Licensed Programs deliver to the Owner all copies of the Source Codes under the User's control or, if required by the Owner, destroy the same and certify to the Owner that they have been destroyed

11   Property rights

(1) The copyright and all other intellectual property rights of whatever nature in the Source Codes shall remain the property of the Owner

(2) If, after the release of a copy of the Source Codes to a User, such User shall correct, modify or enhance the Licensed Programs or the Source Codes the copyright and other intellectual property rights in such corrections, modifications and enhancements shall vest in the Owner and the User as beneficial owner hereby assigns (by way of future assignment) all such copyright and other intellectual property rights to the Owner

12   Assignment

See Clause 30 of Precedent A

13   Termination of agreement

(1) The Owner or the Custodian shall be entitled to terminate this Agreement forthwith by notice in writing to the other party or parties hereto in the event that:

   (a) no Users are from time to time party to this Agreement; or

   (b) all the Users from time to time shall have given their prior written consent to such termination

(2) The Custodian may at any time during the continuance of this Agreement serve on the other parties hereto a written request for a new custodian to be appointed. The Owner and the Users shall thereupon use their respective reasonable endeavours to appoint a mutually acceptable new custodian on terms similar to this Agreement (subject to such modifications as the proposed parties may reasonably require) within *90* days of such written request. If a new agreement is not entered

into within the said period of *90* days then the matter shall be referred to an independent expert to appoint an appropriate new custodian on such terms as he shall think fit. Such expert shall be appointed by agreement between the parties hereto or, failing such agreement within *14* days after the request of any of the parties hereto to the others therefor, nominated at the request of any of the parties hereto by the President from time to time of the *British Computer Society*. Such expert shall act as an expert and not an arbitrator and his decision shall be final and binding on the parties hereto. The fees and expenses of the expert in making his determination and of his appointment shall be borne as to *one-third* by the Users (pro-rata according to the number of them), *one-third* by the Owner and *one-third* by the Custodian. In the case of default by any party in paying his due proportion of such fees and expenses any of the other parties hereto may pay such sum in his stead and any payment made in so doing shall be recoverable from the defaulter as a debt payable on demand. If any User shall fail to pay his due proportion within *30* days after being requested so to do in writing by any of the other parties hereto then that User shall not be entitled to benefit under the arrangement with the new custodian and shall be excluded from the facility thereby established. The parties hereto shall do everything within their power which the expert shall consider necessary or desirable in order to give effect to his decision (including, in the case of the Owner, depositing fresh copies of the Source Codes with the new custodian). This Agreement shall automatically terminate on the appointment of a new custodian pursuant to this sub-clause (1)

(3) If any of the events referred to below occurs the Owner or any of the Users may serve on the other parties hereto a written request for a new custodian to be appointed and the provisions of sub-clause (2) shall apply mutatis mutandis save that the costs of any expert shall be borne as to *one half* by the Users (pro-rata according to the number of them) and the *other half* by the Owner. The events referred to above are the Custodian passing a resolution for winding-up (otherwise than for the purpose of a bona fide scheme of solvent amalgamation or reconstruction) or a court of competent jurisdiction making an order to that effect or having a receiver or administrative receiver appointed of it or over the whole or any part of its undertaking or assets or ceasing to carry on business or entering into a voluntary arrangement with its creditors or becoming subject to an administration order or failing to cure any breach by it of this Agreement within *30* days of being requested so to do by notice in writing from the Owner or any of the Users (such notice to contain a warning of that party's intention to invoke this sub-clause)

(4) This Agreement shall automatically terminate upon the release to all Users of the copies of the Source Codes deposited in their names pursuant to Clause 9

(5) This Agreement shall not terminate except in accordance with the express terms of this Agreement

(6) Any termination of this Agreement (howsoever occasioned) shall not affect any accrued rights or liabilities of any of the parties hereto nor shall it affect the coming into force or the continuance in force of any provision hereof which is expressly or by implication intended to come into or continue in force on or after such termination

14 Confidentiality

(1) The Custodian shall:

(a) keep the Source Codes and the other information, documentation and materials coming into its possession or to its knowledge under this Agreement strictly confidential and shall not divulge the whole or any part thereof to any third party except in accordance with the terms of this Agreement or except to the Custodian's employees who are directly involved with the Facility and have a specific need to know the information concerned;

(b) not release the Source Codes to any person except in accordance with the terms of this Agreement;

(c) ensure that its employees observe the confidentiality, non-disclosure and non-release obligations contained in sub-clauses (1) and (2); and

(d) keep the items deposited with it in its exclusive possession and control and safeguard them from access by any unauthorised person

(2) The provisions of this Clause shall survive the termination of this Agreement

15 Relationship of the parties

The Custodian is an independent contractor and nothing contained in this Agreement shall constitute the Custodian an agent or partner of the Owner or any User

16 Waiver of remedies

See Clause 28 of Precedent A

17 Entire agreement

See Clause 29 of Precedent A

18 Notices

See Clause 32 of Precedent A

[Note: Notices to the Users will be sent to the addresses recorded in the Register.]

19 Interpretation

See Clause 33 of Precedent A

20 Law

See Clause 34 of Precedent A

21 Disputes

See Clause 35 of Precedent A

22 Severability

See Clause 36 of Precedent A

EXECUTED etc

SCHEDULE 1

LICENSED PROGRAMS

SCHEDULE 2

USER'S UNDERTAKING

TO   :   OWNER [LIMITED] [PLC]

FROM   :   USER [LIMITED] [PLC]

Date: 19

1. We refer to the Agreement ('the Agreement') dated
19 made between yourselves and Custodian
[Limited] [PLC] ('the Custodian') relating to the establishment of a facility
for the safe custody of the source codes of your computer programs
which we have been licensed to use by virtue of a Licence Agreement
dated   19

2. We wish to take advantage of the said facility and to become a party
to the Agreement and we set out below the details required by Clause
2(4) thereof:

(a) Name:

(b) Address:

(c) Telephone and fax numbers:

(d) Authorised representative(s):

(e) Version of the Licensed Programs used:

3. We enclose our cheques for £   (in your favour) and £   (in
favour of the Custodian) being the currently applicable fees for the use
of such facility for the first year

4. We confirm that we have been supplied with a copy of the Agreement,
have full knowledge of its terms and conditions and undertake to you
and the Custodian to comply with and be bound thereby as a User

SIGNED for and on behalf of
USER [LIMITED] [PLC]

Signature . . . .

Name . . . .

Title . . . .

COUNTERSIGNED for and on behalf of OWNER [LIMITED] [PLC]

Signature ....

Name ....

Title ....

SCHEDULE 3

DEPOSIT CERTIFICATE

TO   :   USER [LIMITED] [PLC]

- and -

CUSTODIAN [LIMITED] [PLC]

Date: 19

Items deposited:

[Items withdrawn:]

I certify that on   19   Owner [Limited] [plc] deposited with [and withdrew from] Custodian [Limited] [plc] for the benefit of User [Limited] [plc] the source code items specified above. Those items have been inspected by me and I certify that they are the items they purport to be and are complete and that Owner [Limited] [plc] has complied in all respects with its obligations in respect thereof under the Source Code Deposit Agreement dated   19   made initially between Owner [Limited] [plc] and Custodian [Limited] [plc]

. . . .
Director of
Owner [Limited] [plc]

SCHEDULE 4
ANNUAL CHARGES

Owner:

£[   ] plus VAT

Custodian:

£[   ] plus VAT

Precedent O

Turnkey agreement

THIS AGREEMENT is made the   day of   19

PARTIES:

(1) COMPUTER COMPANY [LIMITED] [PLC] whose registered office is at

('the Supplier')

(2) CUSTOMER [LIMITED] [PLC] whose registered office is at

('the Customer')

RECITAL:

The Supplier has agreed to supply and install a fully operational computer system for the Customer and thereafter to maintain the same upon the terms and conditions hereinafter contained

NOW IT IS HEREBY AGREED as follows:

1 Definitions

In this Agreement, unless the context otherwise requires, the following expressions have the following meanings:

'the Equipment' [2.1.1]	means the computer equipment specified in Schedule 1
'the Licensed Programs'	means the computer programs of the Supplier specified in Schedule 1
'the System'	means the Equipment and the Licensed Programs in combination one with the other

'the Specification'
means the specification of the System [dated *31 July 1995*] describing the intended facilities and functions thereof, [a copy of which is annexed hereto]

['the Performance Criteria'
means the performance criteria which it is intended the System shall fulfil as specified in the Specification subject to the tolerances, limitations and exceptions stated therein]

'the Price'
means the price for the System and the services to be provided hereunder as specified in Schedule 1

'the Off-Loading Point'
means the Customer's off-loading point specified in Schedule 1

'the Location'
[2.1.2]
means the Customer's computer room in which the System is to be installed as specified in Schedule 1

'the Implementation Plan'
means the time schedule and sequence of events for the performance of this Agreement (the details of which are set out in Schedule 2) as the same may be amended from time to time pursuant to Clause 14

'the Acceptance Date'
[2.3.4]
means the date on which the System is accepted (or deemed to be accepted) by the Customer pursuant to Clause 14

'Ready for Use'
means fully installed, and tested and accepted in accordance with Clause 14

'the Completion Date'
means the date specified in the Implementation Plan by which the Supplier is to provide the System Ready for Use or such extended date as may be granted pursuant to Clause 14

[**Note:** When fixing the Completion Date the parties should allow sufficient time for acceptance testing.]

| 'the Training Plan' | means the training in the use of the System to be provided by the Supplier for the Customer's staff the details of which are set out in Schedule 3 |
| 'the Operating Manuals' | means the operating manuals to be provided by the Supplier pursuant to Clause 22 |

2   Products and services to be provided [2.1.1; 3.0.2]

(1) The Supplier hereby agrees to:

(a) sell the Equipment to the Customer free from any encumbrance;

(b) grant to the Customer a non-exclusive licence to use the Licensed Programs and the Operating Manuals;

(c) deliver the System to and install it at the Location;

(d) provide the System Ready for Use by the Completion Date;

(e) provide the Operating Manuals;

(f) provide training in accordance with the Training Plan;

(g) provide maintenance for the System after the Acceptance Date;

upon the terms and conditions hereinafter contained

(2) Operating supplies not included—*see Clause 2(3) of Precedent A*

3   Implementation Plan

The Supplier undertakes to perform its obligations under this Agreement in accordance with the Implementation Plan but time shall not be of the essence in relation to the performance of such obligations

[**Note:** This agreement provides for liquidated damages to be paid in the event of a delay by the supplier—see Clause 15(1).]

4   Price and payment [2.2.1]

See Clause 3 of Precedent A

5   Title to and risk in the Equipment [2.8.1]

See Clause 4 of Precedent A

6   Location preparation [2.6.3]

See Clause 5 of Precedent A

7   Information and access [2.6.1]

See Clause 6 of Precedent A

[8   Pre-delivery tests [2.3.2]

See Clause 7 of Precedent A]

9   Delivery of the Equipment [2.3.3]

See Clause 8 of Precedent A

> [**Note:** The phrase 'on the date specified in the Implementation Plan' should be substituted for the words 'on the Delivery Date'.]

10   Installation of the Equipment [2.3.3]

See Clause 9 of Precedent A

> [**Note:** See the note to Clause 9 above.]

11   Post-delivery tests [2.3.4]

(1) The Supplier shall, on the date specified in the Implementation Plan, submit the Equipment to the Supplier's standard installation tests ('the Installation Tests') to ensure that the Equipment and every part thereof is in full working order. The Supplier shall supply the Customer with copies of the specification and results of the Installation Tests

(2) The Customer shall attend the Installation Tests on the said date and shall provide all necessary facilities to enable the Installation Tests to be carried out

(3) If the Equipment or any part thereof shall fail to pass the Installation Tests then, if required by the Customer, the Installation Tests shall be repeated on the same terms and conditions within a reasonable time thereafter but in any event no later than *14* days thereafter. If the Equipment or any part thereof shall fail such repeat tests then the Customer may by written notice to the Supplier elect at its sole option:

> (a) to require (without prejudice to its other rights and remedies) the Supplier to provide such replacement equipment as will enable the Equipment to pass the Installation Tests; or

(b) to accept the Equipment subject to an abatement of the Price such abatement to be such amount as, taking into account the circumstances, is reasonable. In the absence of written agreement as to abatement within *14* days after the date of such notice the Customer shall be entitled to reject the Equipment in accordance with paragraph (c) below; or

(c) to reject the Equipment as not being in conformity with this Agreement in which event this Agreement shall automatically terminate and the Supplier shall (without prejudice to the Customer's other rights and remedies) forthwith refund to the Customer all sums previously paid to the Supplier under this Agreement. Upon rejection as aforesaid the risk in the Equipment shall forthwith pass to the Supplier

(4) Once the Equipment and every part thereof has successfully passed the Installation Tests then the Equipment shall be accepted by the Customer

(5) Any acceptance of the Equipment by the Customer pursuant to this Clause shall be without prejudice to the Customer's right to reject the System pursuant to Clause 14

12   Delivery and Installation of the Licensed Programs [3.3]

The Supplier shall, within *7* days after the Customer's acceptance of the Equipment, deliver the Licensed Programs to the Customer and install the same on the Equipment at the Location. The Licensed Programs so delivered shall consist of one copy of the object code of the Licensed Programs in machine-readable form only, on the storage media specified in Schedule 1

13   Risk in the Licensed Programs

Risk in the media on which the Licensed Programs are recorded shall pass to the Customer on installation. If any part of such media shall thereafter be lost, destroyed or damaged the Supplier shall promptly replace the same (embodying the relevant part of the Licensed Programs) subject to the Customer paying the cost of such replacement. The Supplier shall not make any further or additional charge for such replacement

14   Testing and acceptance of the System [2.3.4, 2.3.6; 3.3.1]

(1) On or before the applicable date specified in the Implementation Plan, the Customer shall submit to the Supplier test data which in the reasonable opinion of the Customer is suitable to test whether the System

is in accordance with the Specification [and the Performance Criteria] together with the results expected to be achieved by processing such test data on the System. The Supplier shall not be entitled to object to such test data or expected results unless the Supplier can demonstrate to the Customer that they are not in accordance with the Specification, in which event the Customer shall make such amendments to such test data and expected results as may be necessary for them to conform to the Specification

(2) After the Licensed Programs have been fully installed on the Equipment, the Supplier shall give to the Customer at least 7 days' prior written notice (or such shorter notice as may be agreed between the parties) of the date ('the Testing Date') on which the Supplier will be ready to attend acceptance tests at the Customer's premises. The Customer and the Supplier shall attend such tests on the Testing Date and shall provide all necessary facilities to enable such tests to be carried out

(3) On the Testing Date the Customer shall process, in the presence of the authorised representatives of the Supplier, the said test data on the System. The Supplier shall if required by the Customer give the Customer's personnel all reasonable assistance in processing such test data

(4) The Customer shall accept the System immediately after the System has correctly processed such test data by achieving the expected results. The Customer shall, if required by the Supplier, sign an acceptance certificate in the form annexed hereto acknowledging such acceptance

[**Note:** See Precedents A and C for specimen forms of acceptance certificate.]

(5) The System shall not be deemed to have incorrectly processed such test data by reason of any failure to provide any facility or function not specified in the Specification

(6) If the System shall fail to process such test data correctly then repeat tests shall be carried out on the same terms and conditions within a reasonable time thereafter but in any event no later than *14* days thereafter

(7) If such repeat tests demonstrate that the System is not in accordance with the Specification [or the Performance Criteria] then the Customer may by written notice to the Supplier elect at its sole option:

(a) to fix (without prejudice to its other rights and remedies) a new date for carrying out further tests on the System on the same terms and conditions (save that all costs which the Customer may incur as a result of carrying out such tests shall be reimbursed by the Supplier). If the System shall fail such further tests then the Customer shall be entitled to proceed under paragraph (b) or (c) below; or

(b) to accept the System subject to an abatement of the Price, such abatement to be such amount as, taking into account the circumstances, is reasonable. In the absence of written agreement as to abatement within *14* days after the date of such notice the Customer shall be entitled to reject the System in accordance with paragraph (c) below; or

(c) to reject the System as not being in conformity with this Agreement in which event this Agreement shall automatically terminate and the Supplier shall (without prejudice to the Customer's other rights and remedies) forthwith refund to the Customer all sums previously paid to the Supplier under this Agreement. Upon rejection as aforesaid the risk in the System shall forthwith pass to the Supplier

(8) Notwithstanding anything else contained in this Clause the Supplier shall be entitled (provided it has complied with its obligations under this Clause) at any time and from time to time after the Testing Date to serve written notice on the Customer requiring the Customer to identify any part of the Specification [or the Performance Criteria] which the System does not fulfil. If the Customer shall fail to identify in writing to the Supplier within *14* days after the receipt of such notice any part of the Specification [or the Performance Criteria] which the System does not fulfil then the Customer shall be deemed to have accepted the System

(9) If at any time the Customer shall commence live running of the whole or any part of the System (as distinct from acceptance testing) then the Customer shall be deemed to have accepted the System.

15   Delays [2.3.7]

Supplier's default

(1)   (a) The Supplier shall provide the System Ready for Use on or before the Completion Date

(b) If the Supplier shall fail to provide the System Ready for Use by the Completion Date then the Supplier shall pay to the Customer as and by way of liquidated damages for any loss or damage sustained by the Customer resulting from delay during the period from the Completion Date to the date on which the Supplier provides the System Ready for Use the sum of *£500* for each week of such delay and pro rata for parts of a week up to a total maximum of *£5,000*. Subject to the provisions of paragraph (c) below, the payment of such sums shall be in full satisfaction of the Supplier's liability for such delay. The payment of liquidated damages shall not relieve the Supplier from its obligation to provide the System Ready for Use or from any other liability or obligation under this Agreement

(c) If the Supplier shall fail to provide the System Ready for Use within *10* weeks after the Completion Date then notwithstanding anything else contained in this Agreement the Customer shall be entitled to terminate this Agreement forthwith on giving written notice to the Supplier and to recover from the Supplier the amount of all [direct] damages and loss suffered by the Customer resulting from such failure. Upon such termination the Supplier shall (without prejudice to the Customer's right to recover the amount of such damages and loss as aforesaid) forthwith refund to the Customer all moneys previously paid to the Supplier under this Agreement. Upon such termination the risk in the System shall forthwith pass to the Supplier

Customer's default

(2) If the Supplier is prevented or delayed from performing its obligations under this Agreement by reason of any act or omission of the Customer (other than a delay by the Customer for which the Customer is excused under Clause 16) then the Customer will pay to the Supplier all reasonable costs, charges and losses sustained or incurred by the Supplier as a result. The Supplier shall promptly notify the Customer in writing of any claim which it may have under this sub-clause giving such particulars thereof as it is then able to provide

16   Force majeure

See Clause 28 of Precedent D

17   Electromagnetic compatibility [2.7.3]

See Clause 13 of Precedent A

18   Telecommunications [2.7.4]

See Clause 14 of Precedent A

19 Licence to use

The parties undertake to enter into a licence agreement on the Acceptance Date in respect of the use of the Licensed Programs and the Operating Manuals in the form of the draft annexed hereto marked 'A'

[**Notes:** (1) Adapt Precedent C.
(2) Alternatively, the parties could undertake to enter into the licence agreement immediately after the signature of this Agreement in which event the licence agreement should be expressed to become effective on the Acceptance Date. The same point applies to clauses 20 and 21 below.]

20 Maintenance of the equipment [2.6.4]

The parties undertake to enter into a maintenance agreement on the Acceptance Date in respect of the Equipment in the form of the draft annexed hereto marked 'B'

[**Note:** See Precedent K.]

21 Maintenance of the Licensed Programs

The parties undertake to enter into a maintenance agreement on the Acceptance Date in respect of the Licensed Programs and the Operating Manuals in the form of the draft annexed hereto marked 'C'

[**Note:** See Precedent L.]

22 Operating Manuals [3.7.3]

The Supplier shall provide the Customer with 2 copies of a set of operating manuals containing sufficient information to enable the Customer to make full and proper use of the System. If the Customer shall require further copies of such operating manuals then these will be provided by the Supplier under licence in accordance with its standard scale of charges from time to time in force

23 Training [3.7.3]

(1) The Supplier shall provide training in the use of the System for the Customer's staff in accordance with the Training Plan

(2) Any additional training required by the Customer shall be provided by the Supplier in accordance with its standard scale of charges from time to time in force

24   Warranties [2.3.8, 3.3.3]

(1) The Supplier warrants that:

(a) the System will after acceptance by the Customer:

(i) provide the facilities and functions set out in the Specification [and will fulfil the Performance Criteria];

(ii) be free from defects in materials, workmanship and installation

(b) the Operating Manuals will provide adequate instruction to enable the Customer to make full and proper use of the System

(2) The Supplier shall have no liability or obligations under the said warranties other than to remedy breaches thereof by the provision of maintenance services in accordance with the maintenance agreements referred to in Clauses 20 and 21. If the Supplier shall fail to remedy any breach of the said warranties as aforesaid then the Supplier shall be liable to the Customer for all [direct] loss and damage suffered by the Customer as a result of such failure provided that the Customer shall have given the Supplier written notice of the breach in question no later than the expiration or termination of the relevant maintenance agreement. The foregoing states the entire liability of the Supplier, whether in contract or tort, for defects in the System and the Operating Manuals notified to it after the Acceptance Date other than liability assumed under Clause 31

(3) The Supplier warrants to the Customer that the Equipment complies fully as to noise heat radiation and all other characteristics with the requirements in the Annex to EC Council Directive 90/270/EEC and in particular that the display screens and keyboards comply fully with the said Annex

(4) *See Clause 18(5) of Precedent A*

25   Customer's warranty

See Clause 20 of Precedent A

26   Confidentiality [2.6.2, 2.7.1]

See Clause 21 of Precedent A

27   Removal of labels [2.6.5]

See Clause 23 of Precedent A

[28   Export control [2.9.1]
See Clause 25 of Precedent A]

29   Intellectual property rights indemnity [2.8.1]
See Clause 26 of Precedent A

30   Termination [2.4.1]
See Clause 18 of Precedent A

31   Liability
See Clause 27 of Precedent A

32   Waiver of remedies
See Clause 28 of Precedent A

33   Entire agreement
See Clause 29 of Precedent A

34   Assignment [2.6.5]
See Clause 30 of Precedent A

[35   Sub-contracts
See Clause 31 of Precedent A]

36   Notices
See Clause 32 of Precedent A

37   Interpretation
See Clause 33 of Precedent A

38   Law

See Clause 34 of Precedent A

39   Disputes [13.1.1]

See Clause 35 of Precedent A or Clause 37 of Precedent D

40   Severability

See Clause 36 of Precedent A

EXECUTED etc

SCHEDULE 1

A THE EQUIPMENT

B THE LICENSED PROGRAMS

C THE PRICE

D THE OFF-LOADING POINT

E THE LOCATION

F STORAGE MEDIA

SCHEDULE 2

THE IMPLEMENTATION PLAN

SCHEDULE 3

THE TRAINING PLAN

Precedent P

Bureau service: general on-line

THIS AGREEMENT is made the   day of   19

PARTIES:

(1) COMPUTER BUREAU COMPANY [LIMITED] [PLC] whose registered office is at   ('the Bureau')

(2) CUSTOMER [LIMITED] [PLC] whose registered office is at
('the Customer')

RECITALS:

(A) The Bureau carries on the business of providing the shared use of a computer by means of [the supply of] on-line terminals through which its customers can obtain direct access to the Bureau's computer for the purpose of running their programs and the processing of their data

(B) The Bureau has agreed to permit the Customer to share the use of its computer and certain of its programs upon the terms and conditions hereinafter contained

NOW IT IS HEREBY AGREED as follows:

1   Definitions

In this Agreement, unless the context otherwise requires, the following expressions have the following meanings:

'the Equipment'	means the Bureau's computer equipment specified in Schedule 1 (situate at the Bureau's Premises) or such other equipment as shall be agreed between the parties

'the Bureau's Premises'	means the Bureau's premises at [ ]
'the Printer'	means the Bureau's *XYZ* [laser] printer situate at the Bureau's Premises
'the Licensed Programs'	means the systems programs specified in Schedule 1 which are to be made available by the Bureau for use by the Customer under this Agreement
'the Specification'	means the specification of the Equipment and the Licensed Programs describing the facilities and functions thereof, a copy of which is annexed hereto
'the Terminal' [10.1.2]	[means the [visual display] [terminal] [personal computer] [and its associated [serial] printer] specified in Schedule 1 which [is][are] to be let on hire to the Customer under this Agreement] [means any suitable terminal or personal computer of the Customer [installed at the Location]]

[Note: The customer might provide his own terminal in which case the second alternative should be used.]

'the Location'	means the Customer's computer room as specified in Schedule 1
'the Commencement Date'	means the date on which this Agreement shall become effective as specified in Schedule 1
'the Initial Period'	means the initial period of this Agreement as specified in Schedule 1
'business day'	means a day other than a Saturday, Sunday or a public holiday

2   Services to be provided [10.1.2]

The Bureau hereby agrees to:

(1) permit the Customer to use the Equipment and the Licensed Programs by means of the Terminal for the storage and processing of the Customer's programs and data;

[(2) install the Terminal and let the same on hire to the Customer for the purpose of obtaining access to the Equipment and the Licensed Programs;]

(3) print, copy and dump the Customer's programs and data or any part or parts thereof as required by the Customer from time to time;

(4) provide the other services hereinafter described;

upon the terms and conditions hereinafter contained

3   Access and use

(1) On or before the Commencement Date the Bureau shall supply the Customer with:

(a) a set of operating instructions containing sufficient information to enable the Customer to make full and proper use of the Equipment and the Licensed Programs [and the Terminal];

(b) a security password to enable the Customer to obtain access to the Equipment and the Licensed Programs;

(2) The Bureau shall periodically change the Customer's security password in accordance with its standard security procedures and shall notify the Customer accordingly. If the Bureau shall become aware, or shall suspect, that any unauthorised person has obtained or has attempted to obtain access to the Customer's programs or data then the Bureau shall promptly notify the Customer and shall forthwith change the Customer's security password

[Note: The customer may have its own password which it can change without reference to the Bureau, in which case this clause will need to be modified.]

[(3) Subject to Clauses 8, 14 and 15, the Customer shall be entitled to use the Terminal for the purpose of inputting, storing, running and retrieving such of the Customer's programs and data as the Customer shall require

(4) The Customer shall use the Terminal only for inputting and processing its own programs and data for its own internal business purposes and shall not make the use of the Terminal available to any third party nor use the Terminal on behalf of or for the benefit of any third party]

(5) The Bureau shall make the Equipment and the Licensed Programs available to the Customer [for use by means of the Terminal] during the hours of *8.00* am to *7.00* pm each business day

(6) The Bureau hereby grants to the Customer all necessary rights by way of licence to use the Licensed Programs in accordance with the terms of this Agreement but not further or otherwise

(7) The Customer undertakes not to attempt to obtain access to, use or interfere with any programs or data of the Bureau (other than access to and use of the Licensed Programs in accordance with this Agreement) or of any other customer of the Bureau and shall indemnify the Bureau against any loss, damage or liability which the Bureau may sustain or incur as a consequence of the Customer failing to comply with such undertaking

4   Charges and payment [10.2.2]

(1) The Customer shall pay the following charges for the services to be provided by the Bureau hereunder:

[(a) for the use of the Equipment and the Licensed Programs—the hourly connect time rate set out in Part A of Schedule 2 and the on-line storage rate per Megabyte per [business] day set out in Part B of Schedule 2;

(b) for dumping any of the Customer's programs and/or data on to magnetic media and for loading any of such programs or data back on to the Equipment—at the rate per Gigabyte set out in Part C of Schedule 2;

(c) for off-line storage of the Customer's programs and/or data—at the rate per magnetic [tape] [disk] per day set out in Part D of Schedule 2;

(d) for print-outs from the Printer—at the rate per page set out in Part E of Schedule 2;

[(e) for the hire of the Terminal—at the monthly rate set out in Part F of Schedule 2]]

[**Note:** The bureau may also charge a joining fee to cover the cost of installing the terminal.]

(2) The Bureau shall invoice the Customer monthly in arrears for the charges referred to in sub-clause (1). Each invoice will be paid by the Customer within *30* days after the Customer's receipt of such invoice

[(3) Notwithstanding the provisions of sub-clause (1)(a) the use of the Equipment and the Licensed Programs shall be subject to the minimum charge per month specified in Part G of Schedule 2 which charge shall be payable whether or not the Equipment and the Licensed Programs are actually used during the month in question]

(4) Right to increase charges—*see Clause 3(4) of Precedent K* [10.5.1]

[**Note:** If a minimum charge is provided for then the bureau will also wish to reserve a right to increase that minimum charge from time to time.]

(5) Charges exclusive of VAT—*see Clause 3(4) of Precedent A*

(6) Interest on overdue amounts—*see Clause 3(6) of Precedent A*

5 Duration

This Agreement shall commence on the Commencement Date, shall continue for the Initial Period and shall remain in force thereafter [unless or] until terminated by either party giving to the other not less than 6 months' written notice of termination [given on] [expiring on]the last day of the Initial Period or at any time thereafter but shall be subject to earlier termination as provided elsewhere in this Agreement

[**Note:** See the note to Clause 8 of Precedent K.]

[6 The Terminal [10.1.2]

(1) The Bureau shall let and the Customer shall take on hire the Terminal for the duration of this Agreement

(2) The Customer shall be responsible for providing proper accommodation and operating conditions for the Terminal in accordance with the Bureau's instructions before the delivery of the Terminal

(3) The Bureau shall deliver the Terminal to the Location and shall install the same at the Location on or before the Commencement Date

(4) Prior to the delivery of the Terminal the Customer shall:

(a) arrange for the provision of a telephone line and appropriate modem to connect the Terminal to the Equipment; and

(b) obtain and produce to the Bureau any necessary consents for such connection

(5) The Terminal shall at all times remain the sole and exclusive property of the Bureau and the Customer shall have no right or interest therein except for quiet possession and the right to use the same upon the terms and conditions contained in this Agreement

(6) The Terminal shall be at the risk of the Bureau which shall be responsible for insuring the same against all normal risks. The Customer shall notify the Bureau immediately of any loss of or damage to the Terminal and shall give all necessary information and assistance to the Bureau in connection with any such loss or damage

(7) The Customer shall not create or suffer to exist over the Terminal any mortgage, charge, lien or other encumbrance

(8) The Customer shall not utilise or attempt to utilise any equipment other than the Terminal for the purpose of obtaining access to the Equipment and the Licensed Programs

(9) The Customer shall use the Terminal only for the purpose of obtaining access to the Equipment and the Licensed Programs in accordance with the terms of this Agreement

(10) The Customer shall operate the Terminal in a proper and prudent manner in accordance with the Bureau's operating instructions and ensure that only competent trained employees (or persons under their supervision) are allowed to operate the same

(11) The Customer shall be responsible for obtaining at its own expense all consumable supplies for use on the Terminal. The Customer shall only use such consumable supplies as the Bureau shall recommend

(12) The Bureau shall provide preventive and corrective maintenance for the Terminal during the hours of *8.00* am to *7.00* pm on business days ('Working Hours')

(13) Preventive maintenance shall be performed by the Bureau during Working Hours at such intervals as the Bureau shall reasonably determine to be necessary for the Terminal

(14) Corrective maintenance shall be performed by the Bureau during Working Hours as soon as possible after the Customer's request therefor on the basis of a response time of *8* Working Hours but such response time is an estimate only and shall not be binding on the Bureau

(15) The Customer shall not without the prior written consent of the Bureau permit any person, firm or company other than the Bureau (or a person appointed for such purpose by the Bureau) to carry out or attempt to carry out any maintenance, adjustment, replacement or repair of the Terminal or any part thereof

(16) The Customer shall ensure that the Terminal is not moved from the Location except with the prior written consent of the Bureau

(17) Upon termination of the Customer's right to hire the Terminal (for any reason) the Customer shall forthwith redeliver possession of the Terminal to the Bureau in a condition consistent with the proper performance by the Customer of its obligations under this Clause and the Bureau shall for the purpose have access to the Location (or any other place where the Terminal may be situated)]

7   Preparation of programs and data

The Customer shall have sole responsibility for the preparation of its programs and data and for the scheduling and control of the running and processing thereof. The Bureau shall not be responsible for any fault or error in the Customer's programs or data

8   On-line storage [10.3.1]

The Customer shall be entitled to store on-line on the Equipment such programs and data as it shall require provided that the total storage volume for all such programs and data at any one time shall not exceed *30* Gigabytes and provided also that the total volume of such programs and data resident in the main memory of the Equipment at any one time shall not exceed *50* Gigabytes

9   Off-line storage

(1) The Bureau shall at the request of the Customer dump on to magnetic storage media all or any part of the Customer's programs and/or data from time to time stored on-line on the Equipment subject to the Customer giving to the Bureau at least *2* business days' notice in writing

(2) Upon receiving such a request the Bureau shall take two copies of the programs or data in question one of which shall be kept by the Bureau and one of which shall be delivered to the Customer at the Customer's expense

(3) The Bureau shall keep the media to be held by it [in its fireproof safe] at the Bureau's Premises

(4) The Bureau shall not be liable to the Customer for any loss or damage sustained or incurred by the Customer resulting from any loss or destruction of or damage to any of the media held by the Bureau unless such loss, destruction or damage is caused by the wilful misconduct of the Bureau, its employees, agents or sub-contractors provided however that nothing in this sub-clause shall affect the Bureau's liability under Clause 13(5)

(5) If any of the media held by the Bureau shall be lost, destroyed or damaged then the Bureau shall forthwith make duplicates of such media and for this purpose the Customer shall promptly make available to the Bureau the copies of such media held by the Customer. Where any media held by the Bureau is lost, destroyed or damaged due to the negligence or wilful misconduct of the Bureau, its employees, agents or sub-contractors then the cost of making such duplicates shall be borne by the Bureau

(6) The Bureau shall not be responsible for the loss or spoiling of any of the Customer's programs or data stored on magnetic media if such programs or data were dumped on to that media more than *3* months previously. The Bureau will at the request of the Customer take duplicates of any of the Customer's programs or data stored off-line on magnetic media subject to the Customer giving to the Bureau at least *2* business days' notice in writing. Where any of the Customer's programs or data are lost or spoiled by reason of their deterioration on magnetic media within the said period of *3* months then the Bureau will forthwith make duplicates of such media free of charge and for this purpose the Customer will promptly make available the copies of such media held by it. The foregoing states the entire liability of the Bureau for the loss or spoiling of any of the Customer's programs or data by reason of their deterioration on magnetic media

[**Note:** See Chapter 13 and Appendix 12 of 'Modern Public Records' (Cmnd 8204) for the problems of keeping computer records for indefinite periods. The advent of optical disks suggests a solution, but at present most bureaux still use magnetic media.]

(7) Subject to the provisions of Clause 8, the Bureau shall at the request of the Customer load on to the Equipment all or any part of the Customer's programs and/or data from time to time stored off-line on magnetic media subject to the Customer giving to the Bureau at least *2* business days' notice in writing

10 Security copies

The Bureau shall take each business day a single security copy of all the Customer's data and programs stored on-line on the Equipment at that time and shall keep such security copies for a period of one week after copying. The Bureau shall not charge for making such security copies but their storage and use (subject to the other provisions of this Agreement) shall be subject to such conditions as the Bureau may from time to time impose

11 Maintenance of the Equipment and Licensed Programs [10.7.3]

(1) (a) The Bureau shall be responsible for maintaining the Equipment in good working order and condition

(b) If the Equipment shall fail or breakdown the Bureau shall use its reasonable endeavours promptly to restore the Equipment to its proper operating condition [and shall in the meantime whenever possible provide suitable alternative equipment for the Customer's use]

[**Note:** The Customer may require a more positive commitment to provide back-up equipment in the event of a breakdown. The position is usually clear cut—either the Bureau will have a back-up machine or it will not.]

(2) If the Customer shall become aware of any fault in the Licensed Programs then the Customer shall promptly notify the Bureau. Upon receipt of such notification (or upon receipt of a similar notification from one of the Bureau's other customers) the Bureau shall forthwith use its reasonable endeavours to procure that such fault is corrected as quickly as possible

[**Note:** This Clause assumes that the bureau does not own the licensed programs and that the bureau would have to arrange for the proprietor to correct the fault.]

(3) (a) In the event of any failure or breakdown of the Equipment or any fault in the Licensed Programs with consequent loss or spoiling of the Customer's data and/or programs or any part thereof the Bureau shall use such security copies as described in Clause 10 to reconstitute the Customer's programs and data free of charge as soon as reasonably practicable after the Equipment and the Licensed Programs are available for use again (in accordance with known priorities)

(b) The Bureau shall notify the Customer of any such failure of the Equipment or the Licensed Programs and reconstitution of the Customer's data and programs from such security copies within *24* hours of such reconstitution

(4) Sub-clause (3) states the entire liability of the Bureau for any loss or spoiling of the Customer's programs and/or data caused by any failure or breakdown of the Equipment or fault in the Licensed Programs. The Bureau shall not be liable for any other loss or damage sustained or incurred by the Customer as a result of any failure or breakdown of the Equipment or fault in the Licensed Programs except to the extent that such loss or damage arises from any unreasonable delay by the Bureau in performing its obligations under sub-clauses (1) and (2) above

12   Print-outs

(1) The Bureau shall at the Customer's request make such print-outs of the Customer's data using the Printer as the Customer shall from time to time require

(2) The Bureau shall not be responsible for the delivery of such print-outs but shall make them available for collection by the Customer at the Bureau's Premises within 2 business days after the Customer's request therefor

13   Ownership of programs and data [10.6.3]

(1) The Customer's programs and data shall be and shall remain the property of the Customer

(2) The Bureau shall ensure that all copies of the Customer's programs and data in the Bureau's possession shall bear a notice that such programs and data are the property and confidential information of the Customer

(3) The Bureau shall protect and defend the Customer's title to its programs and data against all persons claiming against or through the Bureau and shall use its reasonable endeavours to keep such programs and data free from any distress, execution or other legal process

(4)   (a) The Bureau undertakes to treat as confidential and keep secret all information ('the Information') contained or embodied in the Customer's programs and data

(b) The Bureau shall not without the prior written consent of the Customer divulge the whole or any part of the Information to any person except the Bureau's own employees and then only to those employees who need to know the same, and to the extent necessary, for the proper performance of this Agreement

(c) The Bureau undertakes to ensure that its employees are made aware that the Information is confidential and that such employees owe a duty of confidence to the Customer. The Bureau shall indemnify the Customer against any loss or damage which the Customer may sustain or incur as a result of the Bureau failing to comply with such undertaking

(d) The Bureau shall notify the Customer promptly if the Bureau becomes aware of any breach of confidence by any of the Bureau's employees and shall give the Customer all reasonable assistance in connection with any legal proceedings which the Customer may bring against any such employees or any other person for breach of confidence

(e) The foregoing obligations as to confidentiality shall remain in full force and effect notwithstanding any termination of this Agreement (howsoever occasioned)

(5) The Bureau will establish and maintain proper security measures and procedures to provide for the safe custody of the Customer's programs and data and to prevent unauthorised access thereto or use thereof.

The Bureau shall indemnify the Customer against any loss or damage which the Customer may sustain or incur consequent upon any of the Customer's programs or data coming into the possession of any unauthorised person as a result of any negligent act or omission or wilful misconduct of the Bureau, its employees, agents or sub-contractors [provided that the Bureau's liability therefor shall not in any circumstances whatsoever exceed £*100,000* in respect of each event or series of connected events]

(6) (a) Upon any termination of this Agreement (howsoever occasioned) the Customer shall have the right to require the Bureau to do any one or more of the following:

    (i) to deliver up to the Customer all or any off-line storage and security copies of the Customer's programs and data then in the Bureau's possession subject to the Customer reimbursing the Bureau for the cost of the magnetic media on which they are stored;

    (ii) to dump on to magnetic media all or any of the Customer's programs and data then stored on-line on the Equipment and to deliver up such media to the Customer subject to the Customer paying the charges for such dumping at the applicable rate for the time being payable hereunder and to reimbursing the Bureau for the cost of such magnetic media;

    (iii) to erase all or any of the Customer's programs and data then in the Bureau's possession from the magnetic media on which they are stored;

    (iv) to make and deliver up to the Customer such print-outs of the Customer's data using the Printer as the Customer may require subject to the Customer paying the charges for such print-outs at the applicable rate from time to time payable hereunder

(b) If upon any termination of this Agreement the Customer shall require the Bureau to deliver up any of its programs and/or data on magnetic media then the Bureau shall:

    (i) deliver up such programs and/or data on industry compatible magnetic media; and

    (ii) supply to the Customer free of charge all information necessary to enable such magnetic media to be read on another computer

[Note: In the case of magnetic tape this might include information as to the occurrence of tape marks, the number of records in a block, the parity and record density and the character set. In the case of disks these ought only to be run on a machine of the same type.]

(c) Except where this Agreement is properly terminated by the Customer as a result of any breach by the Bureau of its obligations under this Agreement, the Bureau's obligations under paragraphs (a) and (b) of this sub-clause shall be conditional upon the Customer having paid all charges then due to the Bureau under the terms of this Agreement

14   Content of Customer's data

The Customer undertakes that the Customer's data (whether stored on-line or off-line) will not contain anything obscene, offensive or defamatory. The Customer will indemnify the Bureau and keep the Bureau fully and effectively indemnified against all actions, proceedings, claims, demands, damages and costs (including legal costs on a full indemnity basis) occasioned to the Bureau as a result of any breach of the said undertaking

15   Data protection [10.3.3]

Version A (The Act does not apply to the Customer's data)

[The Customer hereby warrants and undertakes to the Bureau that the Customer's data will not contain any personal data as defined in Section 1(3) of the Data Protection Act 1984 or that if it does the processing of such data by the Bureau under this Agreement will not be processing as defined in Sections 1(7) and 1(8) of that Act or that the Customer will be exempt from registering in respect of the Customer's data under the said Act by reason of one or more of the provisions for exemption in Part IV of the said Act and the Customer shall indemnify the Bureau against all or any damages, losses, claims, costs and expenses sustained or incurred by the Bureau in connection with any prosecution of the Bureau under the said Act or any civil action brought by any person or persons under the said Act against the Bureau in so far as any such prosecution or civil action may be in respect of the Customer's data]

Version B (The Act does apply to the Customer's data)

[(1)   The Customer hereby notifies the Bureau that the Customer's data contains personal data as defined in Section 1(3) of the Data Protection Act 1984 ('the Customer's Personal Data') and warrants to the Bureau that the Customer has registered under the said Act in respect of the Customer's Personal Data

(2)   The Customer warrants and undertakes to the Bureau that:

(a) The Customer's Personal Data has been obtained and processed (in so far as the Customer's Personal Data has been processed) lawfully

(b) The services to be provided by the Bureau under this Agreement will be entirely consistent with and appropriate to the specified and lawful purposes for which the Customer has registered under the said Act in respect of the Customer's Personal Data ('the Registered Purposes')

(c) The Customer has not hitherto and will not during the continuance of this Agreement use or disclose the Customer's Personal Data or any part thereof in a manner incompatible with the Registered Purposes

(d) The Customer's Personal Data is adequate, relevant and not excessive in relation to the Registered Purposes

(e) The Customer's Personal Data is accurate and [the Customer shall promptly provide the Bureau with all amendments and corrections to the Customer's Personal Data sufficient to enable the Bureau to keep the Customer's Personal Data at all times fully up to date] [the Customer shall keep the Customer's Personal Data fully up to date at all times during the continuance of this Agreement]

(f) The Customer will promptly instruct the Bureau to delete the Customer's Personal Data or any part or parts thereof as soon as it or they shall no longer be required for the Registered Purposes

(g) The Customer will promptly instruct the Bureau to make copies of the Customer's Personal Data or any part or parts thereof to provide access under Section 21 of the said Act

(3)   The Customer shall indemnify the Bureau against any loss or damage which the Bureau may sustain or incur as a result of any breach by the Customer of the provisions of this Clause

(4)   The Bureau warrants to the Customer that the Bureau has registered under the said Act as a bureau

(5)   Upon request by the Customer in writing the Bureau shall provide to the Customer promptly such copies of the Customer's Personal Data or any part or parts thereof as the Customer shall request to the Bureau in order to comply with Section 21 of the said Act. [The Customer shall pay the Bureau's reasonable costs in complying with this obligation]

[(6)   Upon receipt of updating material from the Customer in respect of the Customer's Personal Data the Bureau shall promptly modify the data in accordance with the updating material]

(7)   The Bureau shall indemnify the Customer against any loss or damage which the Customer may sustain or incur as a result of any breach by the Bureau of the provisions of this Clause]

16   Intellectual property rights indemnities [2.8; 3.8]

(1) The Bureau shall indemnify the Customer against any claim by any third party for alleged infringement of any copyright or other intellectual property rights which arises as a result of the use of the Equipment, the Licensed Programs or the Terminal in accordance with the terms of this Agreement provided that the Bureau is given immediate and complete control of any such claim, that the Customer does not prejudice the Bureau's defence of such claim and that the Customer gives the Bureau all reasonable assistance with such claim

(2) The Customer shall indemnify the Bureau against any claim by any third party for alleged infringement of any copyright or other intellectual property rights which arises as a result of the storage or processing of any of the Customer's programs or data on the Equipment provided that the Customer is given immediate and complete control of any such claim, that the Bureau does not prejudice the Customer's defence of such claim and that the Bureau gives the Customer all reasonable assistance with such claim

17   Bureau's confidential information

The Customer shall treat as confidential all information supplied to it by the Bureau for the purposes of this Agreement which is marked as confidential or which is by its nature clearly confidential. Such information shall only be disclosed to those employees of the Customer who need to know the same and the Customer undertakes to ensure that such employees are made aware of its confidential nature prior to such disclosure

18   Warranties [10.7.5]

(1) The Bureau warrants that the Licensed Programs will provide the facilities and functions described in the Specification when used in conjunction with the Equipment. The Customer acknowledges however that the Equipment and the Licensed Programs are not being made available to the Customer to meet the Customer's individual requirements and that it is therefore the responsibility of the Customer to ensure that the facilities and functions described in the Specification meet the Customer's requirements. The Bureau shall not be liable for any failure

of the Licensed Programs to provide any facility or function not specified in the Specification. The Bureau's entire liability for any fault in the Licensed Programs is as stated in Clause 11

[(2) The Bureau warrants that the terminal response times for the interactive processing of the Customer's programs and data shall be those specified in Schedule 3 subject to the tolerances, limitations and exceptions stated therein]

19   Termination [10.4]

(1) *See Clause 10(1) of Precedent L*

(2) *See Clause 10(2) of Precedent L*

[(3) Right of recovery of the Terminal—*adapt Clause 30(3)(a) of Precedent B*]

20   Assignment

See Clause 30 of Precedent A

21   Force majeure

See Clause 16 of Precedent K

22   Customer's warranty

See Clause 20 of Precedent A

23   Liability

See Clause 27 of Precedent A

24   Waiver of remedies

See Clause 28 of Precedent A

25   Entire agreement

See Clause 29 of Precedent A

26   Notices

See Clause 32 of Precedent A

27   Interpretation

See Clause 33 of Precedent A

28   Law

See Clause 34 of Precedent A

29   Disputes

See Clause 35 of Precedent A

30   Severability

See Clause 36 of Precedent A

EXECUTED etc

SCHEDULE 1

A THE EQUIPMENT

B THE LICENSED PROGRAMS

[C THE TERMINAL]

D THE LOCATION

E THE COMMENCEMENT DATE

F THE INITIAL PERIOD

SCHEDULE 2

CHARGES

[SCHEDULE 3

TERMINAL RESPONSE TIMES]

Precedent Q

Bureau service: batch

[**Note:** This precedent is intended to form a general framework. For specialised services, arrangements can vary considerably and it will be up to the parties to specify the exact service to be provided.]

THIS AGREEMENT is made the   day of   19

PARTIES:

(1) COMPUTER BUREAU COMPANY [LIMITED] [PLC] whose registered office is at   ('the Bureau')

(2) CUSTOMER [LIMITED] [PLC] whose registered office is at
       ('the Customer')

RECITALS:

(A) The Bureau carries on the business of providing the shared use of a computer by means of receiving and inputting its customers' data, processing such data in batch mode and then delivering to them the resulting print-outs

(B) The Bureau has agreed to permit the Customer to share the use of its computer and certain of its programs upon the terms and conditions hereinafter contained

NOW IT IS HEREBY AGREED as follows:

1   Definitions

In this Agreement, unless the context otherwise requires, the following expressions have the following meanings:

'the Equipment'   means the Bureau's computer equipment specified in Schedule 1 (situate at the Bureau's Premises) or such other equipment as shall be agreed between the parties

'the Bureau's Premises'   means the Bureau's premises at
                            [   ]

'the Licensed Programs'   means the computer programs spe-
                            cified in Schedule 1 which are to be
                            made available by the Bureau under
                            this Agreement

'the System'   means the Equipment and the
                            Licensed Programs in combination
                            one with the other

'the Services'   means the services to be provided by
                            the Bureau under this Agreement

'the Specification'   means the specification of the
                            Services describing inter alia the
                            facilities and functions of the System
                            and the form, content and layout of
                            the Input and the Output a copy of
                            which is annexed hereto

'the Input'   means the data (in eye-readable
                            form) from time to time submitted
                            to the Bureau by the Customer for
                            inputting on the System

'the Data'   means the Customer's computer
                            records from time to time stored on
                            the System in machine-readable
                            form

'the Output'   means the print-outs resulting from
                            processing the Data on the System

[**Note:** The output to be produced will of course vary with the type of
service being offered. In the case of a payroll service one would expect
payslips, P60s etc, the precise form and content of which should be described
in the Specification.]

'the Timetable'   means the timing and sequence of
                            events for the delivery of the Input,
                            the processing of the Data and the
                            return of the Output as set out in
                            Schedule 2

[**Note:** Again, the timetable will vary considerably with the type of service
being offered. It is essential that the parties define exactly what their
respective responsibilities are. Time limits will usually be expressed as
maxima.]

554

'the Commencement Date' means the date on which this Agreement shall become effective as specified in Schedule 1

'the Initial Period' means the initial period of this Agreement as specified in Schedule 1

'business day' means a day other than a Saturday, Sunday or a public holiday

2 Services to be provided [10.1.1]

The Bureau hereby agrees to:

(a) provide the use of the System to accept the Input, process the Data and produce the Output in accordance with the Timetable;

(b) provide the other services hereinafter described;

upon the terms and conditions hereinafter contained

3 Charges and payment

(1) The Customer shall pay the following charges for the Services:

(a) for inputting the Input and processing the Data—at the rate per *1000 postings* as set out in Part A of Schedule 3;

(b) for the storage of the Data—at the rate per *1000 records* per [business] day as set out in Part B of Schedule 3

(c) for printing the Output—at the rate per *1000 lines* set out in Part C of Schedule 3;

(d) for dumping any of the Data on to magnetic media—at the rate per Megabytes and per magnetic [tape] [disk] as set out in Part D of Schedule 3;

(e) for delivering the Output to the Customer—at the rate set out in Part E of Schedule 3

(2) The Bureau shall invoice the Customer monthly in arrears for the charges referred to in sub-clause (1). Each invoice will be paid by the Customer within *30* days after the Customer's receipt of such invoice. The first month for payment shall commence on the date on which the Customer's initial data records are set-up on the System pursuant to Clause 6(1)

[(3) Notwithstanding the foregoing the Services shall be subject to the payment of the minimum charge per month specified in Part F of Schedule 3 which charge shall be payable whether or not the Services are actually used by the Customer during the month in question]

(4) Right to increase charges—*see Clause 3(4) of Precedent K*

[**Note:** If a minimum charge is provided for then the Bureau may also wish to reserve a right to increase that minimum charge from time to time.]

(5) Charges exclusive of VAT—*see Clause 3(4) of Precedent A*

(6) Interest on overdue amounts—*see Clause 3(6) of Precedent A*

4   Duration

See Clause 5 of Precedent P

5   Warranty

The Bureau warrants and undertakes that the Services will be provided in accordance with the Specification but not further or otherwise. The Customer acknowledges that the Services are not being provided to the Customer to meet the Customer's individual requirements and that it is therefore the responsibility of the Customer to ensure that the services described in the Specification meet the Customer's requirements. The Bureau shall not be responsible for providing any service not described in the Specification

6   Set-up of Customer's records [10.3.1]

(1) The Customer shall be responsible for delivering to the Bureau within 7 days after the Commencement Date the Customer's initial data records described in the Specification. The Bureau shall be responsible for setting-up such records on the System within *one* week after such delivery

(2) The Customer shall pay the Bureau the sum of £500 for setting-up its data records in accordance with sub-clause (1), which sum shall be paid on the execution of this Agreement

7   Preparation of the Input [10.3.1]

(1) The Customer shall be responsible for preparing the Input in the form and layout described in the Specification

(2) The Bureau does not accept responsibility for any loss or damage sustained or incurred by the Customer as a result of the Input being incorrect, illegible or not being prepared in accordance with the Specification. The Bureau shall not however input or attempt to input on to the System any part of the Input which is illegible or otherwise faulty but shall instead request the Customer to correct the fault in

question. The Bureau reserves the right to charge for any additional work required as a result of any fault in the Input

(3) The Customer shall deliver the Input to the Bureau at the Bureau's Premises in accordance with the Timetable. The cost of such delivery shall be borne by the Customer. The Bureau reserves the right to make a charge for any additional costs incurred by the Bureau as a result of the late arrival or non-arrival of the Input

> [**Note:** This clause assumes that there will be a regular delivery of data. Where data is to be provided by the customer on an irregular basis it will be necessary to establish a procedure for booking time on the computer. The timetable will then come into effect once time has been booked.]

(4) The Customer shall be responsible for keeping a duplicate of the Input as delivered to the Bureau for a period of at least *14* days after such delivery

8   Processing of the Data and delivery of the Output [10.1.1]

(1) Following receipt of the Input from the Customer the Bureau shall input the same on the System, process the Data and deliver the Output to the Customer in accordance with the Timetable [. The Bureau shall return the Input to the Customer at the same time as the Output is delivered]

(2) The Bureau shall produce the Output in the form specified in the Specification

9   On-line storage of the Data

See Clause 8 of Precedent P

10   Off-line storage of the Data

See Clause 9 of Precedent P

11   Security copies

The Bureau shall take each business day a single security copy of the Data and shall keep such security copies for a period of one week after copying. The Bureau shall not charge for making such security copies but their storage and use (subject to the other provisions of this Agreement) shall be subject to such conditions as the Bureau may from time to time impose

12 Maintenance of the System [10.7.3]

(1) *See Clause 11(1) of Precedent P*

(2) *See Clause 11(2) of Precedent P*

(3) (a) In the event of any breakdown of or fault in the System with consequent loss or spoiling of the Data or any part thereof the Bureau shall use such security copies as described in Clause 11 to reconstitute the Data free of charge as soon as reasonably practicable after the System is available for use again (in accordance with known priorities)

(b) The Bureau shall notify the Customer of any such breakdown or fault and of such reconstitution of the Data from such security copies within *24* hours after such reconstitution

(4) Sub-clause (3) states the entire liability of the Bureau for any loss or spoiling of the Data caused by any breakdown of or fault in the System. The Bureau shall not be liable for any other loss or damage sustained or incurred by the Customer as a result of any breakdown of or fault in the System except to the extent that such loss or damage arises from any unreasonable delay by the Bureau in performing its obligations under sub-clauses (1) and (2) above

[13 Changes in law [9.1.2]

The Bureau will from time to time make such modifications to the Licensed Programs as shall ensure that the Licensed Programs conform to any change of legislation or new legal requirements which affect the application of any function or facility described in the Specification. The Bureau shall promptly notify the Customer in writing of all such changes and new requirements and shall implement the modifications to the Licensed Programs (and all consequential amendments to the Specification which may be necessary to describe and enable proper use of such modifications) as soon as reasonably practicable thereafter]

14 Loss of the Input or Output [10.7.2]

(1) If the Input or any part thereof shall be lost, destroyed or damaged prior to the inputting thereof whilst in the Bureau's possession then the Bureau shall forthwith notify the Customer who shall promptly supply the Bureau with the copy of the Input retained by the Customer pursuant to Clause 7(4). The Bureau shall thereupon use such copy for inputting the Input. The cost of delivering such copy shall be borne by the Customer unless such loss, damage or destruction of the Input is caused by any

negligent act or omission or wilful misconduct of the Bureau, its employees, agents or sub-contractors

(2) If the Output or any part thereof shall be lost, damaged or destroyed prior to the delivery thereof to the Customer then the Bureau shall produce a further copy as soon as possible thereafter. The cost of producing such further copy shall be borne by the Customer unless such loss, damage or destruction of the Output is caused by any negligent act or omission or wilful misconduct of the Bureau, its employees, agents or sub-contractors

15   Volumes [10.1.4]

The Services shall be performed in accordance with the Timetable unless the volume of the Input shall exceed the maximum specified volumes as set out in the Specification. Any work in excess of the said maximum volumes shall be performed by the Bureau as soon as reasonably practicable having regard to the Bureau's other commitments

16   Rectification of errors [10.7.3]

If the Output or any part thereof is incorrect by reason of a breakdown of or a fault in the System or of a mistake due to the negligence or inadvertence of the Bureau, its employees, agents or sub-contractors then the Bureau shall promptly correct and reprocess the Data free of charge to produce the Output in the correct form provided that the error in question is notified to the Bureau in writing within *14* days after the Customer's receipt of the Output. The foregoing states the entire liability of the Bureau for errors in the Output

17   Ownership of the Input, Data and Output [10.7.1]

(1) The Input, the Data and the Output (hereinafter collectively referred to as 'the Customer's Data') shall be and shall remain the property of the Customer

(2) The Bureau shall protect and defend the Customer's title to the Customer's Data against all persons claiming against or through the Bureau and shall use its reasonable endeavours to keep the same free from any distress, execution or other legal process

(3)   (a) The Bureau shall treat as confidential information and shall keep secret the Customer's Data. The Bureau shall not without the prior written consent of the Customer divulge the whole or any part of the Customer's Data to any person except the Bureau's own employees and then only to those employees who need to

know the same, and only to the extent necessary for the proper performance of this Agreement

(b) The Bureau undertakes to ensure that its employees are made aware that the Customer's Data is confidential and that such employees owe a duty of confidence to the Customer. The Bureau shall indemnify the Customer against any loss or damage which the Customer may sustain or incur as a result of the Bureau failing to comply with such undertaking

(c) The Bureau shall promptly notify the Customer if the Bureau becomes aware of any breach of confidence by any of the Bureau's employees and shall give the Customer all reasonable assistance in connection with any legal proceedings which the Customer may bring against any such employees or any other person for breach of confidence

(d) The foregoing obligations as to confidentiality shall remain in full force and effect notwithstanding any termination of this Agreement (howsoever occasioned)

(4) The Bureau will establish and maintain proper security measures and procedures to provide for the safe custody of the Customer's Data and to prevent unauthorised access thereto or use thereof. The Bureau shall indemnify the Customer against any loss or damage which the Customer may sustain or incur consequent upon the Customer's Data or any part thereof coming into the possession of any unauthorised person as a direct result of any negligent act or omission or wilful misconduct of the Bureau, its employees, agents or sub-contractors [provided that the total liability of the Bureau therefor shall not in any event exceed *£100,000* in respect of each event or series of connected events]

(5)   (a) Upon any termination of this Agreement (howsoever occasioned) the Customer shall have the right to require the Bureau to do any one or more of the following:

(i) to deliver up to the Customer all or any off-line storage and security copies of the Data then in the Bureau's possession subject to the Customer reimbursing the Bureau for the cost of the magnetic media on which they are stored

(ii) to dump on to magnetic media the Data or any part thereof and to deliver up such media to the Customer subject to the Customer paying the charges for such dumping at the applicable rate from time to time payable hereunder and to reimbursing the Bureau for the cost of such media

(iii) to erase all or any of the Data from the media on which it is stored

(iv) to deliver up to the Customer all copies of the Input and the Output then in the possession of the Bureau or to destroy the same

(v) to make and deliver up to the Customer such print-outs of the Data as the Customer may require subject to the Customer paying the charges for such print-outs at the applicable rate from time to time payable hereunder

(b) If upon any termination of this Agreement the Customer shall require the Bureau to deliver up any of the Data on magnetic media then the Bureau shall:

(i) deliver up such data on industry compatible magnetic media

(ii) supply to the Customer free of charge all information necessary to enable such magnetic media to be read on another computer

[**Note:** See the note to Clause 13(6)(b)(ii) of Precedent P.]

(c) Except where this Agreement is properly terminated by the Customer as a result of any breach by the Bureau of any term hereof, the Bureau's obligations under paragraphs (a) and (b) of this sub-clause shall be conditional upon the Customer having paid all charges then due to the Bureau under the terms of this Agreement

18 Intellectual property rights indemnities [2.8; 3.8]

See Clause 16 of Precedent P

19 Bureau's confidential information [10.6.3]

(1) The Customer shall treat as confidential and shall keep secret all information obtained by it under this Agreement concerning the Services and the System provided that such obligation shall not extend to information which was rightfully in the possession of the Customer prior to the commencement of the negotiations leading to this Agreement, which is already public knowledge or becomes so at a future date (other than by a breach of this Clause) or which is trivial or obvious

(2) The Customer shall not without the prior written consent of the Bureau divulge any of such confidential information to any person except:

(a) the Customer's own employees and then only to those employees who need to know the same

(b) the Customer's auditors, H.M. Inspector of Taxes, Customs & Excise and any other persons or bodies having a right, duty or obligation to know the business of the Customer and then only in pursuance of such right, duty or obligation

The Customer shall be responsible for ensuring that the persons and bodies mentioned in paragraphs (a) and (b) are made aware prior to the disclosure of any such confidential information that the same is confidential and that they owe a duty of confidence to the Bureau. The Customer shall promptly notify the Bureau if it becomes aware of any breach of confidence by any such person or body and shall give the Bureau all reasonable assistance in connection with any legal proceedings which the Bureau may bring against any such person or body or any other person for breach of confidence

20   Use of the Services

Except as may be otherwise agreed by the Bureau the Customer shall use the Services only for inputting its own data for its own internal business purposes and shall not use the Services on behalf of or for the benefit of any third party

21   Contents of the Data

See Clause 14 of Precedent P

22   Data Protection

See Clause 15 of Precedent P

23   Termination [10.4]

See Clause 10 of Precedent L

24   Customer's warranty

See Clause 20 of Precedent A

25   Assignment

See Clause 30 of Precedent A

26   Force majeure

See Clause 16 of Precedent K

27   Liability

See Clause 27 of Precedent A

28   Waiver of remedies

See Clause 28 of Precedent A

29   Entire agreement

See Clause 29 of Precedent A

30   Notices

See Clause 32 of Precedent A

31   Interpretation

See Clause 33 of Precedent A

32   Law

See Clause 34 of Precedent A

33   Disputes

See Clause 35 of Precedent A

34   Severability

See Clause 36 of Precedent A

EXECUTED etc

SCHEDULE 1

A THE EQUIPMENT

B THE LICENSED PROGRAMS

C THE COMMENCEMENT DATE

D THE INITIAL PERIOD

SCHEDULE 2

THE TIMETABLE

SCHEDULE 3

CHARGES

Precedent R

Network service level agreement

THIS AGREEMENT is made the   day of   19

PARTIES:

(1) SERVICE COMPANY [LIMITED] [PLC] whose registered office is at

('the Service Provider')

(2) CUSTOMER [LIMITED] [PLC] whose registered office is at

('the Customer')

RECITALS:

(A) The Service Provider carries on the business of providing information technology services for customers

(B) The Service Provider has agreed to permit the Customer to use its Network and Services upon the terms and conditions hereinafter contained

1 Definitions

In this Agreement, unless the context otherwise requires, the following expressions have the following meanings:

'the Network'	means the cabling, equipment and software by which the Service Provider provides the Services as specified in Schedule 1
'the Services'	means the services specified in Schedule 1
'the Helpdesk Services'	means the helpdesk services included in the Services as specified in Schedule 1

565

['the Network Area'	means the area covered by the Network as specified in Schedule 1]

[**Note:** If this agreement is between different divisions of the same company or different companies in the same group, the network area may be defined as the company's building or buildings in a particular place.]

['the Modem'	means [the modem specified in Schedule 1 which is to be let on hire to the Customer under this Agreement] [any suitable modem of the Customer [installed as part of the Customer's Equipment]]

[**Note:** the Customer may provide his own modem in which case the second alternative may be used.]

'the Security Procedures'	means the security procedures specified in Schedule 1
'the Security Passwords'	has the meaning attributed thereto in Clause 3(1)(c)
['the Software'	means the programs specified in Schedule 1 which are to be made available by the Service Provider for use by the Customer to gain access to the Network and the Services]
'the Training'	means the training specified in Schedule 1
'the Documentation'	means the documentation specified in Schedule 1
'the Commencement Date'	means the date on which this Agreement shall become effective as specified in Schedule 1
'the Customer's Data'	means any data input onto the Network by the Customer
'the Customer's Equipment'	means the Customer's computer[s] as specified in Schedule 1
'the Customer's Staff'	means the Customer's staff specified in Schedule 1 and such other members of the Customer's staff as may be agreed in writing between the Service Provider and the Customer from time to time

'the Initial Period'   means the initial period of this
                              Agreement as specified in Schedule 1

'business day'   means a day other than a Saturday,
                              Sunday or a public holiday

2   Services to be provided [10.1.3, 10.7.1]

The Service Provider hereby agrees to:

(1) permit the Customer to use the Services [and the Software] over the Network [within the Network Area] [by means of a Modem];

(2) provide the Customer with the Helpdesk Services;

(3) comply with the service quality criteria set out in Schedule 3

upon the terms and conditions hereinafter contained

3   Access and use

(1) On or before the Commencement Date the Service Provider shall provide the Customer with:

    (a) the Training;

    (b) the Documentation;

    (c) security passwords ('the Security Passwords') to enable the Customer and each of the Customer's Staff to obtain access to the Network and the Services;

    (d) the telephone number of and access to the Helpdesk Services;

    [(e) the Software;]

    [(f) the Modem]

[(2) Subject to Clauses 10 and 11, the Customer shall be entitled to use the Modem for the purposes of gaining access to the Network and the Services thereon]

(3) The Customer shall use the [Modem and] [Software and] Network only for access to and use of the Services for its own internal business purposes and shall not make the use of the [Modem or] [Software or] Network available to any third party nor use the [Modem or] Network on behalf of or for the benefit of any third party

(4) The Service Provider shall make the Network and Services available to the Customer [by means of the Modem] [during the hours of *8.00 am* to *7.00 pm* each business day]

    [**Note:** There may well be no restriction on the hours when the Network is actually available though there is likely to be a restriction on the hours when the Helpdesk is available.]

567

(5) The Service Provider shall provide the Helpdesk Services to the Customer during the hours of *8.00am* to *7.00 pm* each business day

[(6) The Service Provider hereby grants the Customer all necessary rights by way of licence to use the Software in accordance with the terms of this Agreement but not further or otherwise]

(7) Except as expressly permitted by this Agreement, the Customer shall not attempt to obtain access to or interfere with any programs or data of the Service Provider or of any other customer of the Service Provider and shall indemnify the Service Provider against any loss, damage or liability which the Service Provider may sustain or incur as a consequence of the Customer failing to comply with such undertaking

> [**Note:** Breach of this is also likely to be an offence under Section 1(1) of the Computer Misuse Act 1990.]

(8) The Service Provider shall have the right upon giving to the Customer not less than 2 weeks' notice in writing to take the Network down and deny the Customer the use of the Network and the Services [and the Software] on a Saturday, Sunday or public holiday for a maximum of *88 hours* in any one calendar year

> [**Note:** The Network downtime in the above example amounts to only about 1% of the total availability time during the course of the year. An alternative may be to base this on the service quality criteria in Schedule 3.]

(9) The Customer shall not and shall procure that the Customer's Staff shall not without the Service Provider's prior written consent send messages using the electronic mail service comprised in the Services to all users over the Network simultaneously

> [**Note:** Unacceptably heavy traffic may be generated by mass mailing over a network and the irritation among users can be considerable. In most systems there is a bulletin board service which provides the mechanism whereby general messages can be posted to all users and the purpose of this Clause is to encourage the users to use the bulletin board service]

4   Charges and Payment

(1) The Customer shall pay the following charges for the services to be provided by the Service Provider hereunder:

(a) for the Training at the rates set out in Part A of Schedule 2;

(b) for the Documentation at the rates set out in Part B of Schedule 2;

(c) for the use of the Network and Services [including the Software] at the rate set out in Part C of Schedule 2;

[(d) for the use of the Modem at the monthly rate set out in Part D of Schedule 2]

(2) The Service Provider shall invoice the Customer monthly in arrears for the charges referred to in sub-clause (1). Each invoice will be paid by the Customer within *30* days after the Customer's receipt of such invoice.

(3) Right to increase charges—*see Clause 3(4) of Precedent K* [10.5.1]

(4) Charges exclusive of VAT—*see Clause 3(4) of Precedent A*

(5) Interest on overdue amounts—*see Clause 3(6) of Precedent A*

5 Duration

See Clause 8 of Precedent K

[6 The Modem [10.6.2]

(1) The Service Provider shall let and the Customer shall take on hire the Modem for the duration of this Agreement

(2) The Customer shall be responsible for providing proper accommodation and operating conditions for the Modem in accordance with the Service Provider's instructions before the delivery of the Modem

(3) The Service Provider shall deliver the Modem to the Customer on or before the Commencement Date

(4) Prior to the delivery of the Modem the Customer shall:

(a) arrange for the provision of a telephone line to connect the Modem to the Network; and

(b) obtain and produce to the Service Provider any necessary consents for such connection

(5) The Modem shall at all times remain the sole and exclusive property of the Service Provider and the Customer shall have no right or interest therein except for quiet possession and the right to use the same upon the terms and conditions contained in this Agreement

(6) The Modem shall be at the risk of the Service Provider which shall be responsible for insuring the same against all normal risks. The Customer shall notify the Service Provider immediately of any loss or damage to the Modem and shall give all necessary information and assistance to the Service Provider in connection with any such loss or damage

(7) The Customer shall not create or suffer to exist over the Modem any mortgage, charge, lien or other encumbrance

(8) The Customer shall not utilise or attempt to utilise any modem other than the Modem for the purpose of obtaining access to the Network and the Services

(9) The Customer shall use the Modem only for the purpose of obtaining access to the Network [and the Software] in accordance with the terms of this Agreement

(10) The Service Provider shall provide preventive and corrective maintenance for the Modem during the hours of *8.00 am* to *7.00 pm* on business days ('Working Hours')

(11) Preventive maintenance shall be performed by the Service Provider during Working Hours as soon as possible after the Customer's request therefor on the basis of a response time of *8* Working Hours but such response time is an estimate only and shall not be binding on the Service Provider

(12) The Customer shall not without the prior written consent of the Service Provider permit any person, firm or company other than the Service Provider (or a person appointed for such purpose by the Service Provider) to carry out or attempt to carry out maintenance, adjustment replacement or repair of the Modem or any part thereof

(13) The Customer shall ensure that the Modem is not moved from connection with the Customer's Equipment except with the prior written consent of the Service Provider

(14) Upon termination of the Customer's right to hire the Modem (for any reason) the Customer shall forthwith redeliver possession of the Modem to the Service Provider in a condition consistent with the proper performance by the Customer of its obligations under this Clause and the Service Provider shall for the purpose have access to the Customer's premises (or any other place where the Modem may be situated)]

7   Security

(1) The Service Provider shall periodically require the Customer to change the Security Passwords in accordance with the Security Procedures and shall notify the Customer accordingly. If the Service Provider shall become aware, or shall suspect, that any unauthorised person has obtained or has attempted to obtain access to the Services or the Network by means of any of the Security Passwords then the Service Provider shall promptly notify the Customer and shall forthwith cancel one or more of the Security Passwords

(2) The Customer shall and the Customer shall procure that each member of the Customer's Staff shall at all times comply with all the Security Procedures. If the Service Provider shall become aware that the Customer

or any of the Customer's staff has failed to comply with the Security Procedures the Service Provider shall notify the Customer and have the right to exclude the Customer or such of the Customer's Staff as it suspects to have failed to comply with the Security Procedures from all use of the Network and the Services forthwith until such time as the Customer or such of the Customer's Staff as have been so excluded shall have complied with the Security Procedures

8   Maintenance of the Network [and the Software]

(1)   (a) The Service Provider shall be responsible for maintaining the Network in good working order and condition

(b) If the Network shall fail or break down the Service Provider shall use its reasonable endeavours promptly to restore the Network to its proper operating condition

[**Note:** the Customer may require a more positive commitment to appropriate measures in the event of a breakdown. The position is usually clear cut: either the Service Provider will have back-up servers and gateways or alternative cabling routes, or it will not.]

[(2) If the Customer should become aware of any fault in the Software then the Customer shall promptly notify the Service Provider. Upon receipt of such notification (or upon receipt of a similar notification from one of the Service Provider's other customers) the Service Provider shall forthwith use its reasonable endeavours to procure that such fault is corrected as quickly as possible]

[**Note:** This Clause assumes that the service provider does not own the software and that the service provider would have to arrange for the proprietor to correct the fault.]

(3) In the event of any failure or breakdown of the Network [or any fault in the Software] with the consequent loss or spoiling of the Customer's Data or any part thereof the Service Provider shall notify the Customer as soon as reasonably practicable after the Network [and the Software] are available for use again

(4) Sub-clause (3) states the entire liability of the Service Provider for any loss or spoiling of the Customer's Data caused by any failure or breakdown of the Network [or fault in the Software]. The Service Provider shall not be liable for any other loss or damage sustained or incurred by the Customer as a result of any failure or breakdown of the Network [or fault in the Software] except to the extent that such loss or damage arises from any unreasonable delay by the Service Provider in performing its obligations under sub-clauses (1) [and (2)] above

[**Note:** If there is no software provided by the service provider all the bracketed phrases in the above clause must be omitted.]

9   Ownership of Data

(1) The Customer's Data shall be and shall remain the property of the Customer

(2)   (a) The Service Provider undertakes to treat as confidential and keep secret all information ('the Information') contained or embodied in the Customer's Data

(b) The Service Provider shall not without the prior written consent of the Customer divulge the whole or any part of the Information to any person except those to whom the Customer shall direct the data, the Service Provider's employees and then only to those employees who need to know the same, and to the extent necessary for the proper performance of this Agreement

(c) The Service Provider undertakes to ensure that its employees are made aware that the Information is confidential and that such employees owe a duty of confidence to the Customer. The Service Provider shall indemnify the Customer against any loss or damage which the Customer may sustain or incur as a result of the Service Provider failing to comply with such undertaking

(d) The Service Provider shall notify the Customer promptly if the Service Provider becomes aware of any breach of confidence by any of the Service Provider's employees and shall give the Customer all reasonable assistance in connection with any legal proceedings which the Customer may bring against any such employees or any other person for breach of confidence

(e) The foregoing obligations as to confidentiality shall remain in full force and effect notwithstanding any termination of this Agreement (howsoever occasioned)

(3) The Service Provider will establish and maintain proper security measures and procedures to provide for the safe custody of the Customer's Data and to prevent unauthorised access thereto or use thereof. The Service Provider shall indemnify the Customer against any loss or damage which the Customer may sustain or incur consequent upon any of the Customer's Data coming into the possession of any unauthorised person as a result of any negligent act or omission or wilful misconduct of the Service Provider, its employees, agents or sub-contractors [provided that the Service Provider's liability therefor shall not in any circumstances whatsoever exceed £100,000 in respect of each event or series of connected events]

(4)   (a) Upon the termination of this Agreement (howsoever occasioned) the Customer shall have the right to require the Service Provider to do one or more of the following:

(i) to dump on to magnetic media all or any of the Customer's programs and the Customer's Data then stored on-line on the Network and to deliver up such media to the Customer subject to the Customer paying the charges for such dumping and to reimbursing the Service Provider for the cost of such magnetic media;

(ii) to erase all or any of the Customer's Data then in the Service Provider's possession from the Network on which they are stored;

(iii) to make and deliver up to the Customer such print-outs of the Customer's Data as the Customer may require subject to the Customer paying the charges for such print-outs at the applicable rate from time to time payable hereunder.

(b) If upon termination of this Agreement the Customer shall require the Service Provider to deliver up any of the Customer's Data on magnetic media then the Service Provider shall:

(i) deliver up such data on industry compatible magnetic media; and

(ii) supply to the Customer free of charge all information necessary to enable such magnetic media to be read on another computer

(c) Except where this Agreement is properly terminated by the Customer as a result of any breach by the Service Provider of its obligations under this Agreement, the Service Provider's obligations under paragraphs (a) and (b) of this sub-clause shall be conditional upon the Customer having paid all charges then due to the Service Provider under the terms of this Agreement

10   Content of the Customer's Data

(1) The Customer undertakes that the Customer's Data (whether stored on or sent over the Network) will not contain anything obscene, offensive or defamatory. The Customer will indemnify the Service Provider and keep the Service Provider fully and effectively indemnified against all actions, proceedings, claims, demands, damages and costs (including legal costs on a full indemnity basis) occasioned to the Service Provider as a result of any breach of the said undertaking

11 Data Protection [10.6.3]

[**Note:** it is assumed that the services include electronic mail in which case the inputting of the data is very much in the hands of the customer's users. It is highly likely that such employees will sooner or later include personal data within the meaning of the Data Protection Act 1984 so it is prudent for both sides to assume that that Act will apply and to include clauses accordingly.]

(1) The Customer hereby notifies the Service Provider that the Customer's Data contains or will contain personal data as defined in Section 1(3) of the Data Protection Act 1984 ('the Customer's Personal Data') and warrants to the Service Provider that the Customer has registered under the said Act in respect of the Customer's Personal Data and will maintain such registration at all times during the continuance of this Agreement

(2) The Customer warrants and undertakes to the Service Provider that:

(a) The Customer's Personal Data has been obtained and processed (in so far as the Customer's Personal Data has been processed) lawfully

(b) The Services to be provided by the Service Provider under this Agreement will be entirely consistent with and appropriate to the specified and lawful purposes for which the Customer has registered under the said Act in respect of the Customer's Personal Data ('the Registered Purposes')

(c) The Customer has not hitherto and will not during the continuance of this Agreement use or disclose the Customer's Personal Data or any part thereof in a manner incompatible with the Registered Purposes

(d) The Customer's Personal Data is adequate, relevant and not excessive in relation to the Registered Purposes

(e) The Customer's Personal Data is accurate and the Customer shall keep the Customer's Personal Data fully up to date at all times during the continuance of this Agreement

(f) The Customer will promptly delete the Customer's Personal Data or any part or parts thereof as soon as it or they shall no longer be required for the Registered Purposes

(g) The Customer will be responsible for downloading or making copies of the Customer's Personal Data or any part or parts thereof to provide access under Section 21 of the said Act

(3) The Customer shall indemnify the Service Provider against any loss or damage which the Service Provider may sustain or incur as a result of any breach by the Customer of the provisions of this Clause

(4) The Service Provider warrants to the Customer that the Service Provider has registered under the said Act as a bureau and will maintain such registration at all times during the continuance of this Agreement

(5) The Service Provider shall indemnify the Customer against any loss or damage which the Customer may sustain or incur as a result of any breach by the Service Provider of the provisions of this Clause

12 Intellectual Property Rights Indemnities [3.8.1]

(1) The Service Provider shall indemnify the Customer against any claim by any third party for alleged infringement of any copyright or other intellectual property rights which arises as a result of the use of the Network or Services [or the Software] [or the Modem] in accordance with the terms of this Agreement provided that the Service Provider is given immediate and complete control of any such claim, that the Customer does not prejudice the Service Provider's defence of such claim and that the Customer gives the Service Provider all reasonable assistance with such claim

(2) The Customer shall indemnify the Service Provider against any claim by any third party for alleged infringement of any copyright or other intellectual property rights which arises as a result of the storage or processing of any of the Customer's Data on the Network provided that the Customer is given immediate and complete control of any such claim, that the Service Provider does not prejudice the Customer's defence of such claim and that the Service Provider gives the Customer all reasonable assistance with such claim

13 The Service Provider's Confidential Information [10.7.1]

The Customer shall treat as confidential all information supplied to it by the Service Provider for the purposes of this Agreement which is marked as confidential or which is by its nature clearly confidential. Such information shall only be disclosed to those employees of the Customer who need to know the same and the Customer undertakes to ensure that such employees are made aware of its confidential nature prior to such disclosure

[14 Warranties

(1) The Service Provider warrants that the Software will provide the facilities and functions necessary to enable the Customer to gain access to the Network and the Services. The Customer acknowledges that the Network and the Software are not being made available to the Customer

to meet the Customer's other individual requirements. The Service Provider shall not be liable for any failure of the Software to provide any facility or function other than access to the Network and the Services. The Service Provider's entire liability for any fault in the Software is as stated in Clause 8]

15   Termination [10.4]

(1) *See Clause 10(1) of Precedent L*

(2) *See Clause 10(2) of Precedent L*

[(3) Right of recovery of the Modem—*adapt Clause 31(3) of Precedent B*]

16   Assignment

See Clause 30 of Precedent A

17   Force Majeure

See Clause 15 of Precedent A

18   Customer's Warranty

See Clause 20 of Precedent A

19   Liability

See Clause 27 of Precedent A

20   Waiver of Remedies

See Clause 28 of Precedent A

21   Entire Agreement

See Clause 29 of Precedent A

22   Notices

See Clause 32 of Precedent A

23   Interpretation

See Clause 33 of Precedent A

24   Law

See Clause 34 of Precedent A

25   Disputes

See Clause 35 of Precedent A

26   Severability

See Clause 36 of Precedent A

EXECUTED etc

SCHEDULE 1

A   THE SERVICES

[**Note:** this will include the Helpdesk Services]

B   THE NETWORK

[C   THE NETWORK AREA]

D   THE CUSTOMER'S EQUIPMENT

E   THE CUSTOMER'S STAFF

F   THE TRAINING

G   THE DOCUMENTATION

H   THE COMMENCEMENT DATE

I   THE INITIAL PERIOD

J   THE SECURITY PROCEDURES

[K   THE MODEM]

[L   THE SOFTWARE]

SCHEDULE 2

CHARGES

A   TRAINING

B   DOCUMENTATION

C   THE NETWORK AND SERVICES

[D   THE MODEM]

SCHEDULE 3

SERVICE QUALITY CRITERIA

[**Note:** These will involve such criteria as may be appropriate eg:

95% of all electronic mail of less than two pages in length will be despatched over the Network to be received within 5 minutes of despatch

95% of all Helpdesk calls will be answered within 2 minutes

The Network will be available for 95% of the time in any one calendar year

Etc]

Precedent S

Consultancy agreement

THIS AGREEMENT is made the   day of   19

PARTIES:

(1) CLIENT [LIMITED] [PLC] whose registered office is at
('the Client')

(2) CONSULTANT [LIMITED] [PLC] whose registered office is at
('the Consultant')

RECITALS:

(A) The Client wishes to acquire a computer system to meet its requirements as hereinafter mentioned

(B) The Client has agreed to engage the Consultant to provide certain consultancy services in connection with the proposed acquisition of such computer system and the Consultant has agreed to accept such engagement on the terms and conditions hereinafter contained

NOW IT IS HEREBY AGREED as follows:

1   Definitions

In this Agreement, unless the context otherwise requires, the following expressions have the following meanings:

'Completion of the Project' [11.3]   means the acceptance by the Client of the System in accordance with the contract(s) for its supply

'the Consulting Services'   means the consulting services to be provided by the Consultant pursuant to this Agreement

'the Project' [11.1]	means the acquisition by the Client of a fully operational computer system to meet the Client's requirements described in Schedule 1
'the Project Materials'	means any and all works of authorship and materials developed, written or prepared by the Consultant, its employees, agents or sub-contractors in relation to the Project (whether individually, collectively or jointly with the Client and on whatever media) including, without limitation, any and all reports, studies, data, diagrams, charts, specifications, pre-contractual and contractual documents and all drafts thereof and working papers relating thereto, but excluding ordinary correspondence passing between the Consultant and the Client
'the Project Participants'	means those employees and permitted sub-contractors of the Consultant engaged from time to time in providing the Consulting Services and any employees of any such sub-contractors who are so engaged
'the System'	means the computer system proposed to be acquired by the Client pursuant to the Project

2   Engagement

(1) The Client hereby agrees to engage the Consultant and the Consultant hereby agrees to act as consultant to the Client in relation to the Project

(2) The Consultant represents and warrants to the Client that by virtue of entering into this Agreement it is not and will not be in breach of any express or implied obligation to any third party binding upon it

3 Term [11.3, 11.4]

(1) This Agreement shall commence on [the date hereof] and shall continue subject as hereinafter mentioned until Completion of the Project

(2) The Client shall be entitled to terminate this Agreement forthwith by notice in writing to the Consultant given at any time

[**Note:** alternatively the agreement could provide for a period of notice to be given to the consultant, but with immediate termination on the occurrence of certain pre-defined events such as those specified in sub-clause (3).]

(3) The Consultant shall be entitled to terminate this Agreement forthwith by notice in writing to the Client if the Client shall:

(a) commit any serious or persistent breach of any of its obligations hereunder and (in the case of a breach capable of being remedied) shall have failed, within *14* days after the receipt of a written request from the Consultant so to do, to remedy the breach (such request to contain a warning of the Consultant's intention to terminate);

(b) pass a resolution for winding up (otherwise than for the purpose of a bona fide scheme of solvent amalgamation or reconstruction) or a court of competent jurisdiction shall make an order to that effect;

(c) make any voluntarily arrangement with its creditors or become subject to an administration order;

(d) have a receiver or administrative receiver appointed of it or over any part of its undertaking or assets; or

(e) cease, or threaten to cease, to carry on business

(4) If any sum payable by the Client under this Agreement is not paid by the due date the Consultant shall be entitled to suspend provision of the Consulting Services until such time as payment is made

4 Duties [11.1]

(1) The Consultant shall:

(a) review the requirements of the Client and advise it on the most appropriate type of computer system to fulfil such requirements [and whether the Client should rent, lease or buy such system];

(b) assist the Client with the preparation of a detailed requirements specification and a standard form of invitation to tender to be sent to potential suppliers;

(c) recommend a short-list of potential suppliers;

(d) review the tenders received from potential suppliers and assist the Client in choosing the most suitable contractor(s);

(e) assist the Client and its solicitors in the negotiation of the contract(s) for the supply of the System;

(f) assist the Client with the recruitment of appropriate personnel to operate and supervise the running of the System;

(g) supervise the installation of the System and conduct appropriate acceptance tests on behalf of the Client and advise it on the issue of any necessary acceptance certificates;

(h) [*Here set out any other specific duties of the consultant*]

(i) perform such other duties in relation to the Project as may be mutually agreed from time to time

[**Note:** These duties are given by way of example only and will vary according to the particular nature of the consultancy.]

(2) The Consultant shall devote to its obligations hereunder such of its time, attention and skill as may be necessary for the proper performance of those obligations [.The Client and the Consultant shall from time to time agree what is necessary in this respect]

(3) While the Consultant's method of work is its own, the Consultant shall comply with the reasonable requests of the Client and shall use its best endeavours to promote the interests of the Client in relation to the Project

5   Consultant's undertakings [11.0.3, 11.7.2]

The Consultant warrants and undertakes to the Client that:

(1) the Consultant and the Project Participants will have the necessary skill and expertise to provide the Consulting Services on the terms set out herein;

(2) the Consultant will provide independent and unbiased advice to the Client in relation to the Project;

(3) the Consultant will make available (amongst others) those employees of the Consultant named in Schedule 2 to perform the duties of the Consultant hereunder or such replacements of equivalent status as may be approved by the Client (such approval not to be unreasonably withheld or delayed);

(4) the Project Materials will, so far as they do not comprise material originating from the Client, its employees, agents or contractors, be original works of authorship and the use or possession thereof by the Client or the Consultant will not subject the Client or the Consultant

to any claim for infringement of any proprietary rights of any third party;

(5) the Consulting Services will be provided in a timely and professional manner and in accordance with the time schedules reasonably stipulated by the Client, will conform to the standards generally observed in the industry for similar services and will be provided with reasonable skill and care;

(6) the Consultant will not, without the prior written consent of the Client, accept any commission or gift or other financial benefit or inducement from any supplier or potential supplier of the whole or any part of the System and will ensure that its employees, agents and sub-contractors will not accept any such and will forthwith give the Client details of any such commission, gift, benefit or inducement which may be offered;

(7) no announcement or publicity concerning this Agreement or the Project or any matter ancillary thereto shall be made by the Consultant without the prior written consent of the Client;

[(8) the Consultant has in effect and will maintain in effect during the continuance of this Agreement professional indemnity insurance on the terms set out in Schedule 3 and will not do or omit to do anything whereby such insurance way be vitiated either in whole or in part;]

[(9) the fees to be charged to the Client for the Consulting Services will be no greater than the lowest rates charged by the Consultant from time to time to its other clients requiring similar services]

6 Client's obligations [3.6.1; 11.6]

The Client shall:

(1) make available to the Consultant such office and secretarial services as may be necessary for its work under this Agreement;

(2) ensure that its employees co-operate fully with the Consultant and the Project Participants in relation to the provision of the Consulting Services; and

(3) promptly furnish the Consultant with such information and documents as it may reasonably request for the proper performance of its obligations hereunder

7 Personnel [3.6.1, 3.7.1]

(1) The parties shall each appoint a representative who shall have full authority to take all necessary decisions regarding the Project and the provision of the Consulting Services [including the variation of this Agreement]

(2) The parties shall procure their representatives to meet at [regular intervals] [at least once a *week*] during the continuance of this Agreement to discuss and minute the progress of the Project and the Consulting Services

(3) The Client shall be entitled to request and obtain, in its discretion, the removal and replacement of any of the Project Participants which it may designate; Provided that the Client shall not exercise such right frivolously or vexatiously

(4) The Consultant shall ensure that while any of the Project Participants are on the Client's premises they will conform to the Client's normal codes of staff and security practice

8   Ownership of Project Materials [3.8]

(1) The Client shall be entitled to all property, copyright and other intellectual property rights in the Project Materials, which property, copyright and other intellectual property rights the Consultant hereby, as beneficial owner, assigns to the Client

(2)   At the request and expense of the Client, the Consultant shall do all such things and sign all documents or instruments reasonably necessary in the opinion of the Client to enable the Client to obtain, defend and enforce its rights in the Project Materials

(3) Upon request by the Client, and in any event upon the expiration or termination of this Agreement, the Consultant shall at its expense promptly deliver to the Client all copies of the Project Materials then in the Consultant's custody, control or possession

(4) The provisions of this Clause shall survive the expiration or termination of this Agreement

9   Fees and expenses [3.0.3, 3.2; 11.2; D5]

(1) The Client shall pay the Consultant for the time properly spent by the Project Participants in providing the Consulting Services at the hourly charge-out rates specified in Schedule 4

(2) The hourly charge-out rates of any new Project Participants which the Consultant wishes to use from time to time shall be agreed in writing with the Client, such agreement not to be unreasonably withheld or delayed

[(3) The Consultant shall be entitled at any time and from time to time to vary any or all of such hourly charge-out rates to accord with its or its permitted sub-contractors' standard scale rates in force from time to time; Provided that no such variation shall have effect unless and until written notice thereof is given to the Client]

(4) The Consultant shall maintain full and accurate records of the time spent by the Project Participants in providing the Consulting Services and shall produce such records to the Client for inspection at all reasonable times on request

(5) The Consultant shall render monthly itemised invoices to the Client in respect of the said charges and shall show any Value Added Tax separately on such invoices. The Client shall not account to the Consultant for any charges save on receipt of such invoice. Each invoice shall be accompanied by a statement specifying the time spent by each of the Project Participants in providing the Consulting Services during the period covered by the invoice

(6) All charges payable by the Client shall, subject as aforesaid, be paid within *14* days after the receipt by the Client of the Consultant's invoice therefor

(7) If it shall be necessary for any of the Project Participants to visit the Client's premises or make any other journeys in the course of providing the Consulting Services then the Client shall reimburse the Consultant for all reasonable travelling and subsistence expenses properly incurred in so doing. Apart from minor out-of-pocket expenses, claims for reimbursement of expenses shall be paid by the Client only if accompanied by the relevant receipts

(8) *Charges exclusive of VAT—see Clause 3(4) of Precedent A*

(9) *Interest on late payment—see Clause 3(6) of Precedent A*

10   Confidential information [3.7.2; 11.7.2]

(1) The Consultant shall not use or divulge or communicate to any person (other than those whose province it is to know the same or with the authority of the Client):

(a) any confidential information concerning the products, customers, business, accounts, finance or contractual arrangements or other dealings, transactions or affairs of the Client [and its subsidiaries] which may come to the Consultant's knowledge in the course of providing the Consulting Services;

(b) any information concerning the Project or the System;

(c) the Project Materials or the substance of any report, recommendation, advice or test made, given or undertaken by the Consultant in connection with its duties hereunder and the Consultant shall use its best endeavours to prevent the unauthorised publication or disclosure of any such information or documents

(2) The Consultant shall ensure that its employees, agents and sub-contractors are aware of and comply with the confidentiality and non-disclosure provisions contained in this Clause and the Consultant shall indemnify the Client against any loss or damage which the Client may sustain or incur as a result of any breach of confidence by any of such persons

(3) If the Consultant becomes aware of any breach of confidence by any of its employees, agents or sub-contractors it shall promptly notify the Client and give the Client all reasonable assistance in connection with any proceedings which the Client may institute against any such persons

(4) The provisions of this Clause shall survive the expiration or termination of this Agreement but the restrictions contained in sub-clause (1) shall cease to apply to any information which may come into the public domain otherwise than through unauthorised disclosure by the Consultant, its employees, agents or sub-contractors

[11   Restriction [11.7.2]

The Consultant shall not [and will procure that none of the Project Participants shall] (whether directly or indirectly or whether on its [or their] own account or for the account of any other person, firm or company, or as agent, director, partner, manager, employee, consultant or shareholder of or in any other person, firm or company) at any time during the period from the date hereof to the expiry of *one year* after the date of expiration or termination of this Agreement for any reason and in any manner whatsoever work on any project similar to the Project for any person, firm or company which is engaged in or conducts a business the same as or similar to or competitive with the business of the Client as carried on at the date hereof]

> [Note: Consider whether any restrictions make the agreement registrable under the Restrictive Trade Practices Act 1976.]

12   Assignment

(1) Save as provided in sub-clause (2) below, the Consultant shall not be entitled to assign or sub-contract any of its rights or obligations under this Agreement

(2) The Consultant shall be entitled (subject to the prior written approval of the Client, which shall not be unreasonably withheld or delayed) to engage the services of independent contractors of its own to assist it with its duties hereunder; Provided that the Consultant:

(a) shall not be relieved from any of its obligations hereunder by engaging any such independent contractor;

(b) shall secure binding obligations from any such independent contractor so as to ensure that the Consultant can comply with its obligations under this Agreement including, in particular, its obligations under Clauses 8, 10 [and 11] hereof; and

(c) shall, upon request by the Client, first procure that any such independent contractor enters into direct covenants with the Client in terms similar to and covering the provisions of Clauses 8, 10 [and 11] hereof

13   Effect of termination

On the expiration or termination of this Agreement:

(1) all rights and obligations of the parties under this Agreement shall automatically terminate except for such rights of action as shall have accrued prior thereto and any obligations which expressly or by implication are intended to come into or continue in force on or after such expiration or termination;

(2) the Client shall pay the Consultant for all unpaid charges and reimbursable expenses accrued up to the date of expiration or termination;

(3) the Consultant shall give the Client, at its request, all reasonable co-operation in transferring all sub-contracts made by the Consultant hereunder to the extent that sub-contractors approve and provided that the Consultant is fully released from its obligations in relation thereto

14   Indemnity

The Consultant shall indemnify the Client and keep the Client fully and effectively indemnified against any and all losses, claims, damages, costs, charges, expenses, liabilities, demands, proceedings and actions which the Client may sustain or incur or which may be brought or established against it by any person and which in any case arises out of or in relation to or by reason of:

(1) the negligence, recklessness or wilful misconduct of the Consultant, its employees, agents or sub-contractors in the provision of the Consulting Services;

(2) the breach of any of the warranties and undertakings contained in Clause 5 hereof; or

(3) any unauthorised act or omission of the Consultant, its employees, agents or sub-contractors

15   Interpretation

See Clause 33 of Precedent A

16   Notices

See Clause 32 of Precedent A

17   Force majeure

Neither party shall be liable for any delay in performing any of its obligations under this Agreement if such delay is caused by circumstances beyond the reasonable control of the party so delaying and such party shall be entitled (subject to giving the other party full particulars of the circumstances in question and to using its best endeavours to resume full performance without avoidable delay) to a reasonable extension of time for the performance of such obligations

18   General [11.0.2]

The Consultant is an independent contractor and nothing in this Agreement shall render it an agent or partner of the Client and the Consultant shall not hold itself out as such. The Consultant shall not have any right or power to bind the Client to any obligation. This Agreement constitutes the entire understanding between the parties concerning the subject matter hereof and shall be governed by and construed in accordance with the laws of England. No waiver or amendment of any provision of this Agreement shall be effective unless made by a written instrument signed by both parties. Each provision of this Agreement shall be construed separately and notwithstanding that the whole or any part of any such provision may prove to be illegal or unenforceable the other provisions of this Agreement and the remainder of the provision in question shall continue in full force and effect

EXECUTED etc

SCHEDULE 1

CLIENT'S REQUIREMENTS FOR THE PROPOSED COMPUTER SYSTEM

SCHEDULE 2

CONSULTANT'S EMPLOYEES TO BE MADE AVAILABLE TO THE CLIENT FOR THE PURPOSES OF THE PROJECT

SCHEDULE 3

DETAILS OF PROFESSIONAL INDEMNITY INSURANCE

SCHEDULE 4

HOURLY CHARGE-OUT RATES OF PROJECT PARTICIPANTS

Precedent T

Master agreement for programming services

THIS MASTER AGREEMENT is made the   day of   19

PARTIES:

(1) CLIENT [LIMITED] [PLC] whose registered office is at

('the Company')

(2)   of

('the Contractor')

RECITALS:

(A) The Contractor is a self employed computer programmer [11.0.2]

(B) The Company has agreed to engage the Contractor to provide computer programming and related services from time to time and the Contractor has agreed to accept such engagement on the terms and conditions hereinafter contained

NOW IT IS HEREBY AGREED as follows:

1   Definitions

In this Agreement, unless the context otherwise requires, the following expressions have the following meanings:

'this Agreement'	means this Master Agreement and the Subsidiary Agreements both collectively and individually

'intellectual property rights'	means patents, trade marks, service marks, registered designs, applications for any of the foregoing, copyright, design rights, know-how, confidential information, trade and business names and any other similar protected rights in any country
'Project'	means the work undertaken pursuant to any Subsidiary Agreement
'Project Materials'	means any and all works of authorship, products and materials developed, written or prepared by the Contractor in relation to the Projects (whether alone or jointly with the Company or any other independent contractor of the Company and on whatever media) including, without limitation, any and all computer programs, data, diagrams, charts, reports, specifications, studies and inventions and all drafts thereof and working papers relating thereto
'Subsidiary Agreement'	has the meaning attributed thereto in Clause 4(2)
'the Services'	means the computer programming and related services to be provided by the Contractor pursuant to this Agreement

2   Engagement [11.0.2]

(1) The Company hereby agrees to engage the Contractor and the Contractor hereby agrees to provide the Services as an independent contractor on the terms and conditions set out in this Agreement

(2) The Contractor represents and warrants to the Company that by virtue of entering into this Agreement he is not and will not be in breach of any express or implied obligation to any third party binding upon him

3   Term

(1) This Master Agreement shall commence on [the date hereof], shall continue for an initial period of *one year* and shall remain in force thereafter [unless or] until terminated by either party giving to the other

not less than 6 months' written notice of termination [given on] [expiring on] the last day of the said initial period or at any time thereafter but shall be subject to earlier termination as hereinafter provided

(2) In the event that the Contractor is unable to carry out his obligations under this Agreement due to illness or accident and such incapacity continues for a period of more than 3 months the Company shall be entitled to terminate this Master Agreement forthwith by notice in writing to the Contractor given at any time while such incapacity continues

(3) The Company may terminate this Master Agreement forthwith by written notice to the Contractor if he shall:

(a) commit any material or persistent breach of any of his obligations under this Agreement;

(b) be guilty of any fraud, dishonesty or serious misconduct;

(c) be guilty of conduct or a course of conduct, or be convicted of a criminal offence which may tend to bring himself or the Company into disrepute;

(d) become incapable, by reason of mental disorder, of performing his duties under this Agreement; or

(e) become bankrupt

(4) If any sum payable by the Company under this Agreement is not paid by the due date the Contractor shall be entitled to suspend provision of the Services until such time as payment is made

4   Duties

(1) Any work to be undertaken by the Contractor pursuant to this Agreement shall be jointly agreed between the parties and shall be set out in a written proposal describing:

(a) the nature of such work;

(b) the time schedules pursuant to which such work will be undertaken and completed;

(c) the time and other resources which the Contractor will devote to such work; and

(d) the amount and/or method of calculation of the fees of the Contractor for such work

(2) Each proposal will be incorporated into a subsidiary agreement ('Subsidiary Agreement') between the parties substantially in the form of the letter agreement set out in the Schedule hereto

(3) The Contractor is not authorised to undertake any work for the Company which is not the subject of a duly executed Subsidiary Agreement

[(4) If the Contractor shall undertake any work at the Company's request which is not the subject of a Subsidiary Agreement then, unless the parties otherwise agree in writing, the provisions of this Master Agreement shall apply thereto (so far as the same are capable of applying) and if no fee is agreed for such work the Contractor shall be paid on a quantum meruit basis]

> [**Note:** Sub-clause (4) is a safety clause to cover the situation where the company requests the contractor to undertake some programming work but forgets to sign up a subsidiary agreement.]

(5) This Agreement is personal to the Contractor and he shall not be entitled to assign or sub-contract any of his rights or obligations under this Agreement

(6) Subject to the restrictions on disclosure of information contained in Clause 10 and to the other obligations of the Contractor contained in this Agreement, nothing in this Agreement shall prevent the Contractor from engaging in other activities on a self-employed basis or in part time employment.

5   Contractor's undertakings

The Contractor warrants and undertakes to the Company that:

(1) he will have the necessary skill and expertise to provide the Services on the terms set out in this Agreement;

(2) the Project Materials will, so far as they do not comprise material originating from the Company, its employees, agents or contractors, be original works of authorship and the use or possession thereof by the Company or the Contractor will not subject the Company or the Contractor to any claim for infringement of any intellectual property rights of any third party;

(3) the Services will be provided in a timely and professional manner and in accordance with the time schedules stipulated in each Subsidiary Agreement, will conform to the standards generally observed in the industry for similar services and will be provided with reasonable skill and care;

(4) no announcement or publicity concerning this Agreement or any Project or any matter ancillary thereto shall be made by the Contractor without the prior written consent of the Company;

(5) he will conform to the Company's normal codes of staff and security practice while he is on the Company's premises;

[(6) he has in effect and will maintain in effect during the continuance of this Agreement professional indemnity insurance on the terms set out in Schedule [   ] and will not do or omit to do anything whereby such insurance may be vitiated either in whole or in part]

6   Company's obligations

The Company shall:

(1) make available to the Contractor such office and secretarial services as may be necessary for his work under this Agreement; Provided that the Contractor shall not be obliged to make use of such facilities and services if, in his view, to do so would not be the most effective method of carrying out his obligations;

(2) ensure that its employees and other independent contractors co-operate fully with the Contractor in relation to the provision of the Services; and

(3) promptly furnish the Contractor with such information and documents as he may reasonably request for the proper performance of his obligations under this Agreement

7   Supervision

(1) The Company shall appoint a representative who shall have full authority to take all necessary decisions regarding the Project and the provision of the Services [including the variation of this Agreement]

(2) The Contractor and the Company's representative shall meet at [regular intervals] [least once a *week*] during the continuance of each Project to discuss and minute the progress of such Project

(3) While the Contractor's method of work is his own, the Contractor shall comply with the reasonable requests of the Company and shall use his best endeavours to promote the interests of the Company in relation to each Project

8   Ownership of Project Materials

(1) The Company shall be entitled to all property, copyright and other intellectual property rights in the Project Materials which property, copyright and other intellectual property rights the Contractor hereby, as beneficial owner, assigns to the Company

(2)   At the request and expense of the Company, the Contractor shall do all such things and sign all documents or instruments reasonably necessary in the opinion of the Company to enable the Company to obtain, defend and enforce its rights in the Project Materials

(3) Upon request by the Company, and in any event upon the expiration or termination of this Master Agreement, the Contractor shall promptly deliver to the Company all copies of the Project Materials then in the Contractor's custody, control or possession

(4) The provisions of this Clause shall survive the expiration or termination of this Agreement

9   Fees and expenses

(1) In consideration of the services rendered by the Contractor pursuant to each Subsidiary Agreement the Company shall pay to the Contractor fees in the amounts and at the rates set out in such Subsidiary Agreement (plus Value Added Tax, if applicable)

(2) Unless otherwise agreed in a Subsidiary Agreement, such fees shall accrue monthly and the Contractor shall render monthly invoices to the Company in respect of such fees and, where he is registered for Value Added Tax, shall show any Value Added Tax separately on such invoices. The Company shall not account to the Contractor for any fees save on receipt of such invoice

(3) All fees shall be payable to the Contractor without deductions of any kind save in respect of monies owed by the Contractor to the Company. The Contractor shall account for his Income Tax, Value Added Tax and Class 2 and 4 Social Security contributions to the appropriate authorities

(4) [The Contractor shall be responsible for all out-of-pocket expenses incurred by him in the performance of his duties under this Agreement] [The Company shall pay or reimburse to the Contractor (on production of such vouchers and/or other evidence as it may require) all reasonable and proper expenses incurred in connection with his duties under this Agreement].

(5) All charges payable by the Company shall, subject as aforesaid, be paid within *14* days after the receipt by the Company of the Contractor's invoice therefor.

(6) Interest on late payment—*see Clause 3(6) of Precedent A*

10   Confidential information [3.7.2; 11.7.2]

(1) The Contractor shall not use or divulge or communicate to any person (other than to those whose province it is to know the same or with the authority of the Company):

(a) any of the confidential information concerning the products, customers, business, accounts, finance or contractual arrangements or other dealings, transactions or affairs of the Company [and its subsidiaries] which may come to the Contractor's knowledge in the course of providing the Services;

(b) any information concerning any Project;

(c) the Project Materials or the substance of any report, recommendation, advice or test made, given or undertaken by the Contractor in connection with his duties hereunder

and the Contractor shall use his best endeavours to prevent the unauthorised publication or disclosure of any such information, materials or documents

(2) The provisions of this Clause shall survive the termination of this Master Agreement but the restrictions contained in sub-clause (1) shall cease to apply to any information which may come into the public domain otherwise than through unauthorised disclosure by the Contractor or anyone on his behalf

[11   Restriction [11.7.2]

If stipulated in any Subsidiary Agreement the Contractor shall not (whether directly or indirectly or whether on his own account or for the account of any other person, firm or company, or as agent, director, partner, manager, employee, consultant or shareholder of or in any other person, firm or company) at any time during the period from the commencement of the Project specified in such Subsidiary Agreement to the expiry of *one year* after the completion of such Project for any reason and in manner whatsoever work on any project similar to such Project for any other person, firm or company]

[**Note:** Consider whether this Clause makes any subsidiary agreement registrable under the Restrictive Trade Practices Act 1976.]

12   Effect of termination

On the termination of this Master Agreement:

(1) all rights and obligations of the parties under this Master Agreement and each Subsidiary Agreement shall automatically terminate except:

(a) for such rights of action as shall have accrued prior to such termination and any obligations which expressly or by implication are intended to come into or continue in force on or after such termination;

(b) that, in the event that this Master Agreement has been terminated by notice given by the Contractor pursuant to Clause 3(1), the Contractor shall, at the request of the Company, complete any work to be performed under any existing Subsidiary Agreement and to that extent and for that purpose the provisions of this Master Agreement shall continue in effect until the Project under such Subsidiary Agreement has been completed

(2) the Company shall pay the Contractor for all unpaid fees [and reimbursable expenses] accrued up to the date of termination

13 Indemnity

The Contractor shall indemnify the Company and keep the Company fully and effectively indemnified against any and all losses, claims, damages, costs, charges, expenses, liabilities, demands, proceedings and actions which the Company may sustain or incur or which may be brought or established against it by any person and which in any case arise out of or in relation to or by reason of:

(1) the negligence, recklessness or wilful misconduct of the Contractor in the provision of the Services;

(2) the breach of any of the warranties and undertakings contained in Clause 5 hereof;

(3) any unauthorised act or omission of the Contractor; or

(4) any claim that may be made by any competent authority against the Company in respect of any income tax, national insurance or similar contributions or any other taxation, in each case relating to the Contractor's Services under this Agreement

14 Interpretation

See Clause 33 of Precedent A

15 Notices

See Clause 32 of Precedent A

16 Inconsistency

Unless otherwise expressly provided in a Subsidiary Agreement by specific reference to this Clause, if there shall be any inconsistency between the provisions of this Master Agreement and any Subsidiary Agreement the provisions of this Master Agreement shall prevail

17 Force majeure

See Clause 17 of Precedent S

18 General [11.0.2]

The Contractor is an independent contractor and nothing in this Agreement shall render him an employee, agent or partner of the Company and the Contractor shall not hold himself out as such. The Contractor shall not have any right or power to bind the Company to any obligation. This Agreement constitutes the entire understanding between the parties concerning the subject matter of this Agreement and shall be governed by and construed in accordance with the laws of England. No waiver or amendment of any provision of this Agreement shall be effective unless made by a written instrument signed by both parties. Each provision of this Agreement shall be construed separately and notwithstanding that the whole or any part of any such provision may prove to be illegal or unenforceable the other provisions of this Agreement and the remainder of the provision in question shall continue in full force and effect.

EXECUTED etc

THE SCHEDULE

[To be typed on the Company's headed notepaper]

Dated: 1995

Dear [   ]

We refer to the Master Agreement for programming services dated   19   ('the Master Agreement') between Client [Limited] [Plc] ('the Company') and yourself pursuant to which you have agreed to perform certain services for and on behalf of the Company subject to the terms and conditions set out in the Master Agreement.

In consideration of the mutual covenants and agreements contained in this Subsidiary Agreement and in the Master Agreement, we agree as follows:

(1) *Nature of Work.*   The nature and object of each task to be performed by you under this Subsidiary Agreement and the products that will be delivered by you to the Company in connection with such tasks are set out in the Proposal attached hereto ('the Proposal').

(2) *Timing.*   You will perform the services in accordance with the time schedules contained in the Proposal.

(3) *Resources.*   You will devote to the performance of such services the time and other resources described in the Proposal and such additional resources as may be necessary diligently to perform such services in a timely and efficient manner in accordance with the Proposal.

(4) *Fees.*   In consideration of the services to be performed by you pursuant to this Subsidiary Agreement the Company will pay to you the fees set out in the Proposal.

(5) *Confirmation of Master Agreement.*   You agree to perform the services described in this Subsidiary Agreement subject to the terms and conditions of the Master Agreement.

[(6) *Restriction.*   The provisions of Clause 11 of the Master Agreement shall apply in relation to the work to be undertaken pursuant to this Subsidiary Agreement.]

Please indicate your agreement to these terms and conditions by signing the enclosed copy of this Subsidiary Agreement and returning it to the undersigned.

Yours sincerely

Director
CLIENT [LIMITED] [PLC]

On the copy:

I agree the above terms and conditions

. . . .
Dated: 19

[DETAILS OF PROFESSIONAL INDEMNITY INSURANCE]

Precedent U

Non-disclosure agreement

[**Note:** This is a practical way of reminding a supplier/contractor of his duty of confidence in respect of the customer/client's data. The danger arises not only from a negligent contractor or supplier, but also from negligence or worse on the part of his individual employees, even after they have left his service. The agreement is therefore in two parts: a corporate agreement to be signed by a representative of the supplier/contractor, and individual agreements to be signed by each of the employees reminding them of their duty of confidence both during the contractor's service and after they have left it [1.1; 3.7.2].]

For Company:

To: [Insert name and address of disclosing party]

In consideration of your agreeing to disclose to us information and documents in connection with studies for the computerisation of [   ] ('the Project') we [
        ] of [   ] hereby agree that, save as hereinafter provided, such information and documents shall be treated by us as confidential and that we shall be subject to the following obligations:

(1) We will not without your prior written consent disclose any such information or documents to any third party and will use our best endeavours to prevent the unauthorised publication or disclosure of the same

(2) We will divulge such information and documents only to those of our employees who are directly concerned with the Project [and who have been named by us to you in writing on or before the signing hereof]

(3) We will ensure that our employees are aware of and comply with the confidentiality and non-disclosure obligations contained herein and we will indemnify you against any loss or damage which you may sustain or incur as a result of any breach of confidence by any of our employees

(4) We will not use such information or documents for any purpose other than for the Project

(5) All papers furnished to us by you will be returned or otherwise disposed of as you may from time to time direct

The foregoing obligations shall not extend to any such information or documents which were rightfully in our possession prior to the date hereof, which are already public knowledge or become so at a future date (otherwise than through unauthorised disclosure by us or our employees) or which are trivial or obvious

The said obligations shall continue in full force and effect notwithstanding the completion of the Project

This agreement shall be governed by the laws of England

Signed: _____
                 for and on behalf of [receiving party]

Position: _____

Date: 19

For Individual:

To: [insert name and address of disclosing party]

In consideration of your disclosing to me (whether directly or through my employer) information and documents in connection with studies for the computerisation of [   ] ('the Project') I [   ] of [   ] hereby agree that, save as hereinafter provided, such information and documents shall be treated by me as confidential and that I will be subject to the following obligations:

(1) I will not without your prior written consent disclose any such information or documents to any third party and will use my best endeavours to prevent the unauthorised publication or disclosure of the same

(2) I will divulge such information and documents only to those of my fellow employees who are directly concerned with the Project and who have prior to such disclosure entered into an agreement with you in

the same form, mutatis mutandis, as this agreement or in such other form as may be approved by you

(3) I will ensure that any such employees to whom I divulge any such information or documents are aware that the same is confidential to you

(4) I will indemnify you against any loss or damage which you may sustain or incur as a result of any breach of confidence on my part

(5) I will not use such information and documents for any purpose other than for the Project

(6) all papers furnished to me by you (whether directly or through my employer) will be returned or otherwise disposed of as you may from time to time direct

The foregoing obligations shall not extend to any such information or documents which were rightfully in my possession or that of my employer prior to the date hereof, which are already public knowledge or become so at a further date (otherwise than through unauthorised disclosure by me or by my employer or fellow employees) or which are trivial or obvious.

The said obligations shall continue in full force and effect notwithstanding the completion of the Project.

This agreement shall be governed by the laws of England.

Signed: _____
[receiving individual]

Date: 19

Precedent V

Unsolicited disclosure agreement

[**Note:** This is to be used by a company receiving an unsolicited offer of disclosure of new software [1.4.1 and 4.3].]

Dear [   ]

Thank you for your letter of   19   giving details of your [ideas] [programs] relating to [   ] ('the Work').

It is our policy to act fairly towards anyone who submits new ideas to us, but we are unable to accept any disclosure of new ideas unless it is governed by an agreement between us which clearly establishes our respective rights and obligations.

As I am sure you will appreciate, we are actively involved in many areas of research in the high technology field and we often receive disclosures from third parties. It would clearly be unfair to us if we were to be restrained from or otherwise penalised for making use of an idea or invention which has already been developed by us or is already rightfully in our possession merely because it is similar to your own work.

For this reason I must ask you to confirm that you will agree to submit details of the Work to us on the following basis:

(1) Acceptance of your disclosures will not, except as provided in this letter, place us under any obligation towards you.

(2) We will treat as confidential all information and documents disclosed by you which are clearly designated as such and which are not already public knowledge, but this obligation shall not prevent us from making use of any information and documents already rightfully in our possession (except where such use would infringe any patent rights belonging to you) and shall cease to apply to any information or documents supplied

by you which may come into the public domain otherwise than through unauthorised disclosure by us or our employees.

(3) If our negotiations fail then we shall promptly return all written material supplied by you together with our certificate that no copies have been retained by us and that no unauthorised use has been made thereof.

(4) You warrant to us that:

(a) the Work has not been written, prepared or developed in the course of your duties to any other person, firm or company and that you are the exclusive owner thereof free from any encumbrances; and.

(b) you have not disclosed the Work to any third party with a view to its exploitation or acquisition and undertake that you will not do so for a period of *30* days after submitting the Work to us pursuant to the terms set out in this letter.

(5) Prior to the end of that period of *30* days we shall notify you either that we do wish to commence negotiations with you or that we do not, in which latter case paragraph (3) above will apply.

(6) If we inform you that we wish to proceed with negotiations then we shall endeavour to reach a formal agreement with you for the exploitation or acquisition of the Work but in the event that a formal agreement is not signed within *60* days after the commencement of negotiations we reserve the right to withdraw therefrom. While negotiations are proceeding with us you undertake not to approach any third party with a view to offering the Work to that third party. You will notify us if you decide to withdraw from negotiations.

(7) If we consider that the Work is similar to any which we have already developed or had submitted to us by a third party we will inform you accordingly and, if we decide to proceed with that work but not to enter into a contractual relationship with you for the commercial exploitation or acquisition of the Work you will be entitled (at any time during the period of *one month* after we notify you in writing (which we undertake to do) that we are in a position to proceed with the commercial exploitation of our own work), to appoint an independent expert to report to you as to whether our work impinges on your own and, if so, whether it is based solely on information already rightfully in our possession or whether it makes use of any of the information disclosed by you. The following provisions shall govern the appointment of the expert:

(a) he will be appointed by agreement between us, failing which, by the President from time to time of the *British Computer Society* on the application of either of us;

(b) he will be given full access to all relevant documents and information subject to his entering into a confidentiality undertaking in a form acceptable to us;

(c) he will use the information and documents disclosed to him only for the purpose of reporting to you as aforesaid and in particular he will not be entitled to make any disclosure of such information or documents to you;

(d) he will supply one copy of his report to us;

(e) the conclusions set out in his report will (save in the case of clerical or manifest error) be final and binding on both of us and if the report concludes that we have not made use of any information received from you, you agree that you will have no claim against us in respect thereof except for any infringement of any patent rights belonging to you resulting from our activities;

(f) he will act as an expert and not an arbitrator and his fees for so acting shall be borne [as to *one half*] by you [and the *other half* by us].

If you agree the above terms please indicate your agreement by signing and returning to me the enclosed copy of this letter together with all the material which you wish to disclose to us

I return with this letter your letter of   19   [together with its enclosures] and I confirm that no copies have been taken or other use made thereof except for the purpose of writing this letter.

I look forward to hearing from you.

Yours etc.

On the copy:

I agree the terms of the above

. . . .

Dated: 19

Index